Collaborations in Architecture and Engineering

This new edition of *Collaborations in Architecture and Engineering* explores how to effectively develop creative collaborations among architects and engineers. The authors, an architect and an engineer, share insights gained from their experiences and research on fostering productive communication, engaging in interdisciplinary discussions, and establishing common design goals. Together, they share the tools, methods, and best practices deployed by prominent innovative architects and engineers to provide readers with the key elements for success in interdisciplinary design collaborations.

The book offers engaging stories about prominent architect and engineer collaborations—such as those between SANAA and Sasaki and Partners, Adjaye Associates and Silman, Grafton Architects and AKT II, Studio Gang and Arup, Foster + Partners and Buro Happold, Steven Holl Architects and Guy Nordenson and Associates, and among the engineers and architects at SOM. In the second edition, the newly added case studies showcase extraordinary buildings across the globe at a range of scales and typologies, tracing the facets of high-quality collaborations. Through the examples of these remarkable synergies, readers gain insights into innovative design processes that address complex challenges in the built environment.

The second edition of *Collaborations in Architecture and Engineering* is a terrific sourcebook for students, educators, and professionals interested in integrative design practice among the disciplines.

Clare Olsen holds a Bachelor of Arts in Environmental Studies from Brown University and a Master of Architecture with distinction from the University of California, Los Angeles. A dedicated educator, she is a Professor of Architecture at Cal Poly San Luis Obispo and has also taught at Tulane University, Cornell

University, and Syracuse University. Her research focuses on interdisciplinarity, design pedagogy, and architectural ceramics. She is a licensed architect and pursues residential, installation, and furniture design projects through her practice, C.O.CO.

Sinéad Mac Namara attended Trinity College Dublin and Princeton University, where she received a PhD in structural engineering. She is an Associate Professor and Associate Dean at Syracuse University where she teaches students of architecture and engineering. Her research interests include creativity and innovation in engineering education, technical design education in architecture, structural art, and shell structures. Her engineering practice includes design+build with students and several award-winning design competitions with architectural colleagues.

Collaborations in Architecture and Engineering

2nd Edition

Clare Olsen and Sinéad Mac Namara

NEW YORK AND LONDON

Cover image: © Dennis Gilbert

Second edition published 2022
by Routledge
605 Third Avenue, New York, NY 10158

and by Routledge
4 Park Square, Milton Park, Abingdon, Oxon, OX14 4RN

Routledge is an imprint of the Taylor & Francis Group, an informa business

© 2022 Taylor & Francis

The right of Clare Olsen and Sinéad Mac Namara to be identified as authors of this work has been asserted in accordance with sections 77 and 78 of the Copyright, Designs and Patents Act 1988.

All rights reserved. No part of this book may be reprinted or reproduced or utilised in any form or by any electronic, mechanical, or other means, now known or hereafter invented, including photocopying and recording, or in any information storage or retrieval system, without permission in writing from the publishers.

Trademark notice: Product or corporate names may be trademarks or registered trademarks, and are used only for identification and explanation without intent to infringe.

First edition published 2014 by Routledge

Library of Congress Cataloging-in-Publication Data
A catalog record for this title has been requested

ISBN: 9780367862862 (hbk)
ISBN: 9780367862855 (pbk)
ISBN: 9781003018179 (ebk)

DOI: 10.4324/9781003018179

Typeset in Minion Pro
by codeMantra

Contents

Preface vii
Acknowledgments ix

1 Introduction: Call for Collaboration and Diverse Voices   1

2 Architects and Engineers in the Academy: The Challenge of the Silos   7

3 Architects and Engineers in the Profession: The Barriers and Benefits of Collaboration   20

Case Studies in Collaboration: Civic Buildings   35

4 National Museum of African American History and Culture: Historical Design Concepts Driving Collaborative Design   37

5 Gilder Center at the American Museum of Natural History: Collaborating on an Architectural–Structural Concept as a Foundation for Design   62

6 Glass Pavilion at the Toledo Museum of Art: Collaboration for Minimalism and Transparency   83

7 Billie Jean King Main Library: Collaborating on Mass Timber and Carbon Accounting   101

8 *Case for Collaboration*: Net Zero—The Frick Environmental Center and the Kendeda Building for Innovative Sustainable Design   125

Case Studies in Collaboration: Institutional Buildings   143

  9 Marshall Building at the London School of Economics: Collaborating to Knit Structure into the Urban Fabric   145

  10 41 Cooper Square at the Cooper Union: Integrated Technologies for a High-Tech Lab Building   164

  11 Antwerp Port House for the Port Authority: Collaborating on Rationalization and Constructability   182

  12 Simmons Hall at the Massachusetts Institute of Technology: Collaborating on Discipline and Play   199

  13 *Case for Collaboration*: Circularity—The People's Pavilion and the Urban Mining and Recycling Unit   214

Case Studies in Collaboration: Transportation Buildings   225

  14 Amman Queen Alia International Airport: Integrating Modularity and Constructability   227

  15 Berlin Hauptbahnhof: Collaborating on Lightness and Large Spans   242

  16 Anaheim Regional Transportation Intermodal Center: Rationalizing Facades for Cost-Effectiveness and Performance   260

  17 Groundwork to Support Collaborations: Owners, Project Goals, and Contracts   280

  18 Tools to Support Collaborations: Software   289

    Appendix: Guidelines for Developing Interdisciplinary Courses   *301*
    Index   *305*

Preface

The authors co-taught architecture and engineering interdisciplinary design courses at Syracuse University, which were enabled through a generous National Science Foundation grant supporting Innovations in Engineering Education. The rewards of the teaching and learning experiences far outweighed the challenges. In this book, we share our collaboration experiences as well as those of numerous practitioners, seeking to provide faculty, students, and professionals with the tools and sensibilities to enable positive collaborative experiences.

Acknowledgments

The research and the interdisciplinary teaching that inspired the first edition of this book were funded through the National Science Foundation Award Number 0935168 in 2010, which was secured with the support of the Dean Laura Steinberg of the College of Engineering and Computer Science and Dean Mark Robbins of the School of Architecture at Syracuse University. Further support for this second edition was provided by Dean Cole Smith, Dean Michael Speaks, Brian Lonsway, and Andria Costello Staniec at Syracuse University and the College of Architecture and Environmental Design at Cal Poly San Luis Obispo.

This project would not have been possible without the engineers, architects, educators, and administrators who gave generously of their time and their insights. The authors wish to thank: David Farnsworth, Rory McGowan, Michelle Roelofs, and Edwin Thie at ARUP; Gert Biebauw of Bureau Bouwtechniek; George Keliris, Greg Otto, Sanjeev Tankha, Kurt Komraus, and Stephen Lewis, all at Buro Happold; Kevin Dong, Thomas Fowler, and Jim Doerfler at Cal Poly San Luis Obispo; Xavier De Kestelier, Johnathan Parr, Katy Harris, Gayle Mault, and Sarah Simpkin at Foster + Partners; Guy Nordenson of Guy Nordenson and Associates and Rebecca Laberenne at the World Bank (formerly of GNA); Daniela Gaede, Bettina Ahrens, and Jürgen Hilmer at gmp; Arnold Lee and Julia Oseland at HOK; Peter Simmonds at IBE; Kurt Clandening at John A. Martin Associates; Richard Garlock at LERA; Leiger Stahl at Morphosis Architects; Neil Denari and Yun Yun Wu of NMDA, Inc.; Virginia Tanzmann at Parsons Brinckerhoff; Mutsuro Sasaki and Chiakra Inamura of Sasaki and Partners; Hans Schober and Rebecca Viet of Schlaich, Bergermann und Partner; Alex Terzich at SHoP Architects and Eric Churchill with SHoP Construction; Craig Hartman, Mark Sarkisian, Ben Mickus, Eric Long, Zarmine Nigohos, Roshanak Mostaghim, and Matthew Dierdorf at SOM; Steven Holl and Julia van den Hout with Steven Holl Architects; Guy Mouton of Studioburo Mouton; Toshihiro Oki of Toshihiro Architect P.C.; Bruce Gibbons, Mark Dannettel, Brian Guerrero, and Ben John with Thornton Tomasetti; Danelle Briscoe at the University of Texas-Austin; Kate Simonen at the University of Washington; Barbara Jackson at the University of Denver; Chandler Ahrens of Washington University and Open Source Architecture; Joris Pauwels, Shaun Farrell, Sara Klomps, and Malin Berden at Zaha Hadid Architects; Ben Rosenberg at Silman; Joe Franchina, Alexandria Galloway, and Marissa Glauberman of Adjaye Associates; Shelley McNamara and Paula at Grafton Architects; Hanif Kara and Arabiya Issa at AKT II; Jeanne Gang, Weston Walker, Ana Flor Ortiz, and Alissa Anderson at Studio Gang; Peter van Assche of bureau SLA; Felix Heisel at Cornell University; Patricia Culley and Ray Calabro at Bohlin Cywinski Jackson; Brian Court and Chris Hellstern at Miller Hull Partnership; Marc Brune at PAE Engineers; and Larry Jones at Atelier Ten.

At Syracuse University, Sean Morgan and Ishita Parmar provided research and administrative assistance, Christina Hoover and Shiori Green were invaluable with graphics production, and Librarian Barbara Opar worked tirelessly on our behalf. At Cal Poly, Doug Leyva provided speedy administrative assistance. Fellow engineering and architecture education colleagues Scott Murray, Uli Dangel, Sigrid Adriaenssens, and Chad Schwartz generously shared images.

Sinéad Mac Namara wishes to thank David Billington and Maria Garlock at Princeton University who set her on her academic path; Clare Olsen for being the most gracious and enthusiastic of collaborators; her students for all that they have taught her, her colleagues at Syracuse University and the women of EOW for their encouragement and advice; agus faoi dheireadh is ba thábhachtaí, ba mhaith liom mo bhuíochas a ghabháil le mo thuismitheoirí, Ber, Bláthnaid, Dónal, Doireann, Darach agus Súin ar son na tacaíochta agus an grá a thug siad dom le linn na blianta.

Clare Olsen wishes to thank her mentors at UCLA and beyond who have influenced her research and teaching; Sinéad Mac Namara for her wit and "plug compatible" brain; her colleagues and students for inspiring continual learning; and her family and Doug for their rock-solid support and guidance.

CHAPTER 1

Introduction
Call for Collaboration and Diverse Voices

Introduction

When one considers the gothic cathedrals, boundary-pushing structures,[1] and exquisite feats of architecture, it is extraordinary to the modern designer that these structures were conceived, engineered, and built under the direction of one profession, that of the stone mason (Figures 1.1a and 1.1b). Ever since the Industrial Revolution, the proliferation of specializations required to realize a work of architecture has continued apace with an expansion of disciplinary knowledge, capabilities, and tactics. There are good reasons for this: modern society requires diverse programs and building types, has high expectations for building performance, and has available an ever more complex range of technologies for design, construction, and operation. But it is worth reminding ourselves that as the professions of the architect and engineer diverged, they also became more reliant on one another for their disciplinary expertise while working toward common goals in the form of safe, habitable, functional, and performative buildings. Writing in the late 1800s, the architectural historian and critic, Viollet-le-Duc, who made careful study of those very same gothic cathedrals, cautioned his contemporaries:

> A little reflection will show us the interests of the two professions will be saved by their union … Whether the engineer acquires a little of our knowledge and love for artistic form … or whether the architect

Figure 1.1a Nave of Wells Cathedral, 1239, England. Gothic cathedrals conceived and executed under the direction of stone masons were structurally innovative and architecturally ambitious. Credit: Michael D Beckwith/Wikicommons.

Figure 1.1b Exterior of Reims Cathedral, 1211, France. The flying buttress, the pinnacle, and other features of the gothic style were actually technical innovations. Credit: G Garitan/Wikicommons.

enters upon the scientific studies and adopts the practical methods of the engineer; whether both thus succeed in uniting their faculties, knowledge, and appliances, and thereby realize an art truly characteristic of our times, the result cannot fail to be advantageous to the public and creditable to the age.[2]

The cathedrals of the gothic era may well have been technologically advanced for their time and remain architecturally significant to this day, but a closer examination shows us why the architecture, engineering, and construction industries have shifted to ever more diversified (if sometimes frustratingly siloed) professions and sub-specialties. Gothic cathedrals took decades to build, and often deployed trial and error to achieve their structural heights, which is to say, they sometimes fell down while under construction or moved a little too much in the wind after they were finished and had to be modified accordingly. They were monstrously expensive to build, and their opulence at a time when the vast majority of the citizens of Europe were abjectly poor was purposeful.[3] Responsible designers today could not and should not deploy financial resources in such a way. At the same time, we have different and higher expectations about the ways buildings perform. For example, control of comfort in interior environments (via temperature, humidity, light, and sound) requires a plethora of technologies unimagined by the gothic stone masons. Material use is also more closely questioned in contemporary practice. (In different renovations of Notre Dame de Paris, for example, it has been found that the stone quarries have long since disappeared under an expanding Paris and the large timbers necessary to replace the recently burned roof are very challenging to find in contemporary France.) In sum, today we have different needs and standards for buildings, requiring an array of specialties to design and realize them.

An evolution over time led to the variety of professions that produce today's buildings, but along with the benefits of increased specialization come the risks of atomization. Throughout the 20th century, disciplinary siloing led to compartmentalized design work. The worst outcomes of this are ill-performing buildings that harm the environments and communities that surround them. Aggregated together, the negative impacts of the building industry continue to deteriorate the planet.[4] Given the crises faced today, it is clear that healing the built environment will require systemic and incisive changes to the processes of design and construction. We must evaluate how architects, engineers, and related professionals coordinate, collaborate, and *create* the built environment. Doing so, doing so well, and doing so with a careful eye on the health of the planet and its inhabitants has never been more critical.

Confronting the entangled and transdisciplinary challenges of carbon, climate, and resource scarcity requires collaborations that leverage all the talents of our fields. Speaking about the gravity of climate change and the challenges for the industry, Rory McGowan, Director at Arup asserted, "Multiple disciplines working together is the only way we're going to solve the big issues."[5] "Wicked problems" like homelessness and environmental degradation require diverse voices and strategies. In *The Designer's Field Guide to Collaboration*, Caryn Brause advocates for public interest design (PID) to address these problems:

> [PID's] practitioners are guided by the belief that access to design is a public right, not a privilege. These practitioners are transforming conventional architectural practice by insisting that responding solely to the needs of paying clients limits the profession's ability to address widespread contemporary challenges.

In addition to interdisciplinary collaboration, she highlights the importance of "meaningful and respectful collaborations with community stakeholders" to accomplish shared goals for the greater good.[6]

Making these connections across boundaries, outside of the normative modes of thinking and practicing, is critical for the intense problem-solving efforts ahead. But collaborations require more than each individual's expertise and perspective: collaborating *well* involves a willingness to embrace different viewpoints and approaches. While new ideas can arise from collaborators with copacetic sensibilities, greater potential lies in co-mingling diverse individuals with different training (experts and generalists), backgrounds (cultural and ethnic), world views (interpersonal skills and values), and genders.[7] Researchers investigating sources of collaborative teams' abilities to produce new knowledge describe the need for individual and collective "readiness."[8] This means coming to the table with relevant expertise (or, the researchers note, a generalist's perspective), and an openness to the transformations that can happen when integrating knowledge. An inclusive model of collaborative work builds team capacities in fruitful and productive ways, not only through the generative potential of combining and building upon diverse talents, but also through the added benefits of mentorship and engagement. Simply put, mobilizing diverse individuals and approaches holds the potential for game-changing revelations that "create something new and wonderful."[9]

In writing about knowledge production, author Thomas Fisher asserts that the mega challenges of today—resilience, affordability, and inequality—require academic and professional partnerships and knowledge-sharing. "The more unanswered questions we have regarding the rapidly evolving world around us, the more we need research to help us answer them."[10] Fisher also discusses the benefits of interdisciplinary research in expanding disciplinary knowledge. Meanwhile, architecture does not have the same "knowledge loop" as other professions like law and medicine.[11] This problem pervades the entire building industry. A 2016 McKinsey & Company study found, "R&D spending in construction runs well behind that of other industries: less than 1 percent of revenues, versus 3.5 to 4.5 percent for the auto and aerospace sectors."[12] At the same time, the competitive and litigious nature of the building industry means that knowledge-sharing (outside of one's circle or office) is not common practice, hindering the ability to build upon research and carry it forward.

Yet architects and engineers are problem solvers by nature and should take care not to allow standard business practices to stymie progress for the greater good. The "wicked problems" faced today require a wholescale reconsideration of this defensive and siloed approach. Collaborations among diverse stakeholders, including architects and engineers, have the capacity to improve the welfare of the people they serve and to create net positive environmental impacts. Put in more prosaic terms, collaborations create efficiencies and other measurable gains that improve the bottom line for people, planet, and profits. The case studies in this book show the whole range of these benefits and clearly articulate the rewards of a more synthetic approach (Figure 1.2).

Figure 1.2 View of the National Museum of African American History and Culture. A collaboration involving Adjaye Associates, GNA, Silman, and others, 2016. For an in-depth discussion about this, please see Chapter 4. Credit: Kalen Martin.

Recognizing the importance and complexity of interdisciplinary collaboration, this book addresses the challenges and rewards of cross-disciplinary partnerships and provides real-world case studies to illustrate multiple approaches to collaborative working methods. We focus on collaborations between architects and engineers, generally structural engineers, but in some cases also mechanical engineers. To understand the challenges and benefits of collaboration, it is helpful to better understand the professions and their contexts, and in Chapters 2 and 3, we discuss differences and commonalities between architecture and engineering in academia and practice. In Chapters 4–16, we share in-depth accounts of projects designed by prominent architects and engineers, demonstrating the power of integrated design to realize innovative and award-winning work (Figure 1.3). In Chapters 17 and 18, we provide an overview of platforms for interdisciplinary collaboration in practice.

More broadly, the book provides a portal into the current state of the professions of architecture and engineering. In conversations with practitioners throughout the world, we asked fundamental questions about design methods and project delivery. How are design teams formed, and how do they work together? What are the challenges and rewards of collaboration? How does research inform design and how is knowledge shared? How do teams achieve project goals or bigger altruistic goals? These topics and more are explored in *Collaborations*.

Figure 1.3 View within the SANAA + Sasaki and Partners collaboration on the Glass Pavilion at the Toledo Museum of Art, Toledo, Ohio, 2007. For an in-depth discussion about this, please see Chapter 6. Credit: Scott Murray.

Notes

1. Gothic cathedrals are compared to modern skyscrapers for their boundary-breaking height and relatively skeletal structures. See: David P. Billington, *The Tower and the Bridge: The New Art of Structural Engineering*, Princeton Paperbacks, Science/Architecture (Princeton, NJ: Princeton University Press, 1985).
2. Eugène Emmanuel Viollet-Le-Duc, *Lectures on Architecture, Volume II*, trans. Benjamin Bucknall (Boston: James R, Osgood and Co., 1881), 72.
3. Ironically, craftspeople whose specialized skills were developed during this period of technological advancement spurred in part by the building of gothic cathedrals ultimately formed guilds (not unlike modern unions) which are credited with building the first version of the middle class in Europe.
4. "Why The Building Sector?–Architecture 2030," accessed May 17, 2021, https://architecture2030.org/buildings_problem_why/.
5. Rory McGowan, Interview with Arup, Rory McGowan and Michelle Roelofs, Zoom, March 4, 2021.
6. Caryn Brause, *The Designer's Field Guide to Collaboration*, 1st edition (New York: Routledge, 2017).
7. Richard B. Freeman and Wei Huang, "Collaboration: Strength in Diversity," *Nature* 513, no. 7518 (September 2014): 305–305, https://doi.org/10.1038/513305a.
8. Michael O'Rourke et al., "Disciplinary Diversity in Teams: Integrative Approaches from Unidisciplinarity to Transdisciplinarity." In Kara L. Hall, Amanda L. Vogel, and Robert T. Croyle eds. *Strategies for Team Science Success: Handbook of Evidence-Based Principles for Cross-Disciplinary Science and Practical Lessons Learned from Health Researchers*. Cham: Springer International Publishing, 2019. 21–46, https://doi.org/10.1007/978-3-030-20992-6_2.
9. Warren G. Bennis and Patricia Ward Biederman, *Organizing Genius: The Secrets of Creative Collaboration* (Reading, MA: Addison-Wesley, 1997), 2.
10. Thomas Fisher, "Research and Architecture's Knowledge Loop," *Technology|Architecture + Design* 1, no. 2 (November 1, 2017): 131–134, https://doi.org/10.1080/24751448.2017.1354601.
11. Fisher, "Research and Architecture's Knowledge Loop."
12. "Imagining Construction's Digital Future | McKinsey," accessed May 6, 2021, https://www.mckinsey.com/business-functions/operations/our-insights/imagining-constructions-digital-future#.

CHAPTER 2

Architects and Engineers in the Academy
The Challenge of the Silos

The curricula of architecture and engineering differ greatly and are attractive to students for a range of reasons. A 2018 study on the total number of engineering bachelor graduates in the US included 31,936 mechanical, 13,767 electrical, and 12,221 civil degrees awarded.[1] By contrast, in 2018, there were 2,464 bachelor of architecture degrees awarded by accredited US institutions.[2] Although architects and engineers alike are fundamentally engaged in problem-solving and design, the pedagogical methods employed in their training could not be more different.

Architecture and Engineering Pedagogy

Open-ended problem-solving using multiple methodologies in pursuit of competing goals marks architectural teaching and contrasts with the deterministic, one-problem-at-a-time approach of many engineering courses. Even the physical space where the students work is different (Figures 2.1 and 2.2). While most engineers have little exposure to design and big-picture thinking during their schooling, architecture students are not always expected to integrate complex technological building systems in their design proposals. These content differences between the disciplines are somewhat understandable given the diversities in practice; the methods of relaying content also have a profound effect on the different ways that architects and engineers approach work.

Figure 2.1 Engineering classroom. Credit: Sinéad Mac Namara.

Figure 2.2 Architecture studio. Credit: Clare Olsen.

The division between architecture and structural engineering practice crystalized after the industrial revolution. Similarly, the educational experience in both disciplines has diverged over time. Initially, in both disciplines, training for the profession came in the form of apprenticeships rather than through university education. In the past century, the polar divide in the approach to educating architects and engineers has become quite pronounced in a large number of architecture and engineering programs across the US. In Europe, on the other hand, some architecture schools, particularly German and Swiss schools, have more significant mathematics requirements for entry and focus on more technical courses within the programs. It is argued that this contributes to European dominance in technologically innovative architecture.[3]

Despite this increasing reliance on architecture–engineering collaboration in the professional world, in the US, students from the disciplines generally have few opportunities to mingle. Although the National Architectural Accrediting Board (NAAB) 2020 Conditions for Accreditation encourages Leadership and Collaboration,[4] and design teams in schools are becoming more common,[5] engineering and architecture educational collaborations are historically not as widespread.[6] ABET (Accreditation Board for Engineering and Technology), the analogous organization in engineering, similarly advocates for multidisciplinary learning, specifically in a team context. Departmental isolation in the modern university, however, puts many obstacles in the way of such collaborations. The emphasis on increasing specialization, overloaded curricula, budgetary models that discourage cross-enrollment, and the fact that there are vastly different pedagogical approaches to teaching architecture and engineering, all contribute to keep engineering and architecture students apart in their formative education. John Ochsendorf, a professor of both Architecture and Civil Engineering at MIT, encapsulates the fundamental dissonance between the two educational models and illuminates perhaps the biggest obstacle that the two groups have in working with one another at the academic level. "In engineering education today the problems are over constrained, but in architecture education I really believe that the problems are under constrained."[7]

Architects and engineers interviewed for this book were asked how well the academies are preparing architecture and engineering graduates for collaborative practice. It is worth noting that many of those interviewed also teach, and thus are very well positioned to comment. A common answer came from architects and engineers alike, with many responding "not very well." Faculty and institutions recognize the crucial need to address these pedagogical issues, especially in professional degree programs that are obliged to prepare students for the practice. Here, we identify some of the primary concerns that pervade contemporary architecture and engineering curricula with the goal of identifying opportunities to enhance student learning.

Open-Ended versus Single-Solution Problem-Solving

The typical problem or assignment tackled in an engineering course will have a single answer (often found in the back of the textbook!), while the typical problem or assignment in an architecture course will ideally result in as many solutions as there are students in the class. One of the primary reasons for this difference is the types of problems assigned to engineering students. Inputs, dimensions, boundary conditions, and other specifications are given and the goal of the assignment is to solve (usually mathematically) for one or two

Figure 2.3 First-year architecture and architectural engineering students viewing their studio work at Cal Poly San Luis Obispo. Credit: Clare Olsen.

unknown parameters. Because the problems are generally linear in nature, the methods used to solve them can be almost identical for each student. In an architecture design studio, on the other hand, course problems are more loosely and broadly defined, and there are multiple goals inherent in the problem. Students often have agency in how they approach the problem, and there are numerous acceptable methods for providing solutions (Figure 2.3).

There are very good reasons why this is so. Engineering education is obligated to cover a high volume of technical material, focusing on codes, constraints, and mathematical problem-solving. Engineering courses are both more like one another and more narrow in their focus, as befits the attempt to convey specialized knowledge. Eric Long of Skidmore, Owings & Merrill (SOM) describes that the industry looks for technical competence when hiring graduates saying, "Engineering candidates need to be extremely technically sound. We usually hire graduates with masters degrees that come from schools with solid technical classes and thesis work."[8] By contrast, architecture courses will often draw on disparate ideas and theories with the goal of preparing students for the breadth of experiences and design opportunities they may encounter in the working world. In architecture, there is necessarily more emphasis on the capacity to weave together multiple strands of information and ideas since there are generally multiple problems to address within a single assignment (and in professional practice).

Edwin Thie, Arup Senior Structural Engineer, shared,

> Architects talk about what the project will mean for the people who use it - they are storytellers. I enjoy working with architects from the

start because I like the blank sheet of paper. It is important for engineering students to learn to be okay with this, even in school. Having more collaborative experiences in education will help prepare engineering students for the design challenges of the world.[9]

He went on to say that architecture students would also benefit from collaborative experiences to better understand the engineering challenges of the world. These comments highlight the general differences between engineering pedagogy and architecture pedagogy as one of depth versus breadth. Given their respective roles in design and construction, the differences in curricula are understandable; however, the strict adherence to these deterministic versus open-ended methodologies during education can lead to difficulties in communication when working together in the professional realm and missed opportunities for joint problem-solving.

Synthesis and Design

For engineering students in the US, the curricular emphasis on technical skills and bounded problems means that synthesis of those skills through a complex design problem typically comes late in the undergraduate student career. Increasingly, engineering education researchers are concerned that so much time is spent on skill building and knowledge acquisition that there is little or no time in the curriculum for this vital synthesis. This approach assumes that they will

> be able to develop a solution by combining them … eventually … the effort involved in learning about the small pieces is so overwhelming that we can no longer synthesize the original problem–the parts become more important than the whole.[10]

Further, the engineering curricular focus on solving one problem at a time, assuming a singular answer or solution, stands in direct contrast to what noted historian of science, Thomas Hughes, calls "the history of modern technology and society in all its vital messy complexity."[11]

In most civil engineering programs throughout the US, there are fewer design opportunities for students. Most will have a freshman design course (often the only engineering course in that math and science filled first-year curriculum) and a final capstone design course, which is required by ABET. In the Criteria for Accrediting Engineering Technology Programs, 2019–2020, ABET requires that curricula "must provide a capstone or integrating experience that develops student competencies in applying both technical and non-technical skills in solving problems."[12] The intervening years are described by engineering education researchers as "the valley of despair" in terms of design experience or exposure to engineering creativity.[13] The capstone course typically comes in the last semester or two of the program, consisting of about five to seven hours of work per week with three hours or less in contact with advisor(s).[14] The contact hours and number of occurrences in the curriculum demonstrate the marked differences in design education in architecture and engineering. Engineering education researchers argue that the stark differences between the highly defined problems encountered in the typical lecture or lab and the more complex, less defined, open-ended projects in capstone present a significant challenge to student success.[15] Similarly, students' relative lack of experience with finding appropriate design problems for capstone makes faculty mentorship and contact time extremely important.[16] For an experience that should act as a bridge to a more independent work life, this is an issue of concern. In fact, the lack of design skills stemming from a traditional engineering education has long been an issue of concern. Legendary engineering designer and collaborator Ove Arup is reported to have responded to a young engineer seeking a position who listed his impressive academic and technical expertise as follows: "I'm sure that's very important, but if you meet an architect, can you design things … can you design a structure?"[17] (Figures 2.4a and 2.4b).

Engineering interviewees for this book had differing responses to this issue of design readiness. Hans Schober of SBP argued strongly that engineering students should undertake more design courses and specifically interdisciplinary courses with architecture students.[18] Rich Garlock of LERA (who also teaches engineers at Princeton) emphasized that engineers, like architects, need to be prepared to sketch ten ideas and then throw away eight if they are to

Figure 2.4a Bust honoring Ove Arup at Durham University, UK. Credit: Tim Green/Wikicommons.

Figure 2.4b The Millennium Bridge (architects Foster and Partners), one of the many landmark structures engineered by Arup the firm founded by Ove Arup. Credit: Brian Jeffery Beggerly/Wikicommons.

really take part in the design process.[19] Both Kurt Clandening of John A. Martin and Guy Nordenson similarly asserted that engineering graduates have to break the habit of arriving at one workable solution for a problem, then refusing to pursue further alternatives.[20,21]

Unlike engineering curricula, in architecture, design *is* the primary pedagogical focus. Architecture students continuously engage in creative thinking, keeping an eye on the big picture, while attempting to sort the aesthetic, functional, environmental, cultural, and social implications of their design proposals. In the professional realm, architects must reconcile numerous, sometimes competing goals for a project, making big-picture thinking a crucial part of everyday practice. Because of this, a range of methodologies for design is offered to students and they learn different techniques or combinations of techniques to approach similar problems. In these design-focused curricula, not all architecture students are taught the same depth of building systems expertise. The NAAB requires only two semesters of structures education, and often architecture students take few college-level mathematics and science classes. Naturally, there are exceptions to this mode, and requirements vary across different programs and types of institutions. Architect and educator Neil Denari supports increased discussions about technical integration saying,

> It's very important to get the message across to the student that all the elements of building are part of a palate of tools that are instrumental to constructing a set of ideas and sensibilities … Structures, in particular, should be taught as much poetically and conceptually as it is professionally.

He further argues that architects need to be taught how to talk about architectural values and specific project design objectives with engineers.[22] This is essential because there are ever-increasing technical complexities at play in contemporary architecture and architects in training will grapple with these issues through collaboration once they have entered the professional realm.

There is no question that architects gain significant technical knowledge through working in the practice, and similarly, structural engineers who work closely with architects gain insight and skill in design. However, collaborations during their education represent a rich opportunity to better equip both groups to better succeed in the working realm.

Exposure to Practice

In architecture schools, students are exposed to the best examples of creative endeavor and cutting-edge design practice. Through history and theory courses, they learn how notable moments in history occurred when architects challenged norms, and how new styles, forms, and technologies evolved. By the same token, students in design courses often study precedents to learn about similar site conditions, program types, or technologies that they wish to use. Architecture students are thus very familiar with a wide array of exemplary contemporary and historical projects. Many full-time architecture faculty are actively engaged in design and making, and most schools have practicing architects who teach part time. Travel for the purposes of sketching, investigating, and analyzing existing works of architecture old and new is a fundamental aspect of architecture education. Site visits every semester and longer trips abroad for a semester or a year at a time are standard in many architecture programs. Lectures from notable practitioners or critics are a frequent feature in schools of architecture.

In contrast, in engineering programs, history courses are very rare, and exposure to contemporary practice is far less consistent than it is in architecture. Eric Long from SOM laments, "One thing engineering education lacks is exposure to history and precedent studies. It would be wonderful to study the bridges of Robert Maillart, for example" (Figure 2.5).[23]

Although practicing engineers are often drafted to help teach capstone design courses, most engineering academics engage in primary research rather than design. The authors found in surveying their own engineering students, for example, that second- and third-year students struggle to name engineers,

Figure 2.5 Salginatobel Bridge by Robert Maillart. Maillart's bridges are much admired by engineers and architects alike for their efficient, economic, and elegant designs. Credit: David P. Billington.

buildings, or products of engineering that they admire, in fact they were more likely to have some favorite architects![24] It is difficult to imagine a medical student who could not name a disease that modern medicine had cured, or a music student without a favorite composer or performer, yet the engineering education system seems to leave students entirely divorced from the products of their profession. This surely hinders communication during future collaborations with architects.

Interdisciplinary courses, where each group must teach the other to some degree, represent an opportunity for engineering students to become more familiar with their intended profession and the design world more generally, and for architecture students to learn how to better communicate with those with technical expertise who may not initially share their interests or concerns in the larger design realm.

Visual Representation in Engineering Curricula

While well versed in the language of mathematics, and at a minimum competent in verbal and written communication, engineering students are less trained in the other (and arguably the most important) mode of communication in the design world: the visual, i.e. drawing, sketching, and modeling. Many engineering programs incorporate some CAD software instruction and some training in how to read plans and sections into a first-year introduction course and perhaps again in a capstone course. Electives giving further training in CAD or BIM are not uncommon (and indeed very popular among career-minded students), but visual representation is not formally part of the majority of engineering curricula. It might surprise engineering students to learn that practicing engineers interviewed replied with one voice to the questions "Do you draw? Is drawing an important tool for communication in your practice? Should engineering students be taught to draw?" "Yes, yes, and yes" was the almost universal response.

Drawing and other forms of visual representation are important for developing spatial reasoning and the capacity to visualize the un-built in three dimensions. It is also a tool for developing one's own design concepts and communicating those concepts to colleagues and interdisciplinary collaborators. Garlock observes that drawing is fundamental to the development of design ideas for engineers and laments that not enough engineering students develop their freehand drawing skills.[25] Schober reports that he often makes a rough 3D model in Rhino, which he can then print and sketch over to help him conceptualize a new problem.[26] Guy Nordenson (who also teaches structures to architecture students at Princeton) notes that the engineers at his firm use drawing *and* models to investigate and communicate design ideas amongst themselves and with their architecture collaborators.[27] Xavier De Kestelier reports that when Foster + Partners incorporated in-house engineers, they were quick to adopt the 3D printer and laser cutter as tools for communication and design.[28] Thus, it is clear that in the professions the tools of visual representation *are* important to both in-house and collaborative practice, and that many engineers learn the value of those tools on the job. Interdisciplinary courses can begin this process and better prepare engineering students for effective communication with their architecture collaborators. This concern for the engineer's capacity to engage in visual culture as a way to better engage in design is not new. Writing in 1959 about the obstacles to collaboration between architects and engineers Ove Arup declared, "The Author believes firmly that the civil engineers should learn more solid geometry, freehand sketching, and appreciation of architecture."[29]

Technical Rigor in Architectural Curricula

If one looks at the work of many prominent historical figures in architecture such as Antoni Gaudi, Louis Kahn, and Buckminster Fuller, it is clear that architects of the modern period were well versed in mathematics and structural principles. However, if engineering students are deficient in exposure to practice and visual culture, architecture students are often critiqued as lacking in technical rigor.

One defense of the perceived lack of technical depth in architecture education is that there is simply too much material to learn it all comprehensively, and further that some technical knowledge is best gained through practice. Architect Toshihiro Oki claims that it is only when "you see the reality of working in the field, and you wake up and figure out how to work with consultants,"[30] positing that it is only through practice that architecture graduates have the need or the motivation to fully engage detailed technical requirements.

A complicating factor here is that although architecture students do take technical courses (certainly more than engineers do design courses), there is good evidence to suggest that students do not absorb this knowledge (or indeed many other types of knowledge) when it is presented in lecture format without a design context. John Folan, professor at Carnegie Mellon University, asserts,

> Delivered outside the context of a design scenario, already abstract concepts of social, legal, economic, and contractual performance become entirely opaque, or even impenetrable for most students. As a result, the content remains entirely irrelevant in the academic setting and many students emerge into the profession without capacity to evaluate priorities as they relate to performance.[31]

This observation is supported by education research that demonstrates the value of "just in time" learning where students learn complex tools and skills (a specific math concept for example) best when they have immediate need of that tool to achieve some other immediate work goal.

When the teaching of technical material is relegated to lectures and not emphasized in studio culture, or when rigorous technical standards are seen only as a barrier to creative design, it is a missed opportunity. This aspect of architectural education culture present at many (but by no means all) schools can lead to naiveté on the parts of architecture students as to what technical knowledge they themselves might reasonably claim and the degree to which real design work is a collaborative practice that requires interaction with other experts. This is the single most important thing about technical education for architects. It is imperative that architects are taught to work well with engineering experts of all kinds, so that they can maximize the design potential of emerging technologies, and where better to start than with the engineering students on their campuses?

Call for Interdisciplinary Coursework

The academy has a profound obligation to not only prepare students for professional practice, but to instill values that define a trajectory and future for the fields. Author and educator Dana Cuff reminds us that "The ethos of a profession is born in schools."[32] Despite this, she goes on to say that there is a "general mismatch between the ethos of professional ideals and values (emphasized in schools) and the circumstances of professional work…."[33] Although interdisciplinary course work is advocated by both the architecture and engineering accreditation boards as one way to address professional preparedness, curricular differences can hinder course outcomes. However, when designed well, interdisciplinary courses can prove to be pivotal in students' educational careers.

For schools that strive to impart creativity and technical skills to produce innovative design proposals augmented by integrated systems, interdisciplinary courses are necessary and crucial in the effort to impart a more holistic understanding of the practices of architecture and engineering. Furthermore, the integration of systems and design through studies of efficiencies in structure, energy or constructability, for example, contributes to a more thorough understanding of sustainability and professional responsibilities. Through the process of sharing and developing expertise, students not only gain confidence in their abilities, but they also become better designers. Without question, interdisciplinary experiences are vital to preparing students for meaningful design collaborations in the professional realm.

Summarizing the Critiques

This critical look at architecture and engineering pedagogies points to gaps in the professional preparedness of students. In 2013, Greg Otto of Buro Happold, trained as both an architect and an engineer, offered this summary of the failings of traditional education for both disciplines.

> My personal comment is that both architecture and engineering educational systems are failing the market. Neither is training people in the way that the industry or market requires. Engineering graduates are too 'silo-ed'—they can design beams and columns but they can't think of the big picture and certainly don't understand business well. Architecture graduates are too caught up in the novel and sensational, and sometimes in doing the digital for the digital's sake. Architecture has lost sight of how to build. Engineers are coming out with a lot of theory, architects with a lot of design. But nobody is coming out with how to make buildings.[34]

Many may argue that today's architecture and engineering graduates remain woefully unprepared for the complexities of practice. Integrating collaborative coursework provides a tangible and rewarding means to overcome this challenge.

Notes

1. Joseph Roy, "Engineering and Engineering Technology By The Numbers" (American Society for Engineering Education, 2019). https://ira.asee.org/wp-content/uploads/2021/02/Engineering-by-the-Numbers-FINAL-2021.pdf
2. National Architectural Accrediting Board, "2018 Annual Report on Architectural Education," 2018.
3. Peter Buchanan, "Why Is Europe Winning?" *Architect* 94 (2005): 17–18.
4. "NAAB Conditions for Accreditation, 2020 Edition," 2020.
5. Robert Smith, "2009 and Beyond: Revisiting the Report on Integrated Practice: Suggestions for an Integrative Education." http://www.aia.org/about/initiatives/AIAB082222. Smith paraphrases Renee Cheng in her comment that "…more and more students all across the country are working on design projects in teams—which has been a big change in the past few years."
6. In a survey of architecture programs (cited in Table 2, p43 of the following article), 4 out of 54 had some form of interdisciplinary coursework. Barbara De La Harpe, J. Fiona Peterson, Noel Frankham, Robert Zehner, Douglas Neale, Elizabeth Musgrave, and Ruth McDermott, "Assessment Focus in Studio: What Is Most Prominent in Architecture, Art and Design?," *International Journal of Art & Design Education* 28 (2009): 37–51. https://doi.org/10.1111/j.1476-8070.2009.01591.x
7. John Ochsendorf, "Teaching Architectonics" Keynote lecture, 2013 Building Technology Educators Society Conference, Bristol, RI, July 11–13, 2013.
8. Eric Long, Interview by authors. Phone interview. San Francisco, CA, August 2, 2013.
9. Edwin Thie, Interview with Arup, Edwin Thie, Zoom, April 1, 2021.
10. Linda Katehi, "The Global Engineer," *Educating the Engineer of 2020: Adapting Engineering Education to the New Century*. National Academy of Sciences 4 (2005): 151–155.
11. Thomas Parke Hughes, *American Genesis: A History of the American Genius for Invention*, 1st edition (New York: Penguin Books, 1990), 5.
12. "Criteria for Accrediting Engineering Technology Programs, 2019–2020 | ABET," accessed May 28, 2021, https://www.abet.org/accreditation/accreditation-criteria/criteria-for-accrediting-engineering-technology-programs-2019-2020/.
13. Daria Kotys-Schwartz, Daniel Knight and Gary Pawlas, "First Year and Capstone Design Projects: Is the Bookend Approach Effective for Skill Gain?" *Proceedings of the American Society for Engineering Education 2010 Annual Conference and Exposition*, June 2010, Louisville, KY, 2010.

14 Robert H. Todd, Spencer P. Magleby, Carl D. Sorensen, Bret R. Swan and David K. Anthony, "A Survey of Capstone Engineering Courses in North America," *Journal of Engineering Education* 84, no. 2 (1995): 165-174.
15 James Palmer and Hisham Hegab, *Developing an Open Ended Junior Level Laboratory Experience to Prepare Students for Capstone Design*. Proceedings of the American Society for Engineering Education 2010 Annual Conference and Exposition, June 2010, Louisville, KY, 2010.
16 William Leonard, Robert Merril and Elizabeth Dell, *An Innovative Method Providing and Alternative to Capstone Courses Using Experiential Learning*. Proceedings of the American Society for Engineering Education 2010 Annual Conference and Exposition, June 2010, Louisville, KY, 2010.
17 Derek Sugden, foreword to *Ove Arup Philosophy of Design: Essays 1942-1981*, edited by Nigel Tonks. (London: Prestel, 2012), 6.
18 Hans Schober, Interview by the authors. Phone Interview. Stuttgart, Germany, June 19, 2013.
19 Richard Garlock, Interview by the authors. Phone Interview. Princeton, NJ, June 25, 2013.
20 Kurt Clandening, Interview by authors. Phone interview. Los Angeles, CA, May 24, 2013.
21 Guy Nordenson, Interview by authors. Phone interview. New York, NY, June 14, 2013
22 Neil Denari, Interview by authors. Phone interview. Los Angeles, June 25, 2013.
23 Eric Long, Interview by the authors. Phone interview. San Francisco, April 23, 2013.
24 Sinéad Mac Namara, C.J. Olsen, Scott L. Shablak and Carolina B. Harris, "Merging Engineering and Architectural Pedagogy–A Trans-disciplinary Opportunity?" *Proceedings of the 2010 ICEE Conference on Engineering Education*, Silesian University of Technology, Gliwice, Poland, July 18-22, 2010.
25 Garlock, Interview by the authors. Phone Interview.
26 Schober, Interview by the authors. Phone Interview.
27 Nordenson, Interview by authors. Phone Interview.
28 Xavier De Kestelier, Interview by the authors, Phone Interview. London, UK, May 25, 2013.
29 Ove Arup, "The Architect and the Engineer," *ICE Proceedings* 13, no. 4 (1959): 499-502.
30 Toshihiro Oki, Interview by the authors. Phone Interview, New York, NY, July 30, 2013.
31 John Folan, "Exclusively Mutual." Performative Practices: Architecture and Engineering in the 21st Century, edited by William Braham & Kiel Moe. ACSA Teachers Conference. New York City, 2011.
32 Dana Cuff. *Architecture: The Story of Practice*. (Cambridge: MIT Press, 1991). 43.
33 Cuff, *Architecture*.
34 Greg Otto, Interview by the authors. In person interview. Los Angeles, June 10, 2013.

CHAPTER 3

Architects and Engineers in the Profession

The Barriers and Benefits of Collaboration

Before delving into the rich stories of interdisciplinary collaborations in the case studies, it is helpful to learn about the disciplinary contexts that contribute to the ethos of architecture and engineering practitioners. This chapter provides a discussion about differences in the practices, highlighting the cultural, economic, and historical contexts for collaboration. It also discusses the rewards of collaboration and long-standing relationships, famed partnerships, and their successes.

Introduction to the Practices of Architecture and Engineering

As discussed in the previous chapter, skills learned in architecture and engineering curricula and graduates' ability to work through problems and provide multifaceted solutions lend well to multiple kinds of employment and working methods. There are a wide range of working modes and many types of firms, defined by size and organizational structure as well as methodologies deployed and types of projects produced. Architecture firms are frequently characterized by the number of people employed in the office since it often correlates to the scale of projects that are being designed. An American Institute of Architects (AIA) report indicates that of 19,000 AIA member-owned firms in 2019, 60% had fewer than five employees and a quarter of total firms were sole practitioners (Figure 3.1). Interestingly, the largest firms with 100 or more employees, which made up 2.5% of the firms surveyed, had 30% of total employees and earned 49% of the total billings.[1]

These statistics indicate that an overwhelming majority of architecture professionals work in smaller firms, and the quality of work life depends upon office culture and organization as well as the type of work being produced. Since architecture is both a creative endeavor and a commodity, architects generally operate within the duality of artist/organizer in the service of clients. Job responsibilities in architectural offices range from technical aspects of

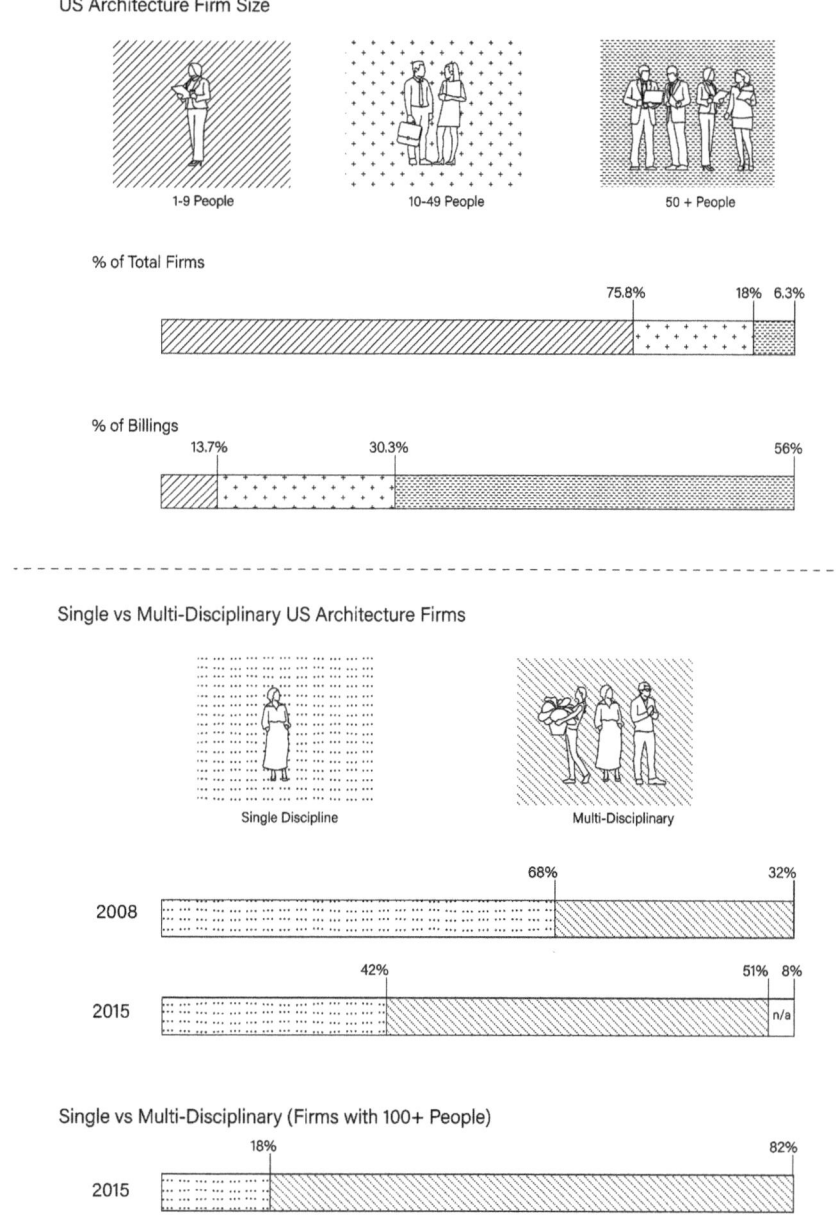

Figure 3.1 Architecture firm structure. Credit: Shiori Green.

architectural production, which include specification writing and code analysis, to creative endeavors such as spatial design and representation. The smaller the office, the more likely that the employees are "wearing many hats" in order to carry out the work.

Similar diversity is found amongst engineering practices. Workplace culture varies widely depending on the scale of the firm and focus of the work. Contemporary engineering practice is wildly diverse both in terms of the type of work and methodological approaches. As diverse as the roles performed in the field of architecture, engineers engage in endeavors including research and development of new technologies and systems, design and analysis, construction management, and marketing. Between 1910 and 2000, engineering jobs' proportion of total employment increased ninefold,[2] and, today, engineers work in many facets of society, not strictly engineering firms. The 2020 Bureau of Labor and Statistics survey revealed that civil engineers, for example, work in areas ranging from architectural, engineering, and related services to natural gas pipelines and social advocacy organizations.[3]

Despite the diversity of work experiences in the disciplines, stereotypes of engineers and architects and their work abound: The engineer makes it stand up, the architect makes it look good. The architect's lofty design ambitions are thwarted by engineers' column grids and bracing. Engineers only value efficiency while architects value the spatial experience. While there might be some kernel of truth at the heart of these caricatures, the reality of interdisciplinary collaboration is more complex and nuanced and these stereotypes can impede working relationships. Since the professions are so interdependent, collegiality and mutual respect must form the basis of any partnership. Traditionally however, there are structural obstacles that hinder successful partnerships between engineers and architects, and both disciplines have much to learn from those on the vanguard of interdisciplinary collaboration.

In the context of the design and construction of buildings, large and small, for the last hundred years, the dominant division of labor between the disciplines is generally understood as an architect-led process with structural engineers, mechanical and electrical engineers, and other experts providing disciplinary expertise along the way. There are many reasons for this traditional arrangement having to do with contracts, costs, and risk allocation. Contracts create a structure for design "control," which in the US, for over a hundred years, was dominated by a design-bid-build contract devised by the American Institute of Architects (AIA); see Chapter 17 for a lengthier discussion. Often in this traditional architect-led process, the design can be relatively well advanced by the architects before other disciplines are engaged.

This work sequence perpetuates the myth of authorship—those outside the disciplines may still believe that buildings are the products of genius creators. In reality, most works of architecture require a "gang of creatives" with diverse skills, open-mindedness, and mutual respect to share ideas and design responsibilities. While architects are often described as generalists and engineers as specialists, the practices both require high levels of expertise, and projects usually necessitate teams of experts to see them through.[4] Integrating aesthetics with structure, sustainability, and systems requires multiple voices at the design table to share perspectives and expertise. When architects and engineers don't work well together, on the other hand, both aesthetics and function suffer. One might find structure in the way of a spatial sequence, or air conditioning that needs to run 24/7 because site strategy and passive cooling systems were not considered early in the design process. The case studies in this book focus on particularly successful collaborations resulting in buildings that would have been impossible without the involvement and expertise of multiple disciplines: in their integration, the buildings are greater than the sum of their parts.

Cost Benefits of Collaboration

Numerous interviewees cited the role of project finances in shaping the nature of collaboration. Richard Garlock, Partner at LERA, noted that the contract structure and the number of engineering hours the client is willing to pay for can dictate whether an engineer is brought on board for early discussions where they might have more design influence.[5] Yet Steven Holl and others noted that waiting until later in the design process to consult with technical experts can be a false economy since design services are a small part of the overall budget in comparison to materials and construction.[6] In larger projects especially, collaborations resulting in minor savings in materials costs would more than compensate for extra engineering fees at the start of the project. Some architects may feel that since the engineer's fee often comes out of the architect's compensation, it makes financial sense to establish early collaboration only on the more technically complex projects. In Chapter 17, a discussion about contract types and alternate project delivery methods addresses some of the structural impediments to collaboration.

Symbiotic Collaborations

Although works of architecture are generally identified by their architect and not their engineer (the Eiffel Tower a notable exception), it is not difficult to argue that notable works of architecture are not achievable without significant contributions by engineering collaborators. Pritzker Laureate, Rem Koolhaas, for example, began collaborating with Cecil Balmond at Ove Arup in 1985. Of this partnership, Koolhaas has said,

> Our growing intimacy with each other's disciplines- in fact, a mutual invasion of territory- and corresponding blurring of specific professional identities (not always painless) allowed us, at the end of the eighties … to defrost earlier ambitions and to explore the redesign and demystification of architecture, this time experimenting on ourselves.[7]

The symbiosis of their relationship has clearly had a profound effect, not only on the work, but also on the growth of Koolhaas and Balmond as creators.

Finding the "right" collaborators—those with copacetic sensibilities—can take the better part of one's career. Numerous factors contribute to the success of collaborations and the composition of the design team can make or break a project. Conversations with almost all of the architects and engineers interviewed for this book described the importance of long-standing relationships; learning how one's collaborators think and communicate forms the basis of successful collaborations. Bruce Gibbons, head of the Building Structure practice for Thornton Tomasetti, Los Angeles, believes strongly in early collaboration, but also recognizes, "It's always easier to collaborate with someone you know. When working with people for the first time, communication can be a major challenge."[8] Engineer Hans Schober of SBP, speaking about the Berlin Hauptbahnhof design, claimed that years of experience working with the architects, Gerkan, Marg and Partners (gmp), prompted them to invite SBP to the design team. Schober also asserted that his firm agreed to be involved because they knew gmp were open to the kind of structurally honest designs that SBP so favors.[9]

Due to the differences in disciplinary training and vocabulary, communicating with experts outside one's discipline can be challenging and sometimes frustrating. So, often when architects find engineers with whom they work well, who understand their design goals and intentions, they partner with the same colleagues for decades. For example, Louis Kahn and August Komendant designed innovative reinforced concrete structures together from the 1950s until Kahn's death in the late 1970s. Many of the structurally expressive skyscrapers of the Second Chicago School were the result of the long collaboration at SOM between architect Bruce Graham and engineer Fazlur Khan (Figure 3.2). Similarly, Renzo Piano and Peter Rice worked on numerous projects together, with the Pompidou

Figure 3.2 John Hancock Center, Chicago, IL, 1970. Skidmore, Owings, & Merrill. Credit: Seth Anderson, flickr Creative Commons, https://www.flickr.com/photos/swanksalot/6106331858

Figure 3.3a-b Pompidou Center in Paris, France, 1971. Designed in collaboration among Renzo Piano, Richard Rogers, Peter Rice, and others. Credit: a and b Sinéad Mac Namara.

Center in Paris an especially successful example of their work (Figure 3.3a-b). Rem Koolhaas and Cecil Balmond have designed numerous structurally ambitious projects including Casa da Musica and CCTV Headquarters (Figure 3.4). Like Koolhaas and Balmond, Toyo Ito and Mutsuro Sasaki's collaborative work is so well integrated that it is impossible to distinguish the engineering from the architecture. Steven Holl and Guy Nordenson have a decades-long working relationship and their writings about their work reflect a deep mutual understanding and reciprocal inspiration in their working methods. Rice, who engineered the shells of the Sydney Opera House, and defined the disciplines saying, "the architect's response is primarily creative, whereas the engineer's is essentially inventive"[10] (Figure 3.5) had this to say about the value of collaboration: "good teams are made up of different people, people whose separateness and attitude complement each other, and who by their willingness to work together and accept …. the contribution of all … make possible real momentum."[11]

Figure 3.4 Casa da Musica by OMA and Arup, Porto, Portugal, 2005. Credit: Clare Olsen.

Figure 3.5 Sydney Opera House. Constructed 1959–1973. Architect Jørn Utzon, Engineer Arup (Peter Rice). Credit: Bernard Spragg/Wikicommons.

In-House Collaborations

The proximity of the engineers and architects working together certainly facilitates a comfort level and ease of communication, crucial aspects of successful collaboration. The contemporary movements toward in-house collaborations and more diversified teams highlight the growing need to work synergistically. With many architects and engineers who work at the cutting edge of their respective disciplines engaging in ever more integrated design work, it is not surprising that some offices are moving towards in-house collaborations. The 2020 AIA firm survey found that in 2019, 56% of architectural offices' employees were single discipline, and 6% of architecture firms' employees were engineers.[12] Architecture journalist B.J. Novitski describes a study of interviews with architects reporting, largely positively, on the creations of in-house positions for engineers to ensure early incorporation of ecological thinking and sustainable systems. One architect quoted by the study's authors, "[believes] this new practice has profoundly changed the firm, concluding, 'We believe the engineers are making us better architects, and architects are making engineers better, too.'"[13]

The trend to employ engineers in-house is nothing new for one of the most prominent integrated firms, Skidmore, Owings & Merrill (SOM is discussed in greater detail in Chapter 7). Since the founding of the firm in the 1930s, SOM's architects and engineers have collaborated from the beginning of the design process, and are internationally known for designing buildings where the architecture and structure cannot be separated—the engineering is critical to the architectural experience and vice versa.[14] As associates at SOM point out, "This spirit of architectural and engineering collaboration feeds the development of conceptual and technical invention to this day at SOM, leading to new structural and architectural paradigms."[15]

Foster + Partners provides a more recent example of integrating in-house engineers, although an integrated approach has been central to Foster + Partners work since the inception of the practice in 1967. The addition of in-house engineers in 2010 was a natural progression from a reorganization in 2005 that restructured the office into multidisciplinary teams. In the first reorganization, the employees were distributed into six design groups, as well as a number of support teams, all led by senior partners. Mouzhan Majidi, Chief Executive, stated in 2008,

> Significantly, the first year of our new collaboration was the practice's most successful ever. During that period we won thirteen international competitions and forty-one design awards—a record for us — and we opened offices in New York, Istanbul and Madrid.[16]

With the success of the team structure, two in-house engineering groups were established a few years later. Having partnered on numerous projects with Piers Heath's firm, PHA Consult, the office was purchased and many of the engineers went to work in Foster + Partners' London Riverside studio. Piers Heath became a Senior Partner and leads the Environmental Engineering group and Roger Ridsdill Smith, previously at Arup, leads Structural Engineering group. Xavier De Kestelier, who was a Partner at Foster + Partners as joint head of one of the support groups, the Specialist Modeling Group described,

> The engineers sit with the architects—they really integrate by proximity—there isn't a separate department. There isn't a different review to look at the engineering and the architecture—they are reviewed at the same time … the integration within our office at all levels has worked quite beautifully.[17]

With the engineering team in-house at Foster + Partners, the collaborators can chat in real time on a daily basis, streamlining communication and therefore the efficiency of project design and development.

Integrating engineers into the practice has resulted in an interesting transformation in the way that the engineers are working and communicating with their architect collaborators. Foster + Partners has a long history of valuing technology and model-making and the firm has one of the largest fabrication shops in London, including numerous 3d printers that run day and night.[18] De Kestelier described that since the engineers are integrated into a highly technological, research-oriented environment that relies heavily on representation, the engineers quickly became adept at visual communication and model-making, as well as utilizing the 3d printers to test ideas. The supporting infrastructure and partnerships have enabled a rich working environment that sparks a "hunger to continuously improve."[19] Significantly, Norman Foster describes the office collegiate structure as one of the design projects of which he's most proud.[20]

Collaboration and Communication

Despite the prevalence of collaboration in the professional realm, working in interdisciplinary groups is not always natural or easy. Numerous factors contribute to who we are, how we work and interact with others. Harvard University experts in group behavior say that

> Different brain systems may have evolved not only to work together within a single head, but also to work together between heads--that is, so that different systems are not only "plug compatible" within a single brain, but also across brains.[21]

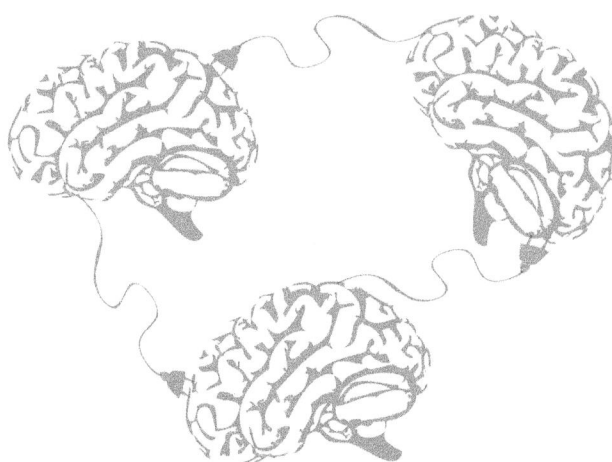

Figure 3.6 Harvard University researchers describe that brains are "plug compatible" to enable collaboration. Credit: Christina Hoover.

Figure 3.6 creates an interesting image, but it also points to some critical issues for understanding collaboration. Firstly, people have different brain systems and are differently skilled. This is what is so wonderful about the nature of collaboration. Individuals have diverse capabilities, desires, and backgrounds so teamwork provides an opportunity to fortify efforts by bringing multiple skill sets together to achieve goals. There is a catch, however. The very differences that can lead to synergies and epiphanies can be a huge source of frustration between collaborators, especially when working interdisciplinarily. People are drawn to study particular fields for a wide range of contextual, environmental, and personal reasons. Subsequently, differences in educational experiences compound dissimilarities in personalities.

This raises an important issue, which is that even though there are certain generalizations that can be made about the differences between architects and engineers, every person is unique, with individual goals, values, techniques, and quirks. Personalities as well as pedagogical and professional training all contribute to the success or failure of working partnerships. Communication across disciplines can be frustrating and even adversarial leading to real and costly project-related problems. A 2018 survey of 600 construction industry leaders found, "Respondents attributed twenty-six percent of rework to poor communication between team members."[22]

Differences in communication and working methods can be very challenging aspects of working in teams. It is important to note that the disciplines of engineering and architecture have different, but overlapping disciplinary vocabularies. The same word might mean very different things to architects and engineers (Figures 3.7a and 3.7b). Words with fluid and useful disciplinary meaning in architecture, such as *differentiation*, *articulation*, *atmosphere*, *continuity*, *discontinuity*, *integration*, and *variation*, have altogether more prosaic

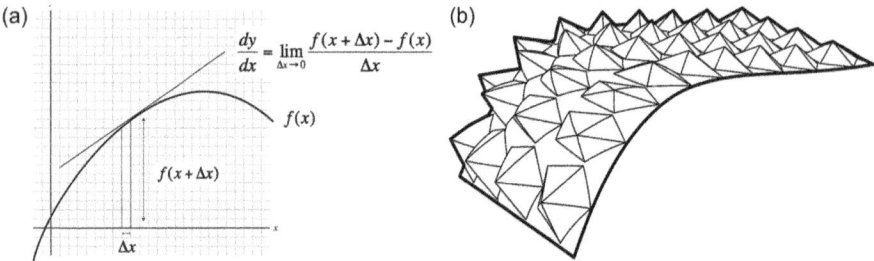

Figure 3.7a A visualization of differentiation as understood by engineers. Credit: Christina Hoover.

Figure 3.7b A visualization of differentiation as understood by architects. Credit: Clare Olsen.

and perhaps more rigidly defined meanings in the world of the engineer. As these examples suggest, the disciplinary vocabulary one learns in school is not necessarily helpful when communicating with colleagues in other fields.

Learning how to communicate effectively is a skill one develops over time through mentorship and observation. Ken Sanders, a Managing Director at Gensler describes, "The most important skill is the ability to collaborate, by far."[23] Sanders also remarks that technical skills can be taught on the job, but the ability to collaborate is "the most important criteria for new hires … The human piece is the harder piece."[24] Of course, communication skills can also be learned on the job, but working well with others does not come naturally to all people. When asked about communicating with his structural engineering colleagues, Ben Mickus, who was an Associate at Skidmore, Owings & Merrill at the time, noted that the burden is on architects to learn how to communicate effectively in order to integrate structural reasoning with architectural goals.[25] SOM has an unwritten mentorship program where junior colleagues and Directors participate side-by-side in roundtable design discussions and after a meeting, a mentor might explain why something was said, thereby passing along communication methods.[26] At the interdisciplinary firm, communication skills are highly valued and assessed in the annual performance reviews.

Many interviewees for this text remarked that clear verbal communication proves vital to the design process. Brian Guerrero, an Associate and engineer at Thornton Tomasetti asserted that communication amongst colleagues and clients is more crucial to the design process than software and by improving communication, "we'll get much farther in the built environment."[27] Eric Long of SOM made a similar statement, saying "innovation in form and thought comes from a community of people at the table and the craft of the individual, not from software."[28] The authors wholeheartedly agree. That being said, representation (analog or digital) can facilitate communication by helping everyone get on the same page. Chapter 18 describes some of the tactics that collaborators are using to further their design goals.

Valuing Relationships

Collaboration requires more than clear communication, however. David Farnsworth of Arup contends: "In today's working environment, one needs to be able to collaborate, be quick to get on the right side of a job, have a willingness to take responsibility, but also know when to share credit."[29] These behaviors can be difficult for some, but extremely important when working in teams. Architecture, especially, has a reputation for ego-driven work, so collaborators need to know when to advocate for their project goals, but also support team members by negotiating and making trade-offs. Stereotypically, architects and engineers value different results, but aesthetics and efficiency don't have to be pitted against one another, and credit given to an engineer's contribution need not diminish the architect's sense of worth. Ideally, researchers claim, "In a true creative collaboration, almost everyone emerges with a sense of ownership."[30] Successes are achieved when multiple experts contribute, moving the project beyond the boundaries of a single discipline. By pushing the field and challenging oneself, each person can feel rewarded in the accomplishment and project's success.

For architects and engineers who value innovation, creative collaboration is pivotal to the design process. Hanif Kara, structural engineer, co-founder and design director of AKT II points out,

> Just as good architecture relies on good clients, good architects make for good engineering. They understand the basic technical role played by engineers, but can also push engineers to think of questions they have not thought of themselves. In this way, good architects know how to get the best out of engineers.[31]

Along these lines, engineer George Keliris of Buro Happold stated, "[Being a good engineer] is not just about structural calculations, but about creativity. [At Buro Happold], we value new ideas, innovation, and difference,"[32] which is a major reason that Buro Happold is widely known for their contributions to innovative projects. Finding the "right" collaborators to contribute to the creative process is of utmost importance.

Collaborative Case Studies

The case studies that follow this chapter provide an in-depth study of collaborative design processes that contributed to notable works of architecture. Seeking an understanding of how projects are realized, the authors interviewed numerous architects and engineers about their design processes and working methods. The second edition includes four new case studies and new short-format stories about "collaboration concepts." Although many—sometimes 20 or more—offices may have worked on a project, each case study typically profiles the partnership of two firms: the architects and structural engineers or mechanical engineers. For a few case studies, a third party was interviewed because one of the initial interviewees suggested that those practitioners (facade consultants, a local collaborating architect, etc.) were a particularly important part of the story. We interviewed innovators—people who are making significant contributions to the fields of architecture and engineering. The case studies themselves were usually chosen by the interviewees. The focus of the case studies are not the projects themselves, but rather the people who designed them and the way in which their collaborative processes manifest in the final outcomes.

Numerous commonalities arose in this qualitative research both in terms of the people we interviewed and the work outcomes. Many of the projects involve innovation and experimentation, where designers developed new forms and experiences through the use of new technologies and materials. Sustainability goals, which are increasingly at the forefront of project goals across the globe, were a primary design driver in the majority of the projects. For example, Cooper Union, Billie Jean King Main Library, and ARTIC have LEED Platinum status, the National Museum of African American History and Culture is LEED Gold, and the Queen Alia International Airport and the Port House achieved similar recognition in their respective environmental compliance schema.

It was also remarkable and encouraging to find considerable loyalty and interdependence among the community of designers. Many of the case studies describe long-standing collaborations—architects, and engineers that have worked together on multiple projects. In projects where new relationships were formed the warmth and appreciation expressed makes clear the mutual regard that developed. Naturally there are challenging aspects of any project, and particular business practices, technical constraints, or diverse stakeholder needs that can and do lead to conflict and friction that interviewees acknowledge. Collaboration is not easy and it's not always productive. There are many methods of working with a team, and the case studies provide insights into the collaborative process through examples of largely successful collaborations that tackled complex technical constraints and laudatory architectural ambitions.

There are eleven full and four shorter project case studies in this book. The longer case studies fall into three broad categories: civic, institutional, and transportation. Civic institutions include the Gilder Center, the National Museum of African American History and Culture, the Glass Pavilion at Toledo Museum of Art, and the Billie Jean King Main Library. With the exception of the Glass Pavilion, the civic and institutional projects are medium to large in scale. Educational or governmental institutions are represented by 41

Cooper Square, the Marshall Building at London School of Economics, Antwerp Port House, and Simmons Hall at the Massachusetts Institute of Technology. The transportation case studies, large infrastructural projects, round out the case studies: an airport in Jordan, and two regional transport stations (in California and Germany). Practitioners interviewed for two focus chapters on Net Zero and Circularity offer insights into the working methods that contribute to exemplary buildings that achieved significant positive environmental and social impacts.

As described in the introduction, practicing in the design world today is extraordinarily complex. The case studies provide a snippet of the design processes that contributed to realizing innovative built work. The case studies presented here do not attempt to exhaustively illustrate the breadth and depth of the long list of collaborators and their input into each project. Rather these studies are an effort to unpack the complex and multifaceted nature of these designs by focusing on two to three of the primary disciplines involved with the goal of understanding the influence those collaborators and their collaborations had on design processes and final outcomes.

It has been incredibly rewarding to connect with the hugely talented individuals that contributed to these projects. We hope you too will find them inspirational.

Notes

1. American Institute of Architects, "Firm Survey Report—The Business of Architecture 2020," 2020, https://www.aia.org/resources/6151-firm-survey-report.
2. Ian D. Wyatt, "Occupational Changes during the 20th Century," *Monthly Labor Review* 129 (2006): 35.
3. "Civil Engineers," accessed May 28, 2021, https://www.bls.gov/oes/current/oes172051.htm.
4. Erin Carraher and Ryan E. Smith, *Leading Collaborative Architectural Practice*, 1st edition (Wiley, 2017).
5. Richard Garlock, Interview by the authors, 2013.
6. Steven Holl, Interview by the authors. Email interview. New York, NY, August 6, 2013.
7. Rem Koolhaas, "Speculations on Structure and Services," reprinted in William Braham and Johathan Hale eds. *Rethinking Technology: A Reader in Architectural Theory*. London: Routledge, 2007. 354–357. 340.
8. Bruce Gibbons, Interview by the authors. Phone interview. Los Angeles, July 8, 2013.
9. Hans Schober, Interview by the authors. Phone interview. Stuttgart, June 19, 2013.
10. Peter Rice, *An Engineer Imagines* (Batsford, 2017), 72.
11. Rice, *An Engineer Imagines*, 31.
12. American Institute of Architects. "2012 AIA Firm Survey Report: The Business of Architecture 2020 on Firm Characteristics." AIA Business Report. www.aia.org/aiaucmp/groups/aia/documents/pdf/aiab095792.pdf.
13. B. J. Novitski, "In-House Engineers make Sustainable Design Work Better," *Architectural Record, Business Practice*. archrecord.construction.com/practice/business/0910practice.asp.
14. SOM, "Fazlur Khan," *SOM Legacy*. https://www.som.com/fazlur-r-khan.
15. Keith Besserud, Neil Katz, and Alessandro Beghini, "Structural Emergence: Architectural and Structural Design Collaboration at SOM," *Architectural Design* 83 (2013): 48–55.
16. Mouzhan Majidi, *Catalogue: Foster and Partners* (Munich: Prestel, 2008), 327.
17. Xavier De Kestelier, Interview by the authors. Phone interview. London, England, June 18, 2013.
18. De Kestelier, Interview by the authors. Phone interview.
19. De Kestelier.
20. *How Much Does Your Building Weigh, Mr. Foster?* Film, New York, Art Commissioners, 2012.
21. Anita Williams Woolley, J. Richard Hackman, Thomas E. Jerde, Christopher F. Chabris, Sean L. Bennett, and Stephen M. Kosslyn, "Using Brain-based Measures to Compose Teams: How Individual Capabilities and Team Collaboration Strategies Jointly Shape Performance," *Social Neuroscience* 2, no. 2 (2007): 96–105. 103.
22. "New Research from PlanGrid and FMI Identifies Factors Costing the Construction Industry More Than $177 Billion Annually," accessed May 13, 2021, https://www.plangrid.com/press/fmi/.

23 Ken Sanders, "Collaboration & Performance/Materials & Building Practices." Lecture, New Constellations, New Ecologies for Association of Collegiate Schools of Architecture, San Francisco, March 20, 2013.
24 Sanders, "Collaboration & Performance/Materials & Building Practices."
25 Ben Mickus, Interview by the authors. In person interview. San Luis Obispo, CA, March 15, 2013.
26 Eric Long, Interview by the authors. Phone interview. San Francisco, CA, April 23, 2013.
27 Brian Guerrero, Interview by the authors. Phone interview. Los Angeles, July 9, 2013.
28 Long, Interview by the authors. Phone interview.
29 David Farnsworth, Interview by the authors. Phone interview. New York City, June 4, 2013.
30 Warren G. Bennis and Patricia Ward Biederman, *Organizing Genius: The Secrets of Creative Collaboration* (Reading, MA: Addison-Wesley, 1997), 28.
31 Hanif Kara, "On Design Engineering," *Architectural Design* 80 (2010): 46–51.
32 George Keliris, Interview by the authors. Phone interview. London, England, June 21, 2013.

Case Studies in Collaboration: Civic Buildings

CHAPTER 4

National Museum of African American History and Culture

Historical Design Concepts Driving Collaborative Design

Architects:	Freelon Group (Perkins + Will), Adjaye Associates, Davis Brody Bond, SmithGroup
Structural Engineer:	Guy Nordenson and Associates, Silman
Mechanical Engineer:	WSP Flack + Kurtz
Construction Management:	Clark/Smoot/Russell
Building Envelope and Curtain Wall Consultants:	Heintges
Manufacturers:	Bendheim, Goppion, Pure + FreeForm, Terrazzo & Marble, Conwed, Sempergreen, Series Seating, Sto, USG Ceilings
Lighting Consultants:	Fisher Marantz Stone
Landscape Architect:	Gustafson Guthrie Nichol
Sustainability Consultant:	Rocky Mountain Institute

Adjaye Associates

David Adjaye was born in Tanzania, with parents from Ghana, and his diplomatic family ultimately settled in London. He founded Adjaye Associates in 2000; the practice has a global portfolio of projects and today, the firm has offices in Ghana (Accra), the UK (London), and the US (New York City). Early work often focused on smaller scale residential projects but as the practice expanded and gained reputation Adjaye Associates was selected to design large-scale civic, housing, and institutional buildings. Recent projects of note include Ruby City, a contemporary art center in San Antonio; the Thabo Mbeki Presidential Library in Johannesburg; a new Art Museum for Princeton University; and the National Cathedral of Ghana (where the structural engineering consultant is Hanif Kara of AKT II, see Chapter 9).

The firm has garnered countless awards, but particularly notable is Adjaye's recognition by the Royal Institute of Architects as the 2021 Gold Medalist.[1] President of RIBA, Alan Jones, described the importance of Adjaye's work,

> At every scale … one senses David Adjaye's careful consideration of the creative and enriching power of architecture. His work is local and specific and at the same time global and inclusive. Blending history, art and science he creates highly crafted and engaging environments that balance contrasting themes and inspire us all … His artistic and social vision has created public projects that perfectly demonstrate the civic potential of architecture - fostering empathy, identity and pride.[2]

Adjaye describes his motivation in pursuing architecture as an intent to add a critical and otherwise missing voice to the field:

> I felt a disconnect between the world I was living in and the world that was being made. I felt the only way of dealing with it was to get involved, to start to make it more relevant and reflect some of the things that I was seeing in culture, and in friends in different disciplines, and in the ideas I was hearing, and to see if that could be somehow infused into form-making.[3]

Trained as an architect at schools that "only taught from the canon of the West,"[4] he was frustrated by the inherent limitations of that approach and consequently his own travel, research, and writing became critical to his evolving practice. Particularly, Adjaye writes about the influence the study of African architecture had on his consideration of climate, light, place, and geography in his architecture.[5] Adjaye Associates' work is noted for buildings "imbued with the qualities of handcrafted objects, structures with a sculptural heft that belies the technical and technological principles by which they were constructed."[6]

Guy Nordenson and Associates

Guy Nordenson studied civil engineering at MIT and UC Berkeley. While in school, he interned with sculptor Isamu Noguchi and, through him, went on to work with architect Buckminster Fuller. After graduating with a master's in structural engineering he worked for prominent engineering firm, Weidlinger Associates, moving shortly thereafter to Arup. He became a director there before opening his own firm, Guy Nordenson and Associates (GNA) in 1997. Since 1995, he has also taught structural engineering to architecture students at Princeton University.

Nordenson believes that engineering and architecture are not autonomous arts.[7] Thus, GNA focuses on collaborative practice with architects and designers. The firm has engaged in structural design for the Museum of Modern Art (MOMA) expansion in New York with architect Yoshio Taniguchi, the Kimbell Art Museum Expansion in Fort Worth, Texas, with Renzo Piano Building Workshop, and Corning Museum of Glass Contemporary Art + Design Wing in Corning, New York, with Thomas Phifer and Partners. Other notable projects include the New Museum of Contemporary Art in New York City, the Glass Pavilion at Toledo Museum of Art, both with SANAA and Sasaki (see Chapter 6), and Simmons Hall at MIT with Steven Holl (See Chapter 12).

Nordenson occupies a prominent role amongst New York City structural engineers and designers. In the aftermath of 9/11, he led a volunteer effort to triage 400 buildings impacted by the World Trade Center's collapse. In 2003, he was the first recipient of the American Academy of Arts and Letters Academy Award in Architecture for contributions to architecture by a non-architect. He served as Commissioner and Secretary of the New York City Public Design Commission from 2006 to 2015. His project "On the Water," researching the risks and potential amelioration strategies in the face of rising sea levels, led to the workshop and exhibit "Rising Currents" in 2010 at the MOMA. Books by Nordenson on structural thinking and GNA's work include *Patterns and Structure* (2010) and *Reading Structures: 39 Projects and Built Works* (2016).

Silman

Silman is an engineering consultancy firm founded by Robert Silman in 1966 in New York City as a sole practitioner; today it is a 160-person firm with offices in Boston, New York, Washington, DC, and Ann Arbor, Michigan. The firm is recognized for their expertise in structural engineering and they have a wide portfolio of work across civic, educational, and corporate clients. They are also considered industry leaders in historic preservation and have led the preservation of noted architectural landmarks, such as St. Patrick's Cathedral in New York City, Frank Llyod Wright's Fallingwater, and UNESCO World Heritage Sites. It is perhaps then not surprising that the firm is held in very high regard across the industry for collaboration with architects and designers. Their philosophical approach to collaborative design set out by founder Bob Silman is, "Work on the best projects. Support great architecture. Provide the highest level of technical excellence. Find joy in what we do."[8] This ethos persists in the company's culture and was recognized by the American Institute of Architects with the 2020 Collaborative Achievement Award.[9] As a firm, Silman also takes particular pride in the significant number of their professionals who also teach at over 20 institutions of higher education in architecture and engineering programs.[10]

The firm collaborates with many prominent architectural practices; recent projects include the Krause Gateway Center in Des Moines with Renzo Piano, 40th Precinct Station House in Bronx, NY with Bjarke Ingels Group, and Hunters Point Community Library with Steven Holl. Interviewed in *Architect Magazine*, the firm's three current leaders Kirk Mettam, Joe Tortorella, and Nat Oppenheimer clarify their approach to working on structures with architects:

> [We] believe in the power of architecture. We understand that architecture can be a vitally powerful mix of art and science ... structural engineering can help bring out inherent order within the architecture or support a critical disorder within a design. At a higher level, a good structural engineer can facilitate evolution within the design by asking questions of the architect, in their language, that forces them to consider, interrogate, and refine the design.[11]

The Project

As early as 1915, there were calls by African American veterans of the civil war for a national museum or memorial to recognize the contributions of their community to US history.[12] Decades of unfunded proposals, unkept promises, and inaction followed. In 2003, the late Congressman John Lewis introduced H.R. 3491 to the 108th Congress of the US. The resolution, which passed almost unanimously, called for the establishment of a new museum by the Smithsonian Institution, the National Museum of African American History and Culture (NMAAHC). The nineteenth of the Smithsonian's portfolio of nationally and internationally significant civic resources, the NMAAHC was intended to function as

> a center for scholarship and a location for museum training, public education, exhibits, and collection and study of items and materials relating to the life, art, history, and culture of African Americans that encompass the period of slavery, the era of reconstruction, the Harlem Renaissance, the civil rights movement, and other periods of the African American diaspora.[13]

Before a building could be designed, the selection of a site and careful consideration of the required program and design parameters had to be undertaken. Multiple sites were considered near the National Mall, and there was some tension between the need to find an appropriately prominent site and the need to preserve views of the historically significant existing fabric of that district.[14] The site ultimately chosen, at the end of the mall, between the National Museum of American History and the Washington Monument, was arguably the most prominent of the sites considered, but it came with the need to carefully study views to and from the Washington Monument,[15] height and setback restrictions, and a footprint limited to a 210 ft by 210 ft (64 m x 64 m) square in a large park-like setting (Figure 4.1).[16]

The Smithsonian Institution appointed historian Lonnie Bunch III in 2005 as the first director of the NMAAHC. Bunch assembled a team of Smithsonian

Figure 4.1 The Museum site overlooks the Washington Monument. The National Museum of African American History and Culture. Freelon Adjaye Bond/SmithGroup, GNA, Silman, 2016. Credit: Ben Rosenberg, Silman.

staff and nationally recognized scholars to refine the museum's mission and approach. He also hired prominent African American architects and educators Max Bond of Davis Brody Bond and Phillip Freelon of Freelon Group Associates to write the programming document outlining the museum's architectural needs that would form the basis of the international design competition launched in 2008.[17] Notable works by the Freelon Group include the Museum of the African Diaspora in San Francisco and the Reginald F. Lewis Museum of African American History and Culture in Baltimore. Davis Brody Bond's significant portfolio includes the Martin Luther King, Jr. Center for Nonviolent Social Change and the Lincoln Center for the Performing Arts Master Plan.

For the competition, Davis Brody Bond and Freelon Group partnered with London-based Adjaye Associates and SmithGroup to form Freelon Adjaye Bond/SmithGroup, and in turn brought in structural engineers Guy Nordenson of GNA and Nat Oppenheimer of Silman. The Request for Qualifications phase of the competition attracted 22 teams of architects, engineers, and other consultants with impressive track records for award winning designs and significant civic projects. After a second phase in which the Freelon Adjaye Bond/SmithGroup team and five others were shortlisted, the team developed the proposal that ultimately won the competition in April 2009 to design and deliver the museum to the people of the US.[18] Freelon Group were the architects of record with Philip Freelon as the design guarantor,[19] while David Adjaye held the role of lead designer.

The groundbreaking ceremony was held in 2012, and it was understood among all the stakeholders in the planning, design, and construction process that the project should be finished while President Barack Obama was still in office so that he could preside over the opening ceremonies. Just four and a half years later, the $500 million project was formally opened in September 2016. The cost included not only the construction of the 350,000-square-foot (32,500-square-meter) building but also the acquisition of many of the artifacts and exhibits that the building would house.

The Collaboration

The collaborators interviewed about the project are in agreement about the most significant and mutually understood goals of the project. Right from the start of the process, David Adjaye's design had several clear and non-negotiable principles that drove the project forward: the shape of the corona (the name the architects gave to the crown-like shape of the building's facade) (Figure 4.2); the separation of that light, transparent lantern-like corona from the rest of the structure; and the connection between the building and the surrounding

Figure 4.2 The crown-like shape of the building's facade is called the corona. The National Museum of African American History and Culture. Freelon Adjaye Bond/SmithGroup, GNA, Silman, 2016. Credit: Chad Schwartz.

landscape including the carefully choreographed entry sequence made by the porch structure. The collaboration and coordination among the disciplines was positive and fluid where necessary, but these facets of the project were sacrosanct and acted as the guide rails to this complex but fast-paced design process.

The scale, significance, and pace of the project warranted a large design team. While Adjaye Associates provided leadership for the architectural design, GNA drove the conceptual aspects of the structural design. After the competition phase, GNA focused on the superstructure, the facade and the structural frame above ground, which encompassed the symbolic function of the corona, the performance functions of solar shading and security, and some of the exhibition spaces. Silman, on the other hand, designed the structure below and at grade, which housed the majority of the exhibits both due to the above-ground height restrictions and the need to mitigate light in the exhibition spaces. Silman also provided design services to support exhibit installation and structure.

In the early stages of the design process, the team met bi-weekly or weekly, often in Washington, DC. Rebecca Laberenne, structural engineer who worked for GNA on the superstructure (the facade and structural frame for the above-ground portion of the building), recalls the early team conversations and design charrettes.

> It was a back and forth process, where we would get some initial input, use it to develop a set of schemes, then have another meeting where we would share those, and get more input. You settle on one or two schemes to develop further, and each time refine it more and more, getting it more in line with what the architect has in mind.[20]

Ben Rosenberg, structural engineer and principal at Silman, advocates similarly for early open dialog with designers and the careful specialized work that follows, noting

> nothing can really beat sitting around the table and sketching things out, rolling out the drawings and some trace paper and working through things together. That process--setting up what we need to then take back to our office and work through so that we could advance the design--is by far the most productive and critical approach.[21]

Laberenne also distinguishes between the work that happens in multi-disciplinary design meetings as opposed to the more detailed discipline-specific work and insists on the importance of engineers being open to developing multiple approaches at once.

> There is in-person collaboration, idea generation and sketching, but I would say that these plant the seed for work that happens more independently. The development of multiple schemes is really important to make sure that we're all confident in the direction that we choose because we've explored these other options.[22]

This collaborative form of charrette worked well for the architects too. Joe Franchina, architect with Adjaye Associates, notes that he values engineering partners who "have a really clear direction on what they want to do and they're not afraid to talk about their ideas." He explains that when complex aspects of projects need to be resolved, if for example, the architectural vision and the structural logic appears to be in conflict, collaboration is especially important. He finds that when engineering collaborators have a clear and articulate concept, and engage and advocate for that concept, collaborative design work is at its best: "those kinds of collaboration are few and far between."[23] Similarly,

Laberenne laments that in the traditional approach engineers are often hesitant to assert their opinions in the design process and really values that Guy Nordenson's practice ensures engineers contribute to design conversations.

> There's actually a difference between collaboration and coordination, and I think oftentimes a lot of an engineer's job is coordination. But it rises to collaboration when it leads to something that's actually better than integration of all the pieces in a way that is logical. We achieved this level of collaboration with Silman on the structure and with Adjaye Associates, Heintges, and our office on the design of the corona.[24]

Adjaye Associates, Silman, and GNA also had existing relationships in place which they argue contributes to the success of projects, and indeed to securing the contract for those projects in the first place. Rosenberg explained that in his experience clients, particularly institutional and government clients, see teams where people have worked together before as a positive. When teams have built up the relationships and trust over time that "ultimately results in a better product."[25] "We have a very nice long standing relationship with [the other members of this design team] on institutional work in higher and governmental institutions like the Smithsonian Institution and we support each other's ethos and work style."[26]

The Corona

The building is a square plan with three inverted trapezoidal tiers (Figure 4.3). The form was inspired by the crown on a Yoruban caryatid sculpture by an artist, Olowe of Ise, who lived in what is now Nigeria in the early 1900s.[27] Adjaye explains,

> I was completely moved by the corona motif. It seemed like a way to start to tell a story that moves from one continent, where people were taken, along with their cultures, and used as labor, then contributed towards making another country and new cultures.[28]

The corona's slopes, slanted up and out, also symbolized "the praise gesture of raised arms"[29] and the angle of 17 degrees was chosen as it is parallel to the downward slope of the Washington Monument "so the two monuments talk to each other."[30] The shape of the Washington Monument itself can be traced to earlier artifacts from the African continent, the ancient Egyptian obelisks whose form inspired so many later European monuments.

The dark filigree panels that form the corona (Figure 4.4) were originally conceived as bronze, but ultimately fabricated from lighter and more

CASE STUDIES IN COLLABORATION: CIVIC BUILDINGS

Figure 4.3 The crown-like shape of the building's facade is called the corona. In the foreground, you can see the steel structure for the porch. The National Museum of African American History and Culture. Freelon Adjaye Bond/SmithGroup, GNA, Silman, 2016. Credit: Ben Rosenberg, Silman.

Figure 4.4 The bronze-colored aluminum panels that make up the facade are inspired by the tradition of metalsmithing by freed slaves. The National Museum of African American History and Culture. Freelon Adjaye Bond/SmithGroup, GNA, Silman, 2016. Credit: Chad Schwartz.

sustainable recycled aluminum with a bronze alloy finish.[31] The panel size and pattern was developed using the Monument stones as a reference.[32] Asked about the decorative patterns on the facade panels that reference the ironwork found on classic southern architecture of cities like Charleston and New Orleans, Adjaye says,

> People keep thinking that the slave trade was about cotton picking. It was also about bridge building, canals, house making. Labor in all its forms ... I said let's really talk about architecture and African-American history, let's go back and look at ... all these places, through a different lens. There, the history is right in front of you, this incredible tradition of metalsmithing by freed slaves. There were no molds. They learned all this by hand. It is part of the history of American architecture.[33]

The transparency of the building's skin (Figure 4.5) facilitated by the lattice panels was deliberate and significant. In addition, specific windows in the galleries are strategically cut and aligned with framed views in the facade (Figure 4.6) of the Washington Monument, the Jefferson Memorial, the White House, among other DC landmarks, where, as Adjaye observes, "history is played out in front of your eyes."[34] It is important to him that the museum does not function like a movie theatre where you suspend reality while you are inside, only to be reminded of your location when you reemerge. He asserts, "[the] experience of being black is not a fiction. There's something important about always coming back to the light of day."

Figure 4.5 The transparency of the facade is facilitated by the lattice panels. The National Museum of African American History and Culture. Freelon Adjaye Bond/SmithGroup, GNA, Silman, 2016. Credit: Chad Schwartz.

Figure 4.6 Specific windows in the galleries are strategically cut and aligned with framed views of DC landmarks. The National Museum of African American History and Culture. Freelon Adjaye Bond/SmithGroup, GNA, Silman, 2016. Credit: Chad Schwartz.

To achieve the lightness and transparency so critical to the function of the corona's design, and to separate it from the rest of the structure, as Adjaye proposed, presented an obvious challenge for the structural engineers. Laberenne recalls thinking in the earliest meetings during the design competition "that was really going to be the challenging piece of this for us, this exterior facade structure."[35] She explains that in typical projects where a non-structural facade is attached to each floor of a building, it would be unusual for the structural engineers to address this issue early, and they might be only lightly involved in that part of the design. Nordenson proposed that hanging the entire facade from the super structure would be the best approach to achieve the design goals, and that would require some structural innovation "it was clear at that point that it was going to be a major feature of the project."[36]

The first iteration of the structure for the corona was a series of horizontal trusses for each tier around the square plan hung by vertical cables from the fifth-floor roof of the building and connected carefully to the ground level to restrain horizontal movement. Hanging the structure was critical to the approach as it would allow the weight of the structure to be carried in tension (always the most efficient use of material when possible) and then in placing the cables under a high tension it would help stiffen the facade against wind and other lateral loads.[37] The wind loads would be picked up by the horizontal trusses on the windward face and transferred into the two sides of the truss parallel to the direction of the wind which "functioned as inverted braced frames to transfer these lateral forces in-plane to the fifth floor of the building."[38] Ultimately this approach changed during the value engineering phase as it proved more cost-effective and saved critical construction time to have a

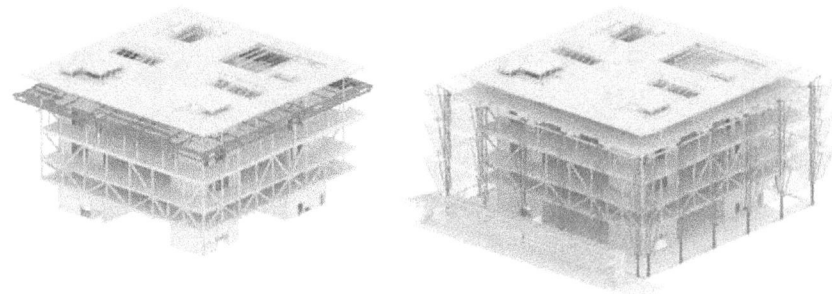

Figure 4.7 The facade is hung from the top floor of the superstructure. The National Museum of African American History and Culture. Freelon Adjaye Bond/SmithGroup, GNA, Silman, 2016. Courtesy of Guy Nordenson and Associates.

more two-dimensional system with trusses hung in the vertical direction and the glazing attached to the inside face and the panels attached to the outside face with a service catwalk in between (Figure 4.7). This system also had to be wind-tunnel tested and carefully designed to consider ice-loading that might build up in the Washington DC winter.[39]

The structural design of the facade involved numerous iterations. Laberenne reflects on the change to the initial design, which she has thought of as a more elegant and simple solution. "It was a lesson for me as an engineer. You think if you come up with this really elegant solution … everyone will buy into it,"[40] but ultimately time and financial constraints were more significant in this instance. However, Franchina insists that his engineering colleagues get due credit, and observes that the concept of the hung facade itself survived multiple rounds of value engineering.

> We always had to meet that budget at the end of each phase … so multiple times they [the contractors] asked us to basically attach the skin to the building to relieve the load of the structure from the top to the bottom and have columns … [but] after the calculations were done there was no savings to be had.[41]

He draws attention to the clarity and logic of the engineer's intent that was so well aligned with the architectural goals for the corona. Franchina observes that the structural innovation required to separate the skin from the rest of the building had other technical benefits. High-profile buildings, of which there are many in DC, typically have blast protection as one of the loading considerations. Franchina recalls,

> we had requirements from the Smithsonian about threat assessment, having the skin detached from the exhibition box, which became the structure of the building, helped protect the building against

progressive collapse, so having the structure set back from the facade and the facade flexible, as Guy's initial design proposed, really helped mitigate that.[42]

It was clear to all collaborators that it was imperative to get the design of the corona right and to achieve both the technical and artistic goals inherent in the original proposal. The metallic surface of the corona reflects back the ambient light as it changes over the days and seasons and at night acts like a beacon as the light from inside shines through the filigreed panels. It deliberately "announces a distinctive presence"[43] among the more opaque white buildings of DC and the National Mall. As Bunch has described it, "this building will sing for all of us."[44]

The Porch

The building is typically approached by a visitor from the south and entered via the porch, a freestanding monolithic cantilevered canopy structure that stretches the full width of the building. In front of the middle section of the porch is a fountain pool (Figure 4.8). The concept is a nod to the porches of the

Figure 4.8 The porch spans over the entry to the building. The National Museum of African American History and Culture. Freelon Adjaye Bond/SmithGroup, GNA, Silman, 2016. Credit: Chad Schwartz.

architectural vernacular of "the African Diaspora, especially the American South and Caribbean."[45] The porch functions, as it does in the domestic sphere, as an intermediate space neither fully inside nor outside, it engages the structure with the landscape and provides refuge from harsh weather. The shade underneath the canopy coupled with the cooling of the air above the pool creates a microclimate that can lower the temperature by 5–10 degrees in summer.[46]

To achieve the thermal performance and fit with the architectural vision of a heavier denser object in contrast to the light open building skin, the porch structure needed an opaque heavy appearance, but to span a beam over 200 ft (61 m) between two columns and then cantilever the roof from the beam would typically call for more open and lightweight structure for efficiency. This was ultimately resolved using a steel structure clad in concrete panels designed by GNA.[47]

The Superstructure

The intent right from the start of the design process was that the structure, which would support, but be separate from, the corona, would also be very open at ground level with no columns, only cores. This was incorporated into Nordenson's scheme for the competition entry. The above-ground structure

Figure 4.9 The above-ground structure consists of four cores, the floor plates of above-grade galleries bridge between these cores and project beyond them supported by cantilevers and perimeter vertical trusses. At the fifth floor, there are outrigger trusses from which the corona facade is hung. The National Museum of African American History and Culture. Freelon Adjaye Bond/SmithGroup, GNA, Silman, 2016. Credit: Ben Rosenberg, Silman.

consists of four cores in a smaller square than the building footprint. The floor plates of above-grade galleries bridge between these cores and project beyond them supported by cantilevers and perimeter vertical trusses (Figure 4.9).[48] At the fifth floor, there are outrigger trusses from which the corona facade is hung. This unusual structural scheme creates open space around the perimeter of the building (Figure 4.10). "This strengthens the relationship between the interior spaces and the context of the Washington Mall, allowing the views to dominate these light-filled atria."[49]

The four structural cores are made from a composite steel and concrete system (Figure 4.11). There are shear studs welded to a steel frame of beams and corner columns, around which a steel-reinforced concrete infill wall is cast. These cores carry all the weight of the above-ground structure, including the facade.[50] This is not a typical system, but the hanging facade called for a structure in the center of the building with high lateral stiffness: the capacity to resist bending of the building due to wind loads and any other lateral load. This system is more typically found in buildings that might be subject to significant earthquake loads.[51] Here it was deployed chiefly because the hanging facade

Figure 4.10 A truss system supports the hung facade of the corona and creates a light-filled atrium inside the perimeter of the building. The National Museum of African American History and Culture. Freelon Adjaye Bond/SmithGroup, GNA, Silman, 2016. Credit: Chad Schwartz.

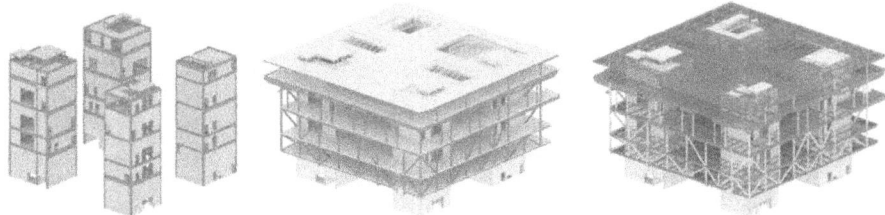

Figure 4.11 The composite core system. Shear studs welded to a steel frame of beams and corner columns, around which a steel-reinforced concrete infill wall is cast. The National Museum of African American History and Culture. Freelon Adjaye Bond/SmithGroup, GNA, Silman, 2016. Courtesy of Guy Nordenson and Associates.

structure of the corona around the perimeter of the building required the deflection or drift of the supporting core structure to be minimized. It also allowed all the steel superstructure of the upper floors to be built off the steel in the cores before the concrete was cast (to stiffen the cores) so there was a significant erection sequencing component to the selection of the system.[52] This system had the added benefit of allowing decisions to be made about penetrations in the core (openings for elevator doors, circulation, mechanical systems, etc.) later in the process than might otherwise be possible, which was crucial in this project where construction needed to start as quickly as possible, but flexibility was needed for the interior and exhibit designs, which were not fully complete at that stage.[53]

The Below-Grade Structure

To deal with the constraints of the footprint on the site, and to ensure gallery spaces that protected the artifacts from light, it was suggested by Ralph Applebaum who designed the exhibit spaces themselves, that a larger below ground structure than originally intended be designed.[54] The final museum design occupies a much larger footprint below ground than it does above, and the site has a relatively high water table, so very careful attention had to be paid to the substructure of the building. Franchina explains the challenge for Nat Oppenheimer and his team at Silman who designed the substructure (Figure 4.12):

> the groundwater was 10 or 15 feet (3 or 4.5 m) feet below grade, so we're essentially putting a huge tub into the earth with 75 foot (23 m) high walls that are cantilevering from the foundation up and holding back the soil and water and someone had to solve that. It was truly amazing what they did.[55]

Rosenberg adds that the foundation design had to be produced quickly due to the tight timeline for the project, and similar to the core of the superstructure, had to anticipate some smaller design changes and accommodate aspects of

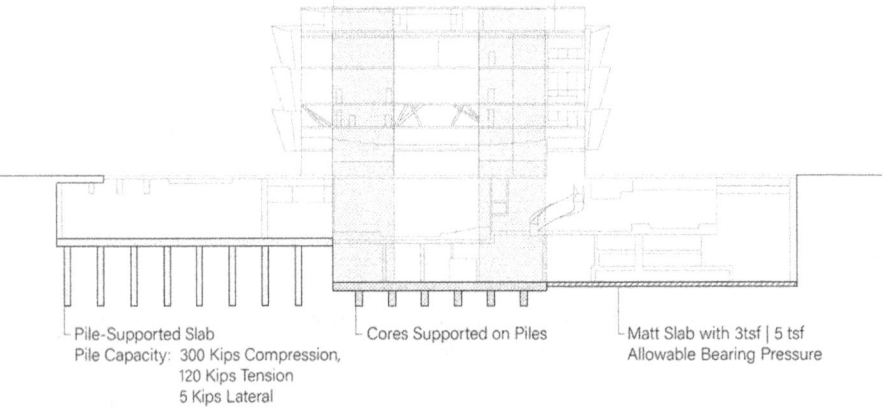

Figure 4.12 The superstructure and the below-grade structural schemes. The National Museum of African American History and Culture. Freelon Adjaye Bond/SmithGroup, GNA, Silman, 2016. Credit: Shiori Green.

the final design that were not fully resolved at that stage. With the significance of the exhibits to be housed, a critical aspect of the substructure design was to prevent water infiltration. Rosenberg explained that for about two thirds of the basement (the section under the corona and the north lawn), the volume extended down to just above bedrock. To mitigate the uplift forces caused by hydrostatic pressure, the perimeter walls were brought down and keyed into the bedrock to hold the surrounding water outside of the building footprint. Per the geotechnical engineers, only minimal water would percolate up through the rock beneath the foundations and this water is easily managed with a sub-slab drainage system. The remaining third (under the south side) only extended down about 35 feet, and as such required a set of pile foundations under the floor that helped to hold the building down against uplift forces as well as support the gravity loads of the structure. He remarks that this final design was chosen after several other options were considered, including excavating all sections down to bedrock and leaving a void below the museum, or making foundation of the southern section from thicker concrete slabs so that its self-weight would counteract the uplift forces. In both sections and in close coordination with SmithGroup, very careful attention was paid to waterproofing materials and the weatherproofing system of the below-grade envelope (Figure 4.13).[56]

The first iteration of the substructure design called for a fully concrete structure below-grade and at-grade and then the steel structure with concrete infill walls and slabs for the above-grade superstructure. However, at an advanced stage in the design process during actual construction, it became clear that if the roof of the permanent history gallery, which is just below grade underneath the north lawn, were to be built in concrete, it would need to be

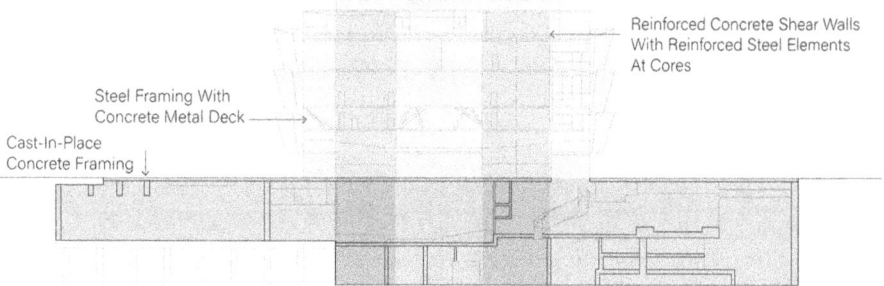

Figure 4.13 The foundations and waterproofing were critical aspects of the below-grade structural design. The National Museum of African American History and Culture. Freelon Adjaye Bond/SmithGroup, GNA, Silman, 2016. Credit: Shiori Green.

supported by 65-foot tall shoring towers to support the concrete as it cured. Between the time required for initial shoring, formwork tower setup, and the concrete curing, this would mean weeks of delay in interior work in the history gallery below due to the presence of the towers. On this project, that scale of a delay to the interior construction was a significant setback and so, with input from the construction manager, the team decided to switch the roof structure to a steel beam with a concrete on metal deck system, which was quicker to erect and eliminated the need for interior shoring and formwork towers. For Rosenberg, this is an example of the flexibility engineers need to be prepared for in good collaborations. "You had to be very nimble in this project, because it was moving very quickly, which was stressful at times, but part of what made the project an interesting challenge."

The Exhibits

In the design of the structure to house a museum, naturally, the exhibits are of primary importance. In this specific case, the task of actually finding, curating, and designing the exhibits was itself both a massive undertaking and one that was ongoing while the structure itself was being designed and even built. Lonnie Bunch describes that the museum staff had to design and implement an outreach process to secure artifacts that had never been collected and others that were in danger of disappearing.[57] The artifacts themselves presented technical challenges, the physical scale of some important pieces and the timeline of the project being such that the interior finish and exhibit construction needed to start as quickly as possible, while the building itself was still under construction. Historic slave cabins brought to the museum had to be internally braced to ensure they survive for generations in their new site. Rosenberg describes going to Louisiana to plan the process of moving the guard tower

Figure 4.14a The "Angola" Guard Tower at the Louisiana State Penitentiary. Credit: Ben Rosenberg, Silman.

Figure 4.14b Engineers from Silman assess how to move the guard tower to the National Museum of African American History and Culture. Credit: Ben Rosenberg, Silman.

Figure 4.14c The guard tower was craned into its permanent exhibition location, while the below-grade structure of the museum was still under construction. The National Museum of African American History and Culture. Freelon Adjaye Bond/SmithGroup, GNA, Silman, 2016. Credit: Graham Seward, Silman.

from the Louisiana State Penitentiary (known as "Angola") as an unusual expedition for a structural engineer (Figures 4.14a and 4.14b).

> To see what it is still like down there was heartbreaking, but the purpose was to look at this guard tower in situ and discover how we could get it to the museum and then make sure that it stayed upright in the museum.[58]

The guard tower and Pullman train exhibits were so large that they would not fit through any door or loading dock of the finished building so they needed to be installed while the site was almost an open hole in the ground. These were significant operations. Rosenberg explains,

> the guard tower was pretty light, they could crane that in with one crane from Constitution Avenue [Figure 4.14c], but the Pullman train car was so heavy that they needed two cranes in tandem to lift it up, swing it into the hole [Figure 4.15a], and they couldn't even swing it all the way over to where it was going to be because the reach was too far for the cranes, so they dropped it down onto a temporary gantry and then slid it over into its place.[59]

The exhibits were protected in plywood and other wrappings and they stayed in their current positions while the building was raised around them (Figure 4.15b).

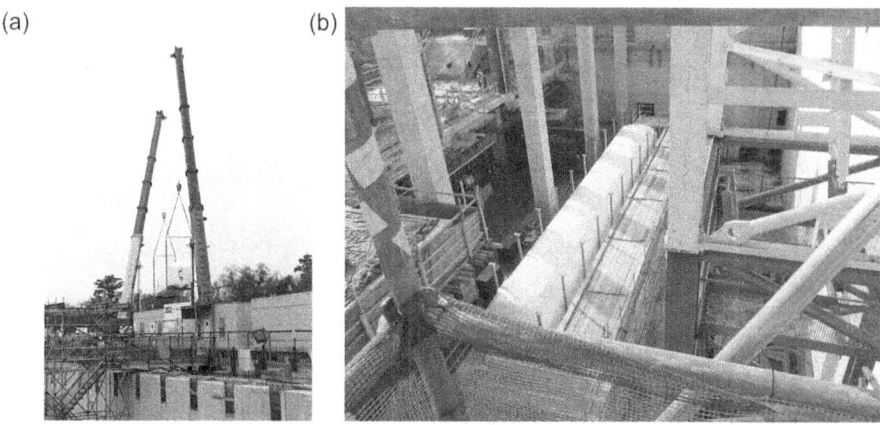

Figure 4.15a-b The Pullman train car was so heavy that two cranes in tandem lifted it up and into the below-grade structure. The National Museum of African American History and Culture. Freelon Adjaye Bond/SmithGroup, GNA, Silman, 2016. Credit: Graham Seward, Silman.

Sustainability

Director Bunch was clear from the outset that a primary design goal for the new museum was environmental sustainability, and called for a design that would be the first of the Smithsonian's new constructions to attain LEED Gold Certification from the U.S. Green Building Council.[60] The limited above-ground footprint, the square form, and the program of the museum itself all lent themselves to energy conservation, but there were also considerable design innovations deployed by the engineers and architects to achieve this goal.

A square has a higher volume to surface area ratio than a longer rectangular shape, meaning less skin through which to lose energy for every square foot of available space. The below ground portion of the building also contributes significantly to its efficient energy usage. About 60% of the floor space is below grade and as such requires less energy to heat and cool over the year due to the insulative capacity of the soil around it.[61] Further, the design strategy of a "box, within a box, within a box"[62] that was deployed to eliminate exposure to the sun for the precious exhibits is also by default a passive energy strategy. The outermost layer of that box (the corona) is also carefully calibrated to control solar gain with denser thicker panels used where heat and light needed to be blocked and more open panels in the spots where transparency to the surroundings was most critical for light and views (Figure 4.16).[63] Strategic use of deciduous trees around the site providing shade in summer while allowing low winter sun to add some heat to the building in winter also contributed to the overall goal.[64]

Figure 4.16 The facade panels during installation. The National Museum of African American History and Culture. Freelon Adjaye Bond/SmithGroup, GNA, Silman, 2016. Credit: Ben Rosenberg, Silman.

The porch structure described earlier is another passive cooling strategy, one that Phillip Freelon describes as inextricably linked to the African American culture of "making something out of nothing and doing more with less … this building is expressive of that."[65] The structure also has photovoltaic panels on the roof to generate power, and an extensive gray water capture system that Brenda Sanchez, an in-house architect at the Smithsonian Institute, estimates saves the city of Washington DC a million gallons of water a year.[66]

Conclusion

Writing about the museum's exhibits, Georgetown University historian Eric Arnsen acknowledges that the NMAAHC is not without its critics. There are those who question the omission of certain more controversial topics among the museum's galleries and those who question the criticality of a museum project when communities of color continue to suffer with more urgent and vital unmet needs. But he argues that the central success of the museum is that it "insists on a recognition of the centrality of slavery and racial oppression to the more traditional narrative of the unfolding of American democracy."[67] The collaborators interviewed were clear about the ways that this project presented special responsibility to collaborate well and carefully to ensure that the museum would fulfill its mission, that the artifacts would find an appropriate, safe, and permanent home, and that the project would be finished in time for its ambitious planned 2016 opening. Adjaye is similarly thoughtful about the responsibilities attached to this specific project: "This is a monumental project and arguably the defining project of my career."[68]

> My hope is that the museum will transcend the uneasy fact of racial tension through an open exploration of history, culture and society— thereby addressing profound aspects of the human condition and the positive value inherent in creating a forum for multiple interpretations of America's history and demography, however uncomfortable those may be.[69]

Adjaye explains that he sees the building operating in three parts, the zone that deals with the early history in the underground level, "a crypt" as he terms it, then as you come up through the building you encounter exhibits about the post–civil war era and then increasingly more contemporary exhibits,

> I wanted the journey from that crypt up into the corona to be analogous to history, as a kind of migratory process, toward the light…. So this tripartite structure relates to the corona's three tiers. It's meant to suggest the link between symbolic form and the museum's content.[70]

The careful collaboration and coordination among the multi-disciplinary team of engineers, architects, and designers who worked together to deliver this project were guided by the principles set out in that vision.

Bunch observes that the museums of the Smithsonian "[open] different portals for the public to enter the American experience."[71] The late Phil Freelon described the pride he had in contributing to the realization of a museum of such historical importance.

> There are some really difficult issues that we're grappling with as a nation and as a global community. I think that this museum can play a really important role in trying to come to that reconciliation that is needed in understanding disparate cultures.[72]

Adjaye echoes that sentiment and argues that the planned purpose of the National Mall is to allow space for the institutions necessary for a country to make sense of itself and its history and that the NMAAHC fills one of the gaps in that plan (literally and figuratively). These "missing chapters" as he terms them and the people whose stories those chapters tell are

> fundamental to the DNA of this country. Creating museums for their stories is not about serving special interests. It's about celebrating the

true diversity of the country, showing how people, even people who moved here under the most traumatic conditions, ultimately thrived…. It's a memorial and also a monument to an incredible contribution.[73]

Notes

1. "Sir David Adjaye OBE to Receive 2021 Royal Gold Medal for Architecture," *Building Design & Construction*, accessed September 30, 2020, http://search.proquest.com/docview/2447558895/abstract/7CB6DCBF1D8345E3PQ/1.
2. "Sir David Adjaye OBE to Receive 2021 Royal Gold Medal for Architecture."
3. Pamela Buxton, "Contribution to the Profession: David Adjaye," *Architects' Journal* 245, no. 11 (June 14, 2018): 130–134.
4. Okwui Enwezor et al., eds., *David Adjaye: Form, Heft, Material*, 1st edition (Chicago: The Art Institute of Chicago, 2015), 17.
5. Enwezor et al., *David Adjaye*, 61–79.
6. Enwezor et al., 16.
7. Nina Rappaport, "Guy Nordenson and Associates." In *Support and Resist: Structural Engineers and Design Innovation*. New York: Monacelli Press, 2007. 137.
8. "Silman - Structural Engineers - Creating, Renewing, Preserving, Sustaining," Silman, accessed April 26, 2021, https://www.silman.com/.
9. "AIA Selects Recipients for the 2020 Collaborative Achievement Award—AIA," accessed May 29, 2021, https://www.aia.org/press-releases/6256964-aia-selects-recipients-for-the-2020-collab.
10. "Teaching – Silman," accessed May 29, 2021, https://www.silman.com/culture/teaching/.
11. Eric Wills, "2020 Collaborative Achievement Award: Silman | Architect Magazine," *Architect Magazine*, May 8, 2020, https://www.architectmagazine.com/awards/aia-honor-awards/2020-collaborative-achievement-award-silman_o.
12. Lonnie G. Bunch, "The Definitive Story of How the National Museum of African American History and Culture Came To Be," *Smithsonian Magazine*, September 2016, https://www.smithsonianmag.com/smithsonian-institution/definitive-story-national-museum-african-american-history-culture-came-be-180960125/.
13. "H.R.3491 - 108th Congress (2003–2004): National Museum of African American History and Culture Act" (2003), https://www.congress.gov/bill/108th-congress/house-bill/3491.
14. Mabel Wilson and Lonnie G. Bunch, *Begin with the Past: Building the National Museum of African American History & Culture* (Washington, DC: Smithsonian Books, 2016).
15. Joe Franchina, Adjaye Associates, National Museum of African American History and Culture, Zoom Interview by the authors, March 2, 2021.
16. Wilson and Bunch, *Begin with the Past*.
17. Wilson and Bunch.
18. The Smithsonian Institution, "The Building," National Museum of African American History and Culture, January 4, 2016, https://nmaahc.si.edu/explore/building.
19. As the more senior architect who led the research and development of the program, Max Bond had been slated to be the guarantor, but received a cancer diagnosis just before the contract was awarded (WALTER Magazine. "WALTER PROFILE: Master Builder: Phil Freelon," June 1, 2017. https://waltermagazine.com/community/people/walter-profile-master-builder-phil-freelon/.)
20. Rebecca Laberenne, GNA, The National Museum of African American History and Culture, Zoom Interview by the authors, April 29, 2021.
21. Silman Benjamin Rosenberg, The National Museum of African American History and Culture, Zoom Interview by the authors, March 17, 2021.
22. Laberenne, GNA, The National Museum of African American History and Culture.
23. Franchina, Adjaye Associates, National Museum of African American History and Culture.
24. Laberenne.
25. Benjamin Rosenberg, The National Museum of African American History and Culture.
26. Rosenberg.
27. Wilson and Bunch.
28. Michael Kimmelman, "David Adjaye on Designing a Museum That Speaks a Different Language," *New York Times (Online)*, September 21, 2016, sec. arts, http://search.proquest.com/docview/1821914165/abstract/95D5398793BB4E7APQ/1.
29. Wilson and Bunch.
30. Bunch, "The Definitive Story of How the National Museum of African American History and Culture Came to Be."
31. Kimmelman, "David Adjaye on Designing a Museum That Speaks a Different Language."
32. "Smithsonian National Museum of African American History and Culture/Freelon Adjaye Bond/SmithGroup," ArchDaily, June 4, 2019, https://www.archdaily.com/794203/smithsonian-national-museum-of-african-american-history-and-culture-adjaye-associates.
33. Kimmelman.
34. Kimmelman.
35. Kimmelman.
36. Laberenne.

37. Rebecca Laberenne et al., "Superstructure of the National Museum of African American History and Culture," *Structural Engineering International* 27, no. 3 (August 2017): 454–461, https://doi.org/10.2749/222137917X14881938991366.
38. Laberenne et al., "Superstructure of the National Museum of African American History and Culture."
39. Laberenne.
40. Laberenne.
41. Franchina.
42. Franchina.
43. Kathleen M. Kendrick, *Official Guide to the Smithsonian National Museum of African American History & Culture* (Washington, DC: Smithsonian Books, 2017).
44. The Smithsonian Institution, "The Building."
45. The Smithsonian Institution.
46. Wilson and Bunch.
47. Laberenne et al.
48. Laberenne.
49. Charles Henry Rowell, "DESIGNING A NATION'S MUSEUM: An Interview with David Adjaye," *Callaloo* 38, no. 4 (2015): 762–770.
50. Laberenne et al.
51. Laberenne et al.
52. Laberenne.
53. Laberenne.
54. Franchina.
55. Franchina.
56. Rosenberg.
57. Bunch.
58. Rosenberg.
59. Rosenberg.
60. Wilson and Bunch.
61. Wilson and Bunch.
62. Ryan P. Smith, "The African American History and Culture Museum Wins Gold for Going Green," *Smithsonian Magazine*, accessed May 14, 2021, https://www.smithsonianmag.com/smithsonian-institution/african-american-history-and-culture-museum-wins-gold-going-green-180968862/.
63. Franchina.
64. Smith, "The African American History and Culture Museum Wins Gold for Going Green."
65. The Smithsonian Institution.
66. Smith.
67. Eric Arnesen, "The Stuff of History Will Be Your Guide: On the New National Museum of African American History and Culture," *Journal of American Ethnic History* 37, no. 2 (2018): 71–81, https://doi.org/10.5406/jamerethnhist.37.2.0071.
68. Rowell, "DESIGNING A NATION'S MUSEUM."
69. Rowell.
70. Kimmelman.
71. Bunch.
72. Perkins and Will, *In Their Own Words: Phil Freelon, Building a Legacy*, 2016, https://vimeo.com/185988396.
73. Kimmelman.

CHAPTER 5

Gilder Center at the American Museum of Natural History

Collaborating on an Architectural–Structural Concept as a Foundation for Design

Client:	American Museum of Natural History
Owner's representative:	Zubatkin Owner Representation, LLC
Design Architect:	Studio Gang[1]
Executive Architect:	Davis Brody Bond
Exhibition Design:	Ralph Appelbaum Associates
Structural engineer, Acoustical and Audio Visual Consultants:	Arup[2]
MEP/FP engineer and facade consultant:	Buro Happold
Geotechnical and Civil Engineer:	Langan
Sustainability Consultant:	Atelier Ten
Construction Manager:	AECOM Tishman[3]

Although multiple experts worked together on the design of the Richard Gilder Center for Science, Education, and Innovation at the American Museum of Natural History, the case study focuses on the collaboration between the Studio Gang design team and the structural engineers at Arup.

Studio Gang

After working in famed practices including the Office for Metropolitan Architecture (OMA) in Rotterdam, The Netherlands, Jeanne Gang founded Studio Gang in Chicago in 1997. Now with offices in New York, San Francisco, and Paris, the firm's portfolio includes urban design, interiors, exhibitions, and ever-larger projects such as the Arcus Center for Social Justice Leadership at Kalamazoo College in Kalamazoo, Michigan; the MIRA high-rise residential tower with affordable units in San Francisco, California; and in the office's hometown of Chicago, Illinois, the rippling high-rise Aqua Tower and a soaring new airport terminal for Chicago O'Hare.

The firm's collaborative and research-based practice is recognized for its community engaged work, environmental stewardship, and high performance buildings.[4] Speaking about the firm's commitment to communities, Gang describes,

> I don't feel engaging the public, helping them envision a new future, is an obligation—it's something I want to do. At our office, we follow our instincts of working toward the greater good....And the issues you choose to advocate for define who you are as a practitioner and as an architect.[5]

Caryn Brause, author of *The Designer's Field Guide to Collaboration*, describes Studio Gang's Arcus Center for Social Justice Leadership as exemplifying these values, where the project developed through "collaborative inquiry" and "trust-building" to create a collective vision that embodies the client's social justice mission.[6]

Jeanne Gang continues to amass recognition as a world leader in the practices of architecture and urban design. Her honors include the MacArthur Fellowship, Architectural Review's Architect of the Year, the Louis I. Kahn Memorial Award, the Marcus Prize for Architecture, and she was named in 2019 by TIME magazine as one of the most influential people in the world. Studio Gang has garnered a plethora of American Institute of Architects awards and other accolades including the 2013 National Design Award from the Cooper Hewitt, Smithsonian Design Museum, and the 2016 Architizer A+ Firm of the Year Award.

Arup

Ove Arup, recognized as a visionary leader in civil engineering, founded Arup Group as a structural engineering firm in 1946. The firm rapidly developed a reputation for innovative approaches to resolving structural challenges. Ove Arup wrote and lectured extensively about the value of structure to the architectural design process, "Great architecture can be created from a tortuous structure or at an inordinate cost, but it would be greater still if structural clarity and ease of construction could be added to its virtues."[7] The success of the firm enabled rapid expansion and today employs over 16,000 staff in a range of disciplines in offices across the world.

The core mission of the firm was described in an address given by Ove Arup to partners in 1970 called the "Key Speech," which remains a touchstone for the firm's practice. Arup described the need for employees to work closely together, especially as the firm expands, and reminded them of his vision for the firm: "our work should be interesting and rewarding…We must therefore strive for quality in what we do, and never be satisfied with the second-rate."[8] It is this philosophy that has made Arup one of the most revered engineering practices in the world, enlisted for design collaborations by prominent architects and on high profile projects. A few of the firm's notable contributions include the National Aquatics Center (The Watercube) with PTW Architects, the National Stadium (Bird's Nest) with architects Herzog & De Meuron, 30 St. Mary's Axe (The Gerkin) with Foster + Partners, as well as the CCTV Headquarters in China and the Seattle Public Library, both with OMA. The firm continues to have a strong reputation for research and innovation leading to creative solutions for boundary-pushing structures.

Introduction to the Gilder Center: Design Influences

In anticipation of the 150-year anniversary of the American Museum of Natural History (AMNH) in New York City, the world-renowned research and education institution held a design competition in 2013–2014 to fulfill a long-standing plan to expand public access to its extensive collections, and ease circulation between the southwest and northwest buildings.[9] Drawn to the competition by the ethos of AMNH and its civic prominence for New York City, Jeanne Gang, Founding Principal and Partner of Studio Gang, describes, "The Gilder Center's holistic mission and the museum's ambitions for the project strongly resonated with our ideas and interdisciplinary practice at Studio Gang, where our architectural work takes cues from nature, adheres to science, and aligns with art."[10] For the competition, Studio Gang studied the museum and began their collaboration with structural engineers at Arup to

Figure 5.1 View of the Central Exhibition Hall of the Richard Gilder Center for Science, Education, and Innovation at the American Museum of Natural History, New York City, NY, 2022. Studio Gang with a team of collaborators including structural engineers at Arup. Credit: Studio Gang and MIR.

develop a design inspired by the museum's mission to "discover, interpret, and disseminate information about human cultures, the natural world, and the universe through a wide-ranging program of scientific research, education and exhibition."[11] Analyzing existing and potential flows of circulation, the design team proposed an organizational strategy characterized by a strong east-west circulation axis that connects the exhibits while simultaneously creating a spatially and visually dynamic atrium space (Figure 5.1). Gang describes, "Designed to inspire a sense of discovery in the visitor, this central space found its form through our study of geological references, such as caves and canyons, which hold the fossil records of life on earth."[12] With this approach that reflected the museum both in form and purpose, the team won the commission (Figure 5.2).

The new Richard Gilder Center for Science, Education, and Innovation addition comprises 190,000 square feet (17,700 square meters) of exhibition, research, and education spaces, and forms connections among ten buildings of

Figure 5.2 Early sketch of the Gilder Center exterior by Jeanne Gang. Credit: Jeanne Gang.

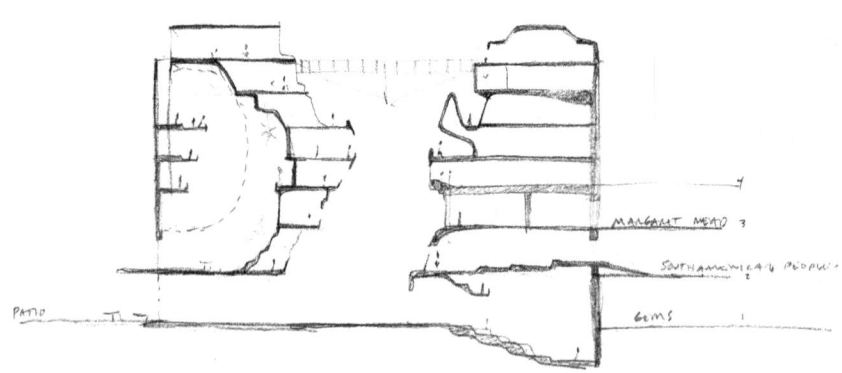

Figure 5.3 Early section drawing for the American Museum of Natural History including the expansion designed by Studio Gang with a team of collaborators including structural engineers at Arup. Credit: Jeanne Gang.

Figure 5.4 Early (2013) sketch of a section through the Gilder Center Central Exhibition Hall by Jeanne Gang. Credit: Jeanne Gang.

the institution (Figure 5.3). The expansion includes exhibition and collection spaces for about 4 million of the museum's 34 million specimens and artifacts, an Insectarium, a live Butterfly Vivarium, the Invisible Worlds Immersive Theater, a new Research Library and Learning Center, laboratories, education spaces for teachers and children of all ages, as well as mechanical and other support spaces.[13] Visitors enter the museum from Columbus Avenue through an accessible, at-grade entrance and immediately encounter the lively Central Exhibition Hall (Figure 5.4). As Gang describes, "Upon entering the space, natural daylight from above and sightlines to various activities inside invite movement through the Central Exhibition Hall on a journey towards deeper understanding of the natural world."[14] The spectacular, five-story "canyon" is an awe-inspiring spatial experience shaped by flowing "geological" structures and daylight streaming from the giant oculi above (Figure 5.5). The visitor's gaze is drawn upwards along the cascading structure while views of the exhibition spaces summon exploration. From the beginning, the designers aimed to create the "kind of space that uplifts your spirits, heightens your senses and makes you want to learn," explains Weston Walker, Design Principal and Partner at Studio Gang.[15]

The structure powerfully reacts to various forces—gravity, the movement of people, openings for the ever-changing natural light—and embodies the flow of knowledge. These architectural–structural ambitions resonated with the scientists and researchers of AMNH. Walker relayed, for example, that Michael Novacek, the museum's Provost of Science, saw many different kinds of natural structures in the design, from bones and tissues to the fibers of a galaxy. "The

CASE STUDIES IN COLLABORATION: CIVIC BUILDINGS

Figure 5.5 Site plan for the Richard Gilder Center for Science, Education, and Innovation at the American Museum of Natural History, New York City, NY, 2022. Studio Gang with a team of collaborators including structural engineers at Arup. Credit: Studio Gang.

Figure 5.6 Park entrance of the Richard Gilder Center for Science, Education, and Innovation at the American Museum of Natural History, New York City, NY, 2022. Studio Gang with a team of collaborators including structural engineers at Arup. Credit: Studio Gang.

architecture isn't just about representing geology," Walker describes, "It's about conductive space and an expression of forces at all scales, which speaks to the cross-scale, cross-disciplinary mission of the education and innovation centers of the museum."[16] The openings or "portals" in the Central Exhibition Hall create human-scaled spaces, while the overall experience is bigger—geological and sublime.

The design for the new Gilder Center not only aligns with the historic institution's focus on science and natural history, but the strength, holism, and clarity of the design's "naturalness" grew out of a five-year collaborative process and feedback from numerous stakeholders. A project of this scale—both in its significance and budget[17]—is too complex to fully describe every contribution and influence. Rather, this case study focuses on key moments in the collaboration between the architects at Studio Gang and the structural engineers at Arup: how they developed the integrated architectural–structural design; how they established the materials and methods for aspects of construction; and how the team overcame challenges during their work on the Central Exhibition Hall for the Gilder Center—a building intended to support AMNH's next 150 years (Figure 5.6).

The Team and Working Methods

The Studio Gang–Arup team worked together from the beginning of the project. Jeanne Gang, whose approach is based on "multi-disciplinary problem solving,"[18] invited Arup Director Rory McGowan to early design discussions during the competition phase. Gang and McGowan had worked together on various projects since the early 1990s during Gang's time at OMA in Rotterdam. Having a long history of collaboration elevated the trust and open communication among team members. Just like Gang, McGowan is firmly committed to this type of working relationship, because "early collaboration and listening to each other results in incredible outcomes."[19] The team for the Gilder Center competition established major parameters for the project, which are discussed in the next section. At the start of the collaboration, the team held several weekend-long, in-person charrettes to develop the design proposal.

After winning the competition in 2014, the architecture and structural engineering teams evolved and expanded. McGowan, who is based in Dublin, Ireland, connected with Arup's New York office, including Associate Principal Michelle Roelofs; Matt Jackson would join the team later. Taking the day-to-day responsibilities for Studio Gang were Design Principal and Partner Wes Walker and Design Principal Ana Flor Ortiz. Other firms were also brought on board including Ralph Appelbaum Associates for exhibition design, Atelier Ten and Buro Happold Engineering for environmental systems and MEP, and

Reed Hilderbrand to design the adjacent landscape that extends into Theodore Roosevelt Park. The executive architect for the project is Davis Brody Bond. After the initial design phase, contract terms were established that bound the team together and provided the benefit of early involvement from the construction manager, AECOM Tishman.

The architecture and structural engineering team talked almost every day and met in person on a biweekly basis. Six in-person charrettes proved critical during the intense design phases of the project from 2015 to 2016, which were each focused on a key topic such as materiality or load paths. The in-person meetings provided team synergy and common ground for design discussions. In these meetings, they used a variety of ideation and communication techniques ranging from sketching to physical models constructed with foam, paper, and 3d-printed interchangeable parts. Analog sketching and model-making have been central to Studio Gang's design methods and are used throughout the design process[20]— this tangible way of working also engaged the engineers and facilitated discussions for the Gilder Center charrettes. Although the physical models with interchangeable parts took time to create and develop, the team found these indispensable in communicating and sharing ideas.[21]

Design Development

Building on the competition charrettes, the next design phase involved informed variations, all guided by the team's shared vision for the project. In the competition phase, as in most competitions, the design team did not yet have access to the client or detailed specifics about the site, institution, or community needs. Therefore, they could not know the full scope of the museum's goals or the project constraints. "The early competition drawings strongly conveyed our concept, but they didn't contain the full intelligence yet—it was like designing in the dark,"[22] Walker notes (Figure 5.7). After the team was hired by the museum, the project evolved through an infusion of information about the institution's long-term goals and programming, details about the site and existing buildings, community involvement, and budget constraints. One of the main methods of gaining this broader and deeper understanding involved many (but engaging) meetings with museum leadership and staff, including researchers and educators who would eventually use the spaces, as well as informative meetings with community groups.[23] Meanwhile, the team also investigated and analyzed the existing conditions of the site and adjacent buildings.

Through this accumulation of information and subsequent analyses, the design naturally evolved, but the main conceptual drivers of the project remained clear: the design team agreed that the Central Exhibition Hall should function both as an awe-inspiring architectural experience and as a

Figure 5.7 Perspective wireframe of the morphology of the Gilder Center. Credit: Studio Gang.

structure that *actually works structurally*. The "canyon" shapes the program and circulation of visitors while providing them with views and natural light, but it also performs very clearly (even to non-engineers) as a system that carries loads to the ground. Walker explained, "The bigger idea is to have a structure that enables the science of the gravity loads to become visible."[24] Maintaining that clarity of intention helped guide the geometric and spatial adjustments eventually needed during the five-year design process.

Post Competition: Bridging the Structure

While the initial design "gained intelligence" through investigations about the site and input from stakeholders, the next phase of the project included "refining in more detail and sculpting the structure to resolve loads, respond to the program, and determine sightlines, all of which are equally technical and architectural tasks."[25] The ground and basement conditions proved highly significant in establishing structural parameters, a discovery that Walker attributes to his structural engineering colleague. Early in design development, McGowan observed the underground infrastructure on the as-built plan drawings and, as Ana Flor Ortiz describes, this "was when we discovered that we cannot just bring the structure down to the ground anywhere. It is not just an empty site—it is very constricted and there are a lot of utilities to avoid."[26] Skirting these utilities meant there were very few areas where the new structure could touch the ground. Arup's Michelle Roelofs explains further how the design evolved through this discovery,

At the site, there was an active loading dock and an existing back-of-house building that were intended to be fully demolished to make way for the new building. After the competition, as we began to work alongside the museum's team, we learned that the basement level of the existing building was chock full of mechanical and electrical equipment that was servicing the whole museum campus. And once the surveys came in, we learned there are tons of mechanical and electrical trenches located there as well. So that became a major challenge: how to maintain all of the active services—this main artery for the campus—while adding a huge new structure on top of them.[27]

This expansive utility corridor also happened to coincide with the site's ancient geology (Figure 5.8). A river historically ran through the ground below the site, leaving silt and clay soils in its geological wake, so bedrock was much lower where the new museum entrance would be. Roelofs describes,

In this area the bedrock is located as deep as negative 30 or 40 feet, because this is where the river used to be, but adjacent to the existing museum buildings, the bedrock is nearly at grade. Spanning over the

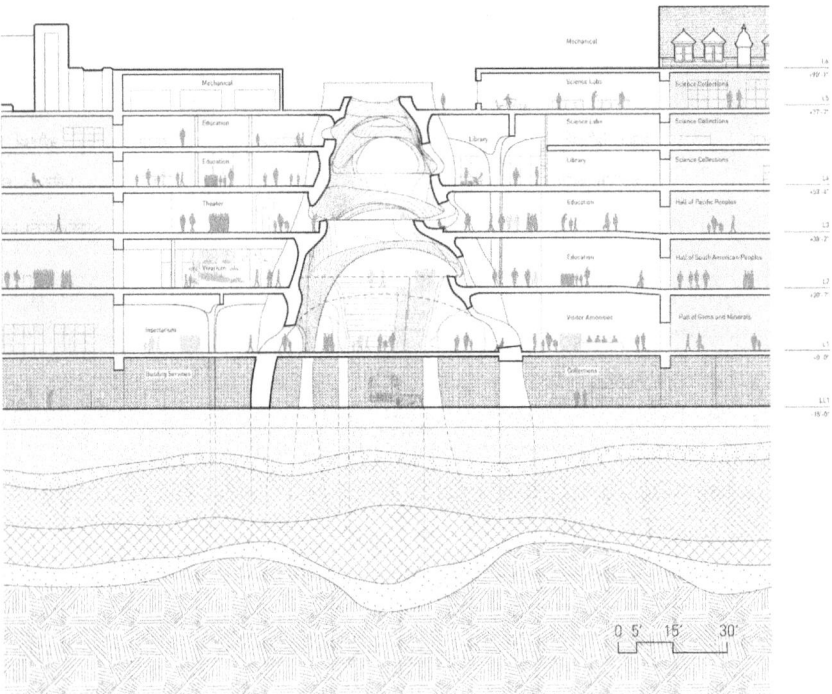

Figure 5.8 Building section cut through the Central Exhibition Hall, adjacent spaces, and ground. The Richard Gilder Center for Science, Education, and Innovation at the American Museum of Natural History, New York City, NY, 2022, designed by Studio Gang with a team of collaborators including structural engineers at Arup. Credit: Studio Gang.

utility zone with the new building was therefore extra beneficial because it also avoided placing any heavy load in the deep riverbed.[28]

By locating the footings outside the riverbed/utility corridor, the footings could connect to the bedrock close to the surface, saving drilling and concrete foundation costs. This is incredibly significant since, depending on soil conditions and loads, foundations can be as much as half of a project's budget. Likewise, circumnavigating the utility corridor for the campus would allow those services to continue to operate during construction, avoiding the high costs of moving them and the associated delays for construction. What might have seemed like constraints or problems became further justification for the "canyon." Walker remarks,

> This notion of arching geometries, using the fluid aspect of concrete to get that flow of load paths around openings to their perfect landing spot, was a nice expression of the concept coming together—the engineering considerations combining with the architectural aspirations.[29]

Continued Teamwork: Means and Methods of Design and Construction

Software

Translating the concept models—made from materials such as paper, foam, ice, wood, and clay—into something the structural team could analyze meant creating new software workflows (Figure 5.9). Studio Gang commonly uses 3d

Figure 5.9 Study model in foam with floors that can be easily taken apart for refinements on the fly during design group discussions on the Gilder Center designed by Studio Gang with a team of collaborators including structural engineers at Arup. Credit: Studio Gang.

modeling software Rhino[30] in the initial design phases of their work, but the fluidity of this design's form called for a program with clay-like modeling capabilities. After testing many options, they selected T-Splines,[31] a plug-in for Rhino, to digitally model a flowing morphology. This process of translating the design vision to the computer model involved a lot of back-and-forth between the architects and engineers. The engineering team also works with Rhino and in the early stages of design would "slice and dice" through the Rhino model to assess geometry and load flows. Roelofs explains that she worked with Walker and Flor Ortiz on,

> various form iterations and looked for load paths in order to come up with sensible advice and guidance that wasn't super prescriptive. We created some rules that the team could come back to as changes were being made, since there were so many factors at play-- including all of the program requirements and all sorts of other issues.[32]

Roelofs helped facilitate the clarity of these guidelines by creating hand-drawn diagrams using prints of screenshots of Studio Gang's Rhino model (Figure 5.10). These drawings included diagrams of load paths, rules about openings in the wall surface, and so forth. As the project developed, there was constant communication between the architects and engineers to refine the form so that it performed well both architecturally and structurally. The workflow involved exchanging the latest Rhino model; Arup would conduct a quick structural analysis and provide diagrams showing "hot spots" that needed form refinements.[33] In response, Studio Gang would fine-tune geometries and

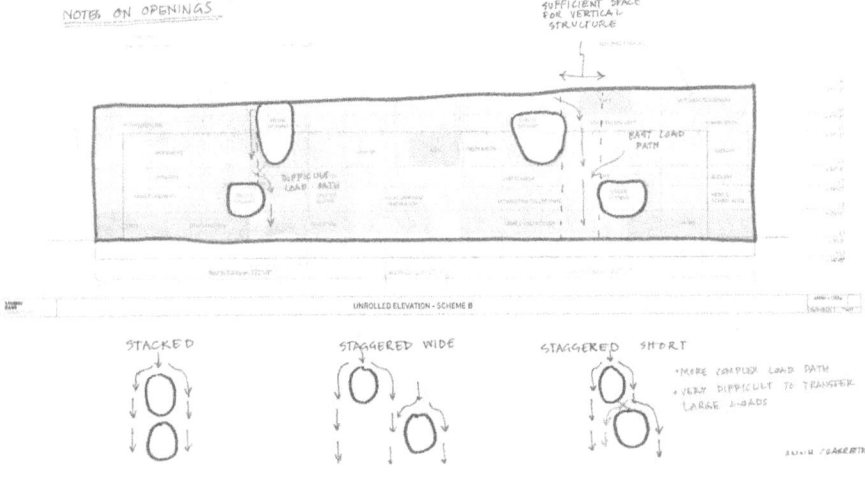

Figure 5.10 Sketch of structural design strategies for load flows around openings by Michelle Roelofs of Arup. Credit: Michelle Roelofs.

integrate them with design developments, continuing the back-and-forth feedback cycle.

As the project progressed, Studio Gang worked with Proving Ground (a digital design consultancy) to develop a customized workflow to translate the complex forms of the design model into a building information model for construction documentation and analysis.[34] The process involved using open-source interoperability programming to convert meshes from Rhino into Revit, a BIM software that is widely used in the US by both architects and engineers. Using a shared model among various disciplines allowed the team to coordinate systems and address clashes, thereby averting potentially costly and wasteful changes in the field.

Various digital models also proved helpful in collaborating and communicating with fabricators and contractors. For example, Arup created a rebar detail model in 3d and shared it with the specialty concrete contractor, COST of Wisconsin. Based on this model, the fabricators then harnessed Rhino to create rebar shop drawings. This benefited the constructors on site too, who used the digital rebar model alongside traditional 2d printed drawings to inform their work.[35]

Constructability

Throughout the design process, the team discussed constructability and investigated various means and methods to translate the digital and physical models into construction systems. Since the feeling of being immersed in a natural rock formation inspired the design, the team agreed on the importance of creating solidity in the structure: The concrete surface did not want to be shiny and smooth, but tactile and solid, and they hoped the cascade of light on the surfaces would "provoke a reaction, something unexpected for the visitor."[36] Given how important this structure–architecture integration was for the project, the team investigated materials and construction methods to realize this vision involving collecting precedents and engaging numerous manufacturers to help to narrow the options.[37] Traditionally, poured-in-place architectural concrete is constructed using wood or steel formwork, but making the formwork requires time, skilled labor, and a huge volume of temporary material that would not be reused. In other projects with more regular structural schemes, repetition of formwork makes it cost-effective, but there is no repetition in the Central Exhibition Hall. To find a more efficient and less wasteful construction method, the architects and engineers investigated options in parallel; McGowan explains, "we looked at maybe a dozen different material and construction approaches to achieving the structure, so a lot of work was put in over six to twelve months."[38]

This investigative process held crucial importance because the construction and material systems for the Central Exhibition Hall had deep implications for the project budget and the visitors' experiences, not to mention the maintenance and longevity of the building. With so many pressures at play, Walker describes that

> more risk-averse voices were initially pushing towards more common construction methods, assuming that the easiest way to build this would be the most conventional: triangulating a steel structure that you can fabricate in any shape and then covering it with GFRC [glass fiber reinforced concrete] panels. But it felt underwhelming to us — and counter to the concept — to imagine knocking on the wall and having it sound hollow.[39]

McGowan agrees, "If we had tried to do something contrived, it would have looked contrived rather than being governed by a natural flow of forces and gravity through its surface. It had to both look and work like structure."[40]

After reviewing costs, weighing material, and constructability options, visiting construction sites, and working with contractors on mock-ups (Figure 5.11), the team ultimately decided the best and most cost-effective material for the Central Exhibition Hall structure was shotcrete. Pneumatically sprayed concrete, an application method for concrete that was invented in 1910, has the benefit of good strength properties (a minimum of 4,000 psi) and requires no formwork.[41] Instead, concrete is sprayed on a cage of reinforcing steel bars

Figure 5.11 A mock-up of a concrete wall and aperture for the Gilder Center. Credit: Studio Gang.

Figure 5.12 A site visit to a Manhattan tunnel project helped the team to agree that shotcrete was the best construction method for the "canyon" in the Central Exhibition Hall of the Gilder Center. Credit: Rory McGowan.

(rebar) configured like a three-dimensional truss covered with a layer of metal mesh. Shotcrete has not been widely used above ground and in architectural applications,[42] yet below ground, in the form of tunnels and swimming pools, it is "everywhere around the world and has stood the test of time."[43]

Gaining full agreement that shotcrete was the solution involved visits to jobsites, including a Manhattan subway tunnel project, which members of the client and construction teams often joined (Figure 5.12). Although the general contractor was initially cautious about employing shotcrete for the Gilder Center, through team meetings and site visits, the contractor grew to trust the process since it is a well-established, "familiar solution." Roelofs explains that in the Central Exhibition Hall (as opposed to the standard structure behind it), "there was no benefit of repetition, so shotcrete was not only more cost-effective, it also provided a freeform, hand-finished structure that had a craft appeal while still being structural. It just ticked all the boxes."[44] Observing the constructors at the shotcrete tunnel and subsequent shotcrete mock-ups, it was clear they took pride in the craft of their fabrication and finishing processes. The shotcrete craftspeople also shared different troweling techniques, sparking fruitful design discussions about the haptic experience of the Central Exhibition Hall surfaces. The designers also consulted with the constructors about local sands and aggregates that could contribute to the surface texture and integrity. These craft-informed decisions contribute to visitors' experiences since textures affect the "geologic" and visceral qualities of the "canyon."

To take advantage of different finishes for the concrete surfaces in the Central Exhibition Hall, the shotcrete was applied in two phases: The first application of concrete filled the rebar cage and formed the bulk of the structure; the second layer, also pneumatically applied, was "rodded" (tamped) to achieve the desired surface texture. Although this top layer still works structurally, it can be a different type of concrete, so for the finished surface, the design team selected a lighter colored mix that would bounce daylight throughout the space from the skylights above.[45] White or lighter colored concretes contain low-iron portland cements, which can add costs and limit the types of admixtures[46] that can be used, so deploying it only in the top layer proved cost-effective and enabled the play of light the team desired.

In all, McGowan commented,

> Another headline of how we arrived where we arrived: It was construction driven. We paid huge attention to how we were going to build the "canyon" and that informed so many decisions. We quite often used construction to inform design.

Roelofs concurred,

> Yes, discussions about sequencing happened in one of the early charrettes, even before the contractor was on board. We didn't want to slow down the whole construction of the project due to the Central Exhibition Hall. So we planned that the standard concrete superstructure would be constructed first, followed by the standard rebar mesh and heavier reinforced areas, then the first layer of shotcrete for the "canyon,"[47]

which was, in fact, the sequence of construction.

Budgetary Effectiveness

Common for architecture of this magnitude and complexity, meeting budgetary constraints means evaluating the project at every scale and detail while assessing costs in relation to shared project goals. This can be a contentious process, but according to the design team, for the Gilder Center, budget constraints made the project better on many fronts.[48] The process involved meetings among the architectural and engineering designers, constructors, and client to compare options and their implications. The architects provided visualizations of the options to help inform the discussions.[49] In the end, the design team brought the project within budget through a few key operations: saving more of an existing building, simplifying some aspects of the structure, lowering the Central Exhibition Hall by one story, and making the skylights smaller. These moves, Roelofs explains, led to the architecture that we have now, which everybody agrees is even better than the previous. There was a breakthrough moment that really hinged on collaboration—we were able to fix a lot of issues for different disciplines with one big move.[50]

The team attributes the positive outcome of the budget analysis process to the solidity of the co-developed design goals. Flor Ortiz remarks, "The cost saving work proved that the concept was so strong that the form could adapt to a big change without losing anything—in fact, it is better."[51]

Through these challenges and others over the five-year design process, the team adeptly navigated project complexities to adapt the design to meet project goals. The design team's responses—including preserving existing buildings and utilities, adjusting to soil conditions to reduce foundations, and working with community groups to safeguard the surrounding park—positively informed this extremely ambitious project. Alissa Anderson reflects on this attitude from Studio Gang, "The office is always optimistic—if you use challenges as opportunities, then the design will improve."[52] Walker agrees, saying,

> We're always trying to listen—not just to our engineers, sustainability experts, and other consultants, but also to our clients and their stakeholders, community leaders, builders and craftspeople. It's really about bringing different people to the table and letting the best ideas percolate up. You have to develop the intuition to recognize those ideas and say yes, if it makes sense, let's go with it.[53]

Listening and refining takes time, however, and though the building was initially slated for completion by the museum's 150-year anniversary in June 2019, it broke ground at that time and is anticipated to open in 2022.

Conclusion—Affirming Common Ground

Through collaboration among the design team as well as with constructors, the client, and community, the Gilder Center is a thoroughly vetted and highly refined manifestation of clear and focused design strategies. The honest approach to the structure is a significant aspect of the Gilder Center design story—it is not a form that the engineers needed to take special pains to make work. Instead, the concept of a fully integrated architecture–structure—based on physics and science—held constant throughout the project's development and ultimate realization.

Having a design vision shared by both the architects and engineers created the foundation for a strong collaboration. McGowan summarizes the value of this working method for the team (Figure 5.13):

> Early on, it was clear that it was important to stick to our guns in terms of the fundamental concept. This was to have a "canyon" or Central Exhibition Hall structure *that is structural*, with openings et cetera that are not contrived, which truly follows the flow of forces and achieves the function by providing separation and bridges. This concept made sense, and you could add and subtract and adjust your budget without losing or compromising it at all…I've seen that happen in great projects, where the concept survives the budget without compromise, and the Gilder Center is certainly an example of that.[54]

Walker agrees, saying that if you have a strong vision that is shared among the interdisciplinary team, "then the concept will survive through all the criteria

Figure 5.13 Entrance of the Richard Gilder Center for Science, Education, and Innovation at the American Museum of Natural History, New York City, NY, 2022. Studio Gang with a team of collaborators including structural engineers at Arup. Credit: Studio Gang and Neoscape.

that are imposed; if you have a good relationship with your collaborators, you can work together to overcome almost any challenge."[55]

Notes

1. Studio Gang design team: Jeanne Gang, Ana María Flor Ortiz, Anu Leinonen, and Weston Walker, with Francisco L. Padron Bolanos, Claire Cahan, John Castro, Juan de la Mora, Natalya Egon, Elif Erez, Dimitra Gelagoti, Spencer Hayden, Jay Hoffman, Maciej Kaczynski, Wei-Ju Lai, Will Lambeth, Lydia Link, Bethany Mahre, Andrew McGee, Gabrielle Poirier, María Risueño Dominguez, Mauricio Sánchez, Mark Schendel, Stanley Schultz, Anika Schwarzwald, Schuyler Smith, Katie Stranix, Art Terry, Michael Vallera, Christopher Vant Hoff, Magda Wala, and Peter Zuroweste.
2. Arup structural engineering team: Rory McGowan, Matt Jackson, Michelle Roelofs, Gabriela Garcia, Charys Clay, Jack Kennedy, James Angevine, Mohammed Hossain, Erika Yaroni, Owen Myers, and Israel Shaw.
3. Additional project team members include Signage Design: Pentagram; Theater Design: Tamschick Media + Space with Boris Micka Associates; Lighting Consultant: Renfro Design Group; Restaurant Design Consultant: Uhuru; Code Consultant: Simpson Gumpertz & Heger; IT Consultant: Shen Milson Wilke; Security Consultant: Ducibella Venter Santore; Kitchen Consultant: Yui Design; Cost Estimator: Cost Plus; Stone Consultant: Vincent Marazita; Historic Preservation Consultant: Higgins Quasebarth; Collections and Laboratory Consultant: Walter Crimm Associates; Interiors Consultant: SpaceSmith.
4. Jeanne Gang et al., *Building: Inside Studio Gang Architects* (Chicago, IL, New Haven, CT ; London, UK: Studio Gang Architects: In Association with the Art Institute of Chicago, Distributed by Yale University Press, 2012).
5. Gang et al., *Building*, 160.
6. Caryn Brause, *The Designer's Field Guide to Collaboration*, 1st edition (New York: Routledge, 2017).
7. Ove Arup, "Architects, Engineers and Builders," *Journal of the Royal Society of Arts* 118, no. 5167 (1970): 390–401.
8. Ove Arup, "Ove Arup Key Speech." *Arup*, 1970, www.arup.com/perspectives/publications/speeches-and-lectures/section/ove-arup-key-speech.
9. Colin Davey, Thomas A. Lesser, and III Kermit Roosevelt, *The American Museum of Natural History and How It Got That Way* (New York: Fordham University Press, 2019). muse.jhu.edu/book/65979.
10. Jeanne Gang, Studio Gang, Email correspondence, June 2, 2021.
11. "About the Museum," American Museum of Natural History, accessed June 5, 2021, https://www.amnh.org/about.
12. Jeanne Gang, Studio Gang, Email correspondence, June 2, 2021.
13. "Richard Gilder Center."
14. "Richard Gilder Center."
15. Weston Walker, Interview with Studio Gang's Alissa Anderson, Ana Flor Ortiz and Weston Walker, Zoom, February 26, 2021.
16. Walker, Interview with Studio Gang's Alissa Anderson, Ana Flor Ortiz and Weston Walker.
17. The budget is approximately $400 million. Source: "Richard Gilder Center: About the Project | AMNH," American Museum of Natural History, accessed June 6, 2021, https://www.amnh.org/about/gilder-center/about-the-project.
18. Gang et al., 164.
19. Rory McGowan, Interview with Arup structural engineers Rory McGowan and Michelle Roelofs, Zoom, March 4, 2021.
20. Gang et al., 10.
21. Michelle Roelofs, Interview with Arup Engineers Rory McGowan and Michelle Roelofs, Zoom, March 4, 2021; Walker.
22. Walker.
23. After extensive community meetings, the Community Board and many other groups endorsed the project in October 2016. "Among the groups that support of the project – some of whose members spoke at the Board meeting—are Friends of Roosevelt Park, Park West 77th street, Columbus Avenue Business Improvement District, Theodore Roosevelt Park Neighborhood Association, West 80th Street Block Association, American Institute of Architects (AIA) New York Chapter, New Yorkers for Parks, and Green Market/Grow NYC." Source: American Museum of Natural History. "Richard Gilder Center: Project News | AMNH," accessed March 20, 2021. https://www.amnh.org/about/gilder-center/project-news.
24. Walker.
25. Walker.
26. Ana Flor Ortiz, Interview with Studio Gang's Alissa Anderson, Ana Flor Ortiz and Weston Walker, Zoom interview by authors, February 26, 2021.
27. Roelofs, Interview by authors.
28. Roelofs.
29. Walker.
30. McNeel, R., & others. Rhinoceros 3D, Robert McNeel & Associates, Seattle, WA, 2010.
31. Autodesk, T-splines plug-in for Rhino, 2015. T-splines has been redesigned by Autodesk as Fusion 360 and is no longer available as a plug-in.
32. Roelofs.
33. This workflow was developed by Gabriela Garcia on the Arup team.
34. Nathan Miller and David Stasiuk, "A Novel Mesh-Based Workflow for Complex Geometry in BIM," in *ACADIA 2017: DISCIPLINES & DISRUPTION*. Proceedings of the 37th Annual Conference of the Association for Computer Aided Design in Architecture (ACADIA) ISBN 978-0-692-96506-1, Cambridge, MA 2–4 November, 2017.

35 Email interview with Alissa Anderson, Studio Gang and Michelle Roelofs, Arup. June 2, 2021.
36 McGowan, Interview by authors.
37 Roelofs.
38 McGowan.
39 Walker.
40 McGowan.
41 American Concrete Institute and ACI Committee 506, *Guide to Shotcrete* (Detroit, Mich.: American Concrete Institute, 2016).
42 Two recent architectural applications of shotcrete include The Museum of the History of the Polish Jews (Wlodzimierz Czajka, "The Museum of the History of Polish Jews," 2013, 6.) and the Taichung Metropolitan Opera (Tackling the World's Most Challenging Building | Industry | 2014-12-22 | CommonWealth Magazine," CommonWealth Magazine, accessed March 22, 2021, https://english.cw.com.tw/article/article.action?id=297.)
43 McGowan.
44 Roelofs.
45 Walker.
46 Admixtures are used in concrete for various purposes including reducing water content, increasing strength and improving durability. "E-4(12) Chemical Admixtures for Concrete," accessed March 22, 2021, https://www.concrete.org/store/productdetail.aspx?ItemID=E412&Language=English&Units=US_Units.
47 McGowan and Roelofs.
48 Walker, Flor Ortiz, and Anderson.
49 Alissa Anderson, Interview with Studio Gang's Alissa Anderson, Ana Flor Ortiz and Weston Walker, Zoom interview by authors, February 26, 2021.
50 Roelofs.
51 Flor Ortiz, Interview by authors.
52 Anderson, Interview by authors.
53 Walker.
54 McGowan.
55 Walker.

CHAPTER 6

Glass Pavilion at the Toledo Museum of Art

Collaboration for Minimalism and Transparency

Client:	Toledo Museum of Art
Architect:	SANAA Kazuyo Sejima + Ryue Nishizawa
Design Team:	Toshihiro Oki, Takayuki Hasegawa, Keiko Uchiyama, Mizuki Imamura, Tetsuo Kondo, Junya Ishigami, Florian Idenburg
Architect of Record:	Kendall Heaton Associates, Inc.
Structure:	Saski and Partners & Guy Nordenson and Associates SAPS
MEP Engineer:	Cosentini Associates, New York
Glass consultant:	Front, Inc.
Lighting:	ARUP/Kilt Planning.

The Toledo Museum of Art Glass Pavilion was a collaboration that encompassed many individuals and companies. This case study will focus on the collaboration amongst SAANA, Sasaki and Partners, and Guy Nordenson and Associates.

SANAA

SANAA, Sejima and Nishizawa and Associates, is a Japanese architecture firm founded by Kazuyo Sejima and Ryue Nishizawa in 1995. Their large and highly lauded body of work demonstrates a refined approach to lightness and transparency through a subtle use of structure and materials. Their designs often involve open, democratic plans with a blurred boundary between exterior and interior, and a relationship with the surrounding natural environment.[1] The practice rose to international prominence with the design for the 21st Century Museum of Contemporary Art in Kanazawa, Japan, the Prada Store in Arezzo, Italy, and their Gifu Kitagata Apartment building. Significant works include the extraordinary rolling shell structure for the Rolex Learning Center in Lausanne, Switzerland, the New Museum of Contemporary Art in New York City, a dynamic stack of subtly radiant shifting boxes, a satellite museum for the Louvre in the French city of Lens, and an impossibly thin snaking roof supported on the thinnest of columns for Grace Farms in Connecticut.

Nishizawa describes their approach to design as "Coherent, consistent, always doing the same thing. One of our constant big concerns is how to create a relation between the inside and outside, this is very important for us to think about."[2] Speaking in 2005, Sejima adds,

> Probably our interest now is more how to organize "a program" within a building - the layout of rooms and how people move inside. But also how to keep a relationship between the "program" and the outside and then how the outside fits to the surroundings. In each project we have different requirements and the site is different, we try to find our way.[3]

They jointly won the Pritzker Prize (architecture's highest honor) in 2010. In awarding the prize, the jury praised them for:

> Architecture that is simultaneously delicate and powerful, precise and fluid, ingenious but not overly or overtly clever; ... creation of buildings that successfully interact with their contexts and the activities they contain, creating a sense of fullness and experiential richness; for a singular architectural language that springs from a collaborative process that is both unique and inspirational.[4]

Sasaki and Partners (SAP)

Mutsuro Sasaki, a Structural Engineer based in Tokyo, has worked closely on numerous projects with SANAA and with other prominent Japanese architects such as Toyo Ito. He studied both architecture and engineering at Nagoya University and went on to receive a Ph.D. in structural engineering. His particular expertise is in resolving complex geometrical forms. To this end his research as professor at Tokyo's Hosei University has led to the development of computational optimization techniques to facilitate form generation that maximizes efficiency of non-regular structural forms and systems.[5,6]

Increasingly, these methods allow for resolving the structure of three-dimensional surfaces that are free and organic, opening up architectural potential and pushing the limits of engineering.[7] For example, at the Kakamigahara Crematorium designed in collaboration with Toyo Ito in 2006, he used a method called sensitivity analysis to design a free form concrete shell roof sitting on 12 columns and four bearing walls. Traditionally, to minimize bending in a concrete shell (and thus avoid a deep, ungainly, and uneconomical cross section) the form must be designed from a series of known optimal forms, or derived from funicular model where a hanging form in tension is inverted to find a form that will only have compression, such as in the work of Antoni Gaudi or Heinz Isler. Sensitivity analysis, on the other hand, is an iterative computer design methodology that bypasses the conventional sequential process and finds directly the optimum structural form that satisfies given design parameters. Starting with an envelope idea of where the roof will be and some other formal constraints for the roof design, the sensitivity method optimizes the exact shape of the roof by continually recalculating the strain energy at a matrix of nodes on the roof and varying the height of the roof in the direction that will minimize that strain energy. Sasaki claims that shape analysis effectively replaces Gaudi's physical experimental method of the hanging model with a modern theoretical method.[8,9] These innovative methodologies are key to the collaborative nature of his work. "This type of multi-objective optimization enables designers and engineers to collaborate in clear and robust frameworks, provides a common basis for the cross-disciplinary teams to make more informed decisions, and fosters the culture of creativity and innovations."[10] Sasaki has a particularly collaborative relationship with his architecture colleagues and works very closely with them in the initial design phases of a project. "When the architect has an idea, we have a discussion directly. All of the ideas of the projects have to be discussed from the structural standpoint because the idea of the structural engineering influences the design itself."[11]

The value he places on the equality of both the architectural and engineering points of view in the process of developing a structural system is also clear: "The structural engineer's role is thereby defined as being more like an architect than an engineer... They must undertake their collaborations from an equivalent standing."[12]

He also notes that collaborative relationships are a function of the relative positions of the collaborators in their careers and fields and that he has both learned a great deal from his primary collaborators and in turn been a teacher at times. He has maintained long-term collaborations with SANAA and other Japanese architects including Arata Isozakin and Toyo Ito. He explains that they have all had a strong influence on his career.

> My relationship with each of them are different, my responsibility for them and with them are different. In the case of SANAA, when we started our collaboration, I was in my 40s while they were in their 30s and 20s. Therefore, my role has been more as a mentor to lead our collaboration. This is how we pass down the values and knowledge.[13]

Guy Nordenson and Associates

Guy Nordenson is a structural engineer practicing in New York City, who works closely with a number of prominent architects. His firm is described in more detail in Chapter 4 where the National Museum of African American History and Culture is presented. Guy Nordenson Associates were consulting engineers in the US for the Toledo Art Museum Glass Pavilion in collaboration with Sasaki and oversaw to the processes of structural design development, construction documentation, local permitting, code compliance, and construction administration.

Cosentini Associates

Cosentini Associates is a New York City-based engineering consulting firm with a long history of partnering with architectural colleagues on innovative and sustainable systems and a wide portfolio of projects across civic, institutional, and commercial clients. Noted collaborations include the 53rd Street branch of The New York Public Library in 2016 with Mexico City-based TEN Arquitectos; Dee and Charles Wyly Theatre in Dallas Texas with REX and OMA in 2011, and Linked Hybrid in 2009 with Steven Holl Architects, and the Guggenheim Museum in Bilbao, Spain, with Gehry Partners in 1999 with whom they also collaborated on the Walt Disney Concert Hall in Los Angeles, the Peter B. Lewis Library at Princeton University, and the Richard B. Fisher Center for the Performing Arts at Bard College.

The Project

Toledo in northwestern Ohio grew rapidly in the latter part of the 19th century with the building first of the Erie Canal and late the New York to Chicago rail lines, becoming an industrial center with a number of manufacturing specialties, among them glass-making. The Glass Pavilion of the Toledo Art Museum was built to house the impressive collection of contemporary and historical glass art amassed by the museum, which was founded by the President of the Libbey Glass Company.[14] The site for the building is among a campus of buildings that includes the original Beaux Arts museum building completed in 1912 and the Center for the Visual Arts, a Frank Gehry project completed in the 1990s. The museum did not hold a competition to find a designer; instead they hired SANAA directly to design the project. Some may have viewed this as a risky move since the firm was relatively unknown in the US at the time. The final project has received much praise from the architectural press, and SANAA went on to design a number of prominent and highly regarded projects in the US and internationally in the years that followed.

Described in *Architectural Review* as a "delicate crystal casket for a major collection of glassware,"[15] the pavilion was designed to house galleries and courtyards on the ground level, along with two glass-making studios used by the art department at the University of Toledo. The low horizontal building is rectangular in plan, measuring 187 by 203 feet (57 by 62 meters), two levels totaling 74,000 square feet (6900 square meters), and sits amid grass and trees on a large town-square-like lot.[16]

In their design for the Glass Pavilion, Sejima and Nishizawa create dramatic tension seemingly out of the air, using the thinnest, most minimal, and most transparent elements of structure and enclosure.[17] The pavilion appears from the outside as a stripe of white roof sitting atop a band of glass (Figure 6.1a-b). Inside, most interior walls are glass with curved corners. Low-iron glass curved panels, 8 feet (2.4m) wide and 13½ feet (4m) high, and up to one inch (25 mm) thick, make up the transparent walls.[18] Iron is what gives glass a greenish hue, so this low-iron glass has greater clarity. The 35 thin solid steel columns (some

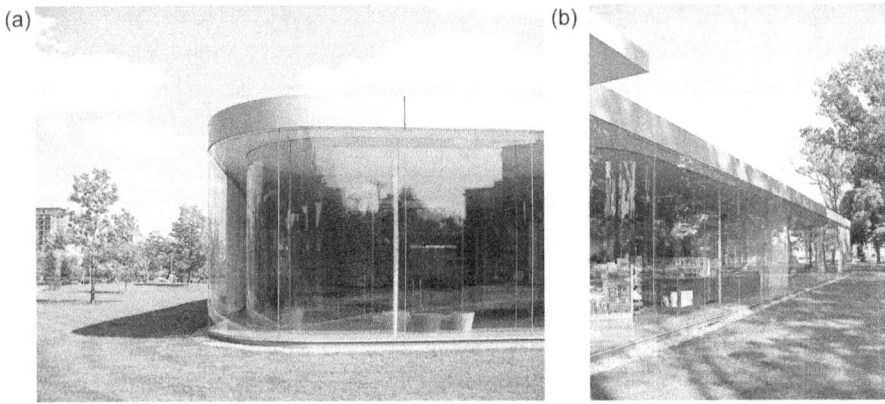

Figure 6.1a-b The pavilion appears from the outside as a stripe of white roof sitting atop a band of glass. SANAA, SAP, GNA, Cosentini Associates, Glass Pavilion at the Toledo Museum of Art, Toledo, Ohio, 2007. Credit: Scott Murray.

Figure 6.2a-b The thin solid steel columns that support the structure recede from view and contribute to the illusion that the roof floats above the glass walls. SANAA, SAP, GNA, Cosentini Associates, Glass Pavilion at the Toledo Museum of Art, Toledo, Ohio, 2007. Credit: Scott Murray.

as slender as 3½ inches (89mm) in diameter)[19] that support the structure recede from view behind the glass or are hidden in the few sections of opaque walls (Figure 6.2a and b) contributing to the illusion that the roof floats above the glass walls.

The all-glass building appears reflective and shiny by day, but at night lit from inside the glass disappears and the patrons and artists emerge in silhouette.[20] *New York Times* critic Nicolai Ouroussoff described the project as

> composed with exquisite delicacy, the pavilion's elegant maze of curved glass walls represents the latest monument to evolve in a chain extending back to the Hall of Mirrors at Versailles ... [a] ...

diaphanous maze. The interior is a series of rounded glass rooms wrapped in a secondary glass skin, which creates a remarkably layered visual experience … creating a more fluid dynamic between the art and the viewer.[21]

There are two opaque galleries, walled in to block light from works that might be damaged by such exposure, which Ouroussoff argues "serve to anchor a structure visually that might otherwise seem about to drift off into space,"[22] an apt description since these walls also hide the structural braces that provide the lateral stability to the building.

At ground level, there are also three courtyard spaces open to the sky above (see the plan and section diagrams in Figure 6.3a–c). These serve to balance light coming from the outer perimeter and minimize glare inside the building. Architectural critic, Clifford Pearson, argues that these spaces along with the interstitial spaces created by the curved glass walls have "a strong visual presence, but remain tantalizingly out of reach."[23] He further posits that "in Japanese architecture, the concept of ma—a gap in time or space—has long played an important role … [SANAA uses] … ma to animate what could be considered just wasted, leftover space"[24] (Figure 6.11).

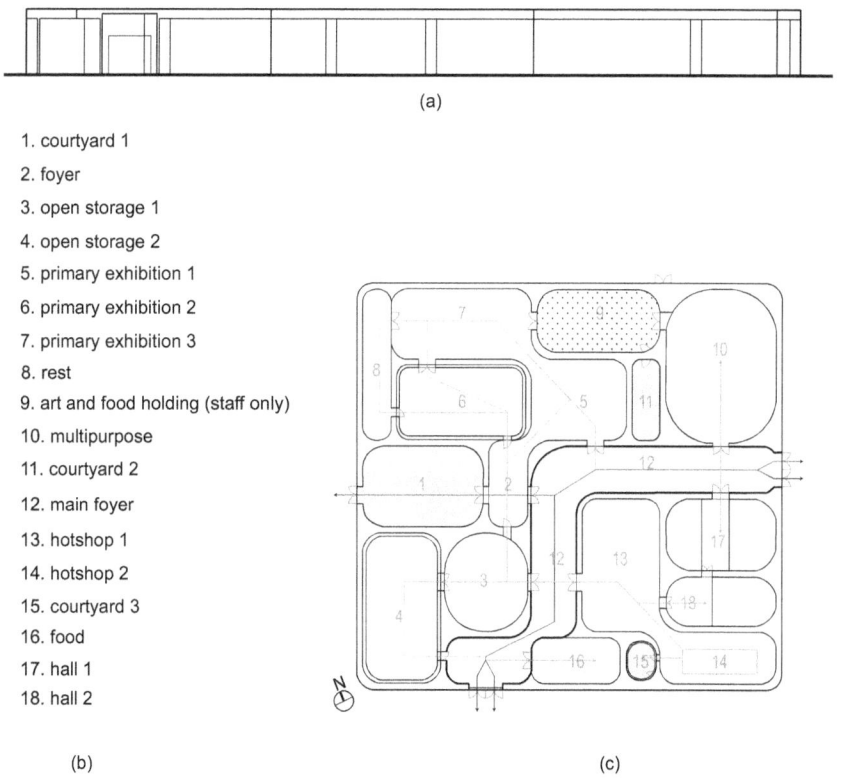

1. courtyard 1
2. foyer
3. open storage 1
4. open storage 2
5. primary exhibition 1
6. primary exhibition 2
7. primary exhibition 3
8. rest
9. art and food holding (staff only)
10. multipurpose
11. courtyard 2
12. main foyer
13. hotshop 1
14. hotshop 2
15. courtyard 3
16. food
17. hall 1
18. hall 2

Figure 6.3a-c Elevation and Plan. SANAA, SAP, GNA, Cosentini Associates, Glass Pavilion at the Toledo Museum of Art, Toledo, Ohio, 2007. Credit: Christina Hoover.

Figure 6.4 Glass workshop. Note the double layer of low-iron glass is clear to provide a view from the outside. SANAA, SAP, GNA, Cosentini Associates, Glass Pavilion at the Toledo Museum of Art, Toledo, Ohio, 2007. Credit: Guy Nordenson and Associates.

Nishizawa himself writes that an exploration of "separating the rooms" has long been a study that he has returned to again and again in his design work (Figure 6.4).[25] Writing specifically about the Glass Pavilion, he explains,

> each function is positioned appropriately then wrapped in transparent curved glass to form an independent space …. the outside connects to the inside, or the rooms in the inside connect with each other, integrating the surrounding green landscape. Here people can stroll about as one pleases, like ranging through the forests.[26]

However, he also notes that the interstitial spaces between the glass walls have additional prosaic functions: they serve as a buffer zone allowing the museum staff to regulate the temperature of each room separately as required, critical with the temperature swings that occur both inside and outside. These spaces also provide sound insulation between the studio programs and between the exhibition areas (Figure 6.5a and b).[27]

Air handling in this building is especially crucial with glass furnaces running at 2300 degrees in the hot glass blowing studios, while adjacent spaces might house delicate and ancient art works that require a cool environment.[28] Combine these complex air-handling needs with the very shallow available cavities for ductwork in both the roof and the floor and you have a considerable logistical challenge.[29] These cavity spaces were shallow in order to minimize both the excavation depth for financial reasons and the visible thickness of the roof for aesthetic reasons. To keep the glass-walled pavilion warm during Ohio's cold winters, Cosentini engineers designed a system to harness heat from the hot shop facilities through heat recovery, while the perimeter is cooled in the summer through a secondary cooling system.[30] These energy-saving measures

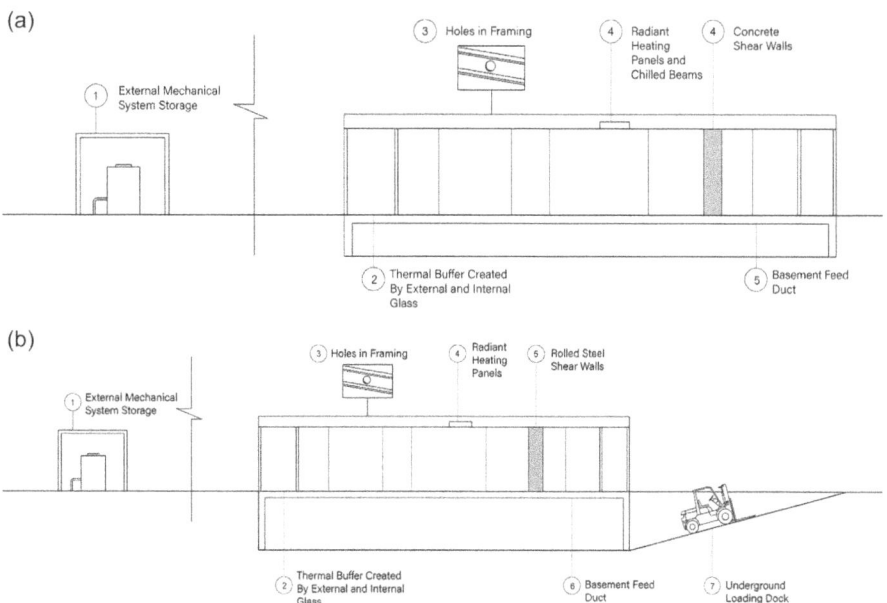

Figure 6.5a-b The shallow cavities for ductwork and the design of the mechanical systems to meet both aesthetic and technical goals presented a complex challenge for the designers. SANAA, SAP, GNA, Cosentini Associates, Glass Pavilion at the Toledo Museum of Art, Toledo, Ohio, 2007. Credit: Shiori Green.

compensate for energy loss through the glazing. The low-slung horizontality of the building, allowing it to sit under the shady tree canopy on the site, clearly contributes to the climatic experience while creating an overall effect that is both unobtrusive and unpretentious. Additionally, neighbors objected to any mechanical equipment being visible on the roof, necessitating the conversion of a nearby building to house the HVAC systems one normally finds on the roof.[31] The services run underground connecting the museum to the outbuilding.

Sasaki designed the structure for the building in collaboration, first with the architects and later with the American engineering team at Guy Nordenson and Associates. Architect Toshihiro Oki worked for SANAA on the Toledo project. He describes the working relationship between SANAA and Mutsuro Sasaki who have completed many projects together as a particularly collaborative one.

> He's always in the office … at any given time when he comes in, he looks at multiple projects that could be at any different phase in the process. He's always involved in projects as an integral part from the very beginning. Everything, right from the conceptual phase.[32]

Oki clarifies that this opportunity for people in the office to just "put things in front of him and get feedback" is very unusual especially in his US experience where engineers are generally hired for a specific project.

That's why I think the architecture and the engineering is so integrated from SANAA's office ... [Sasaki] is not giving design direction, but based on his feedback the design shifts and changes and evolves. He's not saying "we should make a building out of this material" but if architects direct specific questions to him like, "what do you think about this column spacing or this kind of structure, can we do it out of concrete or steel?" he'll come back with some feedback that no one ever thought about.... It's a very specific question and answer process, but based on his feedback, the design tends to evolve.[33]

In the Glass Pavilion, the structure seems simple at first glance, but it is deceptively complex. Sasaki proposed a series of different systems for the roof that had relatively long spans but to be very shallow to align with the architects' vision for the slim, lightweight, horizontal appearance of the project. Some of the initial ideas were too costly to realize. One system initially proposed was a steel plate system similar to one he designed for the Sendai Mediatheque project with Toyo Ito.[34] The early design called for a slab-like system with a horizontal steel plate on the bottom and top with vertical ribs in between that can be customized to the particular load conditions. This orthotropic plate system was an innovative approach to accommodate an irregular column grid. It was inspired by bridge- and ship-building techniques and it was successful in the Mediatheque project, where the project was built by a construction firm with boat engineering history.[35] Unfortunately, this system proved too difficult to achieve in the US as the volume of steel required made it too expensive relative to standard commercially available steel members, there were concerns that it would be difficult to find a local fabricator with the appropriate experience, and there were also code constraints in the US that made it a less attractive solution.[36] Ultimately, Sasaki in collaboration with Nordenson designed a system of girders and beams.

The primary beams (girders) are not aligned to a series of straight axes through the building, as would be typical (Figures 6.6 and 6.7). The beams meander back and forth on a crooked line as the columns are shifted back and forth. This column placement is necessary to align with the architects' plan for the glass walls that enclose a distributed and varied set of programs. The columns also meander to align with the programs in the basement below, which shift in plan to accommodate the equipment required to move heavy pieces of art. The secondary beams run parallel to one another at angles to the girders (Figure 6.8).

In order to keep the roof as thin as possible, the utilities were not hung below the beams and girders as is the norm in standard construction. Penetrations cut in the webs of the secondary beams were used for all the

GLASS PAVILION AT TOLEDO MUSEUM OF ART

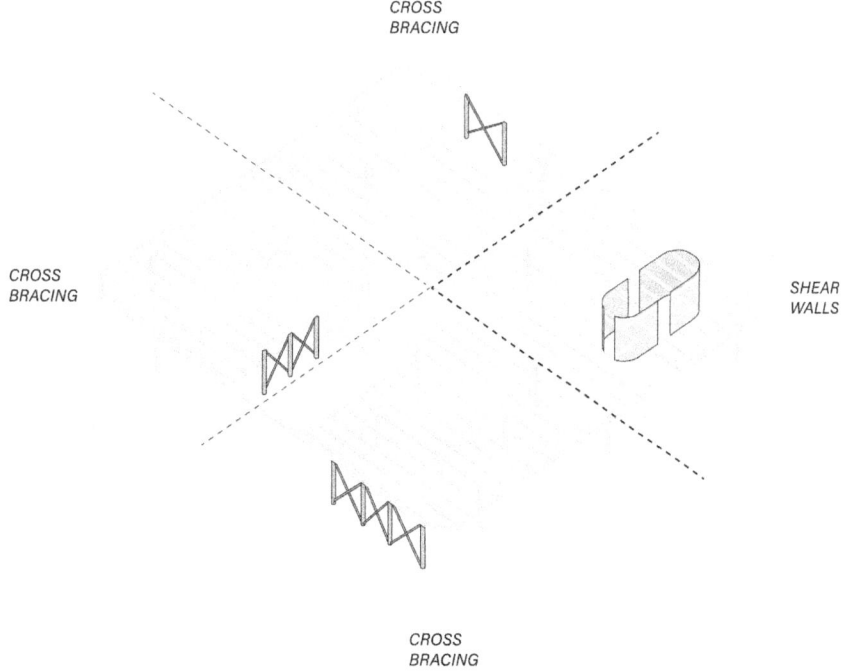

Figure 6.6 Structural frame. The X-braces provide lateral stability as does the curved steel plate wall on the right of the diagram. SANAA, SAP, GNA, Cosentini Associates, Glass Pavilion at the Toledo Museum of Art, Toledo, Ohio, 2007. Credit: Shiori Green.

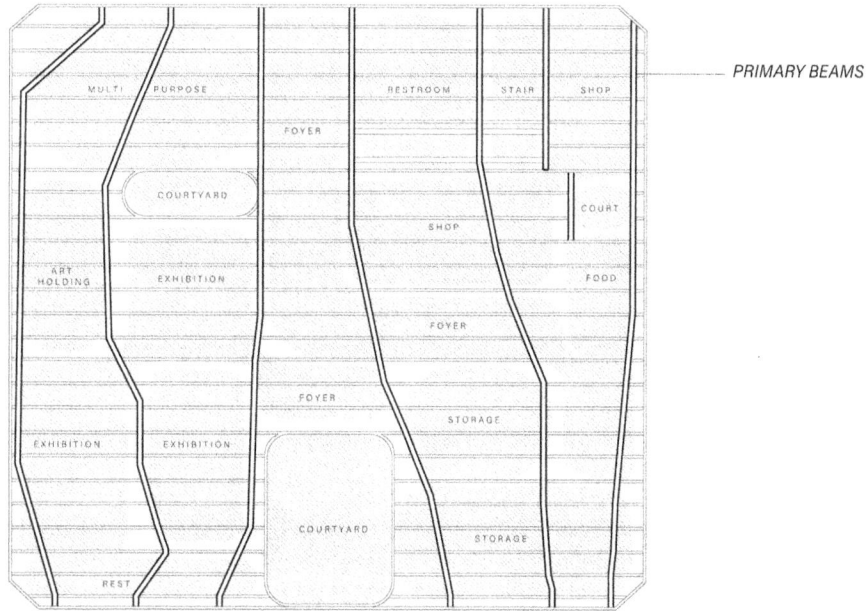

Figure 6.7 Structural frame. The primary beams are highlighted; they meander back and forth with the column locations that are dictated by programmatic needs. SANAA, SAP, GNA, Coentini Associates, Glass Pavilion at the Toledo Museum of Art, Toledo, Ohio, 2007. Credit: Shiori Green.

93

Figure 6.8 Structural frame under construction. SANAA, SAP, GNA, Cosentini Associates, Glass Pavilion at the Toledo Museum of Art, Toledo, Ohio, 2007. Credit: Toshihiro Oki.

Figure 6.9 Glass installation. Note the very shallow available space between the underside of the roof deck and the underside of the ceiling where the mechanical systems had to be carefully inserted. SANAA, SAP, GNA, Cosentini Associates, Glass Pavilion at the Toledo Museum of Art, Toledo, Ohio, 2007. Credit: Guy Nordenson and Associates.

sprinkler lines, drains, and electrical cables, everything was sandwiched in the steel layer (Figure 6.9). A system was devised where most penetrations went through the secondary beams. Only trunk-line penetrations went through the girders. A careful hierarchy had to be created as it was a complex process to fit everything into the steel layer. For example, drain lines need to pitch one eighth of an inch per foot, so when a drain penetrates a beam at a certain point on its cross section, it is passing through the next beam at a lower point, and so on.[37] Cutting into the web of a beam to accommodate utilities is possible because the bending (which is the main structural concern) is largely carried in the top and bottom flanges of the beam. However, cutting a notch in the bottom of the beam is to be avoided, as is cutting a notch in the web at a point where the shear force is high, as the shear is carried in the web (high shear generally occurs in a uniformly loaded beam close to the columns; Figure 6.10). To ameliorate both of these hazardous conditions, some of the beams had to be haunched (made deeper) in certain locations to safely accommodate the penetrations.[38]

A further challenge in the construction process for the roof was the pre-camber that was applied to the beams to minimize deflection. Pre-camber is a deformation of the beam applied in factory conditions in the opposite direction of the anticipated loads that allows a beam to be installed, experience load, and deflect back down to a neutral or near neutral position. It is often used to minimize large deflections of steel beams in long spanning structures like bridges. Here it was deployed to minimize the overall height of the beam, which was so critical to the roof design. Unfortunately, several pieces arrived on site without the correct camber applied. It was crucial given the minimal space into which the structure, enclosure, and utilities were packed that the camber be perfect. At some inconvenience, a crew was hired to "field-camber" the beams, a highly skilled process that required careful oversight to ensure the

Figure 6.10 Structural frame under construction. Note the notches and penetrations for the utilities. SANAA, SAP, GNA, Cosentini Associates, Glass Pavilion at the Toledo Museum of Art, Toledo, Ohio, 2007. Credit: Toshihiro Oki.

beams are not damaged by excessive heat. Ultimately the roof design met the architectural goals: the structural framing was kept to less than 12 inches (30 cm) of height and the white strip of "roof" that contains the structure, all the pipes and ducts, and all the roof finishes is less than 2 feet (60 cm) tall.[39]

This overlap of the programmatic constraints with the structural and mechanical systems meant everything was intertwined. Whenever one thing moved in the design phase, it had an impact on other elements. The hierarchy set up by the structural system accommodated the constant flux in the design phase and helped the architects and engineers to keep track of all the components. This same level of complexity had to be resolved anew for the floor structure over the cellar. This floor was also limited in height, because the further down one excavates the higher the costs. Thus, the ceiling of the cellar was also quite compact with machinery and ductwork. The mechanical needs of the museum along with the extreme temperatures of the glass hot shops, meant that there was significant ductwork and piping that went through the floor system, and in order to maintain the desired floor to ceiling clearance in the cellar everything had to fit right underneath the floor slab. This floor system consisted of one-way slabs with band beams; these one-way slabs were to allow slots to go through the floor. As Oki explains: "so many many different kinds of layering had to take place, the whole structure from the foundation to the top of the roof was like a Swiss watch."[40]

All of the complexity described here was carefully managed by project engineer Brett Schneider working for GNA and the construction documents were used to create a three-dimensional computer model to ensure no clashing of elements, a technique that has become more standard in contemporary practice but was less common at the time.[41]

The incredibly thin columns that are so crucial to the architectural intent of the interiors presented an engineering challenge. The supports are connected to the roof in such a way that they carry only vertical load, a non-normative approach to load distribution.[42] Any lateral load coming from wind, for example, would cause the column to carry bending, and bending requires a stiffer section. Since resistance to bending is a function of the shape of the column's cross section, this would have required a much wider column (which is why most columns are "I" shaped or hollow extrusions of circles and squares). However, even columns loaded only in the vertical direction along their own axis will fail in bending, specifically in buckling. The very careful analysis and design of these slim columns to minimize buckling risk was an interesting research problem according to Guy Nordenson (Figure 6.11).

> For me, one of the things that has emerged from working on the Toledo project is the interest in the consequence of making things

Figure 6.11 One of the courtyard spaces. SANAA, SAP, GNA, Cosentini Associates, Glass Pavilion at the Toledo Museum of Art, Toledo, Ohio, 2007. Credit: Scott Murray.

really thin and dealing with the possibility that they might buckle.... We've had a lot of projects where we are working with things that are on the edge of buckling, either columns or beams that are very thin and so as a result of that we've been doing our own research ... [This problem] has emerged and it is something that seems to recur and has become more and more interesting the more we learn (Figure 6.12).[43]

If every column or wall were connected to the roof in the way described above, the whole structure would rack sideways and collapse under wind load. To take these lateral loads, the vertical structure is locked into the horizontal structure of the roof in each quadrant. In one quadrant, this is achieved by the stiff cross section formed by the curved ¾ inch thick rolled steel wall that forms the enclosure of one of the opaque volumes and provides buckling resistance.[44] It was too costly to replicate this solution in the other portions of the building and so diagonal bracing is used between specific columns that do connect to the roof in such a way as to pick up lateral load. This cross-bracing is hidden in the sheet rock walls that make up the other opaque volumes.[45] Oki argues that this strategy, whereby the vertical and horizontal loads are separated, making columns do only what they are supposed to do (support dead load) and making

Figure 6.12 Interior view. SANAA, SAP, GNA, Cosentini Associates, Glass Pavilion at the Toledo Museum of Art, Toledo, Ohio, 2007. Credit: Scott Murray.

other elements do what they are supposed to do eliminates redundancy and makes the structure more honest and easy to read.[46] Sasaki notes that his deep experience with earthquake engineering in Japan influenced his thinking in this design.[47] This efficiency also contributed to a relatively low cost per square foot of $297—a modest cost for a museum.[48]

It is clear when investigating the technical design of the building, that the experiential quality of the spaces and the ephemeral aesthetic are made possible only by very careful engineering (Figure 6.13). Nordenson argues that this kind of study of buildings is important to understand the results of the collaborative process.

> "The influence of the collaboration is subtle, but it is there … It takes some work to draw it out. It started out pretty much as Sasaki's design of the structure and it went through a series of incremental modifications as we started to have our impact on the way it was done. You really have to look closely at things beyond what people say about them and try to actually study the thing itself to disentangle how it is maybe a different kind of work because of the collaborators who have a hand in it."[49]

Figure 6.13 Note the high degree of precision in the detailing where the glass walls meet the roof. SANAA, Sasakai and Partners, GNA, Glass Pavilion at the Toledo Museum of Art, Toledo, Ohio, 2007. Credit: Toshihiro Oki.

He writes that the drawings of the building when looked at in aggregate resemble a microchip, and finds that the analogy is an apt one. "This feeling of information overlaid … a density both of thought and experience that is embedded in what is at first sight a very simple building. If ever there was a fully conceptual building, this is it."[50]

The Toledo Museum's Director during the time of construction, Don Bacigalupi, appreciates the impact of the architectural "strategy of dematerialization"[51] facilitated by the careful collaboration. The structural and mechanical systems were minimized and streamlined to achieve lightness and the integration with the environment for which so much of SANAA's work strives. "We wanted a showcase for our glass collection…. SANAA's design changes the way you view the artworks, since you're not seeing them against flat walls … they seem to sing in these spaces."[52]

Notes

1. Kazuyo Sejima, Yukio Futagawa, and Ryue Nishizawa, "Creating Principles- Structure, Plan, Relationship, Landscape." In *Kazuyo Sejima Ryue Nishizawa, 1987–2006*. Tokyo: A.D.A. Edita, 2005. 9.
2. "SANAA: kazuyo sejima + ryue nishizawa interview." Designboom. http://www.designboom.com/interviews/sanaa-kazuyo-sejima-ryue-nishizawa-designboom-interview.

3   Ibid.
4   The Hyatt Foundation, "Jury Citation: Kazuyo Sejima and Ryue Nishizawa | The Pritzker Architecture Prize." The Pritzker Architecture Prize, accessed August 6, 2013, http://www.pritzkerprize.com/2010/jury.
5   Mutsuro Sasaki, Toyo Ito, and Arata Isozaki, *Morphogenesis of Flux Structure* (London: AA Publications, 2007).
6   Russell Fortmeyer, "Mutsuro Sasaki," *Architectural Record* 196, no. 3 (2008): 156.
7   Nina Rappaport, "Sasaki and Partners." In *Support and Resist: Structural Engineers and Design Innovation*. New York: Monacelli Press, 2007. 167.
8   Toyo Ito, "Toyo Ito, Liquid Space." *El Croquis* 147 (2009): 70–88.
9   Although others might argue that while the method produces a rational form within a set of formal constraints already established, it is not analogous to the work of Gaudi who was looking to find a formal solution using the resistance of gravity as the only constraint.
10 Mutsuro Sasaki, Interview by the authors. Email Interview. Tokyo, Japan, September 5, 2013.
11 Mutsuro Sasaki, Interview by Marc Guberman and Nina Rappaport. Tokyo, Japan, August, 2006.
12 Sasaki et al., *Morphogenesis of Flux Structure*, 11.
13 Mutsuro Sasaki, Sasaki and Partners, Interview by the authors, Email interview, September 5, 2013.
14 Michael Webb, "Clarity and Light," *Architectural Review* 220, no. 1317 (2006): 66–70.
15 Webb, "Clarity and Light."
16 Julie Sinclair Eakin, "Clearing the Way," *Architecture* 95, no. 10 (2006): 46–51.
17 Clifford A. Pearson, "SANAA's Sejima and Nishizawa Create Layers of Reflections and Perspectives in their Glass Pavilion at the Toledo Museum of Art," *Architectural Record* 195, no. 1 (2007): 78–83.
18 Pearson, "SANAA's Sejima and Nishizawa Create Layers of Reflections and Perspectives in their Glass Pavilion at the Toledo Museum of Art."
19 Eakin, "Clearing the Way," 46–51.
20 Webb, 66–70.
21 Nicolai Ouroussoff, "An Elegant, and Empathetic, Showcase in Glass," *New York Times*, September 1, 2006, sec. Arts and Leisure.
22 Ouroussoff, "An Elegant, and Empathetic, Showcase in Glass."
23 Pearson.
24 Pearson.
25 Sejima et al., "Creating Principles- Structure, Plan, Relationship, Landscape," 10.
26 Sejima et al., 151.
27 Sejima et al.
28 Eakin, 46–51.
29 Toshiro Oki, Toshiro Oki, SANAA, The Toledo Museum of Art Glass Pavilion, Phone interview by the authors, July 30, 2013.
30 "Cosentini Associates—Toledo Museum of Art," accessed May 29, 2021, https://www.cosentini.com/index.php/portfolio-articles/25-cultural/111-toledo-museum-of-art.
31 Eakin, 46–51.
32 Oki, Interview by authors.
33 Oki.
34 Guy Nordenson, *Guy Nordenson: Reading Structures: 39 Projects and Built Works, 1983-2011* (Zurich: Lars Müller Publishers, 2016).
35 Nordenson, *Guy Nordenson*.
36 Nordenson, *Guy Nordenson*.
37 Oki.
38 Oki.
39 Nordenson, *Guy Nordenson*.
40 Oki.
41 Nordenson, *Guy Nordenson*.
42 Oki.
43 Nordenson, Interview by the authors.
44 Oki.
45 Pearson, 78–83.
46 Oki.
47 Sasaki, Interview by the authors.
48 "Toledo," Paratus Group, accessed May 25, 2021, https://www.paratusgroup.com/toledo.
49 Nordenson, Interview by the authors.
50 Nordenson, *Guy Nordenson*.
51 Pearson, 78–83.
52 Pearson.

CHAPTER 7

Billie Jean King Main Library

Collaborating on Mass Timber and Carbon Accounting

Architecture, Structural Engineering, Interiors, and Graphics:	SOM
Civil:	KPFF Consulting Engineers
MEP:	Syska Hennessy Group
Library Programming:	Linda Demmers
Landscape:	Gustafson Guthrie Nichol
Acoustics:	Newson Brown Acoustics
Wood Scientist:	Ron Anthony
General Contractor:	Clark Construction Group[1]

Although multiple experts worked together on the design of the Billie Jean King Main Library in Long Beach, the case study focuses on the collaboration between structural and architectural designers at SOM.

History of Skidmore, Owings & Merrill (SOM)

SOM occupies a unique place in historical and contemporary structural engineering and architecture in the US. Founded by two architects, Louis Skidmore and Nathaniel Owings, and an engineer, John Merrill, it is best known for designing high-end commercial buildings, particularly tall buildings. Two early figures in the firm's history who exemplify the innovative collaboration between structural engineers and architects, for which SOM has become known, are Fazlur Khan and Bruce Graham. Together they designed some of the world's most groundbreaking skyscrapers and were a significant part of the movement referred to as the second Chicago School of Architecture. Their use and refinement of the tube structural system pushed tall buildings ever higher, making them more user-friendly by eliminating much of the interior columns that earlier skyscrapers such as the Empire State and Chrysler buildings had in abundance. Graham and Khan's designs display remarkable structural expression; the structures "were closely integrated with the architecture and, in many cases, became the architecture."[2] Perhaps their most famous collaborations were Chicago's John Hancock Center and the Sears Tower (renamed the Willis Tower), which was the tallest building in the world for decades after its completion. These buildings set the standard for tall building construction for years to come.

This legacy continues for SOM, not just in tall towers, but in their full portfolio of work where interdisciplinary collaboration, integration, and coordination are vital to the firm's identity. In 2020 alone, SOM won over 30 awards including multiple citations from the American Institute of Architects and the Structural Engineers Association. Mark Sarkisian, Structural Partner, describes current sensibilities about integrative design at SOM,

> People say the engineers at SOM look after and protect our architects. Well, I would argue that in many cases it's the opposite: we challenge our architects to think differently, we tell them when it doesn't work, but most of the time we say "yes" to the architects. Usually, the greatest ideas come from the fact that there is no "no" and that's what's exciting, I think, about the relationship.[3]

Significant contemporary projects demonstrating this sensibility include the Moynihan Train Hall in New York City, the Chhatrapati Shivaji International Airport Terminal 2 in Mumbai, Denver Union Station, and the Cathedral of Christ the Light in Oakland.

Introduction to the Project: Contracting Collaboration

The Billie Jean King Main Library, completed in 2019, is an award-winning civic building in Long Beach, California. The project provides a significant case study in collaboration due to the Public–Private Partnership (P3) design-build contract type, mass timber structure, prefabrication construction methods, and ambitious LEED Platinum sustainability goals.

The need for a new main library for the City of Long Beach was identified in the Long Beach Civic Center Master Plan, designed by SOM, with the aim to revitalize and rehabilitate the downtown civic core. The plan for the three-block area includes a new city hall with a connected auditorium, a port headquarters, a main library and a renewed Lincoln Park (Figure 7.1). Executing the plan required new construction rather than remodeling the existing 40-year-old buildings due to the high costs of seismic retrofit: for example, the city hall upgrades would have cost an estimated $55 million more than the new building.[4] Similarly, the old library building, completed in 1976, suffered from considerable water and seismic damages. The sunken concrete structure had originally supported an occupiable roof garden, a continuation of the surrounding landscape of Lincoln Park. However, the waterproofing technology failed over the years, so the roof garden was removed in the 1990s. The library became a public health and safety concern, and with scarce natural daylight, a well-being concern for the librarians, other staff, and visitors.

Lacking the funds to undertake the 22-acre (89,000-square-meter) Civic Center project, the city held a competition for the design, finance, construction, and maintenance of the future buildings with the intent of awarding a contract through a

Figure 7.1 Aerial view of the Civic Center master plan showing the sites for the new park, port headquarters, city hall and main library. Skidmore, Owings & Merrill, Long Beach, California. Credit: © Skidmore, Owings & Merrill.

public–private partnership (P3), the first of its scale undertaken in North America.[5] After winning the competition in 2014, the P3 contract was awarded to Plenary-Edgemoor Civic Partners, a consortium of Plenary, Edgemoor Infrastructure & Real Estate, Clark Construction Group, Skidmore, Owings & Merrill (SOM) and Johnson Controls. P3s offer "technical promises" including, "reducing pressure on public sector budgets, providing better [value for money] VfM for taxpayers, reducing risk to government from projects, better accountability, better on-time and on-budget delivery, and greater innovation."[6] To tackle these expectations, the parties involved in the Civic Center P3—including architects, engineers, and constructors—were not only contracted to collaborate, but they were financially invested in the partnership and the projects' success. In contrast to the traditional delivery method of design-bid-build, collaboration was a baseline necessity, especially given the scope of the civic, social, and environmental ambitions of the projects, which includes the Billie Jean King Main Library, the focus of this chapter (Figure 7.2).

Efficiency, sustainability, and long-term operations drove decisions for the collaborators. The P3 agreement enables the city to lease the buildings from the partnership for 40 years, after which it will have the option to purchase them for $1.[7] At that point, the buildings must be in near-new condition, a deal that ensures protection of the city's future assets, but also embeds into the design process standards for durability and maintenance. The old city hall building lasted just over 40 years and required $12.4 million in maintenance costs per year.[8] So the P3 contract relieves cost burdens (for the city and taxpayers), and in exchange, the partnership will profit from the leases and a mixed-use private development on the property. The maintenance component of the P3 contract also provides financial incentive to invest in the longevity and operational

Figure 7.2 Exterior view of the Billie Jean King Main Library by Skidmore, Owings & Merrill, Long Beach, California, 2019. Credit: © fotoworks/Benny Chan.

BILLIE JEAN KING MAIN LIBRARY

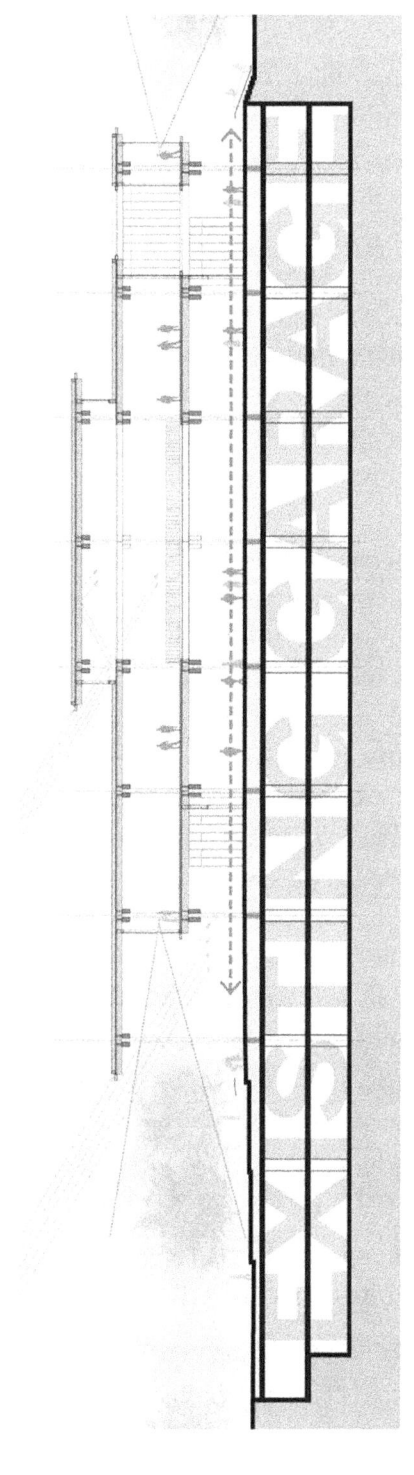

Figure 7.3 Section through building showing open access, daylighting strategies and views to the neighborhood and park for the Billie Jean King Main Library by Skidmore, Owings & Merrill, Long Beach, California, 2019. Credit: © Skidmore, Owings & Merrill.

sustainability of the project. A global accounting of buildings' contribution to CO_2 found that operations comprise 72% of annual emissions,[9] further impetus to use renewable energy and other passive strategies to reduce operation costs. The 40-year maintenance contract also factored into the selection of materials. More durable materials may cost more at the outset but do not need to be replaced as frequently, so materials like wood can win out over shorter lived finishes, overcoming wasteful cycles of maintenance and replacement. Factoring long-term costs into the design decisions anchored the robust sustainability goals for the library, which was awarded LEED Platinum by the US Green Building Council, the highest LEED rating.

Long-term thinking is not only intrinsic to the contract and sustainability goals, but also aligned with the civic mission of the plan. The site's civic programming has been a mainstay for the City of Long Beach for over 100 years. The first library was established in 1896, and soon after, a Carnegie-funded library opened in 1909, located near where the new library stands. Libraries remain vital civic and democratic institutions, although today, they are markedly different in programming. Jose Palacios, SOM Design Director, remarks, "Libraries function very differently now--[they are] more like community centers. They not only house books, but a lot of other purposes that are very public."[10] Civic programming of the building and site drove design sensibilities focused on public access and well-being (Figure 7.3).

Completed in 2019, the Billie Jean King Main Library is a two-story, 93,500-square-foot (8,700-square-meter) mass timber building with exposed structural and mechanical systems on the interior, built on a concrete foundation of an existing underground parking garage on the site. Designed as a "pavilion in the park" to welcome the community, the library not only holds more than 300,000 books, but it also offers maker spaces including 3d printers, robotics, and film editing as well as family and veterans centers, and a dedicated space for special collections. At the heart of the building, a 39-foot-high clerestory-lined central space provides seating, a display of local artists' works, and site lines to other areas of the library (Figure 7.4). In all, the Billie Jean King main library embodies the value and reward of a fully integrated design and construction effort to fulfill civic aspirations with reduced or positive environmental impacts.

The Team and Working Methods

In contrast to some of the other case studies in this book, the contract structure for the Long Beach Civic Center projects required integrative design from the start. Because of this, P3 contracts result in shared decision-making, learning, and innovation.[11] For the design of the main library, the extensive in-house interdisciplinary design team at SOM included architects, structural engineers,

Figure 7.4 Central double-height space with a gallery area, seating, and reception desk. The clerestory provides daylighting and mass timber creates a warm, welcoming space in the Billie Jean King Main Library by Skidmore, Owings & Merrill, Long Beach, California, 2019. Credit: © fotoworks/Benny Chan.

interior designers, technical designers, and timber and sustainability specialists. Given its long history of multidisciplinary practice, integration of systems is a hallmark for SOM. With engineers working down the hall or at a neighboring desk, integration is expected and part of the ethos, but also made easier through the proximity of interdisciplinary partners. Considering the location of the Long Beach project, SOM's Los Angeles office provided the home base for much of the team, but major contributions came from engineers in the San Francisco office and early in the project, the Chicago office. In Los Angeles, Palacios, a lead on the Library project, insisted that the engineers sit with the architects, facilitating team interactions. Engineers Mark Sarkisian, Structural Partner, and Eric Long, Structural Director, who are based in San Francisco but frequent the LA office, would join the team for in-person meetings on a bi-weekly basis.

Starting from the Design Development (DD) phase, the core members of the architectural team[12] each coordinated different areas of the project, allowing the architects to deeply understand, develop, and manage particular aspects in collaboration with engineers and contractors. Zarmine Nigohos, Project Architect, explains:

> Because of the P3/Design Build, we teamed with Clark Construction and subcontractors more than you would on a typical project ... all with the intent to make the design more feasible and efficient. We talked daily with contractors and subcontractors and there was a lot of knowledge sharing,[13]

The team members and project benefited from this frequent communication in multiple ways including more efficient workflows and reduced redundancy. Roshanak Mostaghim, Technical Designer describes,

> The MEP meetings, for example, would include the mechanical engineer and mechanical subcontractor, so we knew that the decisions made were going to get built. At meetings, we would come to an agreement with shared buy-in, which would speed up the process because we weren't drawing things multiple times and the shop drawings showed what we had all agreed on.[14]

Traditionally, architects create a set of drawings and then after the contractor has estimated costs for delivering the project, designs often require value engineering to meet budget expectations. But in this case, the design was developed with collaborators in respect to how to build it efficiently.[15] Members of the design and construction team connected on the phone every day, and during CD and CA (the construction documentation and construction administration phases), met in person two or three times a week, usually at the jobsite. From the start of the design process, the digital model and mock-up at the site were critical tools for collaborative design and detailing.

Physical Mock-Up

A continually evolving physical mock-up at the jobsite proved significant for integrative design and testing, providing a shared understanding among designers and constructors who had a collective drive for efficiency (Figure 7.5). The fast pace of design-build necessitated a mock-up before the building was

Figure 7.5 Mock-up at the site showing experiments with systems relationships including structure, plumbing, and lighting. Billie Jean King Main Library by Skidmore, Owings & Merrill, Long Beach, California, 2019. Credit: © Skidmore, Owings & Merrill.

fully conceived. Palacios notes that this is the reverse of the normal construction process where mockups provide validation. "In our case, we built a mock-up to find out how we were going to design it and the mock-up really helped us in so many ways throughout the project."[16] The mock-up became a vital testbed for materials, techniques, and ideas, beginning with the connections between the wood and steel and to assess various coatings on the timber. Slowly over time, the team added to the mock-up to evaluate aesthetics, systems integration, performance, and economics; for example, the way that the conduit would thread through the structure or how the acoustical panels or lighting would hang amidst the timber. Nigohos provides additional background on the reasoning for the mock-up:

> We wanted to have a platform to test what the subcontractors were proposing and although we had certain aesthetic and performance criteria that they needed to meet, we also considered anything they brought to the table that would benefit and add efficiency to the project.[17]

The physical prototype was especially important since most of the systems were exposed in the building so it provided a "way for the subcontractors to practice and troubleshoot where there were problems."[18] Truly, the mock-up was a highly impactful means to share knowledge and ideas, "and it became this living thing," a pivotal platform for collaboration.[19]

Digital Models

Knowledge gained from the mock-up informed a robust building information model in which the building was digitally constructed before actual construction. Nigohos summarizes the many benefits of a shared digital model,

> Meeting with contractors from the beginning of DD [design development], we were able to leverage their knowledge to inform the drawings. It is so much more efficient to draw what is being built as opposed to drawing a design intent that someone later revises.[20]

The subcontractors drove the decision to use Navisworks,[21] a platform enabling coordination, analysis, and simulation of the project. Starting in the design development phase, the architects supported Clark Construction in coordinating the shared model, which included contributions from the engineers and subcontractors (Figure 7.6). Although the shared digital model required constant monitoring and months of work on integration and updates,

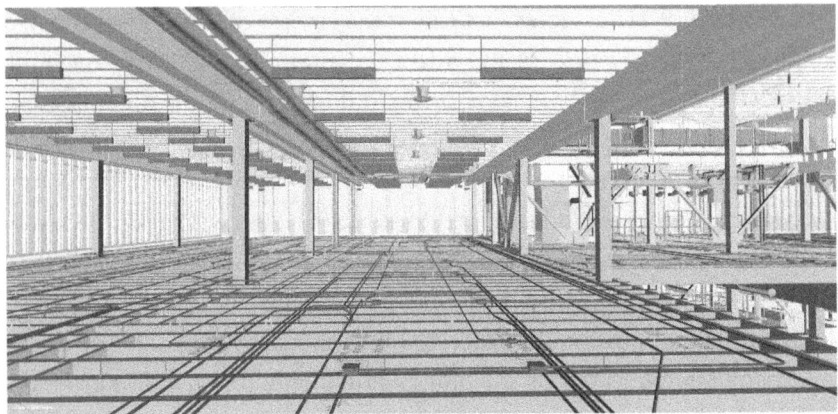

Figure 7.6 View of the integrated digital model. Billie Jean King Main Library by Skidmore, Owings & Merrill, Long Beach, California, 2019. Credit: © Skidmore, Owings & Merrill.

the time invested paid off in eliminating systems clashes, facilitating construction sequencing, and informing construction processes including prefabrication of a kit of parts, and an efficient and clean jobsite. Resulting in "less waste, higher quality, and higher value," this front-end investment in the building information model ultimately led to construction efficiencies that sped up delivery of the library.

Structure–Architecture–Construction Integration

Although the existing main library was too costly to repair, SOM found a viable way to reuse an adjacent underground parking garage for the foundation of the new library, saving significant time, concrete, and budget. Two to three feet of soil had sat on top of the parking structure, equivalent to about 100 pounds per cubic foot when saturated. It had also supported the live load of people using the park on top of it. Concurrent with the engineers' analyses, the architects studied whether the existing column grid of the parking garage (about 30' bays) would work for the library and they found it did (Figure 7.7).[22] This led to the question of whether they could design a building that was equivalent or lighter than the weight of the soil removed. The engineers found that if the new library was composed primarily of mass timber, the gravity loads (the weight of the building) were not an issue and the only intervention required in the existing parking structure were two concrete shear walls that encapsulated two columns each, infilling between them creating a lateral system in line with the braced frames in the new building above. This intervention was necessary to carry the lateral loads of wind, and very significantly in California, earthquake loads. Since not all the underground bays were equal in length, the team designed transitions to transfer the load from the new columns through the garage roof slab to the columns below (Figure 7.8). Notably, the existing

BILLIE JEAN KING MAIN LIBRARY

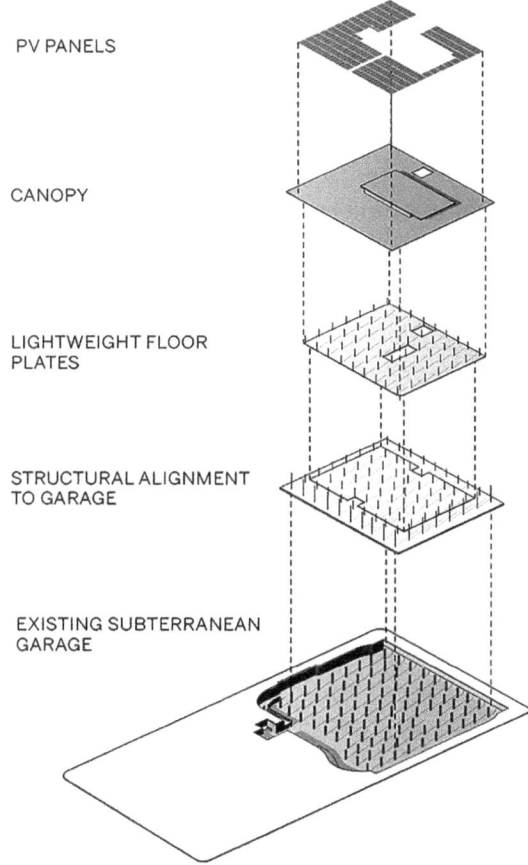

Figure 7.7 Exploded diagram showing the existing parking structure column grid and the new structure for the Billie Jean King Main Library by Skidmore, Owings & Merrill, Long Beach, California, 2019. Credit: © Skidmore, Owings & Merrill.

Figure 7.8 Aerial view of the organized construction site for the Billie Jean King main library showing the kit of parts ready for assembly. Credit: © Clark Construction Group.

111

column grid of the parking garage informed the structural grid for the new building, so the engineering decisions provided the literal and conceptual foundation for the design of the new library.

A mass timber structure was selected not only for its lightness: wooden structures around the world—including some that are thousands of years old—prove wood's resilience and enduring appeal.[23] On a visceral level, studies have demonstrated that the visual, tactile, and olfactory experience of wood can have calming effects[24] and using wood made sense for this civic project, since it has a warm, welcoming, and soothing feel.[25] Structurally, timber is light, strong, renewable if properly sourced, a good thermal and sound insulator, and more fire resistant than many might assume. Engineered timber structural assemblies like glulam and CLT (cross-laminated timber) have come into increasing popularity in recent decades (Figure 7.9).[26] These products layer smaller (more easily sourced) timber pieces and laminate them (using specialized epoxies) into larger structural elements. In glulam, the pieces are arranged in parallel layers typically for beam or column sections, making use of mixed grades of timber by placing stronger layers of wood where the stresses are higher (in a beam this is the very top and very bottom of the cross section) further improving the cost effectiveness of the approach (Figure 7.10). Importantly also, trees absorb carbon, a major contributor to global warming, thereby sequestering it from the atmosphere. Timber production has lowered carbon emissions compared to the manufacturing and transport processes for concrete and steel.[27]

The engineering team for the Billie Jean King Main Library calculated that the foundation would easily support a new mass timber building since timber

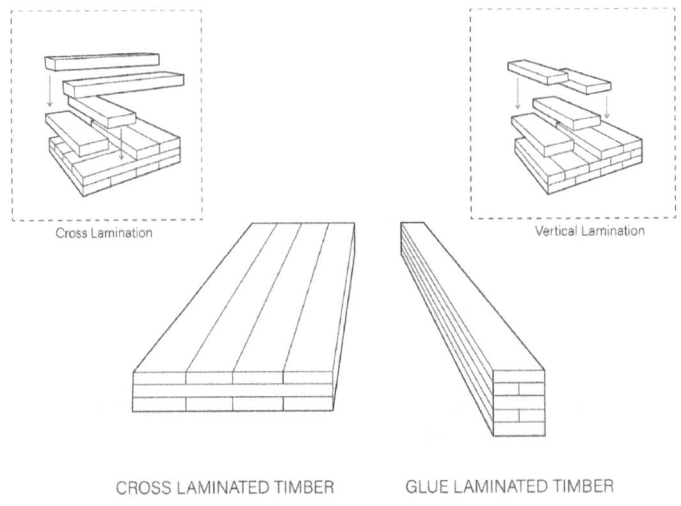

Figure 7.9 Glulam and cross-laminated timber. Credit: © Shiori Green.

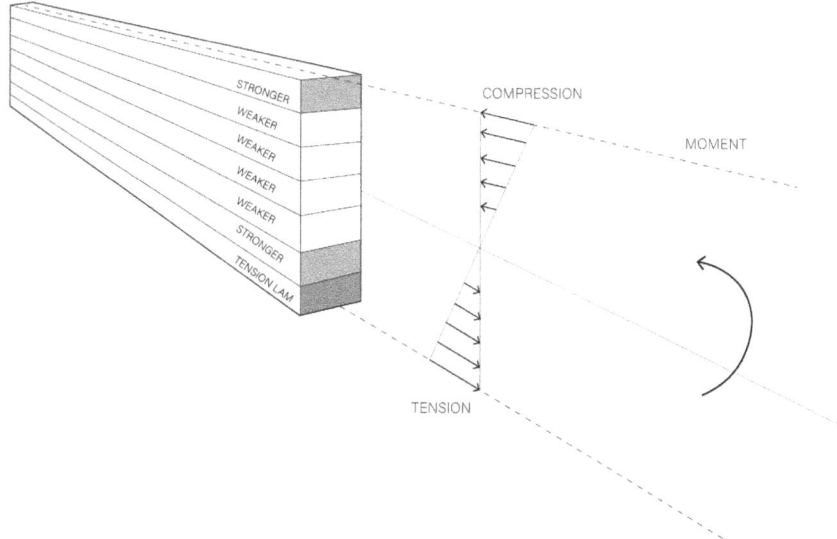

Figure 7.10 Glulam beams use layers of different grades of lumber to carry bending efficiently. Credit: © Shiori Green.

weighs about 35 pounds per cubic foot (in contrast to the alternatives concrete and steel, each of which is much heavier). In addition to excellent strength-to-weight ratios,[28] which allows it to perform well in seismic zones, mass timber is prefabricated, which contributes to decreased construction duration. Eric Long, Structural Director, confirms, "We minimized the retrofit by using timber, and it really made sense to save a lot of money and time required, and by reusing the foundation, it was more sustainable."[29] Many of the partners in the P3 had delivered another P3 project nearby where they had extensively researched an exterior wood finish, instilling confidence in the longevity of the material.[30] Along these lines, a few years prior, engineers Sarkisian and Long had worked together on the Cathedral of Christ the Light, an award-winning timber and concrete landmark building in Oakland, California, so they were comfortable with the nuanced code requirements for mass timber buildings. Furthermore, SOM has a long history of mass timber research buttressed by an in-house timber specialist, Benton Johnson, and the team also consulted wood scientist, Ron Anthony.[31]

The structural designers wanted to harness the best performance out of each material used for the library, so logic drove a hybrid approach. The 30-foot column grid combined with code requirements for fire ratings (in Type IV Heavy Timber construction) led to the use of steel tube columns filled with concrete to support the mass timber girders, beams, and joists. The columns and steel lateral bracing, painted white, virtually disappear in the large open spaces of the library. Spanning between the columns are three-foot deep glulam double girders made of Douglas Fir grown in Oregon and Washington[32] and stained a red tone to emphasize the warmth of the material. A seemingly simple, but hugely impactful structural design move involved shifting the 19.5-inch-deep glulam ceiling joists to sit on top of the girders, as opposed to in-between. With half as many perpendicular connections, this reduces costs and saves time and labor, but also creates a cleaner aesthetic that emphasizes the horizontality and layering of the spaces.[33]

Collaborating on Interior Finishes

Exposing the structure aligned with the ethos of the project, "doing more with less." Palacios comments that "using the wood gave us the opportunity to use the structure as the architecture, or vice versa," a major theme for SOM.[34] Sarkisian explains the benefits of the unity of the structural–architectural experience,

> The success of the building comes from really fundamental ideas of design-- light, material, and repetition-- and, as engineers, we love to see structure but that's not what drives our work--it's something more meaningful. We'd like to think that most of our work [at SOM] speaks this way.[35]

Celebrating the mass timber on the interior meant eliminating more than 58,000 square feet (5,400 square meters) of dropped ceiling systems and their associated emissions, and importantly for the P3, reduced related labor costs and installation time during construction. Furthermore, prefabricated kit-of-parts timber and steel components contributed to an efficient and minimally wasteful construction process (Figure 7.11). SOM calculates, for example, that "durable materials and mass customization of components" led to a "61% reduction in embodied carbon compared to typical new construction."[36] Considering the full life cycle of the building, the library is 80% wood, so when the building is decommissioned, one million board feet of timber can be upcycled.[37]

Collaborating on Enclosure

The "open access" policy of the library manifests quite literally in the building design and siting. Inviting entrances from opposite sides provide convenient access from the neighborhood and park, thereby eliminating a "back" to the building. "We thought of the library as a pavilion in the park[38]--floating with various entrances from multiple sides, which led to a design that is flat and

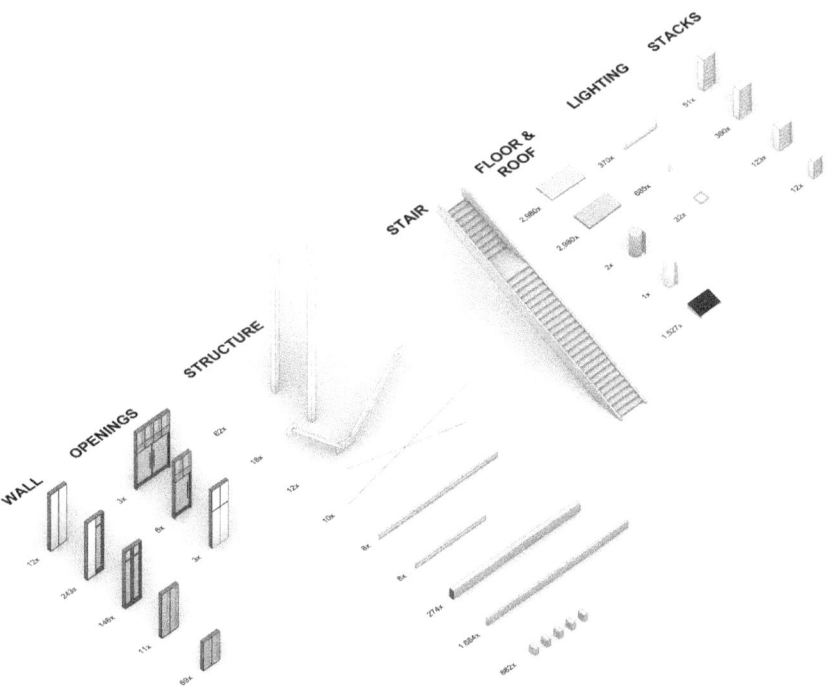

Figure 7.11 A simple kit-of-parts enabled efficiencies in construction. Billie Jean King Main Library by Skidmore, Owings & Merrill, Long Beach, California, 2019. Credit: © Skidmore, Owings & Merrill.

horizontal," explains Palacios. Floor-to-ceiling glass and exposed[39] wood that extends out into the landscape further enhance the connections between inside and outside, the building and the park, while overhangs reduce operational energy required for air conditioning. Long describes the reasons for the structural–architectural move, "It was about shaving the sun with the overhangs and letting indirect light in but providing views out to the park" (Figure 7.12).[40] The California weather allowed the team to create a community space on the south side called the "porch," a covered space large enough for community meetings and events.[41] Views and connections to the lush landscape of Lincoln Park, other civic buildings and surrounding neighborhood provide a feeling of openness and expanse with the intent of creating a welcoming environment for the community (Figure 7.13).

Given the emphasis on openness, the glazing design became another emblem of the architecture–structure–construction integration. Glazing not only reduces energy costs associated with artificial lighting, but studies show that natural light significantly contributes to the well-being of occupants by decreasing stress and improving mood and productivity.[42] Taking advantage of these characteristics, the designers and constructors wrapped glazing around the entire envelope. The curtain wall module aligns with

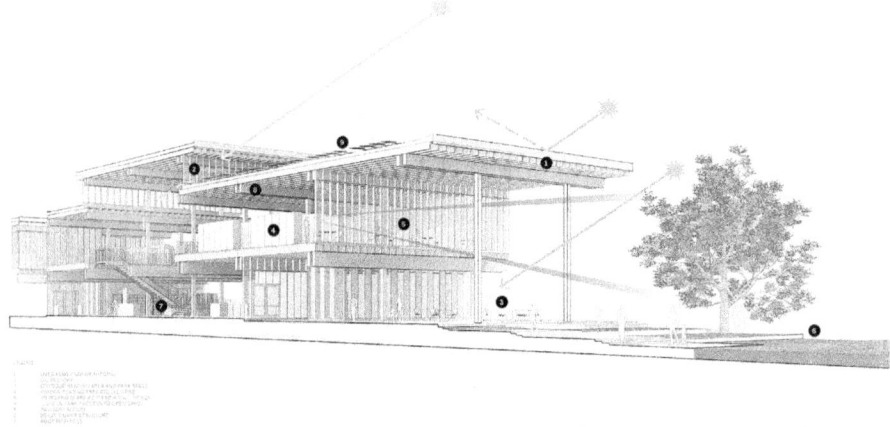

Figure 7.12 Bay section showing large roof overhang for covered gathering space while maintaining daylighting and views to the park and surrounding neighborhood. Billie Jean King Main Library by Skidmore, Owings & Merrill, Long Beach, California, 2019. Credit: © Skidmore, Owings & Merrill.

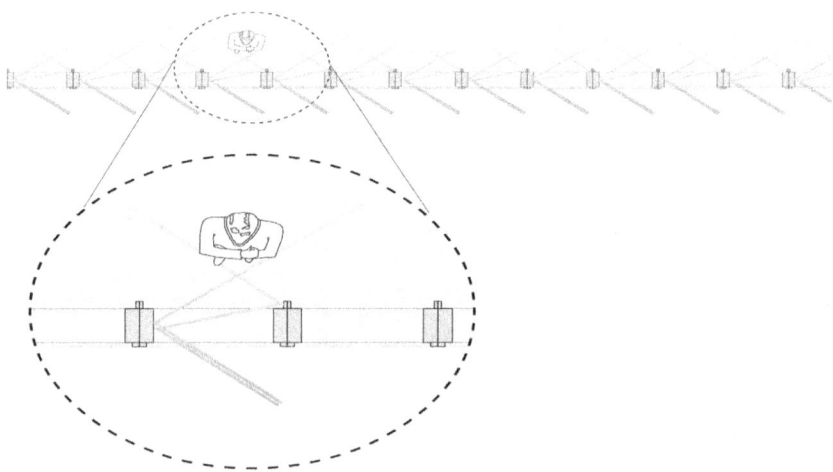

Figure 7.13 The 2-foot curtain wall module also acts as a light diffuser to bounce light into the interior. Billie Jean King Main Library by Skidmore, Owings & Merrill, Long Beach, California, 2019. Credit: © Skidmore, Owings & Merrill.

the two-foot (60-centimeter) separation between the glulam joists. Creating this modularity lent well to the development of a unitized glazing system that was craned in place, speeding up construction of the enclosure ahead of schedule (Figure 7.14).[43] Although a large open-air atrium, which illuminates one of the entrances, did not allow space for a crane, the two-foot-wide module enabled two constructors to lift the glazing into place in those areas. "Collaborating closely with the fabricator and installer Benson Industries, the team designed a joint at the head of each module to accommodate up to a three-quarter-inch deflection of the glulam members,"[44] in case of seismic load and thermal expansion. The unitized system performs

Figure 7.14 Interior view showing the 2-foot window module and the exterior skylight. Billie Jean King Main Library by Skidmore, Owings & Merrill, Long Beach, California, 2019. Credit: © fotoworks/Benny Chan.

holistically—the intrinsic framing system also bounces and diffuses harsh sunlight (Figure 7.15). The prefabricated glazing assembly is another example of the cost and waste-reduction benefits of co-developed, integrated systems.

Coordination with MEP Systems

"Doing more with less" also drove the design and integration of the mechanical, electrical, and plumbing (MEP) systems. With the exposed wood structure, running the fire sprinklers, ducts, and conduit between the joists

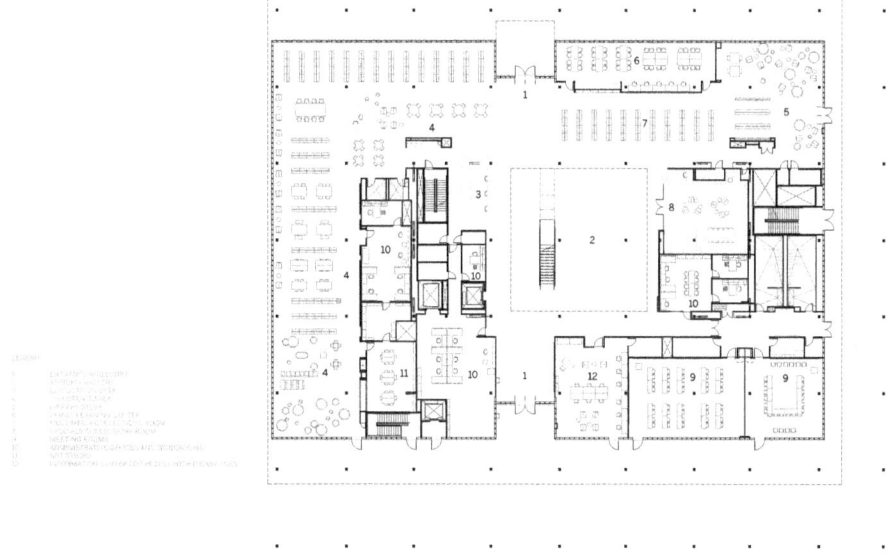

Figure 7.15 First- and second-floor plans for the Billie Jean King main library by Skidmore, Owings & Merrill, Long Beach, California, 2019. Credit: © Skidmore, Owings & Merrill.

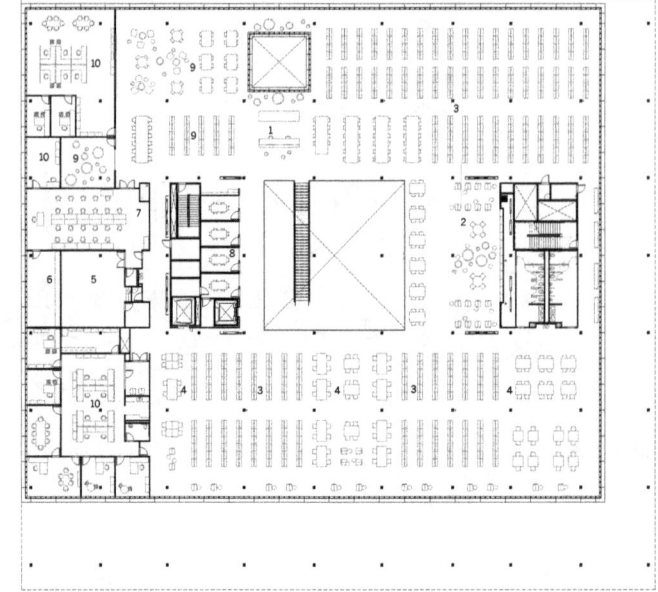

Figure 7.15 (Continued).

maintained a clean aesthetic but doing so would require penetrations. Palacios explains how these design decisions are usually made in the field by subcontractors:

> One of the issues for integration that always gets in the way is that we have silos of expertise and silos of risk. The silos of risk determine how you buy a job. The electricians or plumbers are responsible for x-number of things, and when you buy a contract from the electrician, they are responsible for making the penetrations for the conduit and sprinklers.

So that led Palacios to question this method of contracting and scheduling, which would have meant hand-drilling the timber onsite even though the timber framing was going to be exquisitely fabricated offsite.[45] They asked an electrician to practice making holes to see how they looked (Figure 7.16), leading to the decision to standardize the structural penetrations. The structural engineers provided guidelines about where the openings needed to be and the panels were milled offsite (Figure 7.17). Long describes the advantages of prefabrication,

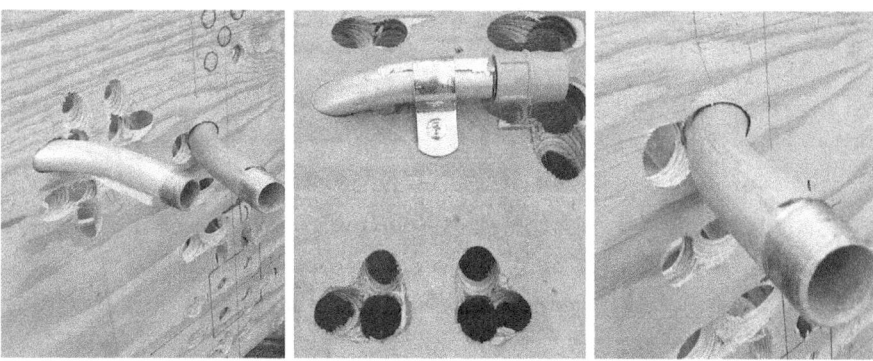

Figure 7.16 Tests on the jobsite to determine if the holes for the services should be drilled through the mass timber on site or off. Credit: © Skidmore, Owings & Merrill.

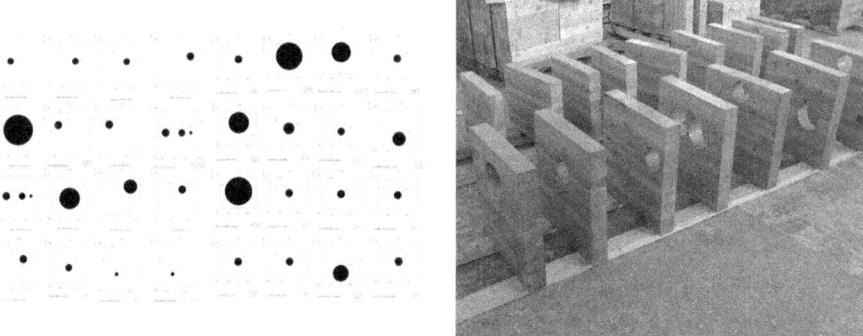

Figure 7.17 Diagram and view of the holes that were CNC milled into the mass timber at structurally determined locations. Credit: © Skidmore, Owings & Merrill.

> The blocking goes between each joist, and they all have the right diameter holes cut in the right locations, so the eventual fire sprinkler conduit could thread right through it and no field drilling or sawing was done so that's how all the lights and sprinklers and everything are tucked up between the joists.[46]

As the field tests demonstrated, offsite fabrication not only saves time on site, but also eliminates potential mistakes associated with onsite work. In fact, a Construction Industry Institute study showed rework averages about 5% of construction costs,[47] which also represents thousands of tons of unnecessary waste bound for landfills. By contrast, due to thorough planning and coordination, the library construction site remained orderly and clean.

Attention to the ceiling plan carried through the acoustical design as well. Working closely with the acoustical engineer, Newson Brown Acoustics, and subcontractor, the design goal was to use a similar language as the exposed ducts. Through many simulation studies and physical tests, they developed a simple, linear panel toned a deep red similar to the wood and installed them between the joists attached to nailers on the underside of the slab. The acoustical treatment is used throughout, but concentrated in the reading rooms, the family center and special collections, areas that need acoustical separation.

Given the fast pace of design-build, the foundation portion of the work was permitted to proceed with construction before the library design was completely finished, which established a non-negotiable limit to the building's above-ground weight. Due to this weight restriction and the desire to minimize the carbon load of the concrete, the thickness of the slab between floors was limited to 3 inches (76 millimeters), including a three-quarter-inch plywood diaphragm plus electrical conduit encased in a topping slab. The conduit layout is not normally an aspect of building design that the architect would get involved with and in a more typical 5" or 6" slab, there is usually plenty of space for multiple layers of tubing. In this case, working closely with the subcontractor and their shared building information model, Mostaghim studied the shear stud locations and other constraints to determine the thinnest possible configuration for the conduit and the moments where two raceways could cross over one another. Nigohos describes,

> Roshanak developed amazing diagrams that were her understanding from the conversations with the contractors about how everything would fit together and then she'd walk over and check with everyone involved in the construction trailer to make sure we were all on the same page (Figure 7.18).[48]

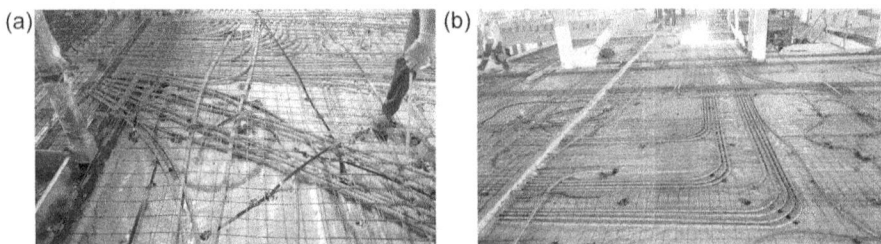

Figure 7.18 Side-by-side comparison of conduit showing the thick, messy configuration on the left, and the organized thin configuration on the right. Credit: © Skidmore, Owings & Merrill.

The diagrams helped to simplify the conduit installation and achieve the impressively thin slabs. Having a clear plan for the conduit ahead of construction also increased installation and material efficiencies.

The electrical engineering design for the library significantly advances the building's sustainability metrics. The solar photovoltaic array on the roof contributes energy for the whole Civic Center campus. Combined with natural daylighting, ventilation, and efficient heating, venting and air conditioning (HVAC) systems, SOM calculates that the library uses 63% less energy than the American Society of Heating, Refrigerating and Air-Conditioning Engineers (ASHRAE) 90.1–2007 Energy Standard for Buildings.

Conclusion: Rewards of Collaboration

The sensibility that drove the team to save the foundation became the design driver for the new building—to "do more with less," minimize carbon and waste, and seek the most sustainable and healthy design solutions. Reusing the foundation also meant that, coupled with a prefabricated timber system, the library could be constructed faster and within budget. The design-build process imposes challenges on teams to design and coordinate systems sometimes at a breakneck pace. But the demands of the integrative process can be rewarding on both a project and professional level. Nigohos explains,

> I really do like this method of working. Design-build drives the practice to a more integrated approach in terms of how projects are designed and delivered. It hasn't been 100% smooth--there were a lot of challenges to overcome and solve, but I appreciated the collaborative nature and working with everyone much earlier in the process and being part of that team.[49]

Owners or architects may have the misconception that early collaboration is a cost burden, but shared knowledge creates efficiencies in both design and construction. Mostaghim found it rewarding that, "Subcontractors and fabricators didn't have to redraw our drawings and then figure out if there were problems or challenges. Since they were in the process with us, then overall it became a more efficient process."[50] From the very beginning of the project, instead of writing a long email or holding on to a list of items or issues, the architecture team was encouraged to communicate with the engineers and contractors and work together to find the most efficient solutions (Figure 7.19).

Design-build engenders a larger sense of collective authorship, making everyone feel invested and rewarded in bringing new ideas to the table.[51]

Figure 7.19 Interior view of the Billie Jean King Main Library by Skidmore, Owings & Merrill, Long Beach, California, 2019. Credit: © fotoworks/Benny Chan.

Although the P3 mandates collaboration and integration, Nigohos describes that the contract was not the only driver for this, "it was also the collection of people that we were working with, and the fact that we were able to have open dialogue and sometimes difficult conversations and find a balance."[52] Multiple team members remarked that design-build projects like the Billie Jean King Main Library take a special group of architects, engineers, contractors, and owners. The successes result not only from people's expertise, but also from an open and generous attitude about knowledge sharing and collective work.

Notes

1. Additional project team members include Lighting: HLB Lighting Design; Fire/Life Safety: Jensen Hughes; Vertical Transportation: Syska Hennessy Group; Roofing/Waterproofing: Curtainwall Design Consulting; Parking: International Parking Design; Operations and Maintenance: Johnson Controls; Project Financier: Plenary Group; Project Developer: Edgemoor Infrastructure & Real Estate.
2. Mark P. Sarkisian, "Perspective." In *Designing Tall Buildings: Structure as Architecture*. New York: Routledge, 2012. 6.
3. Mark Sarkisian, Interview with Eric Long, Jose Palacios, and Mark Sarkisian, Zoom, March 18, 2021.
4. "This Is How Long Beach Will Pay for Its New City Hall Digs," *Press Telegram*, accessed July 27, 2019, https://www.presstelegram.com/this-is-how-long-beach-will-pay-for-its-new-city-hall-digs, accessed April 14, 2021.
5. "SoCal Project of The Year: Nation's Largest Municipal P3 Project Brings Long Beach to Life," accessed April 5, 2021, https://www.enr.com/articles/50252-socal-project-of-the-year-nations-largest-municipal-p3-project-brings-long-beach-to-life?v=preview.
6. Graeme A. Hodge and Carsten Greve, "On Public–Private Partnership Performance: A Contemporary Review," *Public Works Management & Policy* 22, no. 1 (January 2017): 55–78, https://doi.org/10.1177/1087724X16657830.
7. Harry SaltzgaverExecutive Editor, "New Long Beach City Hall Focus on Security, Efficiency," www.Gazettes.com, accessed April 15, 2021, https://www.gazettes.com/news/new-long-beach-city-hall-focus-on-security-efficiency/article_d4d79884-6acc-11e9-856f-ffc9b76ad251.html.

8. "This Is How Long Beach Will Pay for Its New City Hall Digs."
9. "Why the Building Sector? – Architecture 2030," accessed April 14, 2021, https://architecture2030.org/buildings_problem_why/.
10. Jose Palacios, Interview with Eric Long, Jose Palacios, and Mark Sarkisian, Zoom, March 18, 2021.
11. Esther Cheung, Albert P.C. Chan, and Stephen Kajewski, "Factors Contributing to Successful Public Private Partnership Projects: Comparing Hong Kong with Australia and the United Kingdom," *Journal of Facilities Management* 10, no. 1 (February 17, 2012): 45–58, https://doi.org/10.1108/14725961211200397.
12. Jose Palacios (Design Director), Jed Zimmerman (Managing Director, Project Manager), David Renken (Associate, Interior Design), Wilfredo Lima (Project Architect who left at the end of CDs), Zarmine Nigohos (stepped in as Project Architect through CA) and Roshanak Mostaghim (Technical Designer). Various other team members would help with specialty areas as needed, but there were consistently a core group of architectural designers working on the project.
13. Zarmine Nigohos, Interview with Zarmine Nigohos and Roshanak Mostaghim, Zoom, April 16, 2021.
14. Roshanak Mostaghim, Interview with Zarmine Nigohos and Roshanak Mostaghim, Zoom, April 16, 2021.
15. Nigohos, Interview by authors.
16. Palacios, Interview by authors.
17. Nigohos.
18. Mostaghim, Interview by authors.
19. Nigohos.
20. Nigohos
21. *Navisworks*, version 2016 (San Rafael, CA: Autodesk, 2015).
22. Palacios.
23. Timber is one of the oldest structural materials and is used widely today in residential construction.
24. Harumi Ikei, Chorong Song, and Yoshifumi Miyazaki, "Physiological Effects of Touching Hinoki Cypress (Chamaecyparis Obtusa)," *Journal of Wood Science* 64, no. 3 (June 2018): 226–236, https://doi.org/10.1007/s10086-017-1691-7.
25. Additionally, the clients described that the competition proposal's use of wood attracted the jury because of Long Beach's history as a small fishing town with wood houses and boats (Palacios, Interview by Authors).
26. Fast growing, easily harvested, stick frame lumber milled into standard parts has inherent limits when it comes to span, as do even the heavy timbers from older construction modes like those found in barns and warehouses. So, until recently, timber structures have been relatively rare in larger institutional buildings in the US. Engineered timber includes glulam and cross-laminated timber (CLT). In CLT, the layers are arranged at 90 degrees to one another allowing for two-way spanning structural elements like walls and slabs.
27. Given the growing demand for wood in buildings and products, forest resources continue to expand in the US. See Alison Kwok et al., "Seeing the Forest and the Trees: Environmental Impacts of Cross-Laminated Timber," *Technology|Architecture + Design* 4, no. 2 (July 2, 2020): 144–150, https://doi.org/10.1080/24751448.2020.1804754.
28. Force = Mass x Acceleration, and earthquake load is an applied acceleration to a building so a lower mass means that the structure experiences lower loads in an earthquake.
29. Eric Long, Interview with Eric Long, Jose Palacios, and Mark Sarkisian, Zoom, March 18, 2021.
30. Palacios.
31. The wood scientist contributed knowledge and advice about material behavior, transport, and care of the wood on site.
32. Wood should be harvested from sustainably managed forests. Budget constraints did not allow for Forest Stewardship Council (FSC) certification for the mass timber for the Library project, however, Oregon and Washington state forestry laws ensure the longevity and ecology of their forest lands.
33. Sarkisian, Interview with Eric Long, Jose Palacios, and Mark Sarkisian.
34. Palacios.
35. Sarkisian.
36. "Four Projects Receive 2020 AIA/ALA Library Building Award," SOM, accessed April 20, 2021, https://www.som.com/news/four_projects_receive_2020_aiaala_library_building_award.
37. "Billie Jean King Main Library by Skidmore, Owings & Merrill," accessed April 5, 2021, https://www.architecturalrecord.com/articles/14487-billie-jean-king-main-library-by-skidmore-owings-merrill?v=preview.
38. SOM derives the "pavilion in the park" idea from a 1901 deed for a library at the site.
39. The wood was treated with PPG ProLuxe Cetol 1 RE Wood Finish Basecoat and PPG ProLuxe Cetol 23 PLUS RE Wood Finish Topcoat. Exterior and interior treatment was the same except with variations in the number of coats applied.
40. Long, Interview by authors.
41. Palacios.
42. L. Edwards, P. Torcellini, and National Renewable Energy Laboratory, "A Literature Review of the Effects of Natural Light on Building Occupants," National Renewable Energy Lab., Golden, CO. (US), July 1, 2002, 58.
43. "SoCal Project of the Year."
44. "SOM Blends Mass Timber and High Modernism with the Pagoda-like Billie Jean King Library," *The Architect's Newspaper*, October 1, 2020, https://www.archpaper.com/2020/10/facades-som-blends-mass-timber-and-high-modernism-billie-jean-king-library/.
45. Palacios.
46. Long.

47 Bon-Gang Hwang, Stephen Thomas, and Carl Haas, "Measuring the Impact of Rework on Construction Cost Performance," *Journal of Construction Engineering and Management-Asce - J CONSTR ENG MANAGE-ASCE* 135 (March 1, 2009), https://doi.org/10.1061/(ASCE)0733-9364(2009)135:3(187).
48 Nigohos.
49 Nigohos.
50 Mostaghim.
51 Mostaghim.
52 Nigohos.

CHAPTER 8

Case for Collaboration: Net Zero

The Frick Environmental Center and the Kendeda Building for Innovative Sustainable Design

Witnessing an increasing number of global warming-associated catastrophes[1] and driven by both moral obligations and legal commitments such as the Paris Agreement,[2] governments throughout the world are enacting laws and associated policies to achieve climate neutrality by 2050.[3,4] These laws, aimed at reducing or eliminating greenhouse gas (GHG) emissions, impact the building industry in diverse and radical ways. A recent International Energy Agency report confirmed, "Buildings and construction together account for 36% of global final energy use and 39% of energy-related carbon dioxide (CO2) emissions when upstream power generation is included."[5] This translates to more global CO_2 emissions than any other sector.[6] The UN Environment Programme's Global Alliance for Buildings and Construction warns, "Strategies to make buildings net-zero energy and zero carbon are a key part of the global decarbonization strategy and must become the primary form of building construction across all economies to achieve net-zero emissions by 2050" (Figure 8.1).[7]

Since carbon dioxide accounts for three quarters of greenhouse gas emissions,[8] regulations and benchmarks often aim for decarbonization or net-zero carbon emissions (neutrality) over the period of a year. Net-zero 2050 benchmarks established by industry organizations include the World Green Building Council and the Structural Engineers 2050 Challenge, whereas the American Institute of Architects (AIA) has teamed with Architecture 2030 to motivate firms to achieve carbon neutrality by 2030. Although meeting these standards

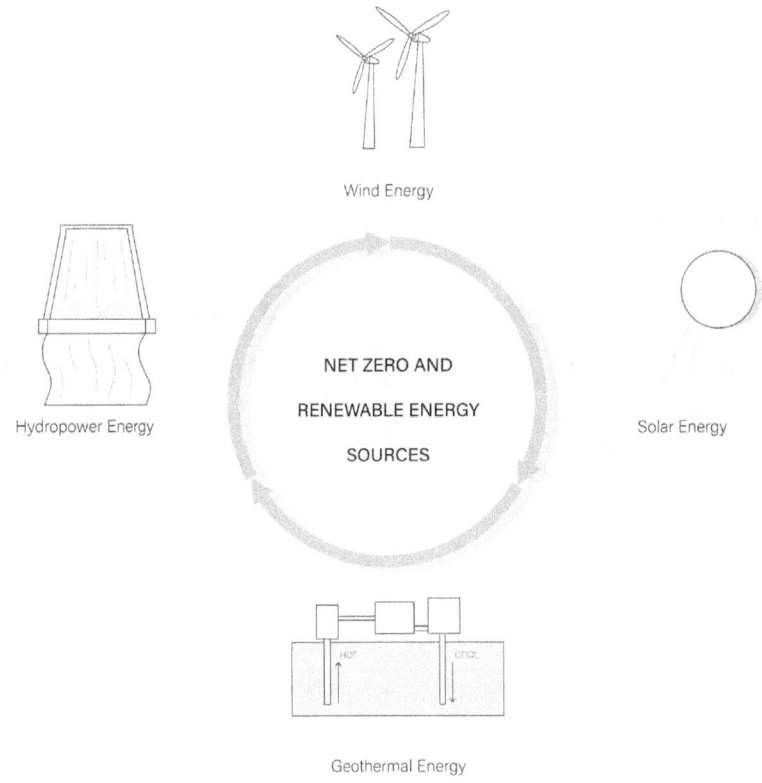

Figure 8.1 Diagram of renewable energy sources. Credit: Shiori Green.

may seem challenging, the design, material, and systems technologies exist to achieve net-zero carbon in buildings.[9] Yet, Tom Smith, executive director of the American Society of Civil Engineers, remarked, "To reach such drastic reductions in emissions requires 'all hands on deck.'"[10]

Net zero simply cannot be achieved as an after-thought; rather, net zero must be considered from the start and throughout the design process. In "Delivering Green Buildings: Process Improvements for Sustainable Construction," the authors describe, "A widely accepted concept in the design community is that high performance projects require intense interdisciplinary collaboration to ensure that building systems are synergistic and 'right sized.'"[11] Similarly, Patricia Culley, Associate Principal at Bohlin Cywinski Jackson, shared experiences working on multiple energy-efficient buildings, "Net-zero energy has to be a priority for owners and designers and integrated in everything that you do because there are so many points within the design process where budget constraints and other decisions could derail the aspirations."[12] Net-zero designs benefit from early engineer-architect collaborations since foundational decision-making significantly impacts a building's carbon footprint, concerning both the *operational carbon* or energy consumed during the building's use, and also the *embodied carbon* or life cycle of the building materials. Researcher and architect Stephanie Carlise of Kieran

Timberlake, states that it is the ethical responsibility of building designers to measure and calculate environmental performance, but this is not a simple process since, "Energy sources have context."[13] Understanding the full life cycle energy consumption of a building is a complex undertaking, nevertheless, a critical one that involves measuring operational and embodied energy.

Operational Energy

According to the US Department of Energy, a net-zero energy building is, "an energy-efficient building where, on a source energy basis, the actual annual delivered energy is less than or equal to the on-site renewable exported energy" (Figure 8.2).[14] Achieving 100% clean electricity commonly means using solar photovoltaic panels, geothermal, water or wind turbines on or nearby the site itself to provide renewable energy for the building since less than 12% of US energy production available via the grid is from renewable (non-fossil fuel) sources.[15] Operational energy can equate to as much as 80% of the life cycle costs of a building, or two or three times the cost of construction,[16] so investing in high-performance design can easily prove both financially effective and carbon reducing in the long run. Early involvement of mechanical-electrical-plumbing (MEP) and environmental engineers helps to ensure an integrated approach to minimizing energy use and maximizing energy production. Many of the architects and engineers interviewed for this book highlighted the importance of early integration of environmental systems engineers to ensure energy efficiency in buildings.

Figure 8.2 Renewable energy resources include sun and wind.

Embodied Energy

By contrast to the energy used to operate a building over its life cycle, "Embodied carbon (kgCO2e) refers to the Greenhouse Gases (GHGs) emitted during the extraction, manufacture, transportation, construction, replacement, and deconstruction of building materials, together with the end of life emissions."[17] Although operational carbon could conceivably change over time for a building through installation of alternative energy sources such as solar panels or upgrades like high-efficiency windows, decisions about embodied carbon involve material selection, procurement, and construction so these must be carefully planned and, perhaps more critically, paid for up front. According to Architecture 2030, "Embodied carbon will be responsible for almost half of total new construction emissions between now and 2050,"[18] so embodied carbon is an increasing concern for architects and structural engineers especially.

Tools for Net Zero

A variety of energy modeling tools are available as stand-alone or plug-in software to provide energy performance projections. Whereas some software involve redrawing the building to conduct energy studies, integrated interfaces facilitate frequent checks on projected performance, which can be especially helpful for architects during concept and schematic phases. These include Ladybug and Honeybee plugins for Rhino's Grasshopper, and Insight for Revit. Stand-alone, advanced energy modelers for fine-tuned studies include DesignBuilder and IES (Integrated Environmental Solutions), which offer interoperability (the ability to import digital or building information models).[19]

Similarly, although measuring the embodied carbon of materials was once an onerous task, reliable data rich tools are increasingly more available and accessible. Life Cycle Assessment (LCA) tools measure the cradle to grave embodied carbon of materials. Carlisle explains, "LCA tools nest individual materials into nuanced assemblies that allow designers to compare results for hundreds of concrete mixes, glazing assemblies, cladding options, or waterproofing systems—rather than merely comparing simple materials like concrete, steel, wood, or cement,"[20] to make informed decisions about selections and trade-offs. After years of research, architects at Kieran Timberlake developed an LCA plug-in for Revit called Tally; similarly, engineers at Thornton Tomasetti created Beacon for Revit. Both are available alongside databases such as Quartz and Athena, which contain the environmental performance metadata associated with different materials and assemblies. The free-to-access Embodied Carbon in Construction Calculator (EC3), developed by the Carbon Leadership Forum and industry partners, provides owners, designers, and constructors with a means to assess low or zero carbon materials using "building material quantities from construction estimates and/or BIM models and a robust database of digital, third-party verified Environmental Product Declarations (EPDs)."[21]

Additionally, whole building ratings systems provide measurement guidelines and awards for lowered carbon footprints such as the World Green Building Council's Net Zero Carbon Buildings Commitment. Another system, the holistic Living Building Challenge sponsored by the International Living Future Institute, rates buildings in seven performance categories called *Petals*: Place, Water, Energy, Health + Happiness, Materials, Equity, and Beauty, that involve 20 rigorous *Imperatives* that are assessed after one year of performance metering and post-occupancy studies. Achieving a "Living Building" entails not just limiting environmental harm, but actual regeneration, self-sufficiency, and positive impact. Levels of recognition include Zero Energy, Net Positive Energy, Net Positive Water, and Net Positive Waste. Depending on the programming and project goals, other ratings systems to aspire to include Passive House, RESET Air, WELL Building, Fitwel, and LEED. While ratings systems provide checklists that may aid in developing designs for net-zero buildings, the following general principles may help guide a collaborative process.

Principles of Net Zero for the Building Industry

Halting greenhouse gas emissions may seem abstract but factors into all design decisions including siting, spatiality, materiality, energy systems, and structural systems. Collaboration on and coordination of these systems is fundamental to a project's net-zero achievements.

Principles of Net-Zero Design:

1. Design for net zero starting with the owner and an interdisciplinary team: Establish shared goals amongst the architects, engineers, contractors, and owners.
2. Design for integration: The drive towards net zero requires a whole building approach, considering both embodied and operational energy.
3. Design for full electrification and onsite clean energy: Use electric appliances and equipment, and generate projected energy needs through renewable energy systems. Consider net positive energy production to serve others and provide resilience. If onsite energy generation is not possible, harness offsite clean energy.
4. Design for net-zero embodied carbon: Use a whole building life cycle analysis (WBLCA) program to facilitate energy calculations for embodied energy. Consider ways to minimize the carbon footprint of the structure,

foundations and enclosure of the proposed project. When possible, use recycled materials or carbon-sequestering materials such as mass timber.
5. Design for net-zero operational energy: Make use of energy analysis software early and periodically in the design process to refine natural daylighting and passive ventilation strategies to minimize energy consumption.
6. Design for energy use adjustments: When possible, integrate building management and/or energy monitoring systems to inform adjustments over time. Consider post-occupancy evaluations to assess where building systems use and maintenance can be more energy efficient.
7. Design empathically for future generations: Create beauty so that people will take care of the building and feel invested in its longevity.

The Drive for Net Zero Necessitates Collaborative Design and Attention to Every Detail

Net-zero energy and decarbonization factor into nearly every design and construction decision, so weighing options and understanding trade-offs can prove challenging and time-consuming. Processes can be smoother when working with the right team and tools to support design development and decision-making. The following stories of the Frick Environmental Center and Kendeda Building provide insights into factors that contribute to achieving net-zero buildings.

Case 1: Frick Environmental Center[22]

The City of Pittsburgh and the Pittsburgh Parks Conservancy partnered to commission the Frick Environmental Center, a public environmental education center with free access and a "welcoming and inclusive" mission.[23] The programming was developed in collaboration with community members who helped the Conservancy envision the new building after the previous Center was damaged by fire in 2002. Bohlin Cywinski Jackson (BCJ), the architects who garnered the commission for the project, are known for their achievements in holistic, high performing, healthy buildings. BCJ teamed with landscape designers and engineers, including environmental consultants Atelier Ten, to integrate the building design with its mission of environmental stewardship. The 16,000-square-foot (1,500-square-meter) building was constructed by PJ Dick and completed in 2016 (Figure 8.3). During the first 18 months of

Figure 8.3 Exterior view of the Frick Environmental Center in Pittsburgh, PA by Bohlin Cywinski Jackson in collaboration with a team including Atelier Ten. Credit: Jeremy Marshall.

occupancy, the Center underwent rigorous monitoring and assessment of both the electric and water usage as part of the performance period review required through the Living Building Challenge (LBC) v2.1. The building is the first free public building to achieve full Living Building status. Patricia Culley, project architect on the Frick Environmental Center describes the five-year design and construction process as "a formative experience, in which the social impact of my work as an architectural practitioner became clearer. It instilled an understanding in me that architects today must balance the demands of the built environment with nurturing the natural environment."[24]

Community members were engaged throughout design and construction and remain the focus of the programming, which includes a public "living room" and gallery, K-12 classrooms for environmental education, offices, and support spaces. To minimize site work and create an energy-efficient massing, the building occupies the former nature center's footprint on the side of a hill where it appears as a single-story building on the north side but opens to three stories of expansive views at the south. As part of the holistic design strategy, which included energy and water reduction, BCJ worked closely with Atelier Ten who developed material report cards, making sure they avoided materials on the LBC red list and selected those materials that contributed to a healthy indoor environment. Larry Jones, environmental engineer and Associate Director at Atelier Ten, describes,

> We asked the design team to choose two alternates for each material and vetted over 1,000 products and their ingredients to meet certain criteria. In order to relay this information, we created weekly scorecards, which included pie charts to easily communicate with the designers and owner.[25]

The team met regularly in person, through all phases of the project, supplementing with virtual meetings when needed. Jones says that Atelier Ten appreciates early involvement in projects, "because that's where we can add the most value. We can bring everyone together to figure out the project sustainability goals and the strategies that make the most sense while keeping costs low."[26] Culley describes the process during the schematic design phase where the team explored many possible strategies to reduce energy usage through ideas ranging from phase-change material to earth tubes that precondition air.[27] Throughout this period, Atelier Ten would compare different options according to life cycle analyses and costs. Culley explains that BCJ has in-house capability to assess the design model for energy-reduction strategies, but for ambitious clients like those for the Frick Environmental Center, they partner with sustainability consultants like Atelier Ten, ARUP and others, for advanced energy modeling and testing.

Given the Living Building goals, passive strategies drove initial design decisions involving a heavily insulated exterior, which is clad in locally and sustainably harvested black locust, a very durable hardwood resistant to decay. Additional energy-reduction strategies include high-performance glazing, a large roof overhang at the south, natural ventilation, ground-source heat pumps (with wells reaching 520 feet deep), radiant flooring, and occupancy sensors for both the lighting and the mechanical systems. A large photovoltaic array shades the nearby parking lot and provides the electricity needs for the main building and the large four-acre site. Culley describes that aligning projected performance with actual performance often proves to be the most challenging aspect of net-zero projects: the number of occupants and their behavior or use patterns are difficult to predict so post-occupancy studies shed light on how assumptions and models match with actual behavior and performance.[28] For the Frick Environmental Center, post-occupancy testing found the solar array exceeds projected production, creating a net positive energy surplus, which is fed back into the grid.[29] Despite icy winters and

CASE FOR COLLABORATION: NET ZERO

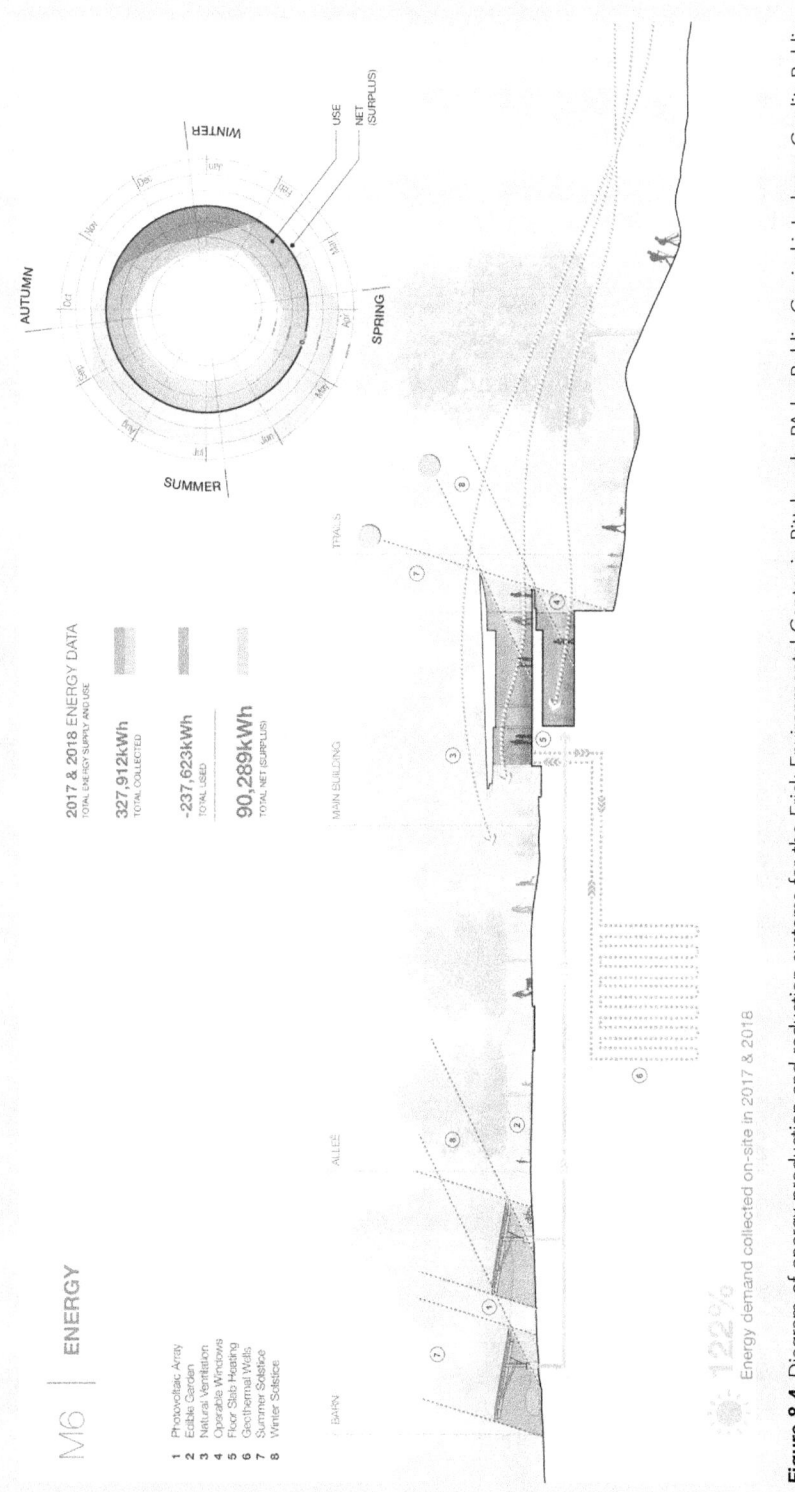

Figure 8.4 Diagram of energy production and reduction systems for the Frick Environmental Center in Pittsburgh, PA by Bohlin Cywinski Jackson. Credit: Bohlin Cywinski Jackson.

sweltering summers, the Center uses 48% less energy than ASHRAE 90.1–2007 Baseline Design.[30] Extensive monitoring includes a full building automation system and point-of-use metering. While monitoring was required to undergo Living Building Challenge Certification, the system continues to provide information that building managers and employees mine to understand and mitigate energy use (Figure 8.4).

Other Living Building measures involved net-zero water, accomplished through Atelier Ten's water budget analysis to determine total annual water demand from the Environmental Center, barn and site; and reducing total

Figure 8.5 Rainwater is used as a biophilic feature and is also collected for use in the Frick Environmental Center in Pittsburgh, PA by Bohlin Cywinski Jackson in collaboration with a team including Atelier Ten. Credit: Jeremy Marshall.

annual potable water use by determining how much could be offset via rainwater capture and reuse. The net-zero water system was achieved through onsite rainwater harvesting, a 15,000-gallon (56,000-liter) underground tank that stores greywater for use within the building and park, and a three-stage treatment process for wastewater disposal. Landscape and biodiversity reclamation measures involved planting more than 7,000 native plants and 200 native trees as well as three demonstration gardens that teach visitors about local histories and ecology (Figure 8.5).

On top of the incredible achievement of LBC Certification, the Center's long list of accolades includes a LEED Platinum rating, and the national 2017 AIA CAE[31] and 2019 AIA COTE[32] Top Ten Plus awards. Even more noteworthy, perhaps, a post-occupancy survey found that the sustainability measures add up to better indoor air quality and comfort, leading "staff [to] feel more collaborative, creative, and relaxed."[33] The vitality of the living building draws annual visitors far surpassing estimates,[34] and continues to serve as a model for positive impact.

Case 2: Kendeda Building for Innovative Sustainable Design[35]

The Kendeda Fund, a philanthropic granting organization in Atlanta, Georgia, offered $25 million (plus $5 million post-occupancy) to fund an LBC-certified education and demonstration building on Georgia Tech's campus (Figure 8.6). Georgia Tech issued public requests for qualifications and proposals, and narrowed the shortlist to three teams who participated in a three-month-long ideas competition that began in 2015. Each robust team included architects, engineers, and landscape architects. Kendeda and Georgia Tech ultimately selected the team that included architects Miller Hull Partnership and mechanical engineers PAE, who had previously partnered on a number of projects including the highly acclaimed Bullitt Center in Seattle, which at the time, was the first office building to earn the stringent LBC Certification.[36] Marc Brune, Principal of PAE Engineers, describes that working with architects at Miller Hull, who are "like-minded" and with whom they have a strong rapport, is not only "more fun but also makes everyone feel like they can give an extra 10 or 20 percent when it's needed."[37] Miller Hull's culture aligns so closely with PAE's, they continue to team up to solve challenges and "set an example of what is possible"[38] for high-performing buildings. This is the very mindset that drove the Kendeda Building design discussions together with local architects Lord Aeck Sargent and other

Figure 8.6 Exterior view of Kendeda Building for Innovative Sustainable Design in Atlanta, Georgia, by Miller Hull Partnership in collaboration with a team including PAE Engineering. Credit: Jonathan Hillyer.

practitioners. Building on the team's expertise, they were well-equipped to create a Living Building in the humid climate of Atlanta.

The communication amongst the team turned out to be one of the major reasons they clinched the contract. Three in-person "touch-point" charrettes held on campus provided the dual purpose of generating ideas and transferring knowledge, while also allowing the clients to observe team dynamics. The client issued competition guidelines describing the "quality of proposed design plan" as 15% of the evaluation, whereas 50% was based on "overall impression of the firm and the overall impression of key team members" and "effectiveness in communication of the team members during the interview process."[39] Brian Court, Partner at Miller Hull describes that the process involved all the teams working in a large room while the clients observed how the teams worked together and interacted.[40] The university wanted to be sure an "alpha-dog architect" was not dictating the design but working collaboratively.[41] Court describes the three-month competition as a long and exhausting process but also a highly productive one in which they essentially designed the building (Figure 8.7).[42]

Shortly after hiring the design team, the clients also secured Skanska, prominent contractors with experience in multiple LBC-certified buildings. They used "connected construction" including collaboration and

CASE FOR COLLABORATION: NET ZERO

Figure 8.7 Exterior view of Kendeda Building for Innovative Sustainable Design in Atlanta, Georgia, by Miller Hull Partnership in collaboration with a team including PAE Engineering. Credit: Gregg Willett Photo.

coordination with a building information model in Revit and construction management software Assemble to evaluate design proposals, materials, energy trade-offs, impacts on sustainability, and cost implications.[43] Also throughout design, PAE harnessed energy modeling software IES to study shading, loads, and thermal mass and to understand the energy impacts of design moves.

Completed in 2019, the Kendeda Building for Innovative Sustainable Design is a living lab for learning, research, and outreach for the campus and community. The nearly 37,000-square-foot (3,400-square-meter) building creates a net positive impact on people and the environment through LBC's 20 *Imperatives* including Energy + Carbon Reduction and Responsible Sourcing of materials. A key feature of the Kendeda Building is the roof, which extends over the landscape to create a west-facing porch, recalling the local vernacular. The roof canopy serves several performance functions: the overhang shades the west wall and an outdoor gathering area allowing a more comfortable connection between inside and outside; it also extends the surface area of the roof needed for the 330 kW solar array that generates net positive energy (120% of energy needed for operation) and collects net positive water, which supplies all the building's needs plus more than 70,000 gallons (265,000 liters) for use at the campus plant.[44]

The team sought to provide ample daylight while also mitigating heat and energy loads. The integrated architecture–mechanical design strategies involve the roof overhang that shades windows for most hours of the day, sizing the west-facing windows to decrease loads, and operable external metal blinds. In sum, Brune says the PAE-Miller Hull-LAS collaboration, "is a partnership where we look at 8,760 hours per year and how the architecture can be tuned for high performance using a minimal low-energy mechanical system" for heating and cooling.

Embodied carbon, on the other hand, is addressed through Forest Stewardship Council (FSC) certified, carbon-sequestering mass timber that creates the bulk of the above-ground structure. "Since the structure of a building is understood to be where 80% of the overall embodied carbon emissions reside, tackling this item greatly helped the team with

Figure 8.8 Interior view of Kendeda Building for Innovative Sustainable Design in Atlanta, Georgia, by Miller Hull Partnership in collaboration with a team including PAE Engineering. Credit: Jonathan Hillyer.

the building's carbon footprint" (Figure 8.8).[45] The concrete foundations sequester carbon too through injected CO_2 by CarbonCure, a carbon-neutralizing measure that Skanska shepherded.[46] Additionally, the team mined local "waste" materials for use in the building or on site. For example, salvaged lumber from local movie sets provided some of the decking in the nail laminated timbers, which were hand-built by Skanska.[47] Also, slate roof tiles from the campus Alumni Association were used on the walls and floors of the showers and restrooms of the new building, while the exterior counters and benches were milled from the campus' felled trees. Skanska estimates that using salvaged materials in the new building saved a few hundred thousand dollars in material costs.[48]

Court describes discussions in the office about the role of architects in the design process, highlighting that these kinds of projects are only possible with a trusted, diverse team, and the architect should "support everyone and try to make sure that each person has a chance to succeed."[49] Chris Hellstern, the Living Building Challenge Services Director for The Miller Hull Partnership, agrees saying, "Living Buildings demand that working style—we all rely on each other and every decision impacts the whole team." Hellstern recommends, "It's really helpful to bring all the experts to the table, including the ownership and the tenants, and make sure everyone has a voice throughout the design process—it's what makes these projects successful."[50]

Court and Hellstern suggest that it is the role of the architects to share a vision and work to optimize systems to remove "all the typical bottlenecks and points of resistance"[51] to realize high-performance buildings. Especially when designing Living Buildings, Court describes,

> We think about the life of the building as an optimal balance where all the systems are operating as efficiently as possible so we can get to this point that the building can live like a tree from the sun and the rain that falls on site.[52]

After one year of occupation, as stipulated in the LBC, the building underwent a rigorous assessment for Living Building Challenge 3.1 Certification. The Kendeda Building is only the 28th to achieve this high honor and the first in the Southeast where the climate is particularly challenging for balancing energy use and occupant comfort (Figure 8.9).

Figure 8.9 Exterior view of Kendeda Building for Innovative Sustainable Design in Atlanta, Georgia, by Miller Hull Partnership in collaboration with a team including PAE Engineering. Credit: Gregg Willett Photo.

Frontiers Ahead

Rapid urbanization and population growth, Architecture 2030 explains, means that,

> we expect to add 2.48 trillion square feet (230 billion m^2) of new floor area to the global building stock, doubling it by 2060. This is the equivalent of adding an entire New York City every month for 40 years.[53]

Translating this projected development to a carbon-neutral built environment poses challenges, but as the Frick Environmental Center and Kendeda Building demonstrate, the challenges are not insurmountable and the technologies and know-how exist to realize net-zero and net-positive buildings. Perhaps one of the biggest hurdles, mitigating CO_2 emissions that result from manufacturing steel and concrete (14% of total global emissions),[54] requires transitioning to novel cements that eliminate or sequester carbon while increasing the use of recycled steel.[55] Research and development in these sectors continues to grow, but it remains that, as Amy Leedham and Claire Maxfield of Atelier Ten assert, "until more stringent regulations are in place, it is incumbent upon designers and contractors to take the lead on [embodied carbon emissions] and achieve GHG emission savings well beyond code."[56]

Collaboration and ingenuity are fundamental to architecture and engineering and they will be vital in upending traditional climate-harming building practices. With "all hands on deck," this will be a productive and transformative period for the industry. Best practices for achieving net zero will evolve as new technologies come to market and practitioners share information. Meeting the net-zero challenge will become easier and more affordable as more owners, designers, and constructors work together to harness whole building strategies. Doing so is an ethical obligation to deliver healthier buildings for people and the planet.

Notes

1. "'Staggering' Rise in Climate Emergencies in Last 20 Years, New Disaster Research Shows," UN News, October 12, 2020, https://news.un.org/en/story/2020/10/1075142.
2. The Paris Agreement is a United Nations-sponsored international climate change treaty signed by 196 countries in December 2015.
3. Grantham Research Institute and Sabin Center for Climate Change LawGrantham Research Institute, and Sabin Center for Climate Change Law, Columbia Law School, "Climate Change Laws of the World," accessed May 18, 2021, https://climate-laws.org/.
4. In January 2020, net zero policies existed in 19 countries, 11 regions, 21 cities according to Diana Ürge-Vorsatz et al., "Advances Toward a Net-Zero Global Building Sector," *Annual Review of Environment and Resources* 45, no. 1 (2020): 227–269, https://doi.org/10.1146/annurev-environ-012420-045843. Ürge-Vorsatz et al., "Advances Toward a Net-Zero Global Building Sector."
5. "Global Status Report 2017," World Green Building Council, accessed May 18, 2021, https://www.worldgbc.org/news-media/global-status-report-2017.
6. "Why the Building Sector? – Architecture 2030," accessed May 17, 2021, https://architecture2030.org/buildings_problem_why/.
7. United Nations Environment Programme and Global Alliance for Buildings and Construction, "2020 Global Status Report for Buildings and Construction: Towards a Zero-Emissions, Efficient and Resilient Buildings and Construction Sector - Executive Summary," 2020, https://wedocs.unep.org/xmlui/handle/20.500.11822/34572.
8. "Global Emissions," Center for Climate and Energy Solutions, accessed January 6, 2020, https://www.c2es.org/content/international-emissions/.
9. Ürge-Vorsatz et al.
10. "A Call to Action for Engineers on Climate Change," accessed May 18, 2021, https://www.enr.com/articles/48389-a-call-to-action-for-engineers-on-climate-change.
11. Michael J. Horman et al., "Delivering Green Buildings: Process Improvements for Sustainable Construction," *Journal of Green Building* 1, no. 1 (February 1, 2006): 123–140, https://doi.org/10.3992/jgb.1.1.123.
12. Patricia Culley, Interview with Bohlin Cywinski Jackson, Patricia Culley, Zoom, May 27, 2021.
13. Stephanie Carlisle, "Getting Beyond Energy: Environmental Impacts, Building Materials, and Climate Change." In David Benjamin ed. *Embodied Energy and Design: Making Architecture between Metrics and Narratives*. Columbia University GSAPP and Lars Mueller Publishers, 2016. 165–177.
14. US DoE, "A Common Definition for Zero Energy Buildings. Report Prepared by The National Institute of Building Sciences for the U.S. Department of Energy; 2015," 2015.
15. U.S. Energy Information Administration, "Frequently Asked Questions (FAQs)—U.S. Energy Information Administration (EIA)," accessed May 20, 2021, https://www.eia.gov/tools/faqs/faq.php.
16. "Design for Maintainability: The Importance of Operations and Maintenance Considerations during the Design Phase of Construction Projects | WBDG—Whole Building Design Guide," accessed May 19, 2021, https://www.wbdg.org/resources/design-for-maintainability.

17 "Embodied Carbon and Cove.Tool," accessed May 17, 2021, http://help.covetool.com/en/articles/3753987-embodied-carbon-and-cove-tool.
18 "New Buildings: Embodied Carbon – Architecture 2030," accessed May 17, 2021, https://architecture2030.org/new-buildings-embodied/.
19 Importing a heavy building information model often slows down calculations, however, so some may find it more efficient to model a simplified version of the building in these software.
20 Carlisle, "Getting Beyond Energy."
21 "EC3," *Carbon Leadership Forum* (blog), accessed May 19, 2021, https://carbonleadershipforum.org/what-we-do/initiatives/ec3/.
22 The Project Team includes: Architect: Bohlin Cywinski Jackson, Wiles-Barre, Pa., Construction Manager: PJ Dick, Landscape Architect: LaQuatra Bonci Associates, Structural Engineer: Barber & Hoffman, Civil Engineer: H.F. Lenz Co., MEP/FP Engineer: RAM-TECH Engineers, Sustainability Consultant: Atelier Ten, Stormwater Management Consultant: Nitsch Engineering, Sustainability Consultant (for Client): Evolve EA, Environmental Artist: Stacy Levy.
23 "Frick Environmental Center | Living-Future.Org," June 29, 2018, https://living-future.org/lbc/case-studies/frick-environmental-center/.
24 Culley, Interview by authors.
25 Larry Jones, Interview with Atelier Ten, Larry Jones, Zoom, June 10, 2021.
26 Jones, Interview by authors.
27 Culley.
28 Culley.
29 "The Frick Environmental Center by Bohlin Cywinski Jackson," Architect, accessed May 27, 2021, https://www.architectmagazine.com/project-gallery/the-frick-environmental-center_o.
30 "Frick Environmental Center | Living-Future.Org."
31 American Institute of Architects Committee on Architecture for Education.
32 American Institute of Architects Committee on the Environment.
33 "Frick Environmental Center | Living-Future.Org."
34 Culley.
35 The Project Team includes: Design Architect: The Miller Hull Partnership, LLP; Collaborating Architect & Prime Architect: Lord Aeck Sargent, a Katerra Company; Contractor: Skanska USA; Landscape Architect: Andropogon; Civil Engineer: Long Engineering; Mechanical, Electrical & Plumbing Engineer: PAE and Newcomb & Boyd; Structural Engineer: Uzun & Case; Water and Ecology Engineer: Biohabitats.
36 DEI Creative in Seattle WA, "Bullitt Center Earns Living Building Certification | Bullitt Center," accessed May 24, 2021, https://bullittcenter.org/2015/04/01/bullitt-center-earns-living-building-certification/.
37 Marc Brune, Interview with PAE Engineers, Marc Brune, Phone, June 2, 2021.
38 Brune, Interview by authors.
39 "Ideas Competition Reforms Architect Selection Process," *Living Building Chronicle* (blog), November 20, 2016, https://livingbuilding.kendedafund.org/2016/11/19/ideas-competition-reforms-architect-selection-process/.
40 Brian Court, Interview with Miller Hull Partnership, Brian Court and Chris Hellstern, Zoom, May 27, 2021.
41 Wanda Lau, "The Kendeda Building for Innovative Sustainable Design's Quest to Become the First Living Building in the Southeast," Architect, accessed December 13, 2017, https://www.architectmagazine.com/technology/the-kendeda-building-for-innovative-sustainable-designs-quest-to-become-the-first-living-building-in-the-southeast_o.
42 Court, Interview by authors.
43 Autodesk Construction Cloud, *Sustainability Reimagined: The Kendeda Building for Innovative Sustainable Design -- Atlanta, GA*, 2020, https://www.youtube.com/watch?v=3NHTz9psifU.
44 "The Kendeda Building for Innovative Sustainable Design | Living-Future.Org," accessed April 22, 2021, https://living-future.org/lbc/case-studies/the-kendeda-building-for-innovative-sustainable-design/.
45 "The Kendeda Building for Innovative Sustainable Design | Living-Future.Org."
46 "Georgia Tech's Kendeda Building Sets a High Bar for Regenerative Design," *Metropolis* (blog), February 24, 2020, https://www.metropolismag.com/architecture/educational-architecture/georgia-techs-kendeda-building-sets-a-high-bar-for-regenerative-design/.
47 Chris Hellstern, Interview with Miller Hull Partnership, Brian Court and Chris Hellstern, Zoom, May 27, 2021.
48 Autodesk Construction Cloud, *Sustainability Reimagined*.
49 Court.
50 Hellstern, Interview with Miller Hull Partnership, Brian Court and Chris Hellstern.
51 Court and Hellstern.
52 Court.
53 "Why the Building Sector?"
54 Chris Bataille, "Low and Zero Emissions in the Steel and Cement Industries: Barriers, Technologies and Policies." In *GGSD Forum*. Paris: OECD, 2019, 44.
55 "Making Concrete Change: Innovation in Low-Carbon Cement and Concrete," Chatham House – International Affairs Think Tank, accessed June 13, 2018, https://www.chathamhouse.org/2018/06/making-concrete-change-innovation-low-carbon-cement-and-concrete.
56 Amy Leedham and Claire Maxfield, "The Role of California's State Regulations in Reducing Building-Related Greenhouse Gas Emissions: Senate Bill 32, Assembly Bill 32, Senate Bill 100, and Assembly Bill 262," *Technology|Architecture + Design* 4, no. 1 (January 2, 2020): 117–119, https://doi.org/10.1080/24751448.2020.1705733.

Case Studies in Collaboration: Institutional Buildings

CHAPTER 9

Marshall Building at the London School of Economics

Collaborating to Knit Structure into the Urban Fabric

Architects:	Grafton Architects
Civil and Structural Engineer:	AKT II
Mechanical, Electrical, and Public Health Engineer:	Chapman BDSP
Transport Consultant:	Steer Davies Gleave
Fire Engineer:	Chapman BDSP
Landscape Architect:	Dermot Foley Landscape Architects
Acoustic Engineer:	AAD-Applied Acoustic Design
Facade Engineer:	Billings Design Associates
Working/Learning Environment/ Loose Furniture, Fittings, and Equipment Consultant:	Burwell Deakins

The Project

Lincoln's Inn Field is a large public space in densely populated London. First laid out in 1630 for the fashionable residents of what was then the outskirts of the city, the park was opened to the public in 1895 and is today situated in a section of the city associated with the nearby Royal Courts, legal offices, and civic and educational institutions. At the southwest corner of the park are the buildings that make up the London School of Economics and Political Science

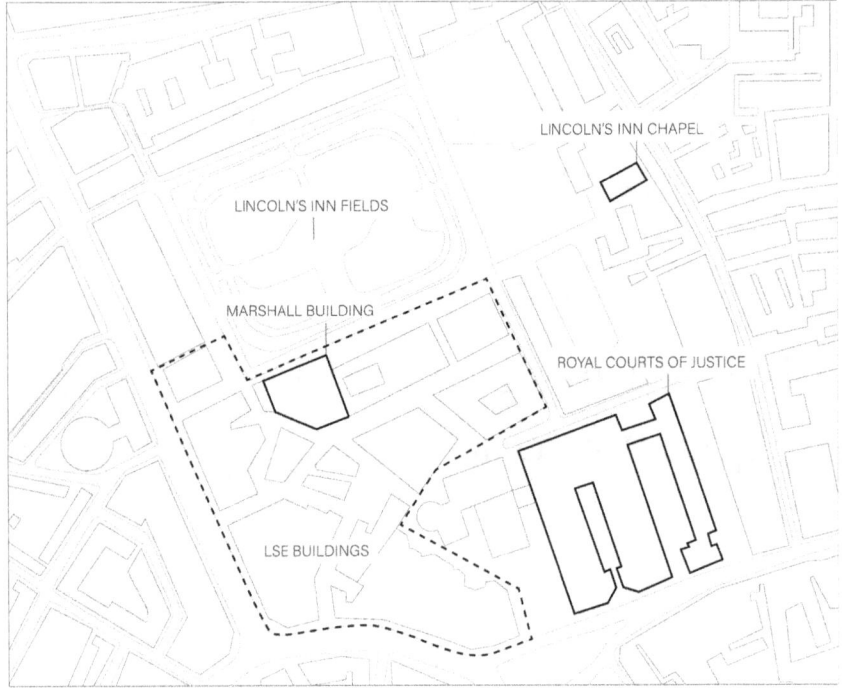

Figure 9.1 Map of LSE and the Lincoln's Inn Fields neighborhood showing the site of the Marshall Building. Grafton Architects, AKT II, London 2021. Credit: Shiori Green.

(LSE). When an international competition to design the Marshall Building was announced in 2015, it was the third major project in recent years and a major renovation for the public research university (Figure 9.1).[1]

The Marshall Building, named for its benefactor, was intended to contribute to the public amenity of the neighborhood, and the competition brief called for a 17,000-square-meter (approximately 180,000-square-foot) sustainably designed building that would provide spaces for academic teaching and research that would serve contemporary education needs[2] and athletic and recreational facilities for the students. The £100 million ($144 million in 2015) project attracted competition entries from prominent international architecture firms and was awarded to Grafton Architects by the jury in early 2016. Jury member Julian Robinson, Director of Estates for LSE, said about the decision

> Grafton's design has the potential to provide LSE with a distinctive and seminal piece of university architecture, which expresses the values and aspirations of the school. Combining modernity and tradition we felt it would enhance Lincoln's Inn Fields and connect well with the rest of LSE.[3]

Grafton Architects

Founded in Dublin, Ireland, in 1978 by a group of five, Grafton Architects is named after the street in the center of that city where they established their first office rather than for the names of the principals. Shelley McNamara and Yvonne Farrell, who met as undergraduates studying architecture, are the remaining founding principals of the firm, and they claim that the choice of name was practical (five names was too many for the answering telephone messages).[4] But many observers have noted how the deep investment in place that typifies their architectural approach resonates in that choice to honor their first professional home.

Known initially for a series of well received houses and smaller civic and educational projects, all in Ireland, their practice expanded over time to encompass much larger scale projects with an international reach. Projects such as the school of economics for Bocconi University completed in Milan in 2008 and the UTEC campus in Lima in 2015 drew considerable attention. Their work, described by one critic as "heroic buildings in sculptural concrete"[5] is notably lauded for its attention to the civic realm and a careful and generous consideration of both the urban environment and the people that it serves.

In 2018, Farrell and McNamara served as curators of the prestigious International Architecture Biennale of Venice. They won the Gold Medal from the Royal Institute of British Architects and were named as Pritzker Prize Laureates in 2020. They were among the first all-female winners of both of these honors. The Pritzker Prize jury citation describes their approach as one with

> a profound understanding of place gained through their research, keen powers of observation, open and ever curious explorations and deep respect for culture and context, Farrell and McNamara are able to make their buildings respond to a setting and city most appropriately, while still being fresh and modern. This deep understanding of "spirit of place" means that their works enhance and improve the local community. Their buildings are "good neighbors" that seek to make a contribution beyond the boundaries of the building and to make a city work better.[6]

Farrell and McNamara advocate that "spaces should represent a vision of diversity, openness, inclusiveness, and a 'love of humanity.'"[7] But, they also display a deep vein of practicality in their approach to constructability.

"Rather than thinking of a space and then finding a structure for it, we make a structure and that, in turn, makes a space."[8] They argue that their "simultaneous engagement with the practical and the poetic"[9] serves to "allow the culture of [the city] to permeate the new [building], to encourage life to happen in the new territory made, to create a new geography."[10]

AKT II

Founded in London, UK, in 1996, the engineering consultancy firm AKT II is led by Robin Adams, Hanif Kara, and Albert Taylor. The firm has become known for innovative design-focused structural and civil engineering practice and has a long history of collaboration with prominent architects. Their work deploys imaginative technical solutions and creative integration of engineering and architectural constraints. Notable projects include the Heydar Aliyev Center in Azerbaijan with Zaha Hadid, a Serpentine Pavilion project in 2016 with Bjarke Ingels Group, the Ghana National Cathedral with Adjaye Associates, and two projects with Heatherwick Studio: the UK Pavilion at Expo 2010 and the Vessel in New York City.

Kara describes his approach to what he defines as "design engineering" as representing not just the disciplinary expertise of engineering, but also as a philosophical approach that encompasses the full design process. "This attitude emerges out of AKT's restlessness to contribute to design, as well as a curiosity to find new ways to relate engineering with other design practices."[11] Kara rejects the "service model in which the engineer simply rationalizes the architect's forms."[12] He argues for early contributions of the structural engineer in the design process, and that "the disciplinary contribution is integrated throughout the design, rather than residing in a particular system or element."[13] He emphasizes that engineers' contribution to the research phase of a design process is as important if not more important than the application of complex digital methods to resolve the technical issues that come later in the process.[14]

Writing about the work of the AKT II in the catalog for a 2009 exhibition of the firm's work at the Architectural Association in London, critic Michael Kubo notes their approach to collaboration.

> In this pluralistic model the engineer is neither wholly creator nor solely problem-solver but instead operates at their intersection, adopting different roles depending on the needs and working

methods of each project ... [it] requires inhabiting the mind of the architect ... while thinking with the knowledge of the engineer ... [in] contrast to other contemporary models that seek to equate the engineer to the role of the architect, ignoring the real differences between them.[15]

The Collaborative Relationships: Architects, Structural Engineers, and the Client

Grafton Architects have long had a strong investment in the role of engineering experts in their design work and specifically in working with structural engineers who can help achieve complementary goals. Shelley McNamara explains "we've always been interested in the power of structure"[16] and remarks that it is her belief that "the separation of engineering and architecture has impoverished both."[17] In talking about her firm's work, she lists the names of engineers she has worked with and speaks effusively about their contributions to the projects.

> We like to work with people who are excellent, but who also have an ambition bigger than just doing a job. If they become engaged with us and engaged with the project, we get the best out of them, they get the best out of us.[18]

In working with engineering partners, she places a particular emphasis on the value of those relationships where there is mutual learning, an openness to questions and critique, and a common understanding of the mutual interdependence of different disciplines when it comes to achieving project goals.[19]

Engineering consultants AKT II first worked with Grafton Architects on an unbuilt competition entry in London, and later had their first built project together: Town House, an educational building for Kingston University on the outskirts of London.[20] In that project, a deceptively simple and incredibly efficient orthogonal exposed concrete frame with precast elements was deployed to great effect, creating a dramatic central public space that serves as courtyard, café, foyer, assembly, and performance space. Of working with AKT II, McNamara says: "[they] are fantastic engineers to work with because they understand architecture."[21] Hanif Kara, lead engineer for AKT II on both the Kingston and LSE projects, comments how open Grafton's architects are to good collaborative practice: "Shelley and Yvonne, they're very giving ... their starting position is beneficial to engineers because they're respectful and inclusive."[22]

LSE is a public university in the UK system, primarily funded by government support of research and teaching, and by student fees.[23] A not-for-profit client comes with certain constraints and, conversely, with certain opportunities. Value for the investment entrusted in the organization by the taxpayers, the students and, in this case, the donor is naturally a primary and immutable objective. But institutions like LSE often take a longer range view of their facilities than a private or commercial enterprise like a developer or corporate client might do. Institutions tend to think in terms of 50 to 100 years, while the life cycle of a typical corporate building is closer to 20 or 30 years. Clients can lack the expertise to evaluate and adjudicate design decisions and sometimes fail to see the beyond immediate budgetary consequences or specific programmatic desires. In many instances it is incumbent on the design team to educate their client and help them understand the stakes of different investments and the potential in alternative designs in their architectural projects. Not so in this case.

Both the architects and the engineers on this project drew attention to the importance of the client as a collaborator and report that in LSE they had a particularly valuable partner. Hanif Kara has worked with this client for over 20 years and appreciates the perspective they bring to the process. "LSE is a very educated client. They have a track record of selecting great architects … and an impressively developed idea about how to get the value of design into a project."[24] He notes that their approach has become a model for many other educational institutions in the UK. McNamara agrees: "LSE are pretty sophisticated as a client, they are very ambitious in terms of the architecture. They make a demand for a high-quality building, but also facilitate the architects in trying to deliver that."[25] The department at LSE in charge of their facilities is known as "Estates" and McNamara observes that the partnership with that department was instrumental in the success of the project and that a number of that team are honorary members of the Royal Institute of British Architects in recognition of their contributions to architecture.[26]

Kara reflects that one of the most important aspects of how a client like LSE approaches a project is that they don't (as is often the case in strictly budget-based processes) hire the design team for the first phase and then transition to the in-house team of the construction firm to deliver (refine, resolve, and construct) the project. He believes strongly that this does not save the money it is intended to, rather that "the wastage comes in not thinking deeper…. [LSE] insisted we all work together to deliver, and I think that is what ultimately gets the result the client wants."[27]

Design Approach

Grafton's keen attention to the constraints and requirements of a project across multiple scales and stakeholders is highly regarded by their collaborators and architectural critics alike. McNamara presents a candid and clear vision of the way her and Farrell's practice operates when working with their collaborators. There is a multi-disciplinary inclusivity inherent in their process:

> It's not that the architect comes along with a pretty design and everybody else has to break their backs trying to deliver it. [The project] is something that grows out of practicality, out of need, and out of the imagination. The most practical or restrictive component of the project can be the thing that feeds the invention.[28]

Kara points out, however, that the constraints for this project were no small matter, and that in the hands of a less skilled team of architects might have produced a much less flexible and celebratory space: "On this project, it was very clear that if you work off the constraints of the project, you remain with something that is very tight. And for the architect to unlock that needs a lot of cleverness."[29]

To approach the design of the Marshall Building at LSE, the team worked through the challenge of the site and the complex needs of the client's program, all while remaining true to their own ethos of design work that carefully integrates into its urban context and making buildings that are something more than the sum of their parts. The constraints of the site were among the most significant challenges of the project. The site appears square at first glance, bounded by Lincoln's Inn Fields to the north, Portsmouth Street to the west, Portugal Street to the south, and a neighboring building to the east. But Portsmouth Street and Portugal Street do not meet at a right angle, rather Portsmouth Street takes a turn and cuts a sizable section of the plan off at a 45-degree angle, rendering the site almost triangular, which makes the layout of a column grid challenging (Figure 9.2).

Paramount in the design process were the specifics of the site in a central and historic part of London, the client's role in anchoring the edge of the public amenity that is Lincoln's Inn Fields, and the need for this specific building to mediate that relationship. Kara comments on the importance of this building to the larger LSE master plan for its facilities and its future. "The conflict of the LSE is that it's in a premier district and it's not a [traditional] campus. So, strategically this client is trying to smuggle a campus in, through a series of very nice buildings."[30] Having already worked with LSE on neighboring buildings for many years, AKT II had a nuanced understanding of the client's needs,

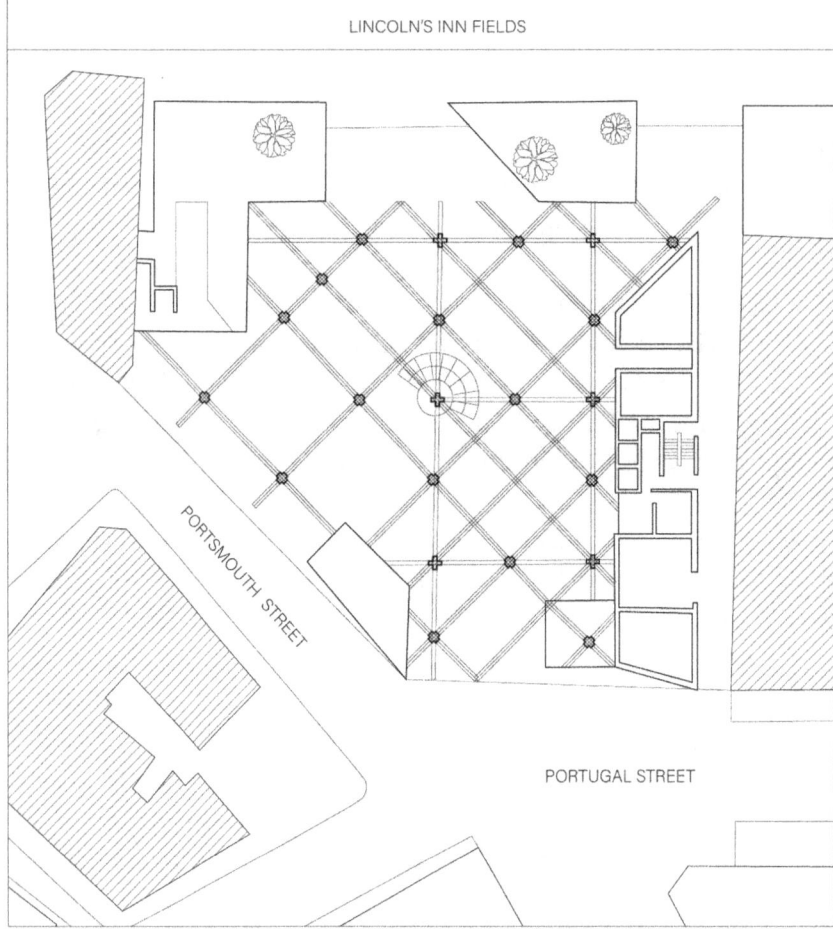

Figure 9.2 Plan of the Marshall Building, Grafton Architects, AKT II, London 2021. Credit: Shiori Green.

which was an advantage in the design competition phase for the whole team.[31] For McNamara, the position of the building between the park of Lincoln's Inn Fields and the rest of the LSE buildings meant the design would have to function as a "kind of the shoreline between the city and the landscape … and so we kept wanting to make the ground floor free."[32]

Grafton has a process early in design competitions called the "ideas wall," where anyone in the office can post ideas they think are interesting or relevant to the project. Some inspirational precedents that emerged at that stage included the large span concrete structures of Italian designer Pier Luigi Nervi, and from an early site visit before the competition, two buildings nearby to the site. The team looked at the Royal Courts buildings that had very interesting circulation patterns designed to serve the different users of the building (lawyers, judges, defendants etc.) and Lincoln's Inn Chapel (Figure 9.3). McNamara explains,

Figure 9.3 The undercroft of Lincoln's Inn Chapel. Credit: Wikicommons.

> it's a little building, just raised up in the air. It's a baroque, groin vaulted structure, in stone. The street level is completely open, and we just thought "that is so beautiful, just to make this building lifted up in the air."[33]

The concept of opening up of the ground floor would also suggest how to arrange the programs of the building. "We started thinking about the university being lifted up in the air, the sports being down below, and the city could flow between."[34] The athletics facilities are a more public facing program and would require more open space (and consequently longer spans) so designing them as more directly accessible to the city made sense. Of the final design McNamara considers

> there is something useful about delaying the point where you have a door ... the ground floor space is open ... you have this open stair up to two floors of lecture space and then there's no security control until you move up to the offices.

This is a strategy that the designers have deployed before, speaking of their project for Bocconi University in Milan, Farrell asks "how long can you delay that moment when you close the door on the city?"[35]

The concept of a very open porous public ground level with multiple paths through the building and connecting the park with the rest of the LSE campus to the south emerged as a foundational principle for the project. This approach fits well with Grafton Architect's philosophy for civic and institutional buildings. As McNamara explains, it is important "that we make a space that gives something back to the city, something that's not in the program."[36] She argues that the architect owes something to everyone who encounters the building, even if they are just walking past. This focus on the potential of the building to go beyond the prescribed program, and the care they take to celebrate the extra spaces that sometimes result, has proven to be fertile ground for the practice in this and previous projects: "it's the spaces between the things that interest us, there are the requirements of course, but it's the cartilage that you make to connect them that is the most important thing."[37]

McNamara and Farrell both teach students of architecture and have been faculty or visiting professors at University College Dublin, Harvard University, Yale University, École Polytechnique Fédérale de Lausanne, and the Accademia di Architettura, in Mendrisio, Switzerland. It is perhaps then not a coincidence that some of their most acclaimed works are buildings for universities. They pay keen attention to the relationships inherent in educational practice and note the influence of the monastery, the original educational institution, on their designs. The colonnades and galleries of those typologies achieve a particular interplay between the privacy and individual endeavors of research and the civic and teaching functions of an educational building. They create space to observe and space to encounter in one scheme.

> The Benedictine monasteries, for instance, are fantastic, there are these galleries that you're very aware of where the monks could move and see what was happening down below. And we believe that education is about serendipity and accidental overlap as well as structured exchange of knowledge.[38]

Stacking the programs from most public to most private, most porous to most secure, and largest spans to smallest spans, but ever mindful of the connections, physical and visual between the two, set the stage for what architectural critic Barry Bergdoll calls "extraordinary sectional complexity" of Grafton's work. "They create spaces of incredible visual richness, but also spaces that solve problems in terms of lighting, connecting public spaces, and really creating a zone for encounters in buildings, from Lima to Milan."[39] Others have noted that this capacity for complex sections offers the deep interior spaces sightlines to the outside and reciprocally the penetration of natural light.[40] The same sensibility is reflected in the section for LSE.

The Design

With sectional complexity, invariably there comes a demand for structural ingenuity, as gravity must be made to travel down through the section of the

Figure 9.4 The Great Hall of the Marshall Building. Grafton Architects, AKT II, London 2021. Credit: Grafton Architects.

building. Such complexity, where the spans are larger in the lower floors of the building, where columns are not continuous from roof to basement is typically navigated by way of heavy transfer structures (large trusses or beams). These are expensive, add to the weight on the foundations, take up space, and are often a barrier to other architectural goals. But Grafton Architects, never shy about using bold structural moves, in partnership with structural engineer Hanif Kara, developed a solution for the Marshall Building that is both technically innovative and aesthetically striking (Figure 9.4).

Others writing about Grafton's work have noted the reverence for gravity, mass, and weight inherent in their approach to structure.[41] McNamara acknowledges this, citing the importance of "feeling weight being held up, because historic buildings, ancient buildings always have a sense of the forces of gravity."[42] In apparent contrast, Kara summed up the structural challenges posed by the proposed section of the building, the ground floor with fewer columns and large spans, and more closely spaced but lighter columns above, as "the inverse of what gravity wants."[43] But it is in Grafton's embrace of the bold large structure required to resolve this problem, that the project finds its identity. Mc Namara explains,

> one of the first things we discussed with Hanif when we visited the site is how are we going to make the transfer structure over the huge sports hall? The span is enormous ... I always thought that it was a really interesting question.[44]

This question was complicated because they wanted to minimize the scale of the basement below and thus did not want a huge truss system as there was a minimum floor to ceiling height for the sports facility, and limits for the overall height of the building. To address these issues, they looked again to the Lincoln's Inn Chapel's vaulted structure as an inspiration.

CASE STUDIES IN COLLABORATION: INSTITUTIONAL BUILDINGS

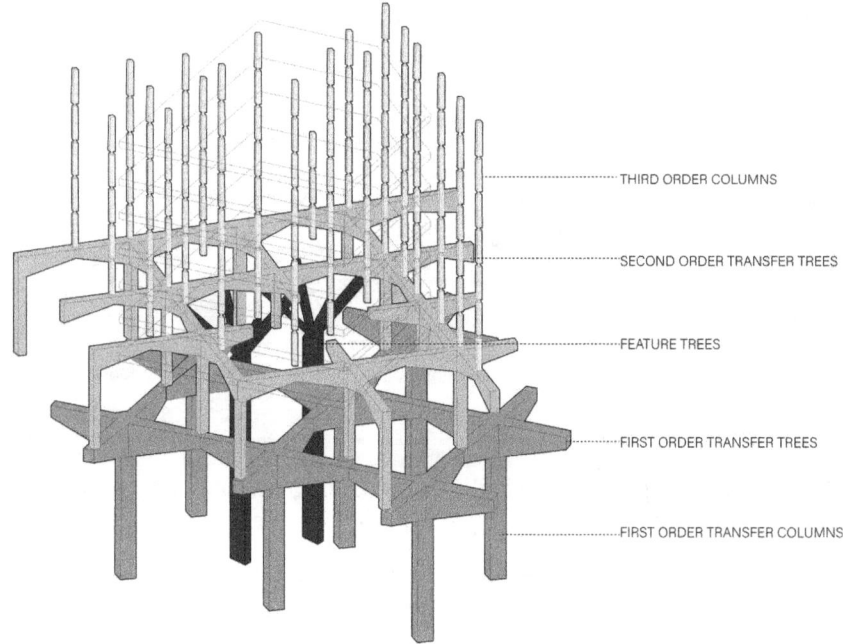

Figure 9.5 The three-part structural scheme for the Marshall Building. Grafton Architects, AKT II, London 2021. Credit: Shiori Green.

The structure in the LSE building changes thrice in the section of the ten-story building through shifts in the span sizes and layout of the column grids (Figure 9.5). For the top six floors there are vertical concrete columns on a square grid of 7.6 meters (25 feet) supporting the floor slabs. That grid is oriented at 45 degrees to the primary streets and parallel to the "cut" corner. This zone is where there are faculty offices and a suite of rooms for the entrepreneurial center inspired by the donor Paul Marshall. These columns are supported by a set of trees on a 10.8 m (35 ft) square grid, oriented parallel to the primary street. These second order trees house the zone of the building with large lecture halls and other quasi-public teaching spaces. They are made up of columns with four tapered cantilevers that fan out in each direction north, south, east, and west to collect the large point loads from the more frequent structure of the upper stories and funnel them back to the columns. These trees in turn sit on the very ends of the cantilevers of a yet smaller number of much larger (first order) trees whose columns are on a 15.2 m (50 ft) square grid (the grid rotates 45 degrees once more) opening up the ground floor for the large spans required.

There is one additional layer of complexity that opens up connections between the three zones of the building. The three "order" system is disrupted twice by the "Christmas trees," Hanif Kara's name for the two steel columns, clad in concrete to match the rest of the structure and for fire protection, that punch through the floor slabs opening up sightlines from the more private upper floors down to the more public Great Hall below (these columns are identifiable by their four diagonals at the top, differentiating them from the all concrete trees, which have tapered concrete cantilevers at the top, see Figures 9.6–9.8).

Figure 9.6 The Marshall Building under construction. Grafton Architects, AKT II, London 2021. Credit: Dennis Gilbert.

Figure 9.7 The "Christmas Tree" columns at the Marshall Building allow sightlines between the private and more public programs of the building. Grafton Architects, AKT II, London 2021. Credit: Dennis Gilbert.

Figure 9.8 The stair to the Great Hall of Marshall Building under construction. Grafton Architects, AKT II, London 2021. Credit: Dennis Gilbert.

McNamara describes the strategy,

> [it] is extraordinary, because we have an orthogonal structure on the ground floor where we've got these big beams and the big, big columns. And then it comes up and it twists diagonally. That sets up a smaller grid of smaller modules. So, it means the structure gets more frequent as you move up, but it also rotates; it's kind of a mad structure in a way.[45]

She appreciates the way that the design reflects the fractal structural performance of real trees in the nearby park, and acknowledges the collaborative process from which the design emerged: "it was very much a to and fro between engineers and ourselves on the spatial idea, the structural idea, the practical idea."[46] The shifting grid facilitated the primary goal of an open porous ground floor, and was key to the success of the strategy.

> The geometry of the site in LSE was interesting because it was at a funny twist in the street. And we decided to twist the structure diagonally, to collect people from all angles … it would feel like you are entering into something that didn't have one single direction but could collect people moving along the south and moving along the

north. And that way we could rationalize the strange geometry of the site and create an interesting relationship between the twisting structure and the orthogonal structure.[47]

The complexity of the structural scheme above ground notwithstanding, it ultimately sits on a very small number of columns. An advantage of the bulk of the building's weight being drawn into the central first order columns is that it simplifies the design of the retaining wall for the basement. Kara explains, "you take the loads away and the edges can be freed from the critical path and that for us was a freeing moment."[48] He explains that in the older cities of Europe "our problems are always under the ground"[49] especially when working in the historical center, as a project is often right up against the street edge and the walls of the neighboring building(s). Engineers and the construction crew are intervening on a site for what might be the fifth or sixth time and find themselves "digging up not only real bodies but also the man made bodies ... the previous three generations of engineers put pile foundations upon pile foundations ... we wanted to avoid creating a future problem."[50] The structural approach simplified the retaining walls and also the foundation systems. McNamara finds Kara's concern for the "violence" of the below ground structure important and observes that the "lack of respect for how we sit buildings on the ground ... how much we damage, the impact on water tables, flooding and so on"[51] simply cannot continue as their respective professions move forward.

Because the primary load carrying structure draws the weight of the building into the center to the large first order columns of the Great Hall, there was also more flexibility in designing the facade. The vertical precast concrete panels and piers[52] that make up the facade, broadcast the structural orders that they conceal and signal the three programmatic zones of the building to the passers-by (Figure 9.9). On the Lincoln's Inn Fields side of the building, there are large panels and large windows framing the Great Hall zone on the ground floor, with the entrance to the building choreographed as an "inward-folding recess" framed by the edges of the cantilevers of one of the ground floor trees (Figure 9.10).[53] The teaching floors and upper floors have a differentiated set of vertical piers framing the windows into their spaces. Kara reflects on the bespoke design of the facade and how significant he thinks it is for this project

> [Grafton] were quite keen to take on the skin as well; there is a rhythm of columns that speaks to each elevation. So on Lincoln's Inn Fields, we have some primary vertical columns that inform the elevation in beautifully made precast concrete, and then as you come around the corner, they change into whatever that street wants it to be.[54]

Figure 9.9 The three orders of the facade echo the three structural and programmatic zones of the Marshall Building. Grafton Architects, AKT II, London 2021. Credit: Grafton Architects.

Figure 9.10 The entrance of Marshall Building is framed by the cantilevers of one of the structural trees. Grafton Architects, AKT II, London 2021. Credit: Grafton Architects.

He also rejoices in how the architects really invested in this part of the design, that they did not use a standard system or curtain wall "I've been trying to glue the architect back to the facade for a long time" (Figures 9.11 and 9.12).[55] He does not believe that the architect should cede control of that part of the design. McNamara for her part asserts that defaulting to a standard

Figure 9.11 The facade of the Marshall Building from John Watkins Plaza. Grafton Architects, AKT II, London 2021. Credit: Grafton Architects.

Figure 9.12 The facade of the Marshall Building from Lincoln's Inn Fields. Grafton Architects, AKT II, London 2021. Credit: Grafton Architects.

facade system is a missed opportunity in terms of sustainability, as the enclosure of a building has a huge and often overlooked impact on the sizing of the mechanical systems and their operational energy loads.[56]

The thoughtful exchanges about the long-term impacts of the facade and below ground design of the building is emblematic of the attitude with which both AKTII and Grafton approach the concept of environmental sustainability. Their discussions of this increasingly central facet of all engineering and architectural design are more synthetic and ambitious than mere adherence to regulatory standards and governmentally imposed targets. McNamara argues that there should be more emphasis on value as opposed to cost when designing buildings. She points out that the structure and the facade are the most important aspects of a building if it is to have the longevity required to justify the quarried materials and embedded carbon required to build it and give it the flexibility to be later repurposed. Frustratingly, much of the conversation about sustainability is focused on mechanical systems that have much shorter lifespans.[57] Kara comments that his firm undertook a detailed study of the carbon footprint of the Marshall Building and found that the design of the transfer system to minimize the structural concrete (along with other careful refinements such as prestressing some of the floor slabs to minimize thickness and remove weight) brought the building well under the current UK carbon targets.[58]

Conclusion

The LSE's motto is *rerum cognoscere causas* (to understand the causes of things). It is fitting then that the Marshall Building is a product of the research-driven approach of Grafton Architects working in collaboration with AKT II and their wider design team of specialists. The careful consideration of the role of architecture in civic space, coupled with the detailed research on the history, significance, and constraints of the site set up the collaboration. The work of the team, integrated and mutually invested from the very start, confronted the project constraints to meet ambitious goals that build on and extend the client's brief. The structure, born out of the architecture and engineering designers' imaginations, where "gravity abounds, gravity is defied,"[59] creates exuberant spaces embodying the history and flows of the site, program, and place.

Notes

1 Rosenfield, Karissa. "Call for Entries: LSE Launches Third Major Competition for £100m Facility," *ArchDaily*, September 29, 2015, accessed April 17, 2021. https://www.archdaily.com/774548/call-for-entries-lse-launches-third-major-competition-for-ps100m-facility.

2 Royal Institute of British Architects. "London School of Economics Launches Its Third RIBA International Design Competition," LSE 44 LIF. September 23, 2015, accessed April 17, 2021. https://www.ribacompetitions.com/lse/index.html.

3. James Taylor-Foster, "Grafton Architects See Off "Stellar Competition" to Design the LSE's New Paul Marshall Building," *ArchDaily*, April 21, 2016, accessed April 17, 2021. https://www.archdaily.com/786009/dublin-grafton-architects-sees-off-stellar-competition-to-design-the-london-school-economics-new-paul-marshall-building.
4. Robert McCarter, *Grafton Architects* (London: Phaidon Press Limited, 2018).
5. Edwin Heathcote, "Pritzker Prize 2020 – Ireland's Grafton Architects Win Award," *FT.Com*, accessed March 3, 2020, http://search.proquest.com/docview/2370253225/citation/E28CD3F189A24BEEPQ/1.
6. Stephen Breyer et al., "Jury Citation." Yvonne Farrell and Shelley McNamara the Pritzker Architecture Prize. March 3, 2020, accessed April 21, 2021. https://www.pritzkerprize.com/laureates/2020.
7. "London School of Economics - Grafton Architects," accessed April 22, 2021, https://www.graftonarchitects.ie/London-School-of-Economics.
8. Oliver Wainwright, "Inside Peru's Modern-Day Machu Picchu – Is This the Best New Building in the World?" *The Guardian*, October 2, 2019, sec. Art and design.
9. McCarter, *Grafton Architects*.
10. Yvonne Farrell et al., eds., *Dialogue and Translation: Grafton Architects*, GSAPP Transcripts 3 (New York: GSAPP Books, 2014).
11. Hanif Kara, "On Design Engineering," *Architectural Design* 80, no. 4 (2010): 46–51, https://doi.org/10.1002/ad.1105.
12. Kara, "On Design Engineering."
13. Kara.
14. Kara.
15. Kara.
16. Shelley McNamara, Grafton Architects, The Marshall Building LSE, Zoom Interview by the authors, January 29, 2021.
17. McNamara, Grafton Architects, The Marshall Building LSE.
18. McNamara.
19. McNamara.
20. Hanif Kara, AKT II, The Marshall Building LSE, Zoom Interview by the authors, March 30, 2021.
21. McNamara.
22. Kara, Interview by authors.
23. Universities UK, "University Funding Explained," Issuu, August 23, 2016, https://issuu.com/universitiesuk/docs/university-funding-explained.
24. Kara, Interview by authors.
25. McNamara.
26. McNamara.
27. Kara, Interview by authors.
28. Kara.
29. Kara.
30. Kara.
31. Kara.
32. McNamara.
33. McNamara.
34. McNamara.
35. Manon Mollard, "Retrospective Grafton Architects," *Architectural Review* no. 1462 (June 2019): 44–52.
36. McNamara.
37. McNamara.
38. McNamara.
39. Miriam Sitz, "Founders of Grafton Architects Win 2020 Pritzker Prize," *Architectural Record* no. 4 (April 2020): 23–24.
40. Agata Toromanoff et al., *Raising the Roof: Women Architects Who Broke through the Glass Ceiling* (1, 2021).
41. McCarter.
42. McNamara.
43. Kara, Interview by authors.
44. McNamara.
45. McNamara.
46. McNamara.
47. McNamara.
48. Kara.
49. Kara.
50. Kara.
51. McNamara.
52. McCarter.
53. McCarter.
54. Kara.
55. Kara.
56. McNamara.
57. McNamara.
58. Kara.
59. Ellen Rowley, "Grafton Architects on the Move," *Irish Arts Review (2002–)* 35, no. 4 (2018): 118–123.

CHAPTER 10

41 Cooper Square at the Cooper Union

Integrated Technologies for a High-Tech Lab Building

Client:	The Cooper Union
Architects:	Morphosis: Thom Mayne, Silvia Kuhle, Pavel Getov, Chandler Ahrens, Jean Oei, plus team
Associate Architects:	Gruzen Samton, LLP
Structural Engineers:	John A. Martin Associates, Inc.
Mechanical Engineers:	IBE Consulting Engineers, Syska Hennessy Group
Facade Consultants:	Gordon H. Smith Corporation
Lighting Consultants:	Horton Lees Brogden Lighting Design, Inc.
Graphics:	Pentagram
Construction Management:	F.J. Sciame Construction Co., Inc.

41 Cooper Square was designed and constructed in collaboration with the above-named individuals and many more designers, engineers, and specialists. This case study will focus specifically on the collaboration between the architects at Morphosis, structural engineers at John A. Martin, and mechanical engineers at IBE.

Morphosis

Morphosis was founded by Thom Mayne in 1972, an architect educated at the University of Southern California and the Harvard Graduate School of Design. Morphosis began as a small, renegade practice focused on thinking through making and became widely known in the architectural community and beyond for exquisite drawings and models of the early restaurants and houses they designed, mostly located in the Los Angeles area. The firm has become known for large institutional and governmental projects, including the passively cooled and naturally lit Federal Building office tower in San Francisco and the iconic California Department of Transportation headquarters (CalTrans) in downtown Los Angeles. As the firm became more prolific, so did the international acclaim, highlighted by Thom Mayne's receipt of the Pritzker Prize in 2005.

Architectural theorist and critic Jeffrey Kipnis characterizes the firm: "Morphosis' schemes have been aggregates of discrete, articulated components arranged in machinelike contrivances."[1] Recent behemoth-scale projects seem to draw energy from the surrounding context, hovering in a state of becoming, in the form of giant metal-clad towers, cantilevered extensions, and dynamic, moving skins. Through partnerships, research, and invention, Morphosis has created bold, expressive structures while pushing the field through advancements in sustainability and technology. The firm triumphed over a slew of international offices in a competition to design the first building for Cornell's Tech campus on Roosevelt Island in New York City. Mayne explains that the commission marks an opportunity to imagine the future of higher learning[2] for the highly technological, net-zero campus. Mayne once described his design process as "a deliberate schizophrenia between instinct and logic,"[3] or art and function. Both are clearly present in the subject of the following case study.

John A. Martin

Based in Los Angeles, John A. Martin, founded in 1953, specializes in structural design services and undertakes much of their work at the institutional and infrastructural scale, i.e. high-rise offices, transportation facilities, retail, government, healthcare, and educational buildings. They employ over 500 people in eight offices across the US and China. They describe their focus as "efficiency, constructability and value."[4] Notable projects for which they have provided structural design include: the

Staples Center and LA Live Complex in Los Angeles, the Frank Gehry designed Walt Disney Concert Hall in Los Angeles, the new international airport in Bangkok, Thailand, and the recent Tom Bradley Terminal expansion to LAX airport.

IBE Consulting Engineers

IBE stands for "Ideas for the Built Environment," founded in 1999 in Los Angeles by engineers Alan Locke and John Gautrey, who began their careers at ARUP in London. It is an interdisciplinary practice that provides services in mechanical engineering, energy systems, lighting design, and facade performance among others, all with a strong emphasis on sustainability through conservation of resources and energy.[5] Notable recent projects include Hall Estate Winery designed by Frank Gehry, Nevada Museum of Art with architect Will Bruder, Charles David Keeling Apartments, a housing complex at UC San Diego's Revelle College designed by Kieran Timberlake, and the Coop Himmelb(l)au building for the Akron Art Museum in Ohio. The relationship between IBE and Morphosis is a long-standing one, with Thom Mayne having worked with both principals for many years, starting when they worked in the LA offices of ARUP.[6] The Advanced Technology group at IBE, which specializes in designing intricate buildings and their systems, worked on the design of 41 Cooper Square.

The Collaboration

In 2004, Morphosis was commissioned by the Cooper Union for the Advancement of Science and Art to design a new building located at 41 Cooper Square in New York City. Recognizing the complexity of the program and systems required, the architects enlisted structural engineers from John A. Martin and MEP engineers from IBE to partner with them from the beginning of the project. Chandler Ahrens,[7] the Lead Designer for Morphosis, argues (as have many others in this text) that successful collaboration between architects and engineers is often a product of an ongoing relationship. "It takes time to educate your engineers about how a company like Morphosis works. It is not a typical company—it takes a few projects, so it is hard to switch and work with someone you don't know."[8] Speaking generally about the selection of engineering collaborators, he argues that the choice is more important for some projects than others, and that cost consideration plays a role.

> The typical relationship between architects and engineers is that the engineer is a consultant to the architect, so their fee is coming out of your fee. You want to use that wisely … Not every project requires a really elegant solution.[9]

He clarifies that in more straightforward projects, he might work with an engineer that is particularly good at optimizing cost, especially if the structure is relatively simple and is ultimately planned to be clad by facade and interior finishes and thus hidden. "With a more experimental project, you are going to tend to go with a higher-end engineer and if it is an experimental project that probably means you have the budget to support that."[10]

For a relatively complex project like 41 Cooper Square, Ahrens makes the case for collaboration as early as possible in the process. He describes both the structural engineer, Kurt Clandening from John A. Martin, and the mechanical engineer, Peter Simmonds from IBE, who collaborated on the project as "engineers who really know how to work with architects."[11] Describing the early weeks and months of the project he notes the height restrictions on the site, the very particular mechanical needs of a university building with labs, and the impact those would clearly have on the structure. Given these needs it was incredibly important to have mechanical and structural experts in the very first meetings. "You want to identify what the limitations are going to be as early in the process as possible. Cooper Union is in New York City, thus you are extremely confined."[12] In older parts of cities there are often height restrictions, in crowded cities like New York City every square inch matters, and the building was planned to house labs, so there were really specific mechanical, plumbing, and air-handling constraints. Under contemporary codes, in labs using chemicals every individual space needs its own dedicated exhaust, a stainless steel duct going from every fume hood going all the way up the building, welded and sealed off. This constraint drove the design in this case according to Ahrens. The zoning envelope had already been established, they needed to fit nine stories in the envelope, which established the maximum floor to floor height, the labs have a lot of equipment and consequently required a ten foot ceiling, all the ductwork had to be carefully choreographed not to overlap, and ultimately a structure that could fit in the remaining space needed to be designed.

> So you have all of these requirements pushing against each other. We had the structural engineer in the room, and he's saying that this can't be a steel building, it is just not possible with all these constraints, it has to be flat slab concrete, which is not typical for this building typology in New York City.[13]

Ahrens describes these early in-person meetings as "absolutely critical." While architects have enough training and experience to have some idea of the answer it is important not to "go too far down the road" without having the engineers involved, he says

> I think pride can get in the way; you don't want to sound stupid, or naive, but it so important to ask the slightly naive questions, because if you ask a different question, you get a different answer. I think that is where a lot of exploration happens.[14]

Structural engineer Kurt Clandening observes that it is important for engineers not just to give the architects what they ask for, but rather to engage them in such a way as to establish what they *need* for the project to succeed, to understand the big picture. This is something he learned in his first engineering position where he worked with a number of engineers who had previously worked at SOM where collaboration is very much part of the culture (see Chapter 6).[15] He echoes Ahrens' sentiment that earlier is better in terms of collaboration and appreciates the team at Morphosis' willingness to engage in the beginning stages, arguing that it improves the project in the long term. "Morphosis is probably one of the few architectural firms that I've had the opportunity to work with that really understands the benefit of a collaborative design very early on."[16] He describes weekly sessions for about 4 hours every Friday morning where he and the architects would sit together and talk about what they were thinking, and how they were evolving one area of design, and clarifying the goals for the project.

> Instead of just telling me what they wanted from me, they would communicate their big idea and let me provide structural input that complimented that idea – and that allowed me to come up with fairly creative (and what I considered unique) solutions to things they likely didn't even know were problems yet, but they knew they had problems they wanted to solve. They included me in that problem solving iteration.[17]

Clandening also agrees with Ahrens that context drives the nature of the collaboration. The kind of collaboration he describes with Morphosis is by no means universal for his practice. "You have a shorter leash with certain types of projects ... definitely as sub consultants we absorb and mimic a little bit of our clients' style."[18] When working with architects on projects that are a little more driven by program he finds there are fewer opportunities for the kind of "out of the box" thinking that happened on the Cooper Union project. For example, when the firm designs hospitals, the programmatic needs, the code requirements, and the clients' outlook mean the process is far more constrained. Since early collaboration is not the norm for most firms, Clandening contends that it is not a process with which all engineers feel truly comfortable.

> For a lot of engineers this is a difficult process because there is no answer. They [the architects] are not giving you direction, they are asking you to think way outside the box, think way beyond just details and calculations.[19]

On the Cooper Union project Clandening based most of the preliminary structural concepts on intuition and experience as opposed to generating detailed calculations,

> because they [Morphosis] were looking for more conceptual input. It really was a collaborative process, and I believe it allowed me to provide valuable input as opposed to just telling them the column size for a predetermined grid, and I think they realized the value early on. It [41 Cooper Square] is really an integrated design.[20]

He further asserts, as have other engineers interviewed for this text, that engineers sometimes have to prove their merit in earlier projects to convince their architecture partners of their value to a project in order to spur greater collaboration in the future.

> I think that the engineers here at JAMA, including myself, find the Morphosis type of collaborative processes much more rewarding and we take more ownership of the process and the project at the end. So I encourage everybody to do that extra little bit and you may find that the architects will respond by including you more in that up front process.[21]

Mechanical engineer for the building, Peter Simmonds, has worked for IBE with Morphosis on many projects, and also teaches students of architecture at USC. He concurs that their collaborative process is very open and communicative, "It was very successful in as far as there was a complete understanding among the design team of what the goals were."[22] He remarks, as did Ahrens, that although the project is critically acclaimed in contemporary architecture for the formal and experiential quality of the work, the average person might not realize that, because it is a laboratory building, mechanical concerns and the attendant code requirements were a driving force in the design. He also asserts, the significance in effective collaboration of a shared respect for disciplinary expertise.

> We have a good understanding, there is also a respect for each trade. They [Morphosis] have respect for how we work ... they always had time to listen to our point of view, when you work with someone who is listening and who is understanding what your constraints are, that makes it a lot easier.[23]

Speaking about the value of communication and the importance of appreciating the "other" discipline's goals, he jokes about the stereotypical position of an engineer "I am an engineer, things are black and white, the last thing you want to do is discuss it with the architect," but for truly successful collaboration, he insists:

> I think the one thing I have learned, not from my education, but in my experience, is that you have to know how to discuss the project with the architects. There is no point in coming with a lot of math to an architect. That is just not effective. They are looking for the big picture, or the artistic solution; you have to learn how to communicate with them.[24]

It is clear from the responses of these team members that the collaborative process for 41 Cooper Square was truly integrated from the very beginning and that the communicative approach of the architects and engineers involved was key to the success of the projects.

The Project

Completed in 2009, 41 Cooper Square (Figure 10.1) houses laboratories, an exhibition gallery, an auditorium, lounge, and multipurpose spaces for the Cooper Union for the Advancement of Science and Art, a 150-year-old, highly selective college in downtown Manhattan that educates engineers, architects, and artists. According to Clandening, well-integrated collaboration also requires the right kind of client. The Cooper Union, as an architecture and engineering school, wanted

> to create an image that the school itself is forward thinking, and then they were fortunate enough to get an architect like Morphosis who has that same philosophy, so you have a client that wants something unique, they want something that makes a statement. Morphosis is good at doing that, it is really a function of finding the right architect, the right client, and the right project.[25]

Figure 10.1 The Cooper Union for the Advancement of Science and Art, Morphosis Architects, 41 Cooper Square, New York, 2009. Credit: Iwan Baan.

Nine stories high, the building has a double height entrance leading to a dramatic atrium stair, 20 feet wide (6.1 meters), that ascends through the first four floors of the organically shaped void (Figure 10.2) which extends the full height of the building, drawing daylight through the entire structure. Writing in *Architectural Design*, critic Jayne Merkel describes this space: "It is as if an inverted tornado had blown through the structure, tearing apart a neat concrete staircase so that the steps were bent and the roof of the building was blown away."[26] This central volume is lined with a steel lattice scrim giving vertical form to the space and privileging the staircase as a defined space of circulation and social condensation (Figure 10.3).

The exterior of the building is wrapped in a double layer facade, an inner glazed layer with an outer skin of stainless steel perforated panels. This outer layer is lifted one story above ground level and is slashed open in rough vertical and horizontal cuts on the front facade. These moves symbolically open the structure to the city with which the institution is so entwined.[27] At moments of openness in the facade, hints of the concrete structure behind can be seen.

CASE STUDIES IN COLLABORATION: INSTITUTIONAL BUILDINGS

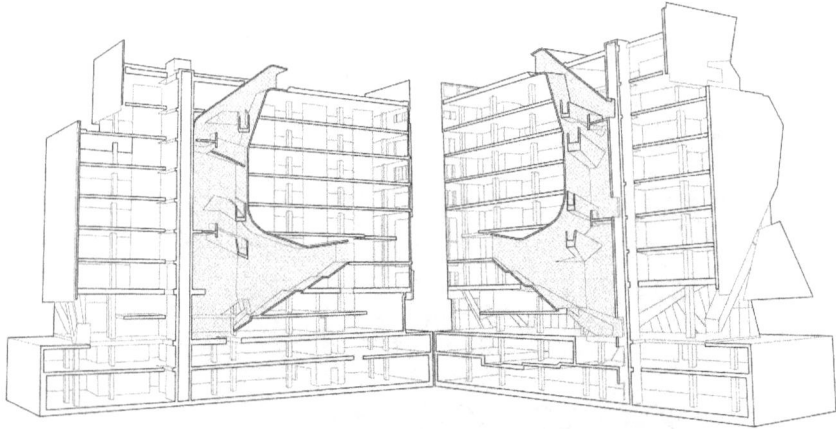

Figure 10.2 Model of the design showing the structural system and the atrium. Morphosis Architects, 41 Cooper Square, New York, 2009. Credit: Shiori Green after model by Morphosis Architects.

Figure 10.3 The atrium with the steel mesh scrim surrounding the void. Morphosis Architects, 41 Cooper Square, New York, 2009. Credit: Iwan Baan.

These dual strategies of layering and slicing can be seen in the original architect's concept drawings for the building (Figures 10.4 and 10.5). The outer surface has operable panels, which are deployed to allow additional daylight and solar gain into the space during certain times of the year. During peak

41 COOPER SQUARE AT THE COOPER UNION

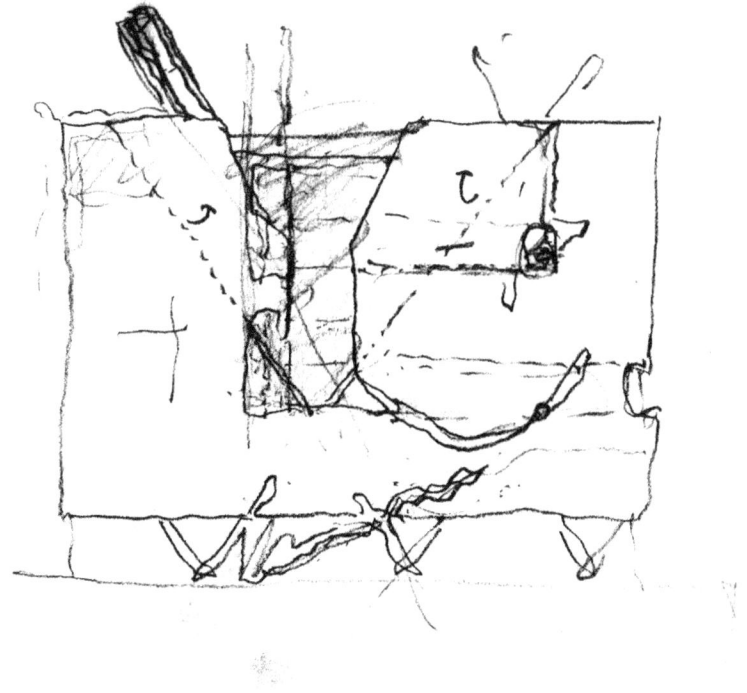

Figure 10.4 Architect's concept sketch. Morphosis Architects, 41 Cooper Square, New York, 2009. Credit: Morphosis Architects.

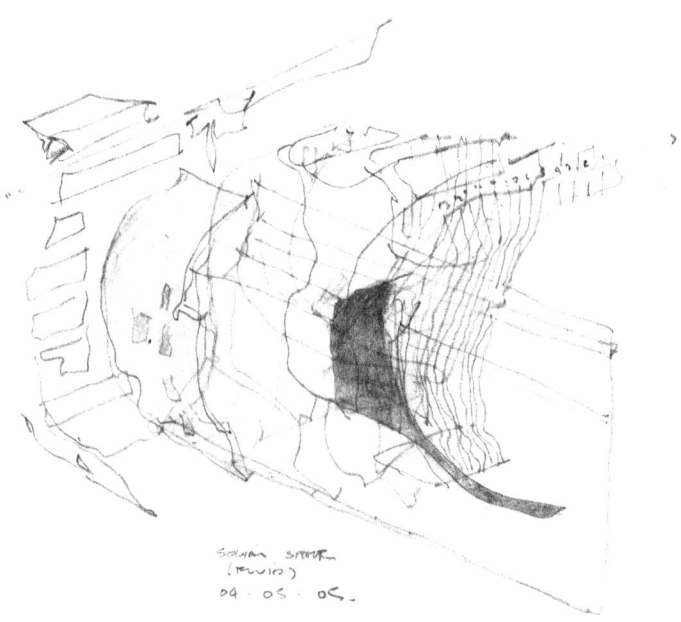

Figure 10.5 Architect's concept sketch. Morphosis Architects, 41 Cooper Square, New York, 2009. Credit: Morphosis Architects.

CASE STUDIES IN COLLABORATION: INSTITUTIONAL BUILDINGS

Figure 10.6 Note the diagonal columns at the base are out of plane. Morphosis Architects, 41 Cooper Square, New York, 2009. Credit: Sinéad Mac Namara.

heating and cooling days the panels are closed. The exterior is a living membrane that is utilized to reduce the energy consumption of the building.[28]

The structure of the building is largely a conventional flat plate concrete structure with vertical columns 30 feet (9.1 meters) on center. The four deviations from standard construction are the columns at the ground level which are aggressively diagonal and also out of plane (Figure 10.6), the entry corner where the column was removed (Figure 10.7), the central atrium for which the slabs must cantilever out to form the edges, and the south west corner where the concrete structure is notched out to make a light glass box that holds an exit stair.

Clandening reports that the design of the cantilevered slabs that surround the atrium (Figure 10.8) provides an example of the way the early and collaborative conversations amongst the design team led to design solutions that addressed multiple concerns at once. It is a cast-in-place concrete building, but in the atrium for the stairs, Morphosis wanted to have the ability to attach a lot of steel elements,

> but they didn't want a lot of ugly imbeds [where steel is bolted into a concrete surface]. I suggested we take all of the slabs that cantilever

174

out into the atrium and taper them down to 8 inches, and then embed an 8-inch (20.3-centimeter) channel, which also serves as a form stop when you pour the concrete.[29]

Figure 10.7 Note the column free corner. Morphosis Architects, 41 Cooper Square, New York 2009. Credit: Sinéad Mac Namara.

Figure 10.8 The Atrium under construction. The slab edges, the connecting stairs and the installation of the steel lattice. Morphosis Architects, 41 Cooper Square, New York, 2009. Credit: Morphosis Architects.

This allowed the contractors and stair fabricators to weld anything necessary to the edge of the structure. It was a very simple solution that allowed very accurate dimensional control because concrete formwork can be difficult to specify precisely while keeping costs low. Clandening's proposal was for a prefabricated channel that could be bent in the shop to Morphosis' tolerances.

> It was a very convoluted shape: it was an amoebic shape in the building and the opening changed on every floor. So this strategy allowed Morphosis to get what they wanted, which was a very high degree of control on a slab edge and attach things to it and you didn't have to see the attachment.[30]

To make this strategy work the engineers had to carefully check all slab thicknesses at the edges (some edges were just 5 feet (1.5 meters) past a column and some were up to 12 feet (3.7 meters) away, so the structural depth requirement would have been different) so they ultimately just made the last five feet of all cantilevering slab the same size. While this approach might sound complex, the contractor reported that it was ultimately a very economical solution. It was an effective tactic because it allowed the builders control in the construction process and they could avoid everything that normally goes wrong in buildings that are geometrically complicated.[31] Even though this was amongst the most complex slab edges they had ever built, it was actually cheaper than comparable projects. Clandening contends that the reflexive response of some engineers (even some of his own colleagues) to this issue would have been to tell the architect to use the imbeds and not to bother looking for another solution; but his philosophy, which he tries to impart to the junior engineers that work with him is,

> If someone asks you a question, don't answer the question, answer the reason behind the question. So I was asking myself, not just how do we connect to the slab edge? But rather, how do we develop a system that gives them complete flexibility and complete control?[32]

The architects at Morphosis were pleased with the solution and ultimately requested that the engineers oversize the channel a little bit so all the slabs have a short toe-guard lip on the edge that became part of the architectural language of the building.[33]

The entrance to the building is on the northwest corner and from the beginning of the design process the architects were clear that they did not want a column at that corner. The floors above have a very regular column grid, and it would have been very expensive to cantilever each of the corner slabs and associated edge beams, so there is a six-story column that is supported on the very

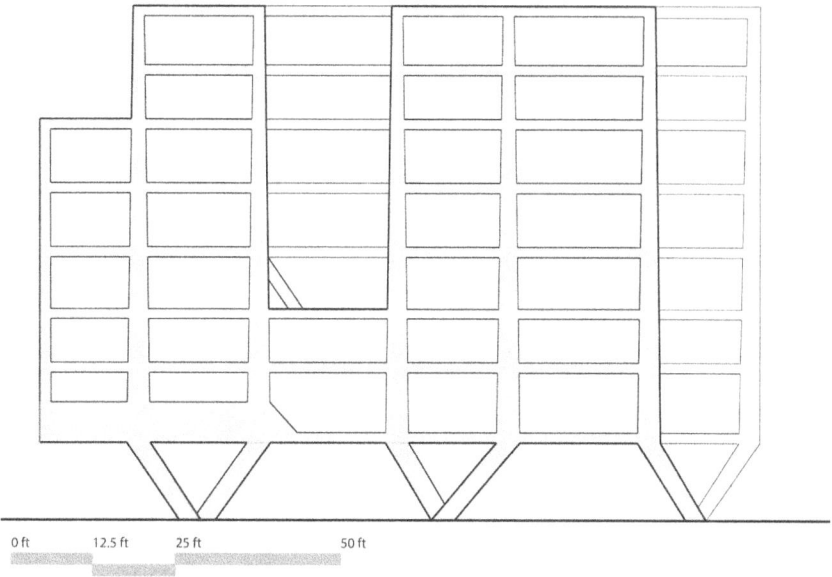

Figure 10.9 Structural grid just behind the front facade. Note the lighter pieces are recessed. Note the deep transfer cantilever under the columns free corner and the recessed zones of structure that correspond to the vertical opening in the stainless steel skin (center) and the notch for the stair tower (right). Morphosis Architects, 41 Cooper Square, New York, 2009. Credit: Christina Hoover.

tip of the cantilevered floor that carries the weight of the corner on each of those floors above. The difference between one of the edge beams in the upper floors at this location and the cantilevering transfer girder that would be necessary at the first floor to make the column free atrium is a 20-fold increase in bending moment (Figure 10.9). Thus the transfer girder would have to be very deep, potentially lowering the ceiling in the lobby, which was not in keeping with the open entrance that the architects envisaged.

> We worked with them for a long time; I understood their overall goal was not to have a column on the corner. But I had to work within the geometry they had and there was some suggestion [from engineering colleagues] that we would tell them "you have to have a column over here" but I resisted that.[34]

Clandening found out that the location on the second floor directly above the entrance was all faculty offices, as opposed to the other floors which were labs. Assuming that in those offices everybody would have a desk so they'd need a four-foot-high wall at the edge of the floor, he suggested that instead of a transfer girder below the slab, they could invert the structure and take advantage of the space no one would be using.

This way we could give them a very high vaulted opening for the lobby, and when you look at it you can't tell that there is a transfer girder there because it doesn't stick down below the slab, it pops up into the space above, where it works with the program.[35]

This cantilever was a pretty adventurous move structurally. The day before the construction supports were removed from underneath, Clandening says the onsite team was worried about its safety. He told them it would deflect ¾ of an inch (2 centimeters) when they took out the shoring, and when they called him back afterwards they reported only ⅝ of an inch (1.6 centimeters) in deflection.[36] Instances like these, Clandening asserts, demonstrate why it is so vital that engineers and architects build up trust in one another. The consequences of structural failure are potentially catastrophic and neither side wishes to be held responsible, but there is also a danger that too much conservatism can stymy innovation.

Another successful detail of the building that was facilitated in collaboration between the structural engineers and architects working on the design was the stair tower on the southwest corner (Figure 10.10). In early meetings with

Figure 10.10 The translucent stair tower on the south west corner of the building. Morphosis Architects, 41 Cooper Square, New York, 2009. Credit: Sinéad Mac Namara.

Clandening, Ahrens was clear that the intent was to have a glowing beacon of light on that corner. To that end, they wanted a light translucent structure. It was decided to notch out the concrete structure from the corner bay and build the stair tower from steel. Even then, Clandening explained that the columns would have to get bigger on the lower floors to handle the potential for buckling from the increasing compressive force as you move down through the building. This was not satisfactory for the architects who wanted the lightest and most regular structural geometry possible. Clandening proposed putting one big cantilever beam at the roof and then hanging the stair from that; thus, the hangers are very small because they are all in tension and each piece can be the same size all the way. The entire nine-story stair is hanging from the roof. "This way we gave the architects what they wanted: it was light, it was airy, it wasn't made out of concrete, and it was all the same, all the treads and all the hangers are the same size."[37] In the final design, he reports, this stair was cheaper than a standard exit stair would have been, because the hangers used so much less material than the columns would have done. Cost considerations may seem like a lamentably pedestrian or functionary aspect of a highly acclaimed project on which to focus, but as Clandening observes, "You can only do great architecture and keep doing it if you can consistently deliver for the price that the client is willing to pay."[38] In fact, Morphosis is noted in the industry for their capacity to deliver high-end architecture without the budget overruns commonly associated with high profile work.[39] Doubtless a contributory facet of this ability is their integrated and collaborative approach to technical aspects of the design.

As noted above, the mechanical engineering for this building was a significant part of the design process and in particular the venting of fume hoods required significant and complex ductwork. To stay within the allowable building envelope and still retain 10 feet (3 meters) floor-to-ceiling heights the mechanical systems had to be carefully designed. One of the innovative systems employed were radiant ceilings. Simmonds explains that 41 Cooper Square was one of the first projects to use the re-emerging technology of the radiant ceiling for heating and cooling. A significant issue when designing a radiant ceiling system is condensation; Simmons reports that it can make a lot of designers and clients nervous.

> Morphosis and The Cooper Union were 100% behind us to design that system, which we did and there haven't been any problems with it. Morphosis worked to integrate the ceiling: they designed a ceiling with perforated steel panels (Figure 10.11) that works with the radiant system. We put the heating and cooling panels above that – the whole thing went together like a Swiss watch.[40]

Figure 10.11 Interior being winched into place, note the perforated steel ceiling panels behind. Morphosis Architects, 41 Cooper Square, New York, 2009. Credit: Morphosis Architects.

Simmonds observes that the radiant ceiling eliminated enough ductwork that it allowed an extra floor to be included over what a normative system would have supported within the constraints of the site. He also remarks that all the systems in the building were so carefully designed with LEED platinum status in mind, that the building uses 46% less energy than the minimum code compliance threshold. For the clients this meant a saving in energy costs of over $200,000 per year.[41] A high-tech building for a storied institution of innovation and art, at 41 Cooper Square the collaborative disposition and disciplinary expertise of all its designers combined to make an extraordinary building. Morphosis' vision is skillfully executed by a diverse group of designers working in collaboration.

Notes

1. Jeffrey Kipnis, "Cincinnati Impressions." In Thom Mayne, ed. *Morphosis IV*. New York: Rizzoli, 2006. 14–19. 14.
2. Robin Pogrebin, "Thom Mayne of Morphosis Is Chosen for Cornell NYC Tech - NYTimes.com." Breaking News, World News & Multimedia, http://www.nytimes.com/203/05/09/arts/design/thom-mayne-of-morphosis-is-chosen-for-cornellnyc-tech.html.
3. Thom Mayne, Yukio Futagawa, and Yoshio Futagawa, *Morphosis* (Tokyo: A.D.A. Edita, 1997).
4. "Mission." John A. Martin & Associates, Inc., accessed August 22, 2013, http://www.johnmartin.com/about/mission.
5. "History." IBE Consulting Engineers: Ideas for the Built Environment, accessed August 22, 2013, http://www.ibece.com/about/history/.
6. Chandler Ahrens, Interview by the authors. Phone interview. St. Louis, MO, May 2, 2013.
7. Chandler Ahrens has since left Morphosis to focus on teaching at Washington University and his practice: Open Source Architecture.
8. Ahrens, Interview by the authors. Phone interview.

9   Ahrens.
10 Ahrens.
11 Ahrens.
12 Ahrens.
13 Ahrens.
14 Ahrens.
15 Kurt Clandening, Interview by the authors. Phone interview. Los Angeles, CA, May 24, 2013.
16 Clandening, Interview by the authors.
17 Clandening.
18 Clandening.
19 Clandening.
20 Clandening.
21 Clandening.
22 Peter Simmonds, Interview by the authors. Phone interview. Los Angeles, CA, May 30, 2013.
23 Simmonds, Interview by the authors.
24 Simmonds.
25 Clandening.
26 Jayne Merkel, "Morphosis Architects' Cooper Union Academic Building, New York," *Architectural Design* 80, no. 2 (2010): 110–113.
27 Morphosis Architects, "Cooper Union." Morphopedia—The Online Encyclopedia of Morphosis, accessed August 21, 2013, http://morphopedia.com/projects/cooper-union.
28 Simmonds.
29 Clandening.
30 Clandening.
31 Clandening.
32 Clandening.
33 Clandening.
34 Clandening.
35 Clandening.
36 Clandening.
37 Clandening.
38 Clandening.
39 Pogrebin, "Thom Mayne."
40 Simmonds.
41 Simmonds.

CHAPTER 11
Antwerp Port House for the Port Authority
Collaborating on Rationalization and Constructability

Architects:	Zaha Hadid Architects
Executive Architect and Cost Consultant:	Bureau Bouwtechniek
Structural Engineers:	Studieburo Mouton Bvba
Restoration Consultants:	Origin
Services Engineers:	Ingenium Nv
Acoustic Engineers:	Daidalos Peutz
Fire Protection:	FPC
Contractors:	Interbuild (Main), Victor Buyck Steel Construction, Groven+ (facades construction)

Although multiple experts collaborated on the design of the Port House in Antwerp, the case study focuses on the roles of Zaha Hadid Architects, Studieburo Mouton, and Bureau Bouwtechniek. Background on the design firms.

Zaha Hadid Architects

Zaha Hadid Architects (ZHA) is one of the most prominent, widely influential, and recognizable design firms in the world. The office, based in London, was founded in 1980 by Baghdad-born Zaha Hadid, who, just two decades later, became the first woman to win the Pritzker Prize, the highest prize in architecture. The Pritzker Prize Jury Citation states,

> Clients, journalists, fellow professionals are mesmerized by her dynamic forms and strategies for achieving a truly distinctive approach to architecture and its settings. Each new project is more audacious than the last and the sources of her originality seem endless.[1]

With a quickly expanding global reach, the office grew from 40 to over 400 employees and transitioned from a democratic office structure to one with directors overseeing clustered working groups. The award-winning work demonstrates continual experimentation and technological refinements to realize spectacular forms and experiences. Notable projects include the Phaeno Science Center in Wolfsburg, Germany; the Guangzhou Opera House in China; the London Aquatics Center, completed for the Olympic Games; the Heydar Aliyev Center in Azerbaijan; and the MAXXI Museum in Rome. Zaha Hadid Architects has won dozens of architectural competitions throughout the world; the Port House project in Antwerp is another competition winner and serves as the subject of the following case study.

Hadid passed away suddenly in 2016, leaving an incredible legacy of trailblazing work. The office continues to develop projects at all scales, from furniture to landmark structures, which at the time of writing, entailed 60 ongoing projects in 28 countries.

Studieburo Mouton

Based in Ghent, Belgium, Guy Mouton positions Studieburo Mouton as a design-oriented engineering firm with a reputation for collaborating with architects early in the design process to achieve aesthetic goals as well as efficiency standards in structural and stability design. The firm is a small practice of both engineers and architects working on projects throughout the Flemish region. Trained first as an architect and then as an engineer, Mouton describes himself as an "engineer architect" with an intimate understanding of the architect's approach. "It is important to harmonize the structure and architecture into a unified concept,"[2] says Mouton. Several past projects exemplify this approach to design, including the Sport Center of Boerekreek with Coussee & Goris Architecten and the Cultural Centre De Grote Post in Ostendwith B-architecten. Other projects include Cultural Centre De Waalse Krook in Ghent with

RCR Aranda Pigem Vilalta and Coussee & Goris, Nature Reserve Het Zwin in Knokke-heist with Coussee & Goris and Gafpa; and the Erasmus School in Brussels with Bevk-Perovic arhiktekti and B-architecten.

Studieburo Mouton's work was featured in an exhibition at Witte Zaal in Ghent entitled, *Designing Together*. In the catalogue, Mouton writes about the need for collaboration from the very start of a project.

> Conducting a stability study for a design goes much further than simply calculating a given situation. The office is ready to be involved in the architect's very earliest design stage. It is the intense cooperation between the architect and the engineer in which architecture and structure both reinforce and challenge one another: this is designing together.[3]

This was the approach taken by Mouton in the Port House design with Zaha Hadid Architects in this case study.

Bureau Bouwtechniek (BB)

Bureau Bouwtechniek (BB) is a well-established multidisciplinary research and consulting firm specializing in building techniques. BB was founded in 1995 by Professor-Architect Jan Moens and now employs 75 architects and engineers who work on an average of 300 projects per year ranging from technical renovation advice and assessments to in-depth guidance on energy and constructability. BB has completed projects throughout Belgium, often in international collaborations. The portfolio includes the Museum aan de Stroom (MAS) in Antwerp with Neutelings Riedijk, the City Hall in Montigny-Le-Tilleul with V+, the Queen Elisabeth Hall in Antwerp with Ian Simpson Architects, and the Royal Museum for Fine Arts in Antwerp with Claus and Kaan Architecten.

Port House Case Study, Antwerp, Belgium, Design-Build Contract

In 2008, the Port Authority of Antwerp held an open call competition to design new office spaces for administrative and technical employees and to envision a building that would act as a gateway to the second largest port in Europe (Figure 11.1). Located at Quay 63 at the site of an existing historic fire station, the port area, known as Het Eilandje, is part of a massive redevelopment effort supported through funding from the Belgian government (Figure 11.2). Nearly 100 firms entered the competition and the team led by Zaha Hadid Architects was one of five finalists selected. The jurors ultimately chose the proposal

ANTWERP PORT HOUSE

Figure 11.1 View of Port House, Antwerp, Belgium, 2016. Zaha Hadid Architects in collaboration with a team including Studieburo Mouton and Bureau Bouwtechniek. Credit: Sigrid Adriaenssens.

because it "preserves as much as possible of the dignity of the present building as a monument, adding a new object to the site" and because of Zaha Hadid Architects' reputation and proven ability to design and construct buildings of outstanding quality. ZHA had worked closely with preservation consultants, Origin, to research the site's history and heritage. The tower form of ZHA's competition-winning proposal derives from plans for an unrealized tower for the firehouse, and highlights the north-south axis that connects the port to the city (Figure 11.3). Creating the Port House extension as a tower and hovering object preserves the historic building and the plaza that surrounds it.

The Team

When questioned about the trajectory of ideas in her work, Hadid said that

> The idea of flotation led to research in structure, and therefore, our work with engineers and structures is really important, not because we need them to figure out how to make the building stand up, but to interpret how these [ideas can] happen.[4]

A floating bar above the existing firehouse was the original design idea for the Port House, and this concept was further developed by the project team (Figure 11.4). From the beginning of the competition, Zaha Hadid led the design process with director Patrick Schumacher and associate Joris Pauwels, who worked as the project architect. ZHA teamed with engineers and an executive architecture firm, Bureau Bouwtechniek, enlisted for their local expertise

CASE STUDIES IN COLLABORATION: INSTITUTIONAL BUILDINGS

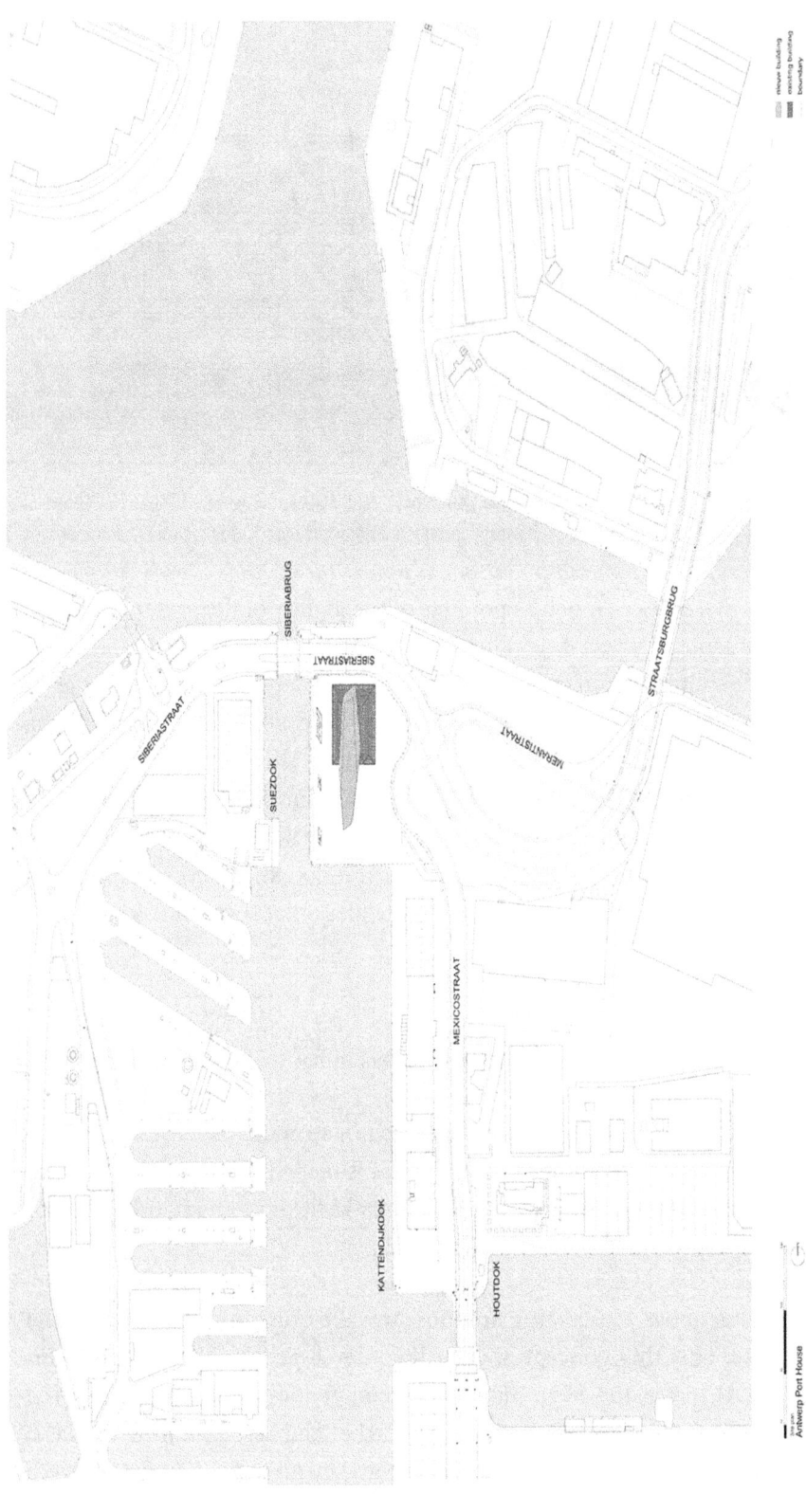

Figure 11.2 Site plan showing the expansive port and the roof plan of the Port House at Quay 63. Zaha Hadid Architects in collaboration with a team including Studieburo Mouton and Bureau Bouwtechniek, Port House, Antwerp, Belgium, 2016. Credit: Zaha Hadid Architects.

ANTWERP PORT HOUSE

Figure 11.3 An early concept for the existing historic fire station involved adding a tower and spire. Drawing after an archival elevation from the city archives. Credit: Shiori Green.

Figure 11.4 The Port House hovers above the existing firehouse and aligns with the north-south axis that connects the port to the city. Credit: Zaha Hadid Architects.

and ability to provide onsite management in the local language. The team that won the competition continued to work together throughout the design and construction processes, meeting regularly in person and daily on the phone.

Pauwels described the team that worked together from the very first concept meetings, which is "crucial for a successful delivery." He discussed that generally for the office, partnerships based on mutual respect lay the groundwork for trust and fruitful collaborations. Although ZHA had not worked with Bureau Bouwtechniek prior to the project, they

> form an important part of the team in advising us technically in relation to local building customs and regulations, dealing with local authorities, etc. They are also our cost consultants and in charge of the day to day site supervision.[5]

Pauwels enlisted his former professor at Sint-Lucas as the structural engineer, who heads Studieburo Mouton.

> Knowing each other is comfortable in the sense that there is already that basis of trust from the start. It speeds up the decision making process and is a bonus when needing to resolve stressful situations that inevitably occur during a lengthy design and construction period.[6]

Evolution of the Design: Form and Structure

The 20,800-square-meter (224,000 square-foot) project involves 12,800 square meters (138,000 square feet) above ground including restoration of the fire station and 6,200 square meters (67,000 square feet) for the new extension plus a 300-car capacity underground parking structure. The new headquarters for the Port Authority holds offices and meeting rooms to serve 500 employees who had previously worked in offices dispersed throughout Antwerp. The historic building's courtyard was enclosed in glass to create an atrium, serving as the main entrance (Figure 11.5). Staircases to the plaza level and underground parking garage are dramatically contained within two giant concrete cores that support the new structure; while a lift battery integrates into the drying tower of the former fire station to provide easy access across the floors (Figure 11.6). The super cores are not unlike the double-duty (structure and circulation) extrusions that support the Phaeno Science Center, which ZHA completed in 2005. Like the Science Center, the new Port House addition hovers above the ground, opening up a plaza space below for the public. Programming in the extension and refurbished fire station includes a library and reading room, restaurant, meeting rooms, and offices (Figure 11.7).

ANTWERP PORT HOUSE

Figure 11.5 A glass roof encloses the courtyard to create an entry for the Port House. Zaha Hadid Architects in collaboration with a team including Studieburo Mouton and Bureau Bouwtechniek, Port House, Antwerp, Belgium, 2016. Credit: © Tim Fisher.

The design concept changed very little after the competition phase aside from the number of supporting cores on which the new structure rests (shifting from three to two). The team had already determined during the competition phase that the structure should change from all steel to a combination of steel and concrete; the main columns and bridge are concrete, supporting three, three-story high steel trusses that frame the cantilevered bar (Figure 11.8). Mouton describes the structure for the building as

> a ring of concrete made by the bridge, the foundations, and the concrete circulation cores. Additionally, four steel tubes that are configured like an open paper clip 50 meters long support the volume and provide stabilization for the wind load.

Mouton goes on to say that "Joris and Zaha Hadid Architects commented on the structure throughout the process to clarify their design intent. During this

CASE STUDIES IN COLLABORATION: INSTITUTIONAL BUILDINGS

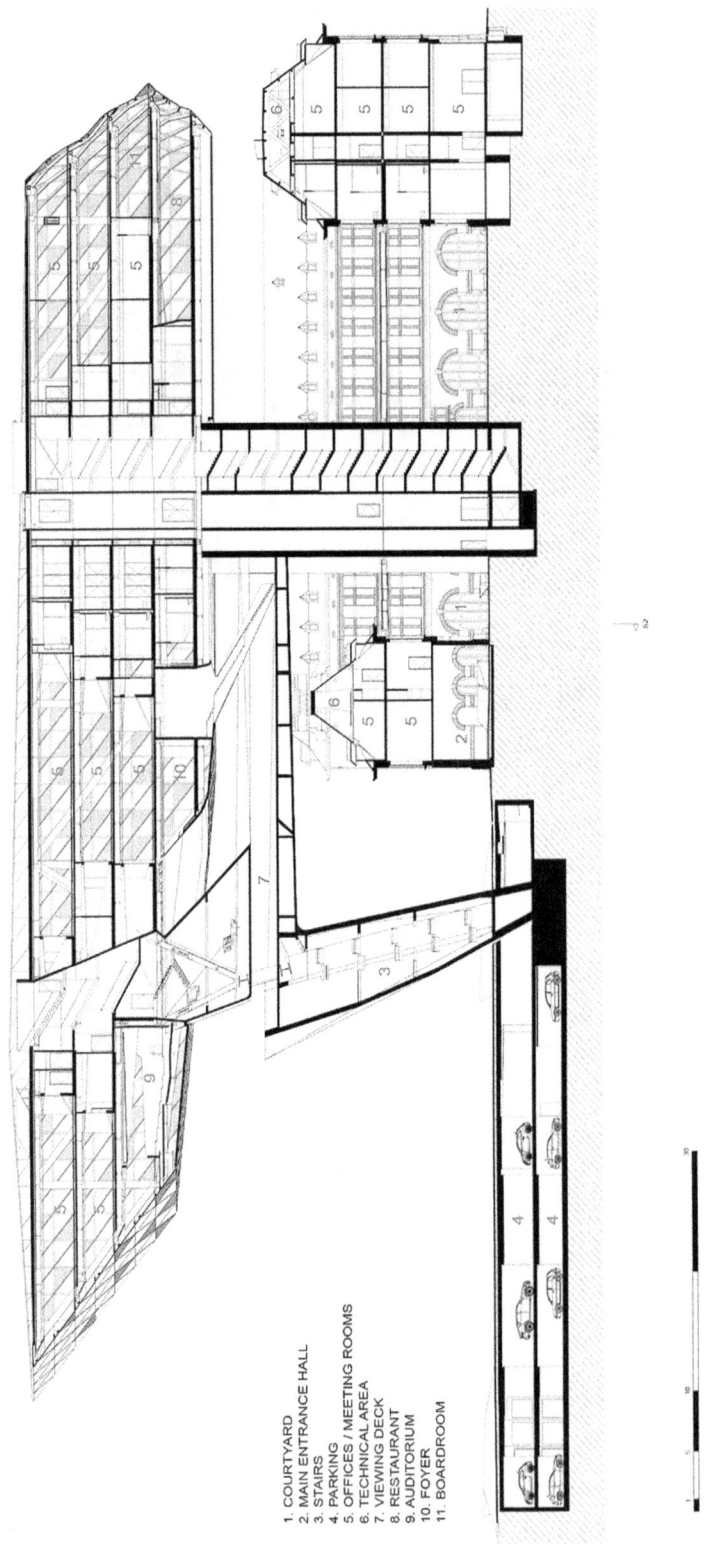

1. COURTYARD
2. MAIN ENTRANCE HALL
3. STAIRS
4. PARKING
5. OFFICES / MEETING ROOMS
6. TECHNICAL AREA
7. VIEWING DECK
8. RESTAURANT
9. AUDITORIUM
10. FOYER
11. BOARDROOM

Long Section S2
Antwerp Port House

Figure 11.6 Section through the fire station, extension and underground parking. Credit: Zaha Hadid Architects.

ANTWERP PORT HOUSE

Figure 11.7 Interior view of Port House, Antwerp, Belgium, 2016. Zaha Hadid Architects in collaboration with a team including Studieburo Mouton and Bureau Bouwtechniek. Credit: © Hufton+Crow.

Figure 11.8 Diagram of the foundation, super cores, and bridge that support the Port House extension. Drawing after illustration by Zaha Hadid Architects. Credit: Shiori Green.

Figure 11.9 View of super column of the Port House extension, Antwerp, Belgium, 2016. Zaha Hadid Architects in collaboration with a team including Studieburo Mouton and Bureau Bouwtechniek. Credit: Sigrid Adriaenssens.

close collaboration, the architectural form-finding in return was informed with sound structural logic" (Figure 11.9).[7]

Evolution of the Facade: BIM and Prefabrication

Influenced by Antwerp's diamond trade and moniker as the Diamond City, the Port House facade envisaged by ZHA uses translucent and reflective glazing to create a shimmering, diamond-like effect (Figure 11.10). The glimmering exterior, visible from great distances, also enables panoramic views from inside the open, expansive interiors. The design for the crystal facade uses triangulated glass panels, and the surface of the facade transitions from flat at the south to three-dimensional and faceted at the north. Both opaque and transparent glass elements amplify the glimmering effect while mitigating heat gain for the interior.

Gert Biebauw, Project Architect at Bureau Bouwtechniek and member of the project team from the start of the competition, understood ZHA's design concepts—their evolution and rationalization for construction. Bureau Bouwtechniek pushed for BIM and prefabrication, which were key to facilitating this process. In the initial competition phase realized through a Grasshopper model, every triangle of the facade was a different size and had a unique placement. Biebauw describes that "One of the biggest challenges was how to achieve the facade design within the constraints of the budget and constructability."[8] Bureau Bouwtechniek rationalized the design by limiting the number of facade

Figure 11.10 Detail view of the faceted, triangulated facade of the Port House, Antwerp, Belgium, 2016. Zaha Hadid Architects in collaboration with a team including Studieburo Mouton and Bureau Bouwtechniek. Credit: Sigrid Adriaenssens.

Figure 11.11 Detail view of the faceted, triangulated facade of the Port House, Antwerp, Belgium, 2016. Zaha Hadid Architects in collaboration with a team including Studieburo Mouton and Bureau Bouwtechniek. Credit: Sigrid Adriaenssens.

panel types and the distances they pull away from the facade plane by setting three fixed distances (Figure 11.11). These modules were then carefully composed to create the aesthetic envisaged by ZHA, "but helped to explain the seeming randomness to the contractors. This way, apparent randomness is contained within constructible boundaries."[9]

BIM was crucial to the rationalization process that actually began with physical modeling. Biebauw describes that "Rhino and Grasshopper helped facilitate the design, but in order to understand the design for constructability, we made physical models—cardboard models—to help to understand what's happening in the Rhino model before moving into Revit."[10] Pauwels was also fully on board with the conversion to Revit, since at the time, a growing number of projects at Zaha Hadid Architects were facilitated through BIM. In 2013, Pauwels described, "Obviously BIM is the way forward and if implemented across disciplines can work extremely efficiently, both during the design process and with the contractors throughout construction."[11] He explained Revit's advantages, which they had harnessed for the project, including cost calculations, project planning, clash detection, and communication with the contractors. The main contractor was asked to integrate services into the Revit model, which originally contained only the architectural and structural information.

Striving for ease of construction and meeting their budget targets for the Port House, architects, engineers, and fabricators pushed for prefabrication on a number of components of the design, reducing costs and the risk of delays due to bad weather. The steel cage, triangulated facade, and roof atrium were constructed in larger, transportable components off site. Victor Buyck Steel Construction, the steel subcontractor, drove the decision to prefabricate the 1500-ton steel cage, composed of six parts. The components were fabricated in a warehouse in Wondelgem and shipped to the Antwerp port site by barge. This reveals some of the challenging aspects of prefabrication: transportation of parts to the site and movement of parts once on site. Minimizing the amount of time that a crane is needed helps to maintain the cost benefits of offsite construction. For the Port House, a crane placed the steel cage, the atrium and facade components. The triangulated facade was partially constructed off site into configurations of four triangles, which are framed in 4 meter × 8 meter (13.1 foot x 26.2 foot) modules. Biebauw describes the facade system as "a giant puzzle and challenging to assemble because each piece will deflect with loads, so in the air, there aren't fixed points since there is no load yet."[12] Nevertheless, the benefits to prefabrication include reduced onsite construction labor costs and shortened construction schedules, which outweigh the costs of planning at the front end of the job.

Construction Process

The construction sequence began with site excavation, construction of the underground parking garage, and then the foundation. The two concrete "legs" were formed and topped off by the prefabricated steel cage and facade. Concurrent with the construction process at the site, the design team worked with fabricators to create mockups for various systems at a range of scales from the concrete pillars to facade prototypes. The componentry and details derived from close collaboration among architects, engineers, and fabricators. Existing

ANTWERP PORT HOUSE

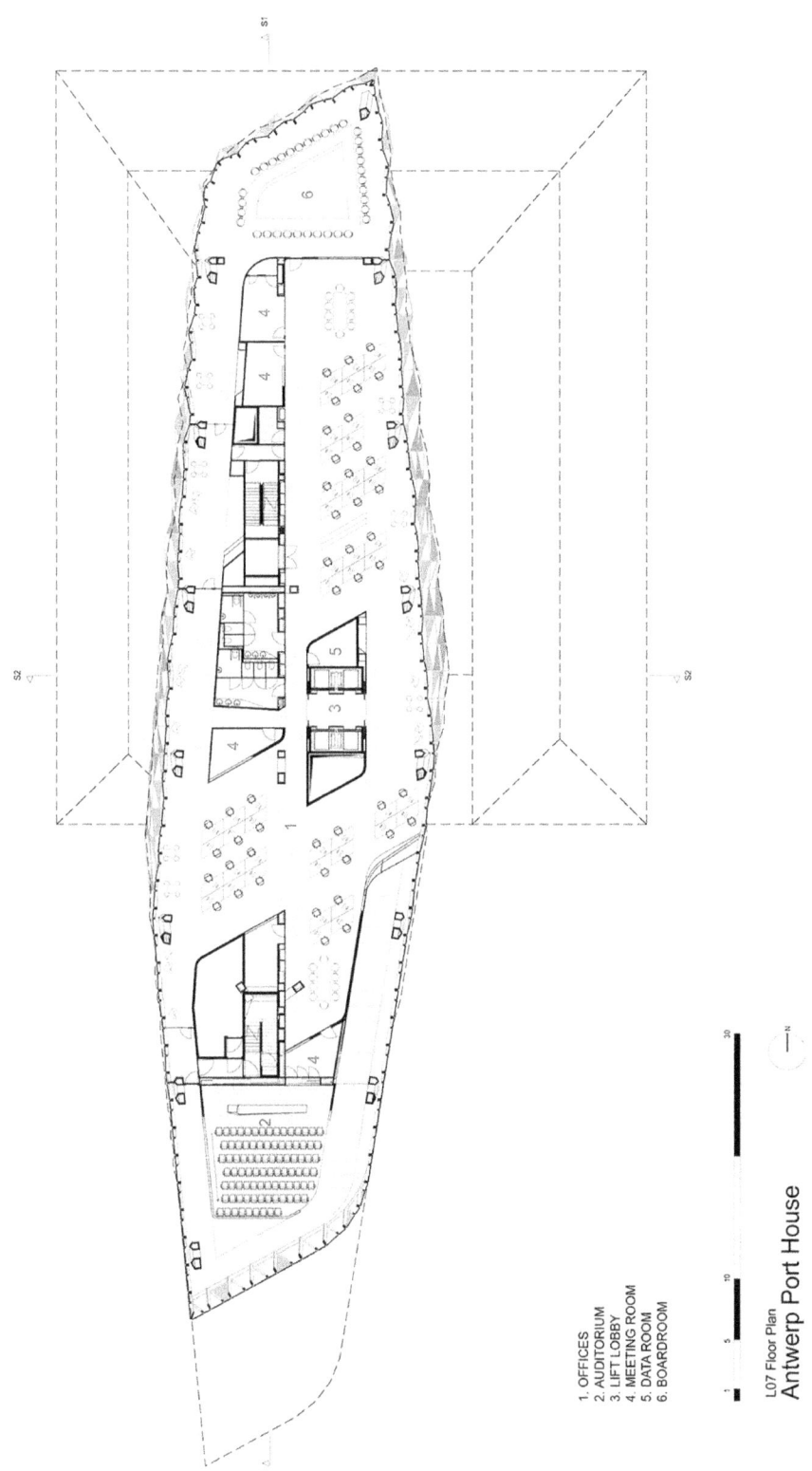

1. OFFICES
2. AUDITORIUM
3. LIFT LOBBY
4. MEETING ROOM
5. DATA ROOM
6. BOARDROOM

L07 Floor Plan
Antwerp Port House

Figure 11.12 Floor Plan Level 7 showing offices, auditorium, lift lobby, meeting room, data room, and boardroom. Zaha Hadid Architects in collaboration with a team including Studieburo Mouton and Bureau Bouwtechniek, Port House, Antwerp, Belgium, 2016. Credit: Zaha Hadid Architects.

ZHA projects, as well as the fabricator's off-the-shelf systems, were mined for design details and constructability, but the two main design concepts for the exterior, the cores and textured facade, are essentially new inventions that required a lot of testing and research. Zaha Hadid Architects' collaborative model of working with engineers and fabricators, and the emphasis on materials and technology research contribute to ZHA's demonstrated capacity to construct groundbreaking buildings such as this one.

After the competition, as is common, the client requested a number of changes to the building's program. Pauwels describes that these involved targeting a "Very Good" BREEAM (British Research Establishment Environmental Assessment Method)[13] rating, and to design the offices based on

> ABO [Activity Based Office][14] principles, which had a significant impact on the layout of the open plan offices and the required number of meeting rooms. Another change to the initial brief was the decision to double the size of the required underground car parking (Figure 11.12).[15]

Despite the changes in the program and the challenges of optimizing the form for construction using new techniques, the project was completed in 2016. The fast track design-build process was partly facilitated by the conversion to BIM and prefabrication for large areas of the building.

Through collaboration with Ingenium on energy efficiency, the Port House in fact achieved a "Very Good" rating from BREEAM. Some of the sustainability measures include a borehole energy system to provide heating and cooling distributed to chilled ceilings in the new extension (and chilled beams in the refurbished building), while sensors minimize water and electricity use. An intricate building automation system, tuned to a weather station, minimizes energy consumption through automated lighting, climate, and facade shading systems (Figure 11.13). The Port House is a textbook example of the benefits of collaboration and technology when constructing complex form and structure. Pauwels offers, "A project succeeds or fails with collaboration and communication. The importance of communication within a design team and with a client body is often underestimated."[16]

Of course, a team of architects, engineers and constructors worked together to design and realize the Port House, but the initial vision for a new structure floating over the old one and freeing the ground below for public space was Hadid's (Figure 11.14).[17] The Port House represents one of the first projects to be fully realized after Hadid's death. Architectural critic Joseph Giovannini describes the project as a continuation of her professional journey, "From the beginning of her career, Ms. Hadid lofted her buildings, defying gravity: Air

ANTWERP PORT HOUSE

Figure 11.13 Port House, Antwerp, Belgium, 2016. Zaha Hadid Architects in collaboration with a team including Studieburo Mouton and Bureau Bouwtechniek. Credit: ©Hufton+Crow.

Figure 11.14 Night view of the Port House, Antwerp, Belgium, 2016. Zaha Hadid Architects in collaboration with a team including Studieburo Mouton and Bureau Bouwtechniek. Credit: © Tim Fisher.

has been her design habitat."[18] Early in 2016, Hadid won the RIBA Royal Gold Medal for architecture and offered these words upon receiving the award,

> I am very proud to be awarded the Royal Gold Medal, in particular, to be the first woman[19] to receive the honour in her own right … This recognition is an honour for me and my practice, but equally, for all our clients. It is always exciting to collaborate with those who have great civic pride and vision. Part of architecture's job is to make people feel good in the spaces where we live, go to school or where we work – so we must be committed to raising standards. Housing, schools and other vital public buildings have always been based on the concept of minimal existence – that shouldn't be the case today. Architects now have the skills and tools to address these critical issues.[20]

Notes

1. "Jury Citation: Zaha Hadid | The Pritzker Architecture Prize," accessed May 31, 2013, https://www.pritzkerprize.com/jury-citation-zaha-hadid.
2. Guy Mouton, Interview by the authors. Phone interview. Belgium, June 5, 2013.
3. Guy Mouton, *Designing Together* (Gent: Witte Zaal, 2009).
4. Zaha Hadid, "AA School of Architecture-Lectures Online," AA School Homepage, accessed March 18, 2014, http://www.aaschool.ac.uk/VIDEO/lecture.php?ID=1951.
5. Joris Pauwels, Interview by the authors. Email interview. Zaha Hadid Architects, March 17, 2013.
6. Pauwels, Interview by the authors.
7. Mouton, Interview by the authors.
8. Gert Biebauw, Interview by the authors. Phone interview. Belgium, May 30, 2013.
9. Biebauw, Interview by the authors.
10. Biebauw.
11. Pauwels.
12. Biebauw.
13. BREEAM in the UK is very similar to the LEED or Leadership in Energy & Environmental Design rating system, which is the dominant environmental ratings system in the US.
14. ABO is a concept for office design in which an open plan encourages collective work and meetings while also saving costs on individual workstations.
15. Pauwels.
16. Pauwels.
17. "Building Zaha Hadid's Bold Afterlife – *New York Times*," accessed May 31, 2021, https://www.nytimes.com/2016/10/02/arts/design/building-zaha-hadids-bold-afterlife.html.
18. "Building Zaha Hadid's Bold Afterlife – *The New York Times*."
19. Hadid was the first woman to receive the award in the 180-year history of the Royal Gold Medal.
20. "Zaha Hadid Receives the 2016 Royal Gold Medal," accessed May 31, 2021, https://www.architecture.com/knowledge-and-resources/knowledge-landing-page/zaha-hadid-receives-royal-gold-medal.

CHAPTER 12

Simmons Hall at the Massachusetts Institute of Technology

Collaborating on Discipline and Play

Client:	Massachusetts Institute of Technology
Architects:	Steven Holl Architects: Steven Holl and Tim Bade
Local Architects:	Perry Dean Rogers and Partners
Structural Engineering:	Guy Nordenson and Associates
Project Engineers:	Guy Nordenson and Associates and Simpson, Gumpertz & Heger
Mechanical Engineer:	Ove Arup & Partners
Lighting Consultants:	Fisher Marantz Stone
General Contractor:	Daniel O'Connell's Sons

The design of Simmons Hall involved many firms and individuals, but the following discussion focuses on the partnership between Steven Holl Architects and Guy Nordenson and Associates.

Steven Holl Architects

Steven Holl Architects (SHA) is a New York-based firm founded by Steven Holl. Holl started his practice, SHA, in 1976 and the firm has gone on to amass a considerable body of work and has won numerous awards.

SHA won its first design competition in 1988, the International Library Design Competition to expand and renovate the Amerika Gedenkbiblothek, the American Memorial Library in Berlin. This was one of Holl's first collaborations with engineer Guy Nordenson.[1] During the 1990s he designed the Chapel of St. Ignatius in Seattle, an AIA National Design Award winner, and Kiasma, the Museum of Contemporary Art in Helsinki. In 1998, he was awarded the prestigious Alvar Aalto Medal for creative contributions to the field of architecture. In addition, Holl won the New York American Institute of Architects Medal of Honor, the French Grande Médaille d'Or, and the Smithsonian Institution's Cooper-Hewitt National Design Award in Architecture. In the 2000s, the firm's designs for the School of Art and Art History at the University of Iowa, the Pratt Institute in Brooklyn, and the Herning Museum in Denmark received much acclaim. Holl was named America's Best Architect by Time in 2001, and in 2010, he was awarded the Royal Institute of British Architects (RIBA) International Award, and in 2012 he was the AIA Gold Medal winner.

Christopher Platt, Head of the Mackintosh School of Architecture, where SHA was commissioned to design a new building on the campus of Charles Rennie Mackintosh's famous Glasgow School of Art, describes the preoccupations of Holl's work as "exploration of place, sensory experience and function ... Holl orchestrates transparency, translucency, texture, opacity, color, material and scale in order to heighten our awareness of who and what we are."[2]

Holl writes extensively about his architectural work and teaches Architecture at Columbia University. He reveals a deep study of the haptic and the experiential as central to his design research. "Architecture intertwines the perception of time, space, light and materials."[3] He argues that the phenomena that a person experiences in a building such as sunlight, color, and reflections and the evolving sensations they invoke across space and time separate from the perceptions of the actual object that is the building is central to his approach and "provides a 'pre-theoretical' ground for architecture ... Phenomenology in dealing with questions of perception, encourages us to experience architecture by walking through it, listening to it."[4]

Guy Nordenson and Associates

Guy Nordenson Associates is a structural engineering practice based in New York City; for a more detailed discussion of the practice, see Chapter 4.

The Collaboration

Steven Holl is an architect with a concern for structural expression in his design work. He rejects the industry reliance on standard structures with a non-structural skin as the differentiating element: "If that is going to be the future of architecture, then I want to do something else."[5] Speaking about the challenges to the integration of architecture and engineering in contemporary design practice, he asserts,

> the tendency today to opt for a complex skin and give in to developers building inexpensive and rapidly constructed interiors has become a challenge … I feel that a concept should integrate structure into the meaning, the basic experience of a work in space and light.[6]

Holl extols the design imperative (that he argues is shared by some of the most significant architects of the 20th century) to attempt to reconcile load-carrying and enclosure systems.

> In most buildings, structure is about 25 percent of the cost and 30 percent of the material. So if you don't bring structure to bear on whatever it is you are doing as an architect, then I think somewhere it's not working.[7]

He reminds us that many of the most important modernist architects of the 20th century including Le Corbusier, Louis Kahn, and Mies van der Rohe were all proponents of incorporating structure into the design. "I am interested in maintaining an integral relation of the idea through the structure, the space, and the experience."[8]

When Holl won the competition in 1988 to expand and renovate the Amerika Gedenkbiblothek, it was to be the beginning of a long-standing collaboration with Guy Nordenson, "We work together on design from the very first concept stage. With watercolor concept diagrams pinned to the wall, we have discussions and debates about alternative design concepts."[9] Speaking specifically about working with Nordenson on Simmons Hall, Holl is quick to acknowledge Nordenson's role in the overall design: "It was a process of true collaboration where the give and take continues through the entire process."[10]

Nordenson argues that the nature of an engineer–architect collaboration depends on the predisposition of the parties involved and is often best achieved in the context of a long-standing working relationship.

> My experience is that collaboration is very site specific, it depends a great deal on who you are working with. Most of the architects I have worked with, I have known for a long time, and started working with them when we were both relatively early in our careers, Steven Holl for example, is someone I have worked with for over 30 years.[11]

Elaborating on the challenges to collaborative practice between architects and engineers, Nordenson expounds

> the fundamental challenge comes up every time you talk to anyone who is not in the field about what it is that engineers and architects do … It inevitably leads to "well what's the difference between you and an architect?" … then that leads to a realization: "Oh I understand now, you make it stand up' which I think is often quite accurate."[12]

However, this linear process of "instrumental application of the engineering disciplines,"[13] where the engineer is required only to get the job done without altering the architect's parti, is not the process that interests Nordenson. "For someone like me that is not all that interesting because there really is no opportunity for interchange."[14] However, he also cautions that in some cases, particularly new collaborations, engineers have to "earn their place" at the design table by proving to their architecture partners that they have the skills and vision to contribute to the process. In another project, the Kimbell Museum with Renzo Piano, which was a first-time collaboration, his firm's input into the complex roof design evolved from a back and forth process. The engineers at GNA produced physical and digital 3D models and deliberately worked in the same medium as the architects to make the case for their proposed scheme "eventually getting to a point where we were working in parallel because they respected what they were seeing and were happy to let it take its course."[15]

Speaking specifically about his working relationship with Holl, he reports that, interestingly, the nature of the collaboration can vary from project to project. "The way we work together is very much a function of the way that Steven works, and the collaboration is best timed within his natural process."[16] There are projects where Holl will initiate conversations on a project with some well-formed ideas of what the material and the structure is going to be and that triggers a design process that leads to that type of solution. A project they designed together in Iowa for an Art History and Art School, for example, has a stair that looks a lot like the initial watercolor Holl made (Holl is known for using his watercolor paintings as inspiration for his architectural designs). In that instance the collaboration was all about working together to execute "what was at the outset was a really beautiful design."[17] But then there are also projects that operate at the other end of the collaborative spectrum such as the design for Simmons Hall, "where the way we made it was something that took some time to develop, and I think [our collaboration] had some impact on how one feels about the building."[18]

It is clear that both designers are predisposed to collaboration and have learned a great deal from each other in a long-standing working relationship.

The Design of Simmons Hall

In 1999, Massachusetts Institute of Technology in Cambridge, Massachusetts, hired Steven Holl to design a new residence hall. Simmons Hall (Figure 12.1) is ten stories tall, 330 feet (100 meters) long, and provides dorm accommodation to 350 students. A primary goal of the project was to promote interaction among the students both around and inside the building.[19] To this end, the program incorporates a theatre, a night café, and a dining hall at street level. The initial design concept was a *"folded street."*[20] That proposal had a street-like ramp that climbed up through the building.

> We took this rather radical design through to 50% schematic design, when the University informed us that a 100 feet [30 meters] height limit would be enforced on the site. We restarted with a concept of porosity, which characterized our entire master plan of four future dormitories along Vassar Street.[21]

Initial concept watercolors for this final design are shown in (Figures 12.2a and 12.2b).

Figure 12.1 Note the filled-in window openings that accommodate areas of higher stress, which occur around openings and in areas where the facade acts as a beam or cantilever to span the openings in the facade. Steven Holl Architects and Guy Nordenson and Associates. Simmons Hall at MIT, Cambridge, Massachusetts, 2002. Credit: Paul Warchol.

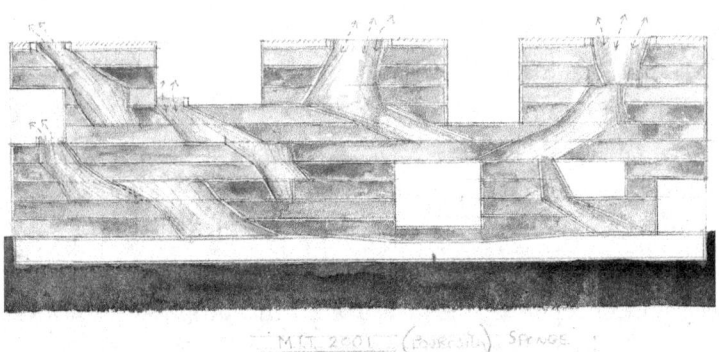

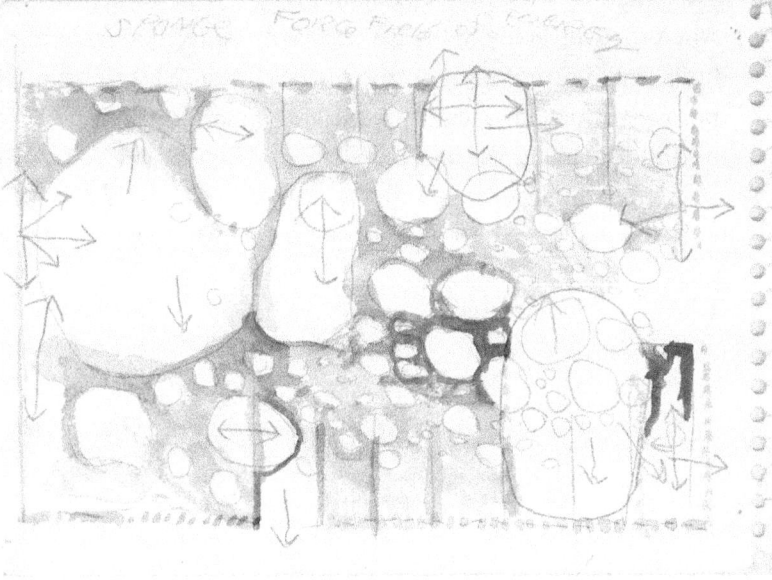

Figure 12.2a-b Steven Holl's watercolor concept drawings showing the initial concept for the final design of the residence hall with organic-shaped atria that puncture the floor plates and act as the lungs of the building. Courtesy of Steven Holl.

The concept is described as "[transforming] a porous building morphology via a series of programmatic and bio-technical functions."[22] Looking at the exterior of the building, one sees five large openings in the facade that faces Vassar Street, these denote the entrance, roof terraces, and other outdoor space. Holl argues that a dormitory is a special housing type, neither permanent like an apartment building, nor transient like a hotel, and as such, must be designed with spaces of social condensation to bring people together. This lead to a design strategy of porosity;[23] inspiration was drawn from sea sponges that are "complex, organic, [with a] structure that exhibits an incredible variety of spaces."[24]

Inside the building, extra wide 11 feet (3.5 meters) corridors function like city streets and they are punctured at strategic locations with free form atria that extend through a number of floors. In and around these atria are the public spaces of the residence hall such as group study rooms and student lounges. These atria also cut from the front to the back of the building and where they intersect with the exterior they cut an organically shaped opening in the wall. Nordenson describes this strategy for the building as a "carved block."[25] There were ten "houses" within the dorm and so ten spaces were included. The glazed openings draw natural light into the interior and public programs of the building (something usually missing from double-loaded corridors of typical residential halls). The free form spaces created by these atria and openings are described as "the lungs of the building bringing natural light down and moving air up through the section."[26] These spaces with heavy concrete walls and large openings are simultaneously cavern-like and filled with light. The free form shapes intrude into some of the corridors (Figure 12.3) and some dorm rooms. These rooms are reported to be among the most coveted by the students (Figures 12.4a and 12.4b).[27]

The site for the building on Vassar Street is about 1000 feet (300 meters) from the Charles River. As is often the case around tidal estuaries, the soil conditions were not ideal; the soil was too unstable for piles and the bedrock was too far down to reach. The weight of the structure is spread out across a 4 feet (1.2 meters) thick solid concrete mat foundation.[28] The mass of the building is largely carried by the precast concrete facade, which allows for structure and enclosure in one. Holl explained "Guy suggested the prefabricated concrete sections of perfcon, which

Figure 12.3 Simmons Hall interior view showing the organic free form atrium interrupting the normative floor-plate construction in a corridor. Note similar incursions exist in some of the dorm rooms. Steven Holl Architects and Guy Nordenson and Associates. Simmons Hall at MIT, Cambridge, Massachusetts, 2002. Credit: Paul Warchol.

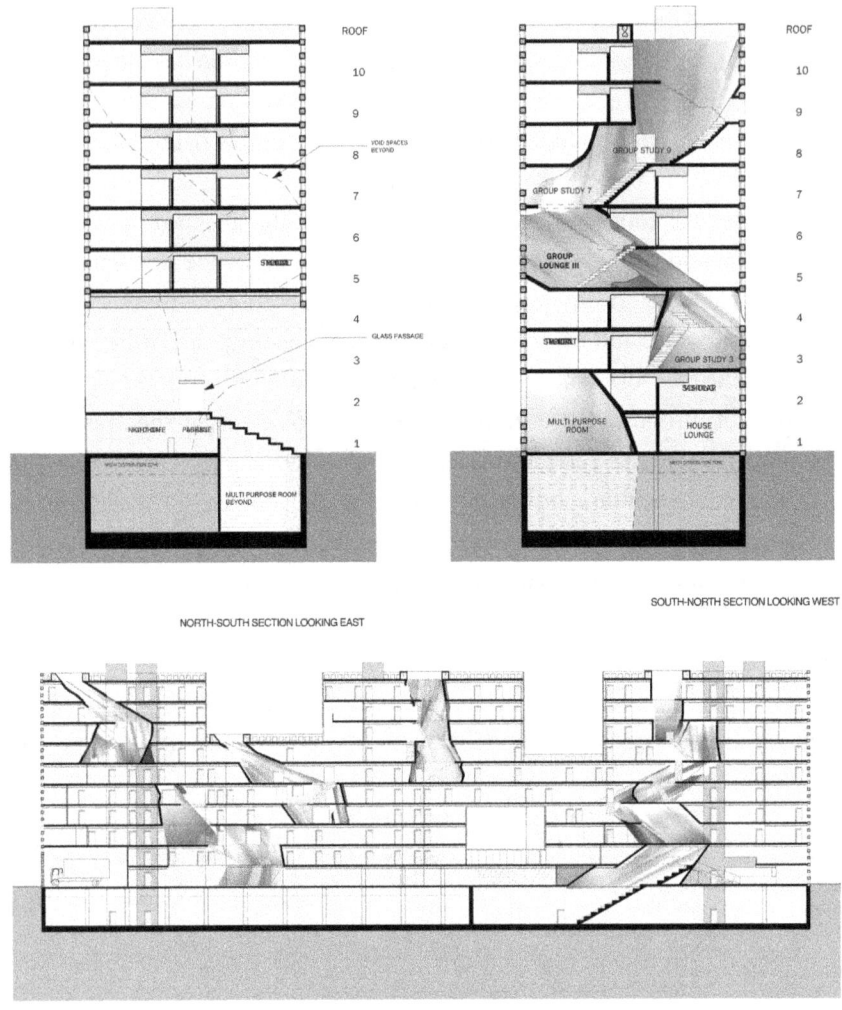

Figure 12.4a-b Sections of Simmons Hall. Steven Holl Architects and Guy Nordenson and Associates. Simmons Hall at MIT, Cambridge, Massachusetts, 2002. Credit: Courtesy of Steven Holl Architects.

fuses window, wall and structure. Guy found the Canadian pre-caster who produced the 291 precast wall panels. They are all slightly different due to the different structural loads (Figures 12.5a–12.5c)."[29]

Around much of the perimeter, the gridded structure acts just like beams and columns do in a normative structure, or like a wall with holes punched for windows. The horizontal pieces span a very short distance and the load flows down the vertical pieces to the foundations below. The horizontals also lend considerable lateral stability against wind loads. It is, however, at the moments where the facade must bridge or cantilever over the larger openings that the true innovative merit of the structural scheme can be seen. In these locations, the grid (all fully moment-connected due to the embedded steel reinforcement) acts like a Vierendeel truss,[30] resolving the large bending forces that would otherwise result into tension and

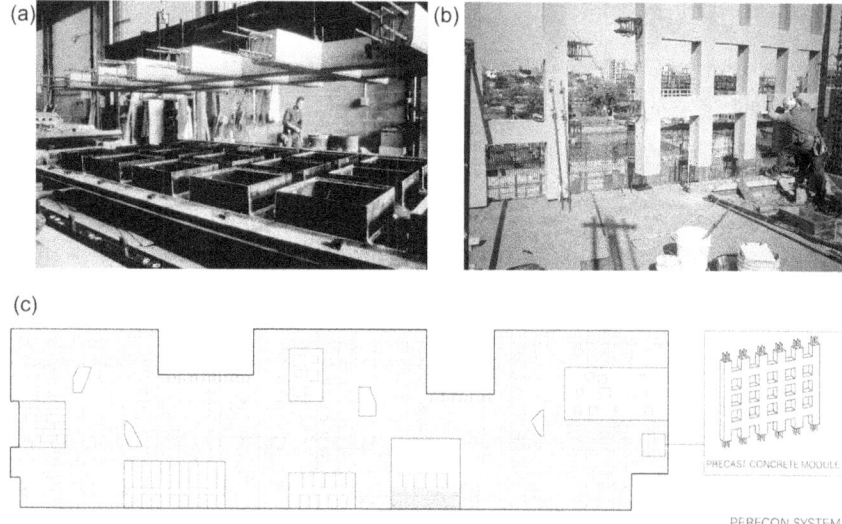

Figure 12.5a Precast concrete modules for the facade of Simmons Hall under construction at the Canadian manufacturing facility. Steven Holl Architects and Guy Nordenson and Associates. Simmons Hall at MIT, Cambridge, Massachusetts, 2002.c. Courtesy of Guy Nordenson and Associates.

Figure 12.5b Installation of Precast concrete modules for the facade of Simmons Hall. Steven Holl Architects and Guy Nordenson and Associates. Simmons Hall at MIT, Cambridge, Massachusetts, 2002. Courtesy of Guy Nordenson and Associates.

Figure 12.5c Precast concrete modules combine to create the load-carrying facade of Simmons Hall. Steven Holl Architects and Guy Nordenson and Associates. Simmons Hall at MIT, Cambridge, Massachusetts, 2002. Credit: Shiori Green after Steven Holl Architects.

compression in the horizontal members (Figure 12.6a). The parts of the grid with larger forces, due to openings large or small, required a combination of filled-in window panels, which Nordenson dubbed "freckles," and increased steel reinforcing (Figure 12.6b).[31] Naturally the irregularity of the structure and the differing loads that each piece would carry required careful study with an iterative computational process. The indeterminate structure required nonlinear structural analysis that was recalculated every time an opening changed or a different window panel was filled in.[32] This process intrigued both designers with Nordenson explaining that "We liked the indeterminacy based on how you activate the information,"[33] while Holl enjoyed the resulting whimsy that could "also meaningfully [make] visible a systematic way of dealing with the variation."[34]

Both Holl and Nordenson pushed for the concrete scheme, while the clients would have preferred steel as they wanted the building finished as quickly as possible.[35] Steel buildings are generally quicker to build and are often cheaper. Several schemes were proposed and the contractor Daniel O'Connell's Sons made estimations of the cost of each and ultimately concluded, albeit apparently somewhat reluctantly, that the precast concrete grid system would be the most cost-effective (Figure 12.7a).[36]

CASE STUDIES IN COLLABORATION: INSTITUTIONAL BUILDINGS

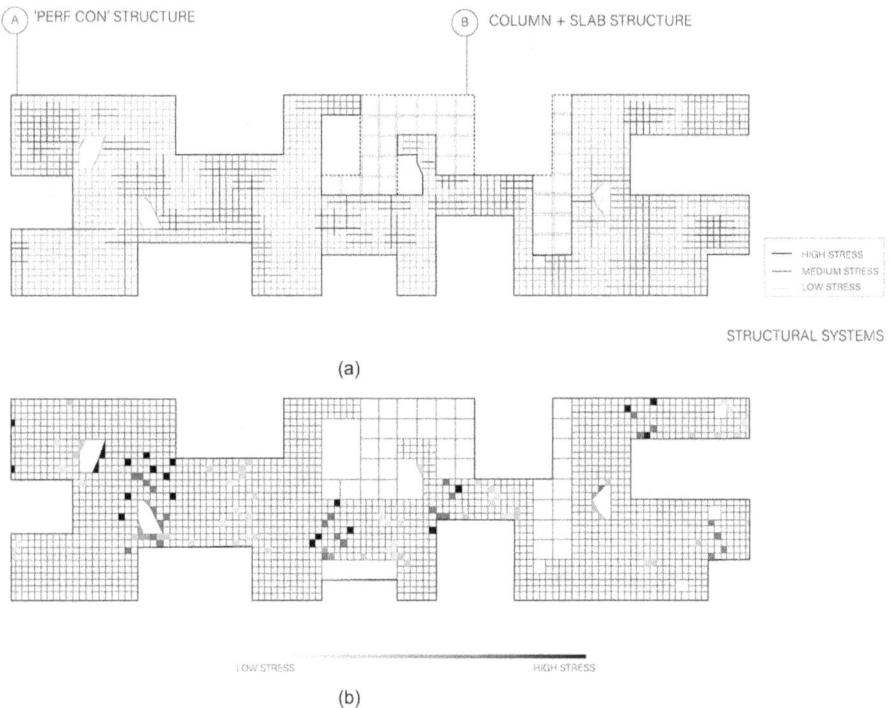

Figure 12.6a Structural engineering plan for the load-carrying front facade. Steven Holl Architects and Guy Nordenson and Associates. Simmons Hall at MIT, Cambridge, Massachusetts, 2002. Credit: Shiori Green after drawing by Amy Schreiber of Simpson Gumpertz & Heger.

Figure 12.6b "Freckles" the filled-in squares of the structural system carry varying levels of stress to help accommodate openings and differentiation in the design. Steven Holl Architects and Guy Nordenson and Associates. Simmons Hall at MIT, Cambridge, Massachusetts, 2002. Credit: Shiori Green after Guy Nordenson and Associates.

But there were a number of additional advantages to a concrete building, particularly one with a load-carrying facade. The building's mechanical design was completed by engineers at Arup and in fact, while the building has limited supplemental air conditioning, it is largely cooled through passive means. The large thermal mass, which is inherently insulating, helps to keep the building cool in summer and warm in winter. The cladding for the concrete also allowed for insulation and further improved the building's response to outside temperature changes.[37] Each single dorm room has nine operable windows that measure over 2 feet by 2 feet (0.6 meters by 0.6 meters) (Figure 12.7b). The size and layout of the windows were designed to allow views for both standing and sitting occupants.[38] The window jambs are 18 inches deep, and the windows panes are inset such that they are shaded from the high summer sun but allow the lower winter sun to penetrate the rooms.[39] Concrete as a structural material is also highly sound absorptive, which makes it a great choice for a dorm building.

Figure 12.7a Simmons Hall under construction. Steven Holl Architects and Guy Nordenson and Associates. Simmons Hall at MIT, Cambridge, Massachusetts, 2002. Courtesy of Steven Holl Architects.

Figure 12.7b Guy Nordenson visits Simmons Hall interior under construction. The precast modules that make up the skin of the building are structure and facade in one system, with the openings providing ample daylight into the residence hall. Steven Holl Architects and Guy Nordenson and Associates. Simmons Hall at MIT, Cambridge, Massachusetts, 2002. Courtesy of Guy Nordenson and Associates.

Holl named the precast grid system "Perfcon," and it proved economical. Digital modeling of the molds in the pre-casting process allowed for incredible precision and refinement in the final product.

> Only one of the six thousand panels was defective—it had a small chip. The site-cast concrete, on the other hand, was very crude. We intentionally played up the difference between the two systems by lining the forms of the site-cast work with random boards.[40]

This contrast is particularly evident in the grand lobby staircase (Figures 12.8 and 12.9). In addition to proving to the client that concrete was the more economical choice, the precast panels (each the height and width of one dorm

CASE STUDIES IN COLLABORATION: INSTITUTIONAL BUILDINGS

Figure 12.8 Simmons Hall interior staircase under construction. Note the use of rough boards to line the formwork of the cast-in-place concrete, in deliberate contrast with the highly controlled and refined finish of the precast elements. Steven Holl Architects and Guy Nordenson and Associates. Simmons Hall at MIT, Cambridge, Massachusetts, 2002. Courtesy of Guy Nordenson and Associates.

Figure 12.9 Simmons Hall interior staircase. Steven Holl Architects and Guy Nordenson and Associates. Simmons Hall at MIT, Cambridge, Massachusetts, 2002. Credit: Paul Warchol.

room) also facilitated a quicker build process relative to cast-in-place concrete, with one panel attached every 35 minutes.[41] Nordenson recounts that the speed of construction of the exterior precast structure outpaced the interior cast-in-place concrete to such a degree that the contractor complained that they had not designed the whole structure to be precast.[42]

After the structure was complete, the facade was wrapped in sanded aluminum giving the building a subtle reflectivity, and the window jambs and headers were assigned a color (Figure 12.10). The design was inspired by a color-coded graph made by site engineer Amy Schreiber of SGH to keep track of the differing diameters of reinforcing steel required at each location.[43] Blue indicates the smallest bars, number fives, approximately 5/8th of an inch (16 millimeters) in diameter, with green indicating number six bars, yellow number sevens, orange number eights, and red indicating the largest bars, number nines and tens. Nordenson saw a copy of her diagram and showed it to Holl who was intending to use color on the facade.[44] Thus, along with the filled-in windows, the color-coded facade can be read as a map of the forces that carry the building's load to the ground.

Simmons Hall opened in 2002 and received considerable praise from architectural critics. Sarah Amelar of *The Architectural Review* notes, "with its

Figure 12.10 Simmons Hall exterior view. The window openings are lined with different colors of the aluminum skin. The color pattern was inspired by a site engineer's spreadsheet that was color coded to help her remember the different steel-reinforcing requirements at different locations in the structure. Steven Holl Architects and Guy Nordenson and Associates. Simmons Hall at MIT, Cambridge, Massachusetts, 2002. Credit: Paul Warchol.

cast-concrete exoskeleton clad in sanded aluminum, the chameleon-like building changes appearance according to light conditions. Holes in the entry canopy play against the grid's regular rhythm, providing a whimsical rendition of the porosity theme."[45] In *Domus*, Yehuda Safran argues that the project is successful as the social condenser imagined by Holl in his design process.

> If student life is in fact a rehearsal for the future life of civil society, this project can be said to revolutionize everyday life in the university, releasing the ordinary street into a world of experiment and play as an alternative to political apathy and personal isolation.

He calls Simmons Hall "a slice of a city that echoes Holl's own earlier preoccupation with the edge of the city" and says that the wide street-like corridors "benefit from the porous morphology in providing unexpected openings, lounges and common halls. These collective spaces are intended to bring students together, to provoke interaction and dialogue" (Figure 12.11).[46]

Simmons Hall's success at resolving structure and enclosure, and crafting an integrated, controlled, and particularized solution to the load conditions and design intentions is emblematic of the successful collaboration between its designers. The long-established relationship and the mutual understanding and respect for each other's talents and goals, led Holl and Nordenson to a remarkable result. For Nordenson, a former MIT undergraduate himself, the building that broadcasts its structural and architectural performance with both logic and whimsy is a "satisfying homage to the institution and its irreverent culture of hackers and thinkers."[47]

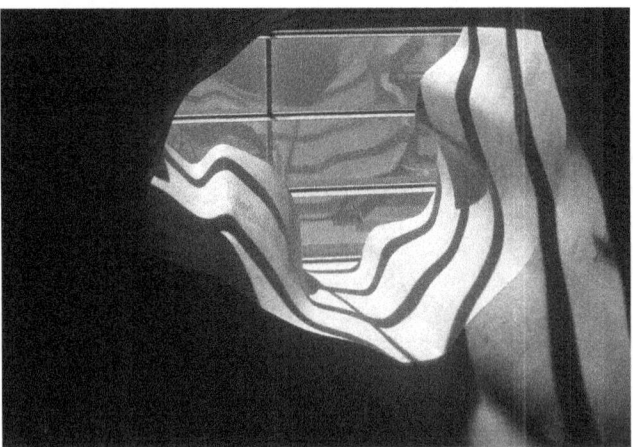

Figure 12.11 Daylight reflecting on a free form opening on the facade at Simmons Hall. Steven Holl Architects and Guy Nordenson and Associates. Simmons Hall at MIT, Cambridge, Massachusetts, 2002. Courtesy of Guy Nordenson and Associates.

Notes

1. Steven Holl, Interview by the authors. Email interview. New York, NY, August 6, 2013.
2. Christopher Platt, "Possibilities of Uncertainty." In Christopher Platt and Brian Carter eds. *Uneasy Balance*. Glasgow, Scotland: MSA Publications, 2013. 43.
3. Shlomi Almagor, "Steven Holl's Words, and Edited Selection." Introduction to *Steven Holl and Chris McVoy: 1999–2012 Volume 2* by Yukio Futagawa, Tokyo: A.D.A. Edita, 2012. 10.
4. Almagor, "Steven Holl's Words, and Edited Selection."
5. Steven Holl, Jeffrey Kipnis, and Todd Gannon, "Execution." In Todd Gannon and Michael Denison, eds. *Steven Holl: Simmons Hall MIT Undergraduate Residence*. New York, NY: Princeton Architectural Press, 2004. 113.
6. Holl, Kipnis and Gannon.
7. Holl, Kipnis and Gannon.
8. Holl, Kipnis and Gannon.
9. Holl, Interview by the authors. Email interview.
10. Holl.
11. Guy Nordenson, Interview by the authors. Phone interview. New York, NY, June 14, 2013.
12. Nordenson.
13. Nordenson.
14. Nordenson.
15. Nordenson.
16. Nordenson.
17. Nordenson.
18. Nordenson.
19. Adelyn Perez, "Simmons Hall at MIT." *ArchDaily*, accessed August 15, 2013, http://www.archdaily.com/65172/simmons-hall-at-mit-steven-holl/.
20. Holl.
21. Holl.
22. Yukio Futagawa, "Simmons Hall, Massachusetts Institute of Technology." In *Steven Holl and Chris McVoy: 1999–2012 Volume 2*. Tokyo: A.D.A. Edita, 2012. 106.
23. Steven Holl and Todd Gannon, "Master Plan." In Todd Gannon and Michael Denison, eds., *Steven Holl: Simmons Hall MIT Undergraduate Residence*. New York, NY: Princeton Architectural Press, 2004. 23.
24. Holl and Gannon, "Master Plan."
25. Guy Nordenson, *Guy Nordenson: Reading Structures: 39 Projects and Built Works, 1983-2011* (Zurich: Lars Müller Publishers, 2016).
26. Futagawa, "Simmons Hall, Massachusetts Institute of Technology."
27. Holl and Gannon, "Master Plan," 62.
28. Holl and Gannon, "Master Plan."
29. Holl.
30. Nordenson, *Guy Nordenson: Reading Structures: 39 Projects and Built Works, 1983--2011* (Zurich: Lars Müller Publishers, 2016).
31. Nordenson, *Guy Nordenson*.
32. Nina Rappaport, "Guy Nordenson and Associates." In *Support and Resist: Structural Engineers and Design Innovation*. New York: Monacelli Press, 2007. 144.
33. Rappaport, "Guy Nordenson and Associates."
34. Rappaport.
35. Steven Holl and Todd Gannon, "Perfcon." In Todd Gannon and Michael Denison, eds., *Steven Holl: Simmons Hall MIT Undergraduate Residence*. New York, NY: Princeton Architectural Press, 2004. 71.
36. Nordenson, *Guy Nordenson*.
37. Nordenson, *Guy Nordenson*.
38. Steven Holl and Todd Gannon, "Student Rooms." In Todd Gannon and Michael Denison, eds., *Steven Holl: Simmons Hall MIT Undergraduate Residence*. New York, NY: Princeton Architectural Press, 2004. 79.
39. Futagawa, "Simmons Hall, Massachusetts Institute of Technology."
40. Holl and Gannon, "Perfcon," 73.
41. Rappaport, 142.
42. Nordenson, *Guy Nordenson*.
43. Rappaport.
44. Nordenson, *Guy Nordenson*.
45. Sarah Amelar, "Steven Holl Experiments with Constructed "Porosity" in his Design for SIMMONS HALL, an Undergraduate Dorm Set in the Scientific Realm of MIT." *Architectural Record* 191, no. 5 (2003): 204.
46. Yahuda Safran, "Holl's of Hall Residence for MIT is his Most Significant Building Yet," *Domus* 858 (April 2003): 40–61.
47. Nordenson, *Guy Nordenson*.

CHAPTER 13

Case for Collaboration: Circularity

The People's Pavilion and the Urban Mining and Recycling Unit

Introduction

Given the increasing number, intensity, and size of natural and social catastrophes in the world today, it is apparent that current sustainability principles are neither explicit nor stringent enough to ignite the kind of societal and economic transformations that are needed for the health, habitability, and biodiversity of the planet. The root of the problem—environmental degradation and injustice—lies in the linear economy, a "take-make-dispose" system, which strips the Earth of natural resources and fills it and the atmosphere with waste.

This is not just an economic problem, but fundamentally, a design problem. Architects, engineers, and the construction and demolition of the built environment contribute significantly to this ecologically destructive process. In Europe, for example, the building industry is responsible for about 50% of total resource extraction while construction and demolition account for 35% of total waste.[1] In the US in 2018, construction and demolition generated 600 million tons of debris.[2] Building construction worldwide also accounts for 11% of energy sector CO_2 emissions.[3]

The environmental impacts from architecture and engineering design decisions are not only detrimental to the Earth's resources and future generations, but pollution and waste from manufacturing and demolition disproportionally affect frontline communities and people of color. Transforming this pervasive linear system into a circular system could, according to the Ellen MacArthur

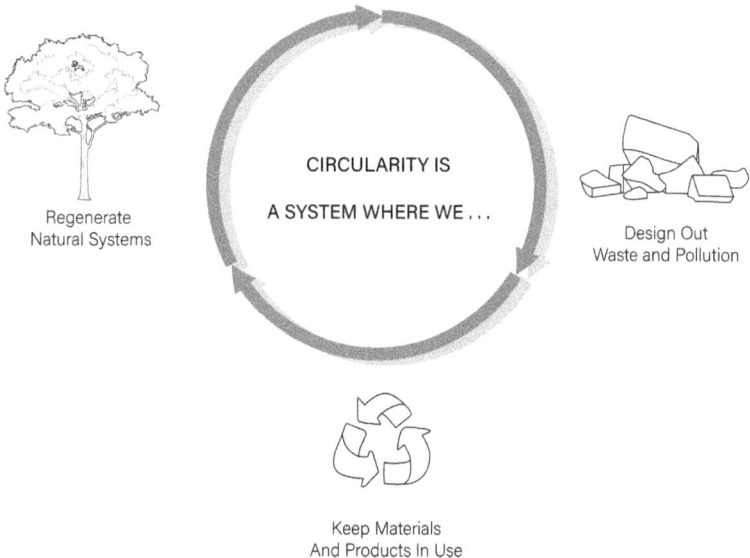

Figure 13.1 Diagram after the Ellen MacArthur Foundation explaining the circular economy. Credit: Shiori Green.

Foundation, "design out waste and pollution, keep products and materials in use, and regenerate natural systems" (Figure 13.1).[4] Increasingly, governments, institutions, and organizations recognize that a circular economy is the way forward for healthier communities and ecosystems.

Parallel with the energy transition to carbon neutrality, circularity is a material transition; both enable a carbon-neutral economy. Recognizing the health, social, environmental, and economic benefits, governments worldwide are moving toward circular systems. One response comes from the European Commission's Circular Economy Action Plan (2020), part of the European Green Deal (2019), which aims for zero waste, carbon neutrality, healthier people and environments, and a strengthened economy by 2050. In the Plan, the circular economy is championed as a vehicle for job and industry creation as well as innovation and competitiveness in the world market.

In line with the European Commission, Amsterdam adopted Circular Strategy 2020–2025, a policy that addresses food waste, consumer goods, and the built environment.[5] Toronto is also "working towards a circular economy" with the aim of achieving zero waste,[6] while Tokyo pledged a circular economy in "Zero Emission Tokyo Strategy."[7] Notably, the people of Kamikatsu, Japan, committed in the year 2000 to become a zero-waste community and twenty years later, they nearly achieved this by recycling or reusing 80% of their waste.[8] These international initiatives will undoubtedly create ripples in nearly every sector of the global economy. But what does this mean for the building industry and how will the circular economy impact the working methods of architects and engineers?

Principles of Circularity for the Building Industry

Understanding the circular economy within the context of the built environment requires reevaluating the means and methods for building delivery and the "cradle-to-grave" full life cycle of materials. The following principles derive from research including a conversation with Edwin Thie, a Senior Structural Engineer at Arup who is co-developing circular design guidelines with a cross-disciplinary Arup team for the Ellen MacArthur Foundation.

Principles of Circular Design:

1. Design for circularity starting with an interdisciplinary team: Establish shared goals amongst the architects, engineers, contractors, and owners.
2. Design for smart use of a building: Consider whether a new building is required or if an existing building can be repurposed to meet the functional needs of the client. In new buildings, minimize the footprint through smart and high utilization.
3. Design for reduced extraction of raw materials: If a new building is required, the full life cycle of the building and all of its materials must be considered. Work with renewable, reused, and recycled materials from the start. Consider the reuse and recycling potential of materials after the service life of the building.
4. Design for clean material use: Use materials that are renewable, nonpolluting, nontoxic, low, or zero carbon. This means understanding the environmental impacts of the material flows from extraction through production, construction, use, reuse, repurposing, and so forth.
5. Design for spatial flexibility: Embed adaptability and flexibility to ensure serviceable use of the building for as long as possible through change over time according to user needs.
6. Design for future use: Construct connections that are reversible to support disassembly and reuse; limit in-situ concrete stitches, steel welds, and glues unless they are biodegradable.
7. Design empathically for future generations: Create beauty so that people will take care of the building and feel invested in its longevity. Support regeneration of natural habitats to ensure a healthy planet for the future.

The Drive for Circular Communities Requires Collaboration, Research, and Entrepreneurship

Recognizing that resource consumption and production are at the core of the waste-based linear economy, this means that designers must consider building materials and assembly methods from the start of a project. Peter van Assche, founder of Amsterdam-based bureau SLA and an early champion of circularity in buildings, explains that circular design requires totally rethinking traditional working methods that have divided the architecture, engineering, and construction disciplines into adversarial silos.

> This layer model of hierarchical organization has to flip 90 degrees into a model where you share responsibilities, where you share communication. Architects need to talk to the building suppliers and the structural engineers talk to installers--everybody should talk to everybody, because you have to develop new methods and processes to facilitate the fluid dynamics of building in this circular way. It demands a whole new way of working.[9]

He speaks from the experience of working on multiple circular projects including the People's Pavilion, a temporary structure, made entirely out of borrowed materials.

Case 1: People's Pavilion[10]

In 2017, bureau SLA & Overtreders W received the commission to design a pavilion to host events during Dutch Design Week in Eindhoven, the Netherlands (Figure 13.2). The commissioners asked the architects to make the temporary pavilion so sustainable that people would be talking

Figure 13.2 Exterior view of the People's Pavilion in Eindhoven, the Netherlands by bureau SLA & Overtreders W in collaboration with a team including Arup. Credit: Filip Dujardin.

about for 10 or 15 years. Bureau SLA's van Assche describes that "It seemed crazy to build something from raw materials for such a short period," so they decided the entire pavilion would be constructed from borrowed materials and returned in the same condition as they received them. Edwin Thie, Arup Senior Structural Engineer, worked with the architects on the project from early design and was challenged by the notion of designing for deconstruction. "So that of course meant that from a structural perspective, the traditional way of connecting materials with nails, bolts or glue would not work because they always involve damaging the material and causing a loss of value."[11] The architects began by developing a sketch design that used standard lengths of materials and contacted suppliers to borrow components starting with a concrete pile supplier (most buildings are built on piles in the Netherlands due to the soft soil conditions, so these are common building components). The supplier agreed to lend 12 piles for the 250-square-meter (2700-square-foot) pavilion, which the team used as columns. Lightweight timber beams were sourced from a supplier premarket and unplaned (timber beams are rough cut to size from trees and then planed into standard sizes before being sold by suppliers), while the hybrid framing system was connected to the columns with tensioned industrial ratchet straps, and the standard-sized timber elements were held together using metal straps (Figure 13.3). "Friction fit" is not something calculable within structural analysis software or a standard way of meeting building code

Figure 13.3 View of a detail of the People's Pavilion structure connections using straps to connect the concrete columns and the wood beams. Credit: Jeroen van der Wielen.

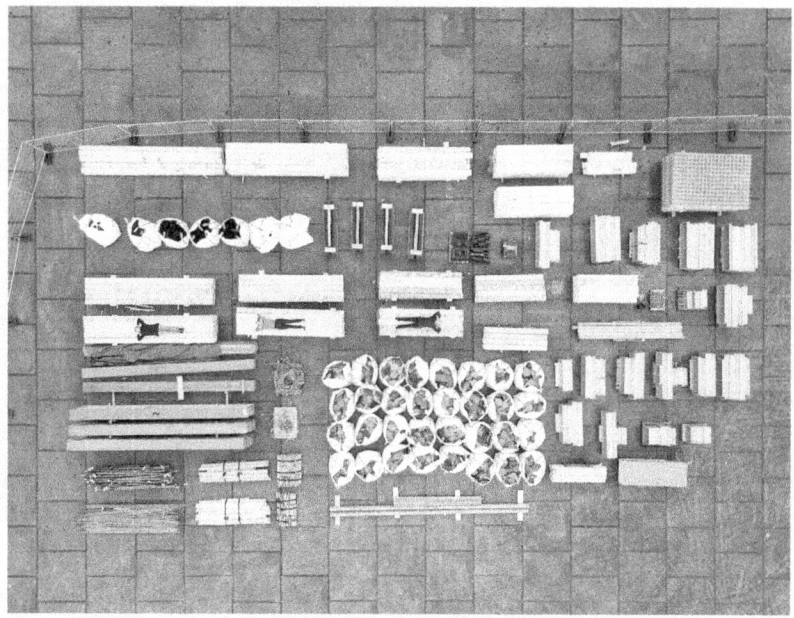

Figure 13.4 Aerial view of all of the materials used in the People's Pavilion after deconstruction. Credit: Jeroen van der Wielen.

requirements, so the design group teamed with the University of Eindhoven where full-scale mockups of these modular beams and strapped connections could be tested for strength and stiffness. Architect van Assche explains the ambitions, "Through this research, we wanted to meet regulations—not only festival regulations, but all building regulations—and it did."[12] For the cladding, they collected plastic waste from Eindhoven residents and extruded it into colored panels to wrap the exterior, later returning the panels to the residents after the festival ended. The rest of the borrowed components were also returned to their suppliers, completing the circle and successfully eliminating waste from the building process (Figure 13.4).

Peter van Assche describes the ethos that guided the People's Pavilion and subsequent work, "At a minimum, a circular building should be generative. Buildings should not die but regenerate either as a building or (6400-square-feet) building elements or building materials."[13] Bureau SLA and Overtreders W continue to develop circular designs including a research center for the University of Amsterdam that is 100% circular. The 600-square-meter (6400-square-feet) building will house labs, office spaces and ten affordable apartments with adaptable elements that allow the users to change the spaces over time. They are also designing a 7,000-square-meter (75000-square-feet) housing complex in Amsterdam with 70 apartments on land owned by the city. van Assche is optimistic and excited about the shift to circularity, "changing the way we live, behave, and use buildings—the implications for design are far stretching and there is a world to gain."[14]

Excited by the People's Pavilion, Edwin Thie is now a Consultant of Circularity for Arup and is currently working on several circular infrastructure projects for the Netherlands highways agency including a timber bridge concept that is carbon-neutral and designed for adaptation. The bridge can be widened if another driving lane is needed in the future, and the main components can be reused at the end of service life of the bridge. Incorporating renewable heavy timber reduces the carbon load and is a material that can easily outlast the government-required 100-year lifespan when protected from weather exposure. By designing for deconstruction, they thought beyond 100 years: Thie explains,

> Because we have built in flexibility, the service life can be extended (currently most highway bridges don't reach their design life, because they cannot easily adapt to changing needs). In the future, we'll either need to adapt it to changing needs or disassemble it to use somewhere else. The main beams that span the road could be used in a new bridge or a sports hall, for example.[15]

These smart measures ensure future resilience, thereby guaranteeing that investing in circular strategies will ultimately pay off many times over.

Case 2: Urban Mining and Recycling Unit

Keeping materials in circulation within the city is the thinking behind the Urban Mining and Recycling (UMAR) Unit designed by Werner Sobek with Dirk E. Hebel and Felix Heisel, as part of the NEST[16] research building at the Swiss Federal Laboratories for Material Science and Technology (Figure 13.5). Keeping the full life cycle of materials in mind means thinking about their sourcing, use in the building, and eventual reuse, recycling, or biodegradability. In this sense, "UMAR functions simultaneously as a material laboratory and a temporary material storage."[17] The project uses modularity and prefabrication in the design of materials and parts that can be borrowed, leased, made, or purchased and then assembled without glue so that they can be harvested from the building cleanly. Included are "cultivated mycelium boards, innovative recycled bricks, repurposed insulation materials, leased floor coverings

CASE FOR COLLABORATION: CIRCULARITY

Figure 13.5 Urban Mining and Recycling (UMAR) Unit by Werner Sobek with Dirk E. Hebel and Felix Heisel. Credit: Wojciech Zawarski.

Figure 13.6 UMAR's pipes and cables were connected reversibly at the module borders. Credit: © Zooey Braun.

and a multifunctional solar thermal installation."[18] A research team continues to monitor the performance of the building and durability of the materials through post-occupancy studies.

The UMAR Unit proves the viability of circular principles, but the researchers recognize that scaling up the processes of material streams to the size of cities will require new systems for tracking, sourcing, and relaying material.[19] The architect and engineer partners also reflected that UMAR demonstrated, "the importance of interdisciplinary teamwork [involving all professions] in design and construction ... from the very beginning of the process until the very end"[20] to create not just a new building, but new procedures for design, procurement, construction, and continued use of the materials. (Figure 13.6)

Frontiers Ahead

A first principle of circularity and waste reduction involves keeping buildings in use for as long as possible. A case study life cycle analysis (LCA) comparison of an adaptive reuse building compared to ground-up construction, "showed 53–75% reductions across 6 different environmental impact categories when the renovation was compared to a new construction scenario."[21] The article goes on to explain "The most significant components added during renovation were the roof, access floors, and new windows, while the new construction scenario was overwhelmingly burdened by manufacturing intensive structural (concrete and steel) and envelope components (brick and terracotta walls)."[22] Furthermore, the study highlighted that although LCA typically assumes a 50- or 60-year lifespan, structural materials like concrete, masonry, and steel can remain in use for much longer,[23] making a compelling argument to extend time periods for cradle-to-grave cost comparisons between adaptive reuse and newly constructed buildings.

By upending traditional industry practices, circular design provides a new frontier for collaboration among architects and engineers to use design innovation and imagination to create healthier, stronger communities. Architect Peter van Assche describes that designers may "feel the weight of guilt of half of the waste coming from building and infrastructure," which may be the impetus for change, but instead of thinking of a major industry transformation as overwhelming, it helps to think of it as a design problem: "Fundamentally rethinking the design process from the start is very exciting ... circular thinking offers opportunities. If you think about disassembly not as waste producing, but as a source for materials, disassembly becomes a positive," and a means to keep materials local and in circulation, thereby eliminating carbon-producing and resource-depleting extraction and manufacturing practices. Collaborating on these new systems opens a world of research and invention for practitioners and students, designers and contractors … Well put by van Assche, "You can feel the expansion of possibilities that this way of thinking allows us."[24]

Notes

1. European Commission—European Commission, "New Circular Economy Action Plan," *Text*, accessed August 5, 2020, https://ec.europa.eu/commission/presscorner/detail/en/ip_20_420.
2. OLEM US EPA, "Sustainable Management of Construction and Demolition Materials," *Overviews and Factsheets, US EPA*, accessed December 2020, https://www.epa.gov/smm/sustainable-management-construction-and-demolition-materials.
3. "Global Status Report 2017," World Green Building Council, accessed May 18, 2021, https://www.worldgbc.org/news-media/global-status-report-2017.
4. "What Is a Circular Economy? | Ellen MacArthur Foundation," accessed May 6, 2021, https://www.ellenmacarthurfoundation.org/circular-economy/concept.
5. Amsterdam, "Policy: Circular Economy," webpagina, English site (Gemeente Amsterdam), accessed May 6, 2021, https://www.amsterdam.nl/en/policy/sustainability/circular-economy/.
6. "Working towards a Circular Economy," City of Toronto (City of Toronto, August 9, 2018), Toronto, Ontario, Canada, https://www.toronto.ca/services-payments/recycling-organics-garbage/long-term-waste-strategy/working-toward-a-circular-economy/.
7. "Zero Emission Tokyo Strategy | 東京都環境局," accessed May 20, 2021, https://www.kankyo.metro.tokyo.lg.jp/en/about_us/zero_emission_tokyo/strategy.html.
8. McCurry, Justin, "'No-Waste' Japanese Village Is a Peek into Carbon-Neutral Future," *The Guardian*, accessed March 20, 2020, sec. World news. https://www.theguardian.com/world/2020/mar/20/no-waste-japanese-village-is-a-peek-into-carbon-neutral-future.
9. Peter van Assche, Interview with bureau SLA, Peter van Assche, Zoom, May 4, 2021.
10. Architects: Overtreders W, bureau SLA; Manufacturers: DEGO, Elektroned, Govaerts, Heezen, IJB groep, Keizersgrachtkerk, Logistiek Concurrent, Morssinkhof, Pretty Plastic, Stiho group, TETRiS, Van Happen; Lead Architects: Hester van Dijk, Peter van Assche, Reinder Bakker; Structural Engineering: Arup; Urban Mining Advice: New Horizon; Main Builders: Ham & Sybesma.
11. Edwin Thie, Interview with Arup, Edwin Thie, Zoom, April 1, 2021.
12. van Assche, Interview by authors.
13. van Assche.
14. van Assche.
15. Thie, Interview by authors.
16. Next Evolution in Sustainable Building Technologies.
17. Circular Construction Lab at Cornell AAP, "Urban Mining and Recycling (UMAR) Unit," accessed May 4, 2021, http://ccl.aap.cornell.edu/urban-mining-and-recycling-umar-unit/.
18. "Urban Mining and Recycling (UMAR) Unit," *Circular Construction Lab at Cornell AAP* (blog), accessed May 4, 2021, http://ccl.aap.cornell.edu/urban-mining-and-recycling-umar-unit/.
19. Felix Heisel, Dirk E. Hebel, and Werner Sobek, "Resource-Respectful Construction – the Case of the Urban Mining and Recycling Unit (UMAR)," *IOP Conference Series: Earth and Environmental Science* 225 (February 2019): 012049, https://doi.org/10.1088/1755-1315/225/1/012049.
20. Heisel, Hebel, and Sobek, "Resource-Respectful Construction."
21. Vaclav Hasik et al., "Comparative Whole-Building Life Cycle Assessment of Renovation and New Construction," *Building and Environment* 161 (August 15, 2019): 106218, https://doi.org/10.1016/j.buildenv.2019.106218.
22. Hasik et al.
23. Hasik et al.
24. van Assche.

Case Studies in Collaboration: Transportation Buildings

CHAPTER 14

Amman Queen Alia International Airport

Integrating Modularity and Constructability

Architects:	Foster + Partners
Collaborating Architect:	Maisam—Dar Al-Omran JV
Structural Engineer:	Buro Happold (Conceptual Engineer and Construction Advisors)
Quantity Surveyor:	Davis Langdon
M+E Engineer:	Buro Happold (Conceptual Engineer)
Landscape Architect:	Dar Al-Handasah
Lighting Engineer:	World of Lights
Additional Consultants:	NACO, ADPi, Zuhair Fayez Partnership, Rahe Kraft
Design + Build Main Contractor:	Joannou & Paraskevaides (Overseas) Ltd, J&P-AVAX S.A.
Client:	Airport International Group, The Hashemite Kingdom of Jordan Ministry of Trans, Joannou & Paraskevaides (Overseas) Ltd, J&P-AVAX S.A., Airport International Group P.S.C.

Although multiple experts worked together on the design of the Queen Alia International Airport, the case study focuses on the collaboration of Foster + Partners and Buro Happold.

Foster + Partners

Foster + Partners was founded by Norman Foster in 1967 in London, but is now a global practice owned by all 140 partners. Over the past four decades, the studio has pioneered integrated, sustainable design solutions through a strikingly wide range of work, from urban plans, public infrastructure, airports, civic and cultural buildings, offices and workplaces to private houses and product design. The practice has an extensive reach, with buildings on six continents and designs for Lunar and Mars Habitats. Since its inception, the firm has received hundreds of awards for excellence including the *Architect's Journal Practice of the Year*.

Projects have included the redevelopment of the Reichstag, the New German Parliament in Berlin and the Hongkong and Shanghai Bank Headquarters, as well as Apple Park, a LEED Platinum building on a 175-acre (71-hectare) green campus powered by 100% renewable energy. The portfolio of work demonstrates decades of accumulated expertise, sparking critic Paul Goldberger to say, "Foster buildings … don't show their effort."[1] In describing the trajectory of the firm's work, Foster said, "The only constant is change and change is about evolution, it's about innovation, it's about new ways of doing things."[2] Foster designed the office's collegiate structure, which focuses on collaboration, innovation, and research, enabling a rigorous approach to the work, and ultimately, longevity for the office.

Attuned to evolving forms of practice, Foster + Partners has restructured the office to align with growing expertise. Starting in 2004, the office was divided into design groups, each led by a Senior Partner; these studios now include Design Management, Environmental Engineering, Industrial Design, Interiors, Research, Structural Engineering, Sustainability, Workplace Consultancy, and Urban Design. These groups are supported by specialist teams including experts in materials, environmental audits, and modeling. In 2010, Foster positioned integrated design at the forefront of the firm's mission and added two in-house engineering groups. Foster + Partners continues to amass recognition and in 2019, was the 14th largest practice in the world.

Buro Happold

Buro Happold was founded by British engineer, Edmund "Ted" Happold, in 1976. Happold worked at Arup before starting an office in Bath to partner with Frei Otto on the King's Office and Council of Ministers project in Saudi Arabia. The early work in form-finding and complex geometries seeded the firm's commitment to research and design innovation, which has continued throughout the office's nearly 40-year history. In Peter Davey's *Engineering for a Finite Planet*, Ted Happold is quoted as saying that engineering, "is intensely creative; at its best it is art in that it extends people's vision of what is possible and gives them new insights."[3] Buro Happold has a formidable record for design innovation, which is why they are enlisted on some of the most complex projects. The firm now employs 1,900 staff offering a wide range of services in 26 offices across the globe.

Buro Happold's first office was located in Bath, and now there are six offices in the UK. Wolf Mangelsdorf, writing as the Head of Structural Engineering in the London office at the time, describes the firm's philosophy in his article *Structuring Strategies for Complex Geometries*,

> …structural engineering has to be a creative contribution to the design process, so that a full integration and coordination of aesthetical and physical aspects can be achieved. This relies completely on the development of engineering concepts that understand and facilitate the design, and at the same time close collaboration with the architect, manufacturer and other design disciplines.[4]

The London office has worked on such world-renowned projects as the British Museum Great Court with Foster + Partners, which won a British Institute of Civil Engineers Special Award, the London 2012 Olympic stadium and the Tottenham Hotspur Football Club stadium with Populous, completed in 2019.

Introduction to Queen Alia International Airport: Design Influences

When examining the diverse body of Foster + Partners' portfolio, there are a few recurrent themes. Exposed structure is often used as a means of providing clarity and elegance to the form and experience of the built work. In the 1970s and 1980s, the firm was viewed as championing the "high-tech" style. In a 1994 article, "Architecture and Structure," Foster described that "The visual dimension of a structure is also its spiritual dimension: how it will look, and how it will work, become conceptually inseparable throughout the process of design."[5] Although the tone and aesthetic of the work has evolved with the firm, exposed structure continues to be a feature of many projects; however, every design is a unique response to the site, demands of the brief, environment, culture, and many different users.

Foster describes the importance of the experiential qualities of the architecture and the goal to "...reinvent concepts like an airport in such a way that the experience of an airport will be uplifting. An airport has gotten to the point of crowds and security that it's a kind of reviled building type."[6] Foster + Partners revolutionized the design of airports, first with Stansted Airport in London (1981-1991) where the designers shifted the services under the floor in order to create a lighter roof structure with skylights. Given the plans for phase growth of Stansted, the architects decided to use a modular system, which proved highly influential for later projects, including the Queen Alia International Airport (Figure 14.1). Foster describes the firm's approach for their first airport:

> At Stansted the base or "trunk" of the trees are literally rooted in the distribution of air and artificial lighting from the undercroft below. The "branches" spread out to support the most elegantly minimal roof, whose function is only to provide shelter from the elements and to let in light from the sky above. Compare this with the massive roof and supporting structure for a traditional airport with its need to carry the weight of the mechanical equipment above the roof and below it all the usual ductwork, fluorescent lighting, cables and suspended ceilings. By comparison, our concept for Stansted is radical even if it does mark a return to an earlier tradition of less mechanistic buildings - to suggest a newer generation which are elegantly comfortable but also energy conscious.[7]

Figure 14.1 Aerial view of the Queen Alia International Airport showing the modular structure. Foster + Partners, Buro Happold, Queen Alia International Airport, Amman, Jordan, 2013. Credit: Nigel Young/Foster + Partners.

In addition to reducing energy consumption and providing flexibility, the design also dramatically transformed the airport experience, and subsequently, the firm has been commissioned to design multiple airports and transport stations. These include Chek Lap Kok Airport in Hong Kong, completed in 1998; Beijing Airport, which, until recently, was the largest building in the world and constructed in just four years by 50,000 workers in time for the 2008 Beijing Olympics; the first station for commercial space transport, Spaceport America; and Tocumen International Airport in Panama completed in 2021.

Project Overview

In 2005, Foster + Partners was approached by the Jordanian Royal Development Company to produce designs for a number of projects, including the airport located 35 kilometers from the capital city of Jordan, Amman. With a growing customer base, the clients envisioned that a new airport would create a gateway and increased tourism for the country (Figure 14.2). The team composed of architects and engineers did an initial 10-week study to show how the existing airport could be expanded. This preliminary scheme, presented to the royal household, was well received. Very shortly into the development, however, the team determined (with full support of the client) that in looking towards the future of the airport, a ground-up strategy would have more longevity than remodeling the existing structure. The World Bank funded further design work, which was developed into a tender package. The project construction was an $800 million, privately funded venture and is operated by Airport International Group (AIG), a consortium of Jordanian and international companies.

Figure 14.2 The airport is envisioned as a gateway to Jordan. Foster + Partners, Buro Happold, Queen Alia International Airport, Amman, Jordan, 2013. Credit: Nigel Young/Foster + Partners.

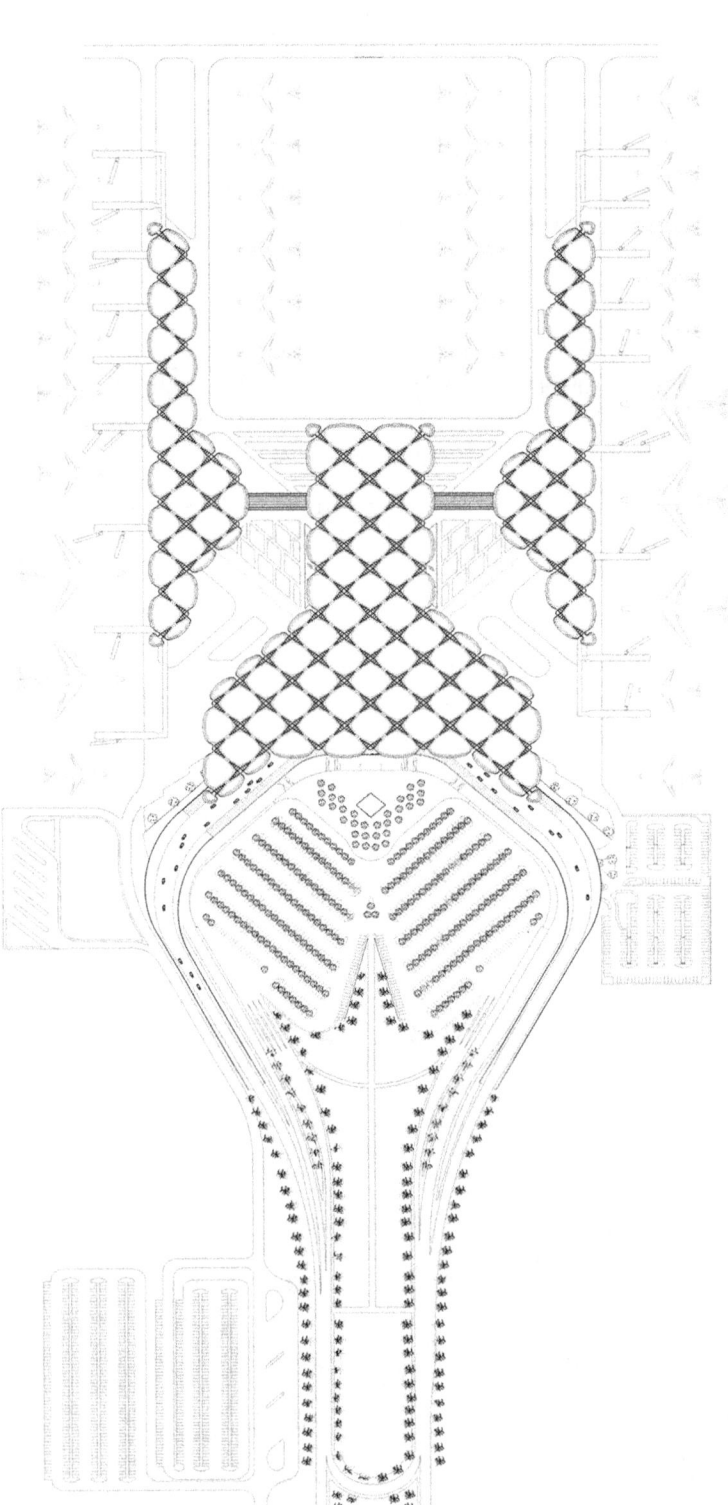

Figure 14.3 The 100,000-square-meter project is organized symmetrically around a central axis. Foster + Partners, Buro Happold, Queen Alia International Airport, Amman, Jordan, 2013. Credit: Foster + Partners.

The 100,000-square-meter (over 1,000,000-square-foot) building is symmetrically organized with two terminal piers extending from either side of a central building that contains duty free shops, newsstands, banks, restaurants and passenger lounges, as well as offices and storage (Figure 14.3). The two piers hug a central courtyard filled with trees that create shade for families greeting visitors and also filter air before it moves through the building. The glazing surrounding the perimeter provides an open feeling and a visual connection to the airport runways as well as natural day lighting. Heat is mitigated with a louver system and the use of thermal mass, essential for an environmentally responsible building in the extreme temperatures of Jordan. The concrete enables passive environmental control through thermal mass as the building slowly warms up throughout the day and releases heat in the cool evening hours. Perhaps for these reasons, the airport consistently wins the Customer Experience Award for the best airport in the Middle East. In 2018, the airport was also the first in the Middle East to achieve carbon neutrality (Figure 14.4).

Figure 14.4 The mullions curve to reflect the domed roof. Foster + Partners, Buro Happold, Queen Alia International Airport, Amman, Jordan, 2013. Credit: Nigel Young/ Foster + Partners.

The Team and Working Methods

The team that designed the building included architects and engineers as well as many of Foster + Partners' in-house specialists. The Partner in charge of the project was Jonathan Parr, a Deputy Group Leader at Foster + Partners, and the project architect was Associate Partner, Darryn Holder. Parr started working with Foster + Partners in 1992 on Hong Kong International Airport the cargo terminal and transportation building. The London office of Buro Happold was also part of the initial design team and included Senior Partner and Chairman, Mike Cook, Senior Partner and environmental engineer, Neil Billett and Group Director and structural engineer, George Keliris. Keliris describes the working relationship with Jonathan Parr and Foster + Partners around the world, including Jordan, "Being in London was quite useful, because much of the discussion was face-to-face, and this allowed Buro Happold to talk through the designs and influence them from the engineering perspective."[8]

The multidisciplinary team would gather around a table, discuss ideas and then they would work through the design ideas through visualization. During this process, Keliris notes, "We were challenged by the architects to not use a typical, normative structure, but something that was iconic and different. That meant that we challenged the architecture as well, ensuring that the solution was the result of our in-depth collaboration."[9] Keliris goes on to describe the rewarding aspects of working as a "creative engineer" and credited offices like Foster + Partners that encourage innovation in structural design.[10]

Foster + Partners has always partnered closely with engineers, and Norman Foster made a decision to integrate engineers into the office in 2010. The QAIA project was designed before this restructuring, but the working mode used on the project was very similar to what is described in the firm's mission of integrated design:

> Foster + Partners understands that the best design comes from a completely integrated approach from conception to completion.... By doing so, we believe that the [disciplines] can learn from one another and combine their knowledge to devise wholly integrated design solutions.[11]

The architecture–engineering design team for QAIA evolved to include members of support groups including the Specialist Modeling Group (SMG). Xavier De Kestelier, a Partner at Foster + Partners and joint head of SMG, worked with the firm from 2002, supporting project teams in areas of computation and geometry at various stages from conceptual development to rationalization and construction. De Kestelier explains the philosophy about involving engineers early,

> The form might be driven by various things at the same time--aesthetics, rationalization, structural optimization—all these things probably have their own perfect shape and it's a conversation amongst everyone to get that right. It's not like we make the shape we want and then give it to the engineer to figure out how to make it stand up—it's always a conversation.[12]

For Queen Alia International Airport, the Specialist Modeling Group worked with the multidisciplinary team to develop modeling strategies, constructability rationalization, and fabrication support.

Development of the Structure and Fabrication

Parr relates that "the decision to make the roof out of largely precast components sitting on an otherwise very straight-forward in-situ concrete slab was decided quite early on" (Figure 14.5a–b).[13] A precast, modular roof structure was chosen for a number of reasons. Firstly, the modular system had proven effective in Stansted Airport, which provided QAIA's "genetic code."[14] Because there was a Design and Build contract, the contractor came into the design process early on and played a pivotal role in moving forward with the decision to employ the modular system to facilitate construction. The systematic approach was also critical to creating the kind of flexibility that had proven so successful in Stansted Airport. As Parr points out, "Airports, like many infrastructure projects, respond to a need at a given time, but they have to be flexible."[15] Stansted grew in scale during construction and the Queen Alia traffic is also growing at a faster rate than expected. Since the number of passengers is

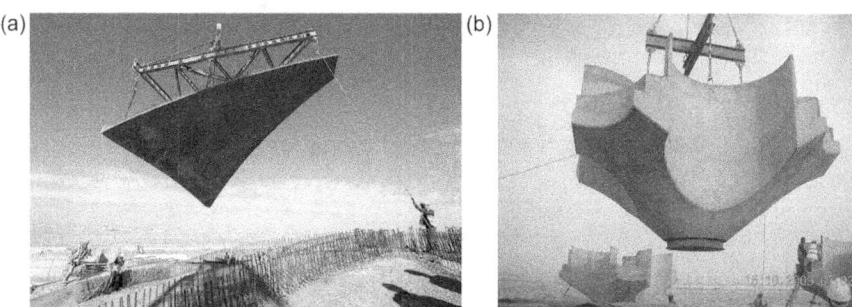

Figure 14.5a, b Precast components craned to the site. Foster + Partners, Buro Happold, Queen Alia International Airport, Amman, Jordan, 2013. Credit: Nigel Young/Foster + Partners.

anticipated to increase from 3.5 million to 12 million by 2030, the modular design allows the airport to grow by 6% each year.

The shape of the modules grew from a desire to create a more fluid and welcoming environment, and the efficient geometry of the umbrella structures enables wider spans (Figure 14.6). The 24-meter (79-foot) column spacing opened up the floor areas for circulation, permitting visitors to see signage from a distance and more easily navigate the airport. The domed, warm-hued concrete creates a grand, monumental space, thereby producing an uplifting and celebratory experience. There are 127 modules composed of a simple set of four module types: a field unit, a half unit, edge, and corner units. Each module has the same cantilever and shared dimensions, which permitted an efficient use of formwork and assured constructability. According to Parr,

> The beauty of the modular system is that once you work out the initial kinks in manufacturing, the rest of the building follows suit. It's a highly repetitive building, which means that it's not constantly setting new challenges; once you figure out how it works, it continues to work the same way.[16]

This approach to structure is consistent with Foster + Partners' search for integrity in their design work and desire to convey buildable ideas to their clients. Parr remarks that constructability and flexibility drove design discussions, so when presenting the modular structure to the client, they

> would have the comfort of knowing that what they see in visualization is eminently practical and buildable and it's not just an image …

Figure 14.6 Interior view showing the openness afforded by the umbrella structures. Foster + Partners, Buro Happold, Queen Alia International Airport, Amman, Jordan, 2013. Credit: Nigel Young/Foster + Partners.

Figure 14.7 Openings in the shells provide natural light and reduce the energy load for the building. Credit: Nigel Young/Foster + Partners.

It's a very honest way of working and part of a process, and we hope that it gives people reassurance. So even in the early days, we were showing a roof made of components.[17]

The form of Queen Alia International Airport has been compared to desert palms and Bedouin tents that give the structure a feeling of place. The openings at the column-beam junctions provide natural light (and also remove weight from the structure), reducing energy loads for lighting the large terminal (Figure 14.7). Keliris describes that the openings were also a strategy to create structural efficiency and make the "enormous, heavy, hard-working roof structure light and elegant." The team arrived at "formed precast X-beams that follow forces and allow for the openings making architecture and structure integrated" (Figure 14.8).[18] Texture on the concrete at the openings diffuses daylighting throughout the airport, reducing electricity consumption and energy loads.

Constructing the Structural Modules

The modular system facilitated prefabrication, offering many advantages including a faster construction process (Figure 14.9). The contractors set up a batching plant adjacent to the site. In describing the concrete, Parr said that it was composed of "locally sourced materials, which apart from the very fact that that's the sensible and sustainable thing to do, it means from an emotive and symbolic point of view, the building is made of Jordan."[19] With a reliable supply of material, this assured that the quality and texture of the concrete would remain consistent throughout the project.

CASE STUDIES IN COLLABORATION: TRANSPORTATION BUILDINGS

Figure 14.8 The precast X-beams and roof shells. Foster + Partners, Buro Happold, Queen Alia International Airport, Amman, Jordan, 2013. Credit: Nigel Young/Foster + Partners.

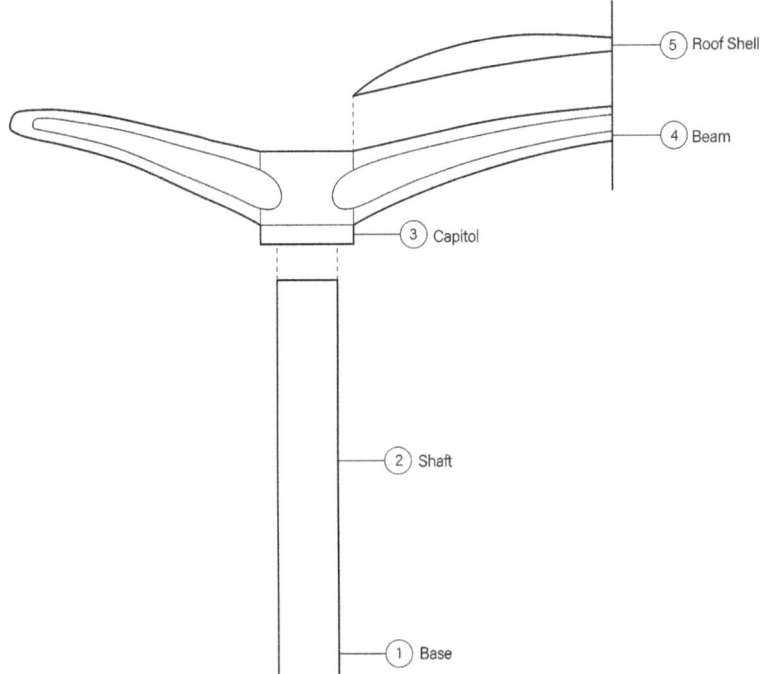

Figure 14.9 Diagram illustrating the cast-in-place columns capped with modular precast concrete elements. A topping slab was poured on the roof for lateral stability. Credit: Shiori Green.

The formwork for prefabrication was manufactured at a ship-building plant in Greece that had experience in molding steel in doubly curved shapes. The steel enabled a very smooth, crisp finish and stature to the concrete and also allowed the contractors to reuse the molds in a way that timber would not have

Figure 14.10 The modular roof allows for a systematic approach to construction. Foster + Partners, Buro Happold, Queen Alia International Airport, Amman, Jordan, 2013. Credit: Nigel Young/Foster + Partners.

permitted. Foster + Partners' Specialist Modeling Group provided a digital model that enabled the ship builders to program their Computer Numerically Controlled (CNC) machines to cut the 5 millimeter (0.2 inches) steel and mold it to create the formwork for the roof shells. They also fabricated the steel formwork for the X-beams, which were 19.4 meters (64 feet) long but needed to be cut in half for transport to the contractor's fabrication plant in Jordan, adjacent to the building site (Figure 14.10).

The 308 X-beams weigh just over 19 metric tons (over 40,000 pounds) each and form a network that supports the roof shells (Figure 14.11). Each of the 127 domes is composed of parts, resulting in 720 shell components that needed to be transported to the site with a crane. The parts were made at the offsite facility in assembly-line fashion, identified with a code number and lifted with the crane a short distance to become part of the building. In order to ensure that these parts were as lightweight as possible (relatively speaking), they used "a high-performance steel fiber-reinforced mix with a maximum aggregate size of 10 millimeters (3/8 of an inch)."[20]

A cast-in-place strategy was used for the concrete to the tops of the columns including the foundation, pile caps, and ground floor slab. One area of columns is double height to allow for a mezzanine level (Figure 14.12). The roof, on the other hand, including the column heads, beams spanning between and roof shells were all precast. Once positioned on site, a layer of in-situ concrete was poured on top of the roof to stabilize the structure and allow for tolerance in assembling each of the dome's multiple precast parts. It was a challenge to level all the columns so that the roof would sit squarely on top, but given the repetition of the system, the leveling strategy could be applied to each column.

Figure 14.11 Foster + Partners Smart Geometry Group developed a very detailed precise model that was used for fabrication and construction administration. Foster + Partners, Buro Happold, Queen Alia International Airport, Amman, Jordan, 2013. Credit: Nigel Young/Foster + Partners.

Despite its remarkable presence and character, raw concrete is not very common in Jordan and the designers needed to do some convincing to preserve the bare material. Parr describes that

> Concrete can do fantastic things, and in our eyes, can produce a beautiful product; it's not merely structural-- it can provide character. We were so pleased with the quality of the finish that was being achieved in the early mock-ups that we became convinced that the concrete should be exposed. The light had a lovely reflection on the concrete, so we believed that it should be left in its natural state, without finishes. It's been appreciated by the world press, the people who go there, and contractors…. At the opening ceremony, people

Figure 14.12 Interior view of one of the terminals. Foster + Partners, Buro Happold, Queen Alia International Airport, Amman, Jordan, 2013. Credit: Nigel Young/Foster + Partners.

said that it was the right thing to do, it makes it special. That's all we were trying to do, we were just trying to make the building special for everyone who will use it and for the people who took part in making it and for the people who run it and the people of Jordan. It really is something that belongs to them in a very special way and on that level is why it succeeds as a building more than anything else, it really does belong there; it comes from Jordan.[21]

Notes

1. *How Much Does Your Building Weigh, Mr. Foster?* Film, New York, Art Commissioners, 2012.
2. ArchDaily, "AD Interviews: Norman Foster," *ArchDaily*, accessed October 12, 2012, http://www.archdaily.com/280814/ad-interviews-norman-foster/.
3. Peter Davey, *Engineering for a Finite Planet Sustainable Solutions by Buro Happold* (Basel: Birkhäuser, 2009), 9.
4. Wolf Mangelsdorf, "Structuring Strategies for Complex Geometries," *Architectural Design* 80, no. 4 (2010): 40–45.
5. Norman Foster, "Architecture and Structure," www.fosterandpartners.com/data/practice-data/essays/essay14.
6. ArchDaily, "AD Interviews: Norman Foster."
7. Foster, "Architecture and Structure."
8. George Keliris, Interview by the authors. Phone interview. London, England, June 21, 2013.
9. Keliris, Interview by the authors.
10. Keliris.
11. Foster + Partners. "Integrated Design | Foster + Partners." Accessed November 9, 2013. https://www.fosterandpartners.com/profile/integrated-design/.
12. Xavier De Kestelier, Interview by the authors. Phone interview. London, England, June 18, 2013.
13. Jonathan Parr, Interview by the authors. Phone interview. London, England, June 18, 2013.
14. De Kestelier, Interview by the authors.
15. Parr, Interview by the authors.
16. Parr.
17. Parr.
18. Keliris.
19. Parr.
20. T.R. Witcher, "Jordan Airport Extension Reflects Local Influences," *American Society of Civil Engineers*, http://www.asce.org/CEMagazine/Article.aspx?id=23622325664.
21. Parr.

CHAPTER 15

Berlin Hauptbahnhof
Collaborating on Lightness and Large Spans

Client:	Deutsche Bahn AG
Architects:	Gerkan, Marg and Partners (gmp) Meinhard von Gerkan and Jürgen Hilmer
Structural Engineering:	Schlaich, Bergermann und Partner, IVZ/ Emch + Berger
Lighting design:	Peter Andres + Conceptlicht GmbH
Mechanical services:	Ingenieurgesellschaft Höpfner

The design of the Berlin Hauptbahnhof involved many firms and individuals, but the focus of this discussion is on the partnership between Schlaich, Bergermann und Partner and von Gerkan, Marg, and Partners.

Schlaich, Bergermann und Partner

Schlaich, Bergermann und Partner is a German engineering firm co-founded by Jörg Schlaich, a German structural engineer who studied civil engineering at Stuttgart University and the Technical University of Berlin and Rudolph Bergermann. Although formally enrolled as an engineering student, Schlaich attended architecture courses and would have tried to qualify in both areas but for the difficulty in resolving the competing timetables of the two schools that were situated in two different campuses in Stuttgart. He was heavily influenced by his sister, who trained as an architect first at Stuttgart University and later at IIT under Mies van der Rohe. She introduced him to many structural engineers whose work was of interest to architects, such as Robert Maillart and Pier Luigi Nervi.[1]

Schlaich is a professor at Stuttgart University and a partner in the firm he founded. In 1972, he was the engineer of the roof for the Munich Olympic Arena designed by fellow German architect/engineer Frei Otto (Figure 15.1). The resolution and construction of the prestressed cable net roof required the development of one of the first computer programs to help design such structures to be used at this scale in professional practice.

Under Schlaich's direction, the firm has designed and built many pedestrian bridges in a spare, elegant style that is always structurally expressive. This work won the firm many accolades including multiple awards for innovation and design. Schlaich emphasizes the importance of the pedestrian bridges to the firm's practice due to their intimate scale. As structures that humans interact with closely, he believes they must be as carefully designed as any building. This humanist concern for the user

Figure 15.1 The cable net structure consists of saddle-shaped surfaces supported by edge cables and masts, which are in turn anchored by cable stays. Frei Otto and Schlaich Bergermann und Partner, Munich Olympic Arena, Munich, Germany, 1972. Credit: Schlaich Bergermann und Partner/Hans Schober.

Figure 15.2 Glass Canopy at the Light Rail Station Plaza, a suspended glass roof, Schlaich Bergermann und Partner in collaboration with architects Auer and Weber, Heilbronn, Germany, 2001. Credit: Schlaich Bergermann und Partner/Hans Schober.

is at the forefront of the firm's philosophy.[2] The engineers were amongst the first to experiment with grid shell glass roofs and facades, concentrating on form-finding to create shapes that would self structure, integrating the load carrying structure and glass mullions as one system. They also experimented with forms that could be stiffened with the minimum of extraneous structure such as prestressed cables and thin struts, thus minimizing structure in order to maximize the transparency. The firm's early work in this area was inspirational to architects and designers internationally (Figure 15.2).

Evident in all the firm's work is the expected concern for efficiency and economy common to most engineering firms, but Schlaich is also clear in his desire to pursue "the poetics of lightness."[3] There is a "stylistic awareness" in their work that has drawn the attention of many in the architectural design field.[4] Schlaich and his colleagues exhibit a distinct preference for structural forms in which the members act entirely in tension or compression, claiming they are the most "honest." The firm's work makes heavy use of cable nets, tensile fabric structures, and other solutions that enable formal expression while minimizing structure. In particular, Schlaich extols the virtue of the shell as the most honest because: "[it] lends itself less than any other structure to attempts to hide inadequate design under camouflage or cladding."[5]

Gerkan, Marg and Partners (gmp)

Based in Hamburg, but with offices across Europe and Asia, Gerkan, Marg, and Partners (gmp)[6] are architects with an established history of innovative work at institutional and infrastructural scales. They are one of the largest and most prominent architecture firms in Germany. Founded in 1965 by Meinhard von Gerkan and Volkwin Marg, they have completed noted designs for stadia, exhibition and conference centers, airports, train stations, and museums internationally. In recent years the firm has completed designs for several airports in Germany, governmental and cultural projects in both Vietnam and India, multiple football stadia in Brazil ahead of their World Cup hosting, and many transportation and institutional projects across China including a number in Liang New City, for which they did the master planning.

Writing about his work, Volkwin Marg asserts that "if there is a general ethos, then it is that investment in architecture is much too expensive, for it just to be short lived."[7] The firm has developed a reputation for work that is neither avant-garde nor populist, preferring instead to emphasize design competence and purposefulness.[8] The partners describe their architectural interpretation as "characterized by the Vitruvian ideals of solidity, longevity and beauty."[9] Their design philosophy is one of simplicity, responsiveness to site and structural rationality.[10]

> With a critical distance from recent architectural expressions, we try to avoid expressionist forms, which are only derived from artistic caprice, without reference to use, construction and functionality.... The development of appropriate and acceptable answers and solutions for problems demands an openness for dialogue and the adaptation of one's standpoint to changing conditions.[11]

Both of the founders are also active in teaching, having held numerous professorships over the years, and gmp sponsors the Academy for Architectural Culture, a Hamburg-based institution that supports education and research in architecture and design.

The Project

When Berlin became the capital once again of a reunified Germany there was a need to create a new transportation hub in the center of the new Berlin, close to the newly reinstated government buildings. This facility would reconnect the tram and underground systems in the city along with the regional, national, and international train systems. On the site of the old Lehrter station, just to the west of where the wall had stood, overlooking the River Spree, the site for the new Hauptbahnhof (Central Station) was found. The proposal called for 175,000 square meters (1.8 million square feet) of space over 5 platform levels.[12] The facility serves over 300,000 passengers on 1,200 trains every day[13] and is the largest train station in Europe.[14]

As is common for many significant public buildings in Germany, a design competition was held. The architects at gmp invited Schlaich, Bergermann und Partner (SBP) to work on the competition with them, and their entry took first prize. The two firms had worked together before numerous times, on projects including bridges, airports, and stadia such as the new roof installed on the 1936 Olympic Stadium ahead of the 2006 Soccer World Cup.

The architects of gmp's winning vision for the station has a pair of axes, the overland tracks run along the east-west axis and the office and retail building that straddles them runs north south to mark the orientation of the underground tracks below (Figure 15.3). These formal gestures of the structure mimic a stitch that is knitting the fabric of East and West Berlin back together.

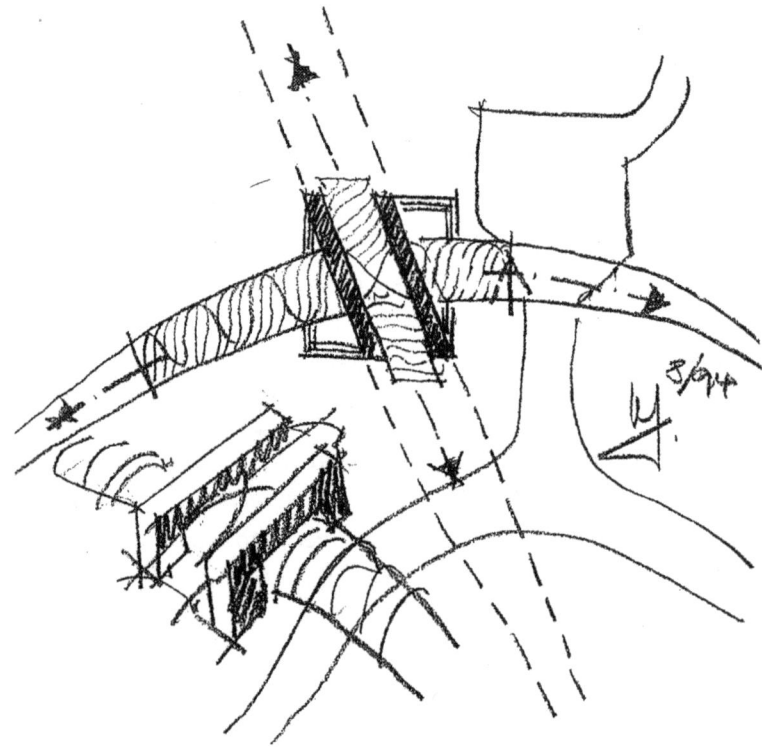

Figure 15.3 Architect's concept sketch for the Berlin Hauptbahnhof. The east-west arched roof spans the overland tracks for the regional, national, and international trains, the office tower runs north south as do the underground tracks hidden below. von Gerkan, Marg, und Partners and Schlaich, Bergermann und Partner. Berlin, Germany, 2006. Credit: Design Sketch by Meinhard von Gerkan, von Gerkan, Marg, und Partners.

BERLIN HAUPTBAHNHOF

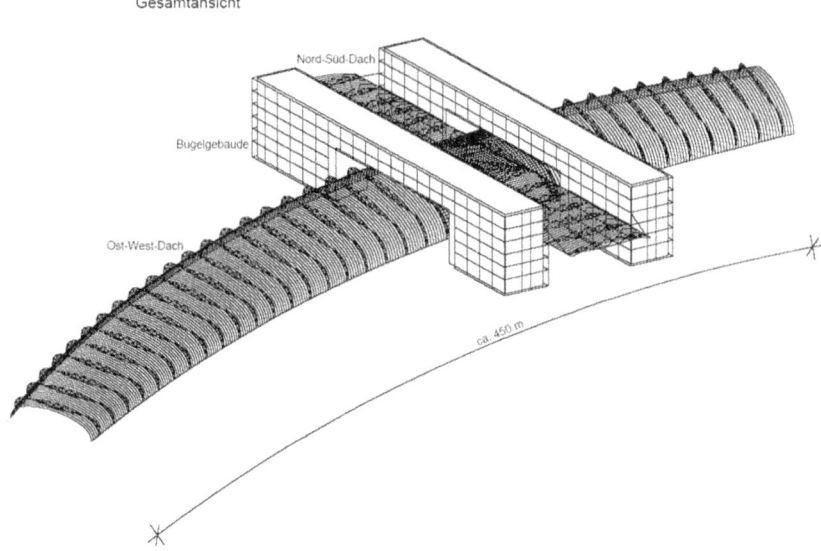

Figure 15.4 Drawing of the Final Design for the Berlin Hauptbahnhof. von Gerkan, Marg, und Partners and Schlaich, Bergermann und Partner, Berlin, Germany, 2006. Credit: Schlaich Bergermann und Partner.

The east-west tracks are under a 320 meters (1000 feet) long arched glass roof reminiscent, in form if not materials, of the great European train stations of the 19th century. Originally designed to be 450 meters (1400 feet) long, the arch starts with a span of 46 meters (150 feet) on the approaching tracks flaring out to a span of 66 meters (216 feet) inside the station to make room for the platforms in between (Figure 15.4). The height of the arch also varies from 14.5 to 16.5 meters (48 to 54 feet) as the arch flares out.[15] The three dimensional variation of this roof would have been all the more dramatic had it been built to its planned length. The client dictated the shorter roof length for time reasons rather than cost, and the architects at gmp were bitterly disappointed by this decision.[16] Nonetheless it is a striking form; from a distance this platform roof that accommodates six train tracks and the associated platforms, looks almost like a singular sheet of glass carefully curved over to span the distance. Only up close does the intricate structure reveal itself, and the primary structural elements are thoughtfully pulled back from the free end of the roof to emphasize this sharp, thin, elegant edge (Figure 15.5). The north south axis consists of a pair of taller buildings that bridge over the surface level tracks, suspended between these buildings is a glass canopy roof that covers the mezzanine levels of shopping and access to the underground lines below. Recessed back from the edge of the canopy roof on both ends is a suspended glass facade. Inside the building, the comparative weight of the office building with its exposed steel exoskeleton contrasts with the light filigree structure of the glass roofs and walls (Figure 15.6).

CASE STUDIES IN COLLABORATION: TRANSPORTATION BUILDINGS

Figure 15.5 Berlin Hauptbahnhof. von Gerkan, Marg, und Partners and Schlaich, Bergermann und Partner, Berlin, Germany, 2006. Credit: Sinéad Mac Namara.

Figure 15.6 The interior of the Berlin Hauptbahnhof looking south. von Gerkan, Marg, und Partners and Schlaich, Bergermann und Partner, Berlin, Germany, 2006. Credit: Marcus Bredt.

The Collaborating Team

Hans Schober, the lead engineer for SBP on the Berlin project, emphasizes the importance of the long-standing relationship between the architecture and engineering firms to the collaboration process, in particular because it often means that the architect will be willing to bring the engineer into the process earlier. Speaking generally about collaboration between architects and engineers he notes: "It is very clear, as the engineer you have to start to work with the architect at the conceptual phase. This is the phase where you can be innovative and contribute new ideas."[17]

He characterizes the traditionally dominant industry paradigm where the architect makes all formal and design decisions in the early stages without any input from the engineer and the engineer merely calculates and sizes members for what the architect has designed as "totally the wrong way." Rather,

> When we work together, it is often the case that the architect has ideas about the structure, different from those of the engineer, and it stimulates the engineer to innovate. In turn, when the architect takes input and learns from the collaboration about good structural ideas, the architect is also stimulated by the engineer.[18]

He goes on to argue that if designers do not exploit this potential inherent in each other's expertise, new ideas and opportunities are missed.

> It is very important that both disciplines work together from the very beginning. I must say, many of our architects come to our office because they know that we work in this way. It is also good for an engineer's reputation, if architects know that the engineer has great input and brings innovation to the design.[19]

Schober observes that the history of gmp working together with SBP influenced both their decision to bring them on to the project, and the choice to involve them from the very beginning. He also credited the architects of gmp and their interest in structural form as an important facet of their work together: "Because we had worked with … [gmp] … many times before…. they knew we would collaborate well."[20] He describes the culture at gmp as "receptive to a structure that expresses the design"[21] which makes for an optimal working environment. "Working with gmp is a very good fit for us, we were a team member from the beginning, this was very, very important. The conceptual design phase was more than one year and we worked very closely with them."[22]

Architect Jürgen Hilmer, who led the project for gmp, concurs:

> In the years we have worked together we have been able to develop a deep sense of professional familiarity and a common general understanding of architecture and construction principles, upon which our

years of teamwork is founded. Our philosophy of design, which can be characterized by simplicity and diversity, uniformity and variety and structural organization, coincides with Schlaich Bergermann und Partner's philosophy. That is the only means by which one can produce a design in cooperation with another planner.[23]

Schober describes the project as an excellent example of collaboration between the architect and the engineer in that there are elements of the final design where the architect's vision is absolutely primary and elements that come entirely from the structural principles of the engineer. The office building design, with its exoskeleton of structure in a square grid sitting markedly proud of the facade, was an important part of the architect's competition-winning proposal. However, Schober describes this design as presenting two significant challenges to the structural engineers. "Here we had a conflict between the aesthetics or the architectural idea and the technical solution"[24] The first is the problem of differential thermal expansion. The structure on the outer sides is exposed to wide variations in temperature and the structure on the interior is exposed to much more modest variations of temperature; however, the concrete slab inside the building must be connected to the structure on the inside, the structure on the inside must connect to the structure on the outside of the 220-meter (720-foot) long building and thermal expansion is a function of length. To understand this problem: imagine a very hot day, and over the course of the day, all the exposed steel members on the outside of the building get hotter, and thus longer, pushing against each other. The movement will never be uniform and all these structural members are attached to other elements in the building. This movement can cause unsafe stresses to build up in both structural and nonstructural elements of the building and could cause problems such as cracking in the concrete slabs and glass to shatter, even if there is no danger of failure of the exposed steel elements themselves.

The solution to this problem is to fix the interior steel members (transverse floor girders) to the vertical members of the exoskeleton and let the horizontal elements in the exoskeleton slide horizontally making them decorative and redundant structurally.

This solution would not have worked for the portion of the building that would bridge over the tracks. A solution that was initially proposed was to use a cable system that would make the structure effectively a suspension bridge with the weight of five spanning floors hanging from the cable in tension with the consequential horizontal reactions at the top of the cables carried as compression in the concrete slab (Figure 15.7a–b). This option did not appeal to the architects in part because this scheme would mean the horizontal elements in the steel exoskeleton were still redundant and effectively decoration. The final

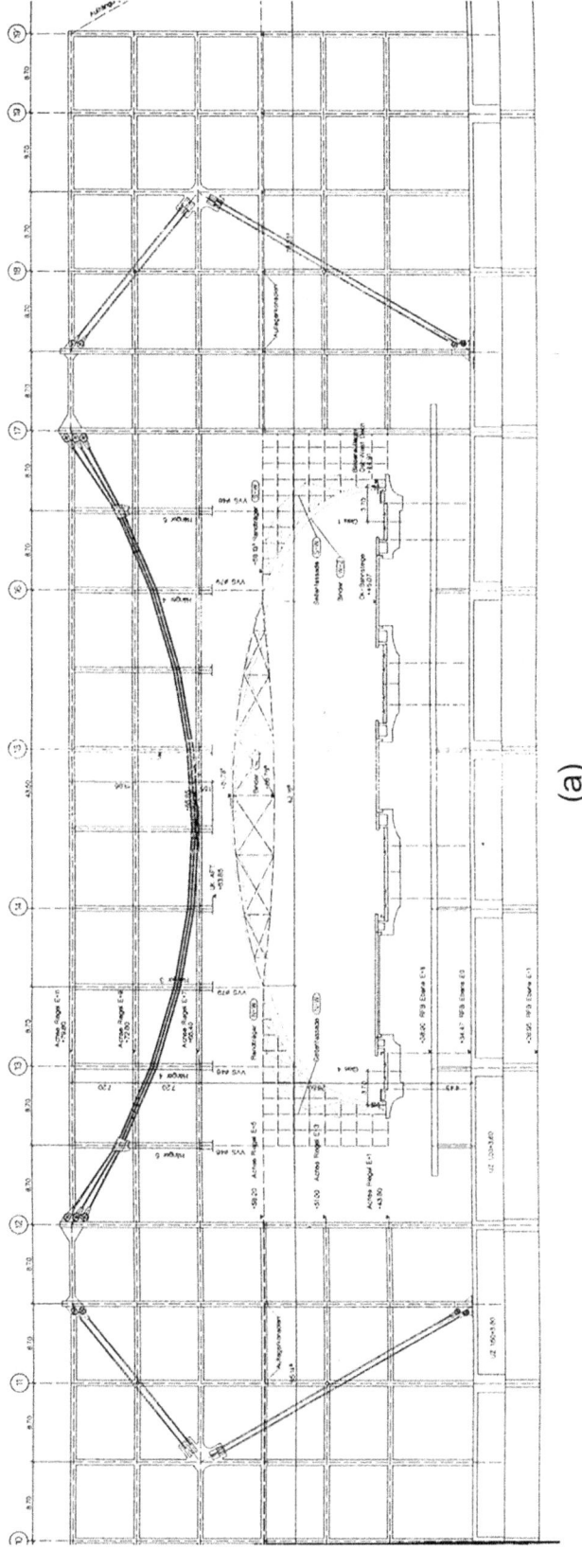

Figure 15.7a–b Structural Options for the bridge portion of the office building at the Berlin Hauptbahnhof. von Gerkan, Marg, und Partners and Schlaich, Bergermann und Partner, Berlin, Germany, 2006. Credit: Schlaich Bergermann und Partner.

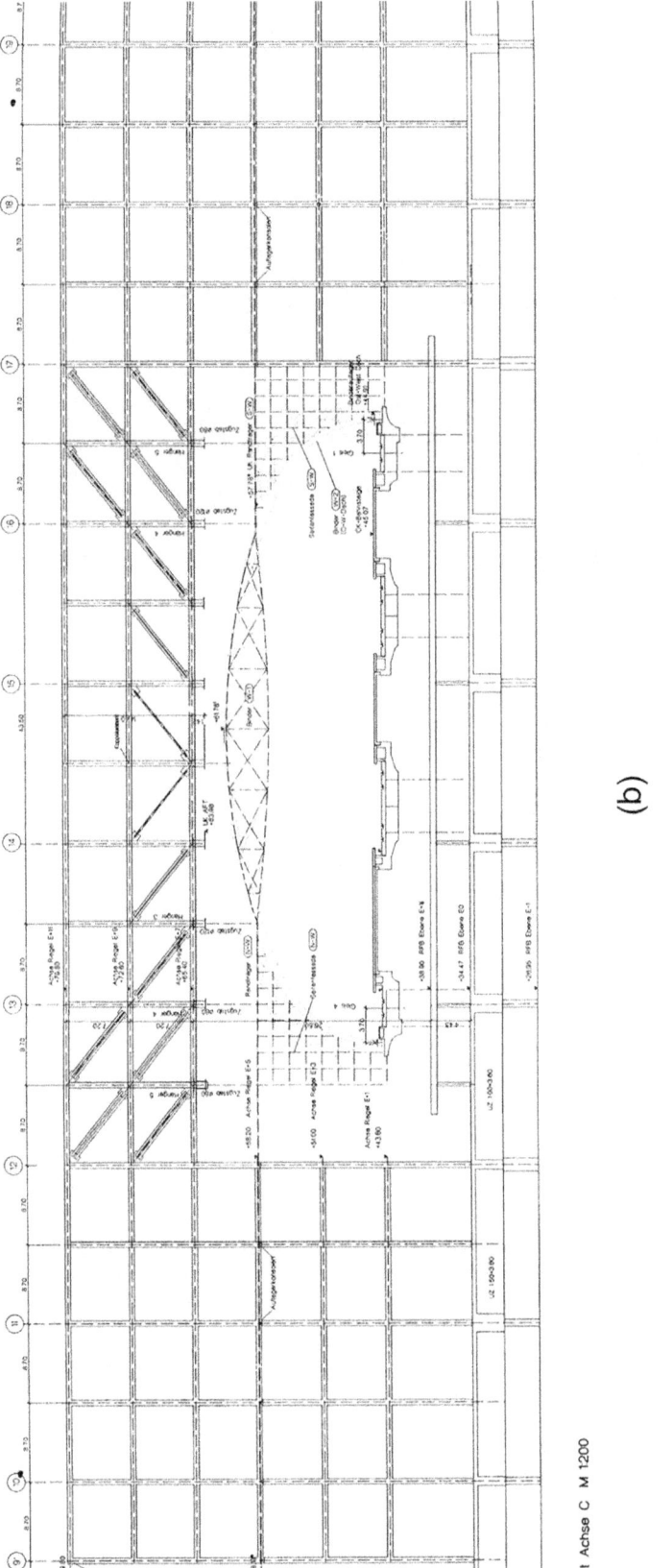

Figure 15.7a–b (Continued).

design that was chosen uses a truss system where the horizontal elements of the exoskeleton are load carrying chords of the truss. As a consequence, the connections between the exterior and interior steel members are specially designed sliding connections. Such connections, however, are not optimal at transferring the load and would never be the engineer's first choice. The engineers and architects discussed the problem back and forth, but eventually the engineers found a way to make the architect's vision work, using carefully designed connections. Schober describes the final compromise as "a distinguished design, but from the engineer's point of view, the structure is not optimal."[25] However, the final design proved to be the best solution for construction of this part of the office building as the train tracks were already in place. The truss could be built vertically in two halves and rotated into place, neatly solving a construction issue at the same time (Figure 15.8).

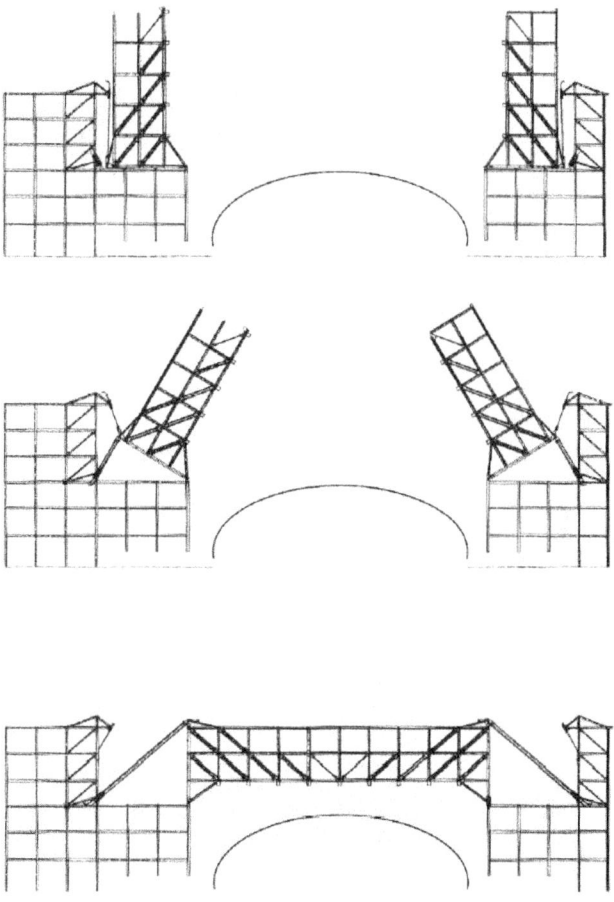

Figure 15.8 The truss bridge portion of the office building at the Berlin Hauptbahnhof, under construction and lowered into place. von Gerkan, Marg, und Partners and Schlaich, Bergermann und Partner, Berlin, Germany, 2006. Credit: Schlaich Bergermann und Partner.

For the entrance facade walls at either end of the north south axis, the architect wanted maximum transparency. Schober initially proposed a cable net wall, where a grid of prestressed cables are pulled to maximum tautness allowing them to then carry the wind load and weight of glass panes in a singular sheet of structure and enclosure at once, but the architect rejected this idea as too minimal and the engineers worked on alternate ideas for the very large wall. Various proposals including beams, beams and cables, and cable trusses with diagonals, etc. were considered but the final solution was an assembly of crisscross cables held apart from a pair of straight cables by glass fins to give structural depth and create a series of vertical vierendeel trusses that lend stiffness to the wall against loads perpendicular to the wall (primarily wind) (Figure 15.9). The architect really wanted to use glass for the struts to maximize transparency, which an engineer might have avoided due to the brittle structural nature of glass, a particular issue in a train station with the potential for vibration and vandalism. However, SBP conducted a series of tests and calculations, building prototypes and making models to design the fins, which are a laminated sandwich of four or five layers of glass with pvb interlayer. They

Figure 15.9 The glass facade wall at Berlin Hauptbahnhof. von Gerkan, Marg, und Partners and Schlaich, Bergermann und Partner, Berlin, Germany, 2006. Credit: Marcus Bredt.

also had to check how the wall might behave if one or more of the fins failed. Schober was very pleased with the result, which looks interesting and shows the flow of forces. Though it is not what he might have done without the architect's rejection of the initial idea, he acknowledges that the final result is better for the collaboration. "Of course our philosophy is that if you do a minimal structure and you show the flow of forces you cannot do it wrong, but it is not necessarily the best solution from an aesthetic point of view."[26] In this vein, Schober is quick to point out that engineers must avoid thinking there is only one solution to a design problem.

> Some engineers might be happy if they find one solution that works. Our experience is that there are a lot of solutions – not only one economic or efficient optimum solution…. We have to train our young engineers to know this.[27]

The final design for the glass wall had the added benefit of less deflection than a simple cable net would have. In this case, the architects' needs ultimately gave the engineers an opportunity to come up with another structural solution that had advantages of its own. Hilmer, too, notes that shared respect and willingness to see the other's point of view is crucial in a long, large-scale project like this one.

> Particularly important is the mutual support concerning the coordination in very long projects, that means projects that span several years, and in this particular case in regards to the glass roofs and the bridge-like office buildings. The longstanding mutual understanding and trust proved to be immensely helpful in the search for acceptable and sustainable solutions to meet the various interests.[28]

The curved glass roof, which spans over five rail lines, appears to be only 13 centimeters (5.1 inches) thick at the steel mullion that runs around the glass panes. To achieve this extraordinary thinness, the roof is supported at intervals by trusses. For this roof, the architect had specified the shape of the curve (a flatter arch than the engineers might have chosen) and that they wanted as much transparency and light as possible (Figure 15.10). So the engineers set out to design as minimal and as filigree a structure as possible. A true parabolic arch (as in the grand tradition of major train stations such as London's Paddington Station and New York's Grand Central Terminal) would have been the ideal structure, allowing for a pure compressive arch, completely eliminating bending under dead load. For a shell roof (Schober is among the world's leading designers of glass shell roofs), he maintains "the design should always strive towards a membrane, which is to say a moment

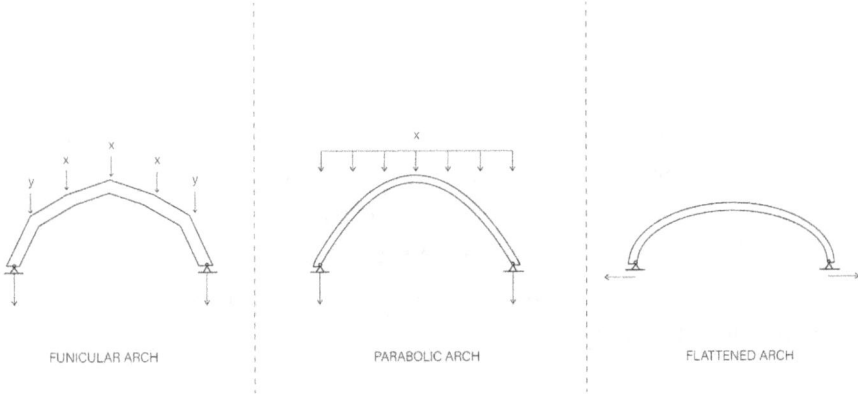

Figure 15.10 A funicular arch shape responds to a specific set of loads, a parabolic arch is in perfect compression if uniformly loaded, the flatter shape of the Berlin Hauptbahnhof meant the section had to be designed to carry bending. Credit: Shiori Green.

free state."[29] However, the architect successfully argued that such a high roof was unnecessary and wasteful when the era of the steam train is so long past. So the engineers were faced with designing a very long single span with a form that would have to resist bending. In order to span such a large distance and minimize the structure, it makes most engineering sense to find a form that can put material exactly where it is needed to resist the loads (and remove it where it is not necessary). Every element of the roof structure is designed with this in mind. The final design for the roof came entirely from the engineering requirements. Schober explains,

> We discussed various options: a frame, a frame with a cable truss, and so on, back and forth. But if you think of the principles of light structures, it is always good if you can dissolve the structure into struts and ties that take only compression and tension, rather than building a bending member.[30]

To carry the bending, a truss was designed to separate the bending into compression and tension members (struts and ties). These trusses are rendered almost invisible by aligning the compression member with the glass plane (where a structure to hold the glass is required in any case) and using thin tension cables above and below the roof in a shape that mimics a fixed-fixed bending moment diagram due to the gravity loads (Figure 15.11).[31] Schober is a strong proponent of using the geometries inherent in fundamental structural calculations which allow even a complex building like this one to be explained with a few simple formulae, even when advanced structural tools allow designers to experiment with less structurally rational forms. "I believe that simple understandable principles, whose basic mathematical and geometric concepts can be reconstructed … mathematically based shapes are justified and

Figure 15.11 Platform Roof Cross-Section Berlin Hauptbahnhof. The truss mimics the bending moment diagram of the flattened arch under dead load. The compression member of the truss is coincident with the arch, with the tension members (thin cables) held off the arch with minimal compression struts. Every effort is made to lighten the section with the compression members hollowed out except in those places where a little extra structure is needed to resist the small amount of bending under non-uniform and lateral loads. von Gerkan, Marg, und Partners and Schlaich, Bergermann und Partner, Berlin, Germany, 2006. Credit: Schlaich Bergermann und Partner.

disciplines and mathematical relationships are timeless. Rational design principles are timeless."[32]

In the design of the supporting truss for the glass roof, to further remove weight from the cross section (in a large structure, self-weight is a significant load) and to maximize transparency, openings were placed in the compression members in the middle of the section where the material is least necessary to resist buckling. These openings are absent only at the supports and at the point of inflection of the bending moment diagram due to the dead (gravity) load. There is a small amount of bending due to wind load, which is largest at the point of inflection, and thus the compression struts must act as beams in those locations need to be deepened slightly and the web filled back in for resistance to bending. This form (Figure 15.12), Schober argues, comes from the engineering imagination.

> This is a good example of a high tech structure that comes mainly from the engineer, because it has only one function, to carry the load, and when this is the case the engineer should be the leading designer and not the architect. Of course the flat form came from the architect – otherwise we might have a different roof.[33]

So, while the engineer might never have started from the form of the non-parabolic arch with its attendant bending, the architect would not have come up

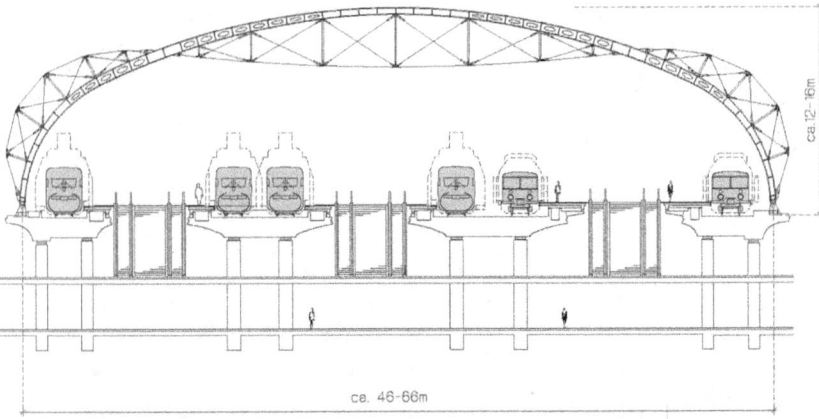

Figure 15.12 The Platform Roof at Berlin Hauptbahnhof spans up to 66 mm and the maximum depth of the compression members in the arch is only 13 cm. von Gerkan, Marg, und Partners and Schlaich, Bergermann und Partner, Berlin, Germany, 2006. Credit: Marcus Bredt.

with the details of the undulating truss form.[34] Working in collaboration however, they produced a novel and successful design. In summing up gmp's successful collaboration with SBP, Hilmer argues that the two firms' common design values were the key to the positive outcomes.

> The most significant aspect of a successful collaboration between architects and engineers is not who assumes the leading role in regards to formal and aesthetic decisions, but rather the congruence not only in the approach to the design but also in the fundamentals of design work. Good design is dependent on a give-and-take basis. On the one hand it requires a fine balance of construction ideas and decisions in regards to fabrication and erection as well as architectural and aesthetic considerations. All considerations must be sufficiently addressed without questioning who is responsible for the one or the other aspect. The design process is solely directed at creating a coherent and comprehensive building. This is dependent on a common philosophy of design. The philosophy includes the efficient use of materials, the simple recognition of the path of structural loads, simplicity in regards to a minimalistic and honest structure and the honesty to show how a structure is connected and how it works, which together provide for an outstanding design and construction like the Berlin Hauptbahnhof (Central Station).[35]

Notes

1. Alan Holgate, *The Art of Structural Engineering: The Work of Jörg Schlaich and his Team* (Axel Mengels, Stuttgart/London, 1997).
2. Nina Rappaport, "Schlaich, Bergermann und Partner." In *Support and Resist: Structural Engineers and Design Innovation*. New York: Monacelli Press, 2007. 181.
3. Jörg Schlaich and Rudolf Bergermann, *Leicht Weit/Light Structures*. Exhibition catalog, Deutsches Architekturmuseum, Frankfurt Am Main. Prestel, Munich, 2003.
4. Rappaport, "Schlaich, Bergermann und Partner," 179.
5. Holgate, *The Art of Structural Engineering*.
6. Note this is the firm's preferred usage.
7. Volkwin Marg, "Immer hart trainieren." *Build* Mai/Juni (2003): 15.
8. Eva Barkhofen, "Bauten für die Sinne, 40 Jahre gmp in Berlin." In *Berliner Bauten und Projekte, 1965–2005*. Berlin: Jovis, 2005. 9–10.
9. "Practice Profile." gmp Architekten von Gerkan, Marg und Partner, accessed July 29, 2013, http://www.gmp-architekten.com/projects.html.
10. Meinhard von Gerkan, "Editorial." In *Von Gerkan, Marg and Partner: Architecture 1999–2000*. Basel: Birkhäuser, 2002. 8.
11. "Philosophy." gmp Architekten von Gerkan, Marg und Partner, accessed July 29, 2013, http://www.gmp-architekten.com/projects.html.
12. "Projects." gmp Architekten von Gerkan, Marg und Partner, accessed July 29, 2013, http://www.gmp-architekten.com/projects.html.
13. "Die Bahnhöfe." Deutsche Bahn, accessed July 29, 2013, http://www.bahnhof.de/?lang=en#station/17620.
14. Eva Barkhofen, "Berlin Hauptbahnhof—Lehrter Bahnhof, 2006." In *Berliner Bauten und Projekte, 1965-2005*. Berlin: Jovis, 2005. 144.
15. Rappaport, 184.
16. Hans Schober, Interview by the authors. Personal interview. Stuttgart, June 19, 2013.
17. Schober, Interview by authors.
18. Schober.
19. Schober.
20. Schober.
21. Schober.
22. Schober.
23. Jürgen Hilmer, Interview by the authors. Email Interview. Hamburg, August 2, 2013.
24. Schober.
25. Schober.
26. Schober.
27. Schober.
28. Hilmer, Interview by the authors. Email Interview.
29. Hans Schober and Claudia Schaffert, *Transparent Shells: Form, Topology, Structure* (Berlin, Germany: Ernst & Sohn, a Wiley brand, 2016), 14.
30. Schober.
31. Hans Schober, "The Berlin Connection," *Civil Engineering* 81 (2006): 43–89.
32. Hans Schober and Claudia Schaffert, *Transparent Shells: Form, Topology, Structure*, 7.
33. Schober.
34. Schober.
35. Hilmer.

CHAPTER 16

Anaheim Regional Transportation Intermodal Center

Rationalizing Facades for Cost-Effectiveness and Performance

Design Architect:	HOK
Executive Architect:	Parsons Brinckerhoff, Los Angeles
Structural Engineer:	Thornton Tomasetti, Los Angeles
MEP and Facades Engineering:	Buro Happold, Los Angeles
Construction Management:	STV, Irvine, CA
Testing and Inspections consultant:	Group Delta Consultants, Irvine, CA
General Contractor:	Clark Construction Group LP

The design of ARTIC involved numerous experts and firms, but the discussion focuses on the partnership between HOK and Buro Happold.

HOK

HOK, founded by George Hellmuth, Gyo Obata, and George Kassabum in 1955 in St. Louis, Missouri, now boasts 23 offices around the world and 1,600 multidisciplinary staff. In 2019, HOK ranked sixth in US architecture firms with the highest revenue, while also that year, it was named one of Fast Company's Most Innovative Companies. Major projects include the Mercedes Benz Stadium in Atlanta, Georgia, the Kentucky International Convention Center, and the LG Science Park in Seoul, Korea. The Anaheim Regional Transportation Intermodal Center in Anaheim, California, the subject of this case study, adds to HOK's impressive portfolio of transportation projects including the 6.46 million-square-foot Hamad International Airport Passenger Terminal Complex in Doha, Qatar; the Indira Gandhi International Airport in New Delhi; the Indianapolis International Airport; the Hartsfield–Jackson Atlanta International Airport modernization; and the Terminal 5 Automated People Mover at London Heathrow Airport.

One of HOK's most ambitious projects to date is the King Abdullah University of Science and Technology (KAUST) campus in Thuwal, Saudi Arabia. The project team—consisting of 300 architects, engineers, interior designers, planners, and laboratory design specialists across 11 HOK offices—had less than 30 months to design and construct 5.5 million square feet of complex space across 27 buildings. The campus is Saudi Arabia's first to garner Leadership in Energy & Environmental Design (LEED)[1] certification and, at the time, the world's largest LEED platinum project.

Sustainability and integrated design are part of HOK's mission, which foregrounds the needs of people and the environment. The firm is consistently ranked as a leader in sustainable design by *DesignIntelligence*. Editor James Cramer explains,

> HOK is a firm often cited for making a difference ... HOK is recognized for breaking new ground with clear, practical and informational leadership. HOK's staff is admired for its compelling case studies, engaging thought leadership and insights that lead to making wise decisions to benefit the planet's future condition.[2]

HOK includes experts in a wide range of fields, including architecture, interior design, engineering, planning, and urban design "to deliver solutions that inspire clients and communities."[3]

Buro Happold

Buro Happold is one of the go-to engineering firms for architects and clients seeking innovation, holistic integration, and constructability in design. Widely viewed as thought-leaders in the industry, Buro Happold was founded in 1976 by Ted Happold (who started his career at Arup, a company featured several times in this book) and today the firm employs 1,900 people with a wide range of expertise in 26 offices around the world. The firm has a long history of lightweight structures, and they were early innovators in the industry on sustainability issues infusing structural engineering designs with passive thermal performance and taking an integrated research-based approach to the environmental impact of their projects.[4]

The Los Angeles office was founded in 2006 by Greg Otto who was educated as both an architect and engineer and believes strongly in collaborative modes of practice. Otto explains his approach to developing a robust team, and thinks carefully about who to hire and how to foster a collaborative environment:

> It's challenging to nurture the ethos necessary to do this type of work, which is between disciplines: it's engineering, but not pure engineering, it's architecture, but not pure architecture. It's the middle ground, which is a challenge for engineers and architects to walk into … We look for people that are [very eager] to take responsibility, take a bit of risk and challenge convention.[5]

The Los Angeles office works at a range of scales from installations to mega structures. Buro Happold Los Angeles completed structural and MEP engineering for the award-winning Helios House, a fully sustainable, prefabricated BP gas station designed by Office dA and Johnston Marklee, completed in 2007. At the opposite end of scale, one of the largest projects for the Los Angeles office to date is San Francisco's Salesforce Transit Center, completed in 2018. The firm provided sustainability and MEP engineering with architectural design by Pelli Clarke Pelli. Similar services were delivered for the Perot Museum of Nature and Science in Dallas designed by Morphosis, which employs, among a multitude of other green infrastructures, a 100% gray water capture system for reuse in the building. The sustainable measures in the Museum contributed to an award of Four Globes, the highest rating issued by the Green Building Initiative. Buro Happold continually receives international praise for design innovation while furthering the engineering fields. Their research-oriented approach is exemplified in the following case study.

The ARTIC Project

The Anaheim Regional Transportation Intermodal Center (ARTIC) is a 67,000-square-foot (6200-square-meter) terminal providing connections for ten different modes of transportation as well as support programs including commercial tenant and dining space, ticketing, lobby, and operation offices (Figure 16.1a–b). The intermodal station serves the Orange County Transportation Authority (OCTA), Metrolink, AMTRAK, local shuttles and buses, international buses, pedestrians and bikers, taxis, and parking for 1,082 vehicles. High-speed rail and light rail are planned to be connected in the future. The hefty $184 million budget was funded through county, state, and federal government transportation support measures, and has not been without controversy for reasons discussed later in this chapter.

Figure 16.1 The Anaheim Regional Transportation Intermodal Center (ARTIC), PB/HOK, Buro Happold, Anaheim, California, 2014. Credit: Sinéad Mac Namara.

Figure 16.2 Interior view. The Anaheim Regional Transportation Intermodal Center (ARTIC), PB/HOK, Buro Happold, Anaheim, California, 2014 [on page credit] HOK. Credit: Sinéad Mac Namara.

ARTIC is located on the north side of the Anaheim Angels Stadium parking lot, a short distance from Honda Stadium, and provides easy public transportation access to the sports arenas and the vicinity while serving as a hub for Anaheim's numerous tourist destinations including Disney Land. More than 40 million tourists visit Anaheim annually, generating $8.7 billion in revenue and creating thousands of jobs for the city, which is the 10th largest in California. In 2006, the city projected the population would grow by 31% by 2035,[6] putting added strain on the county's already-congested roadways, a huge motivation for the intermodal station (Figure 16.2).

The city envisioned an iconic transportation center and the request for proposals called for a sustainable design for a long-term civic landmark and regional gateway to Orange County. Hundreds of firms responded to the RFP, and the Parsons Brinckerhoff (PB)/HOK team was awarded the contract in 2009, beating out such world-renowned firms as Gehry Partners, Pelli Clarke Pelli, Foster + Partners, and Santiago Calatrava. It was a fast-tracked design process. The initial proposals from PB/HOK reflected both firms' design heritage, which include numerous airports and other complex transportation facilities. The team's proposals were firmly committed to the LEED platinum goals. Arnold Lee, Senior Project Designer for HOK, described the competition process,

> Because of the unique shape of the proposal, we did multiple schemes: one was a more traditional repeating bay structure, which you would associate with large infrastructure projects; it was very rational and allowed for flexibility. But the one the client chose was a big soaring design that is very iconic and specific.[7]

The chosen design fulfilled the city's vision for an intermodal hub that would not only support public transportation growth, but also spark commercial development in the region (Figure 16.3).

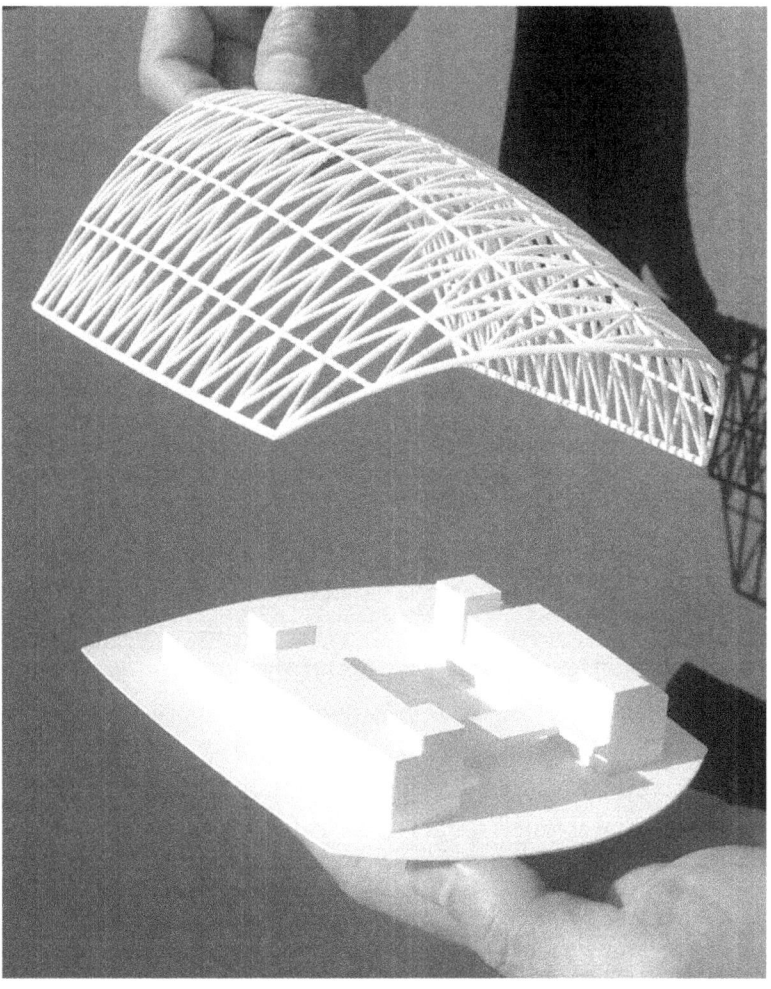

Figure 16.3 Shell geometry demonstrated in a 3D print. The Anaheim Regional Transportation Intermodal Center (ARTIC), PB/HOK, Buro Happold, Anaheim, California, 2014. Credit: Buro Happold.

This case study demonstrates a different kind of collaborative mode than some of the others featured in the text. In this project, the complexity and scale of the design and execution required a very diverse skill set—a matrix of experts. During design development, Eric Anderson, Senior Project Manager from PB Architecture oversaw the PB/HOK collaboration which included design and engineering for the rail infrastructure, traffic planning, and intermodal design. About six months before the bid process, Virginia Tanzmann, FAIA, Architect and Vice President of PB Architecture, took on management of the project and the 20-plus consultants. The collaboration between HOK and Buro Happold showcased here represents just a snapshot of the coordination required to realize ARTIC. The work pushed the boundaries of traditional architectural and engineering practices; the players wore multiple hats during the design process, crossed disciplines, and faced responsibilities outside of the "normal" call of duty. The computation tools that were ultimately required to manifest this project presented an intricate challenge. Meanwhile, it also required specialized expertise to realize the building efficiently and cost-effectively. Given the complexity of the design and site, those interviewed reflected that this project would not have been possible without the collaboration (and cooperation) of the interdisciplinary team.

The Project Team

Achieving the project goals within budget was the feat of a large group of designers and technical experts. Tanzmann remarks,

> This is my 40th year as a licensed architect and this is the most exciting project I've worked on-- a culmination of so many things. Every system in it is wonderful and to accomplish that with success requires successful collaboration … It's extremely complex, but that's part of the fun.[8]

The scale, scope, projected use, and timeline of the project were hugely demanding; add the unique design that uses entirely customized systems and the sum total is a design story that is intricate and innovative.

The initial design proposals were developed by a team composed of architects, planners, landscape architects, and engineers from PB and HOK, structural engineers and facade consultants from Thornton Tomasetti along with mechanical engineers at Buro Happold. Lee explains that transportation facilities, with their very long life spans, require a careful balance of the longevity and permanence that you associate with large infrastructure projects, against a judicious use of the public taxpayer's investment. "It was a very complex job, so for us, the most important thing was to make sure we had a healthy collaboration with structural enclosure, mechanical, and sustainability, which were all front and center from the very beginning."[9]

After the client approved the scheme, the team shifted to develop the design for the project. Given the unusual form of the proposed scheme, the construction challenges inherent in the facade systems, and the tremendous risk involved (including cost and life safety), it was essential for the widely varied team of experts to rationalize the systems and test them virtually. Lee describes the change in the design team responsibilities saying that

> Thornton Tomasetti is an excellent firm and they did the structural enclosure. Buro Happold was doing the mechanical, which is of course really important for a highly sustainable building. Due to the difficult and challenging geometries of the project we realized it was helpful to have all the complex geometry, MEP and enclosure all under one roof.[10]

Given that Buro Happold was deeply involved with the enclosure already, their team's responsibility was expanded to develop and optimize the facade systems. Lee explains the selection of Buro Happold:

> [They are] engineers who have the history, track record and ability to start very, very complex projects where the solutions either weren't readily available or are not conventional market solutions, and we worked together towards designing these solutions. Since it is a small office, they ramped up their staff, wrote their own software and were able to juggle between different kinds of complex programs to get us the right solution. Plus they had resources to tap worldwide. It worked out great.[11]

Greg Otto describes the Buro Happold team that worked on the ARTIC project:

> On complex projects, you really have to have both sides of the equation. Sanjeev [Tankha] is an architect by training, Kurt [Komraus] has worked for an architect for the bulk of his career; Steve Lewis is a pure engineer. That's the way this practice needs to be to do this type of work[12]

Cross-disciplinary design factored heavily into the project, which has an almost entirely customized enclosure.

Defining the Form, Structure, and Materiality

The original competition-winning design was inspired by iconic infrastructure projects, including two that are both now demolished, Broad Street Station in Philadelphia and New York City's Penn Station (Figure 16.4). Both historical

Figure 16.4 Penn Station, Interior, Manhattan 1935. Credit: Abbot Bernice, 1898–1991 (New York Public Library).

projects demonstrate the dynamic effects of a glass and steel shed with free circulation and lots of natural light. These historic influences and the ARTIC project goals led to the design of a long span, gridshell structure to create a grand naturally lit space that allows for open circulation, crucial on stadium event days when the design foresaw surges upwards of 50,000 people (Figure 16.5). The team focused on efficient, parabolic shell geometry through the design of a catenary curve swept on a torus (Figure 16.6). The original competition-winning design had a height of 180 feet (55 meters), which was reduced to a height of 120 feet (37 meters) for the bid package. Lee says,

> Since it was a competition, it was challenging because you don't get to speak to the client. We came up with two or three ideas and they picked one. Once we started the project, we found out more about the site and about the political and economic conditions that were shaping the project. We realized that we had to adapt the scheme almost immediately … It was really a challenging kick-off to the project.[13]

The interdisciplinary team worked through numerous options to maximize the design for aesthetic ambition balanced with efficiency requirements and constructability goals.

Figure 16.5 The grand lobby is enclosed by a soaring grid shell composed of steel and frit patterned ETFE pillows to mitigate heat. The Anaheim Regional Transportation Intermodal Center (ARTIC), PB/HOK, Buro Happold, Anaheim, California, 2014. Credit: Sinéad Mac Namara.

Early on, the soil tests indicated that the level of backfill (uncompacted soil that was not native to the site) would require extremely robust foundations, which would demand a disproportionately large chunk of the budget for the site work and concrete. Thus lightweight materials to reduce the weight of the foundations were investigated. Economic concerns also called for an approach that could be built quickly and efficiently. The designers considered long span structures to reduce the amount of steel. "We looked at efficient shell structures to lighten the weight of the roof and we looked at alternative membrane structures because the foundations were just going to be too big, so ETFE was one of those solutions."[14]

David Herd, Managing Partner for Buro Happold North America, led the MEP team and helped to push forward ethylene tetrafluoroethylene (ETFE) on the project (Figure 16.7a–b). ETFE is a very lightweight translucent plastic that when assembled in multi-layered panels is used as a highly energy efficient facade component, particularly in roofs. Since ETFE is 1/100th the weight of glass, the material was key to enabling lighter foundations and reduced costs. It also contributes to the project's LEED certification as the material is responsibly manufactured, helps lighten the load during transport to the site (thereby reducing emissions), provides excellent insulation for temperature regulation, and is recyclable. At the time it was built, ARTIC was the largest ETFE project in North America with the material covering 200,000 square feet (18600 sqaure

CASE STUDIES IN COLLABORATION: TRANSPORTATION BUILDINGS

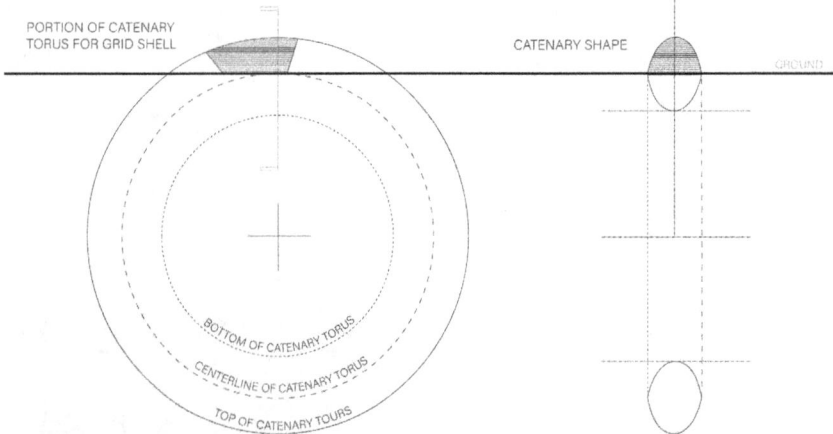

Figure 16.6 The geometry of a parabola swept on a torus enables a very efficient and light structure. The Anaheim Regional Transportation Intermodal Center (ARTIC), PB/HOK, Buro Happold, Anaheim, California, 2014. Credit: Shiori Green after drawing by HOK.

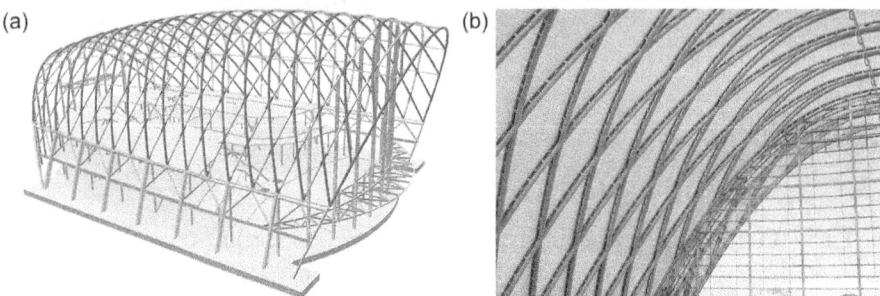

Figure 16.7 Steel frame for ARTIC. The use of ETFE, which is 1% the weight of glass, enables the reduction in steel. The Anaheim Regional Transportation Intermodal Center (ARTIC), PB/HOK, Buro Happold, Anaheim, California, 2014. Credit: (a) Buro Happold and (b) Sinéad Mac Namara.

meters) of roof surface. Engineers at Buro Happold worked closely with their colleagues throughout the world as well as the material fabricators to hone the system details to ensure constructability. Incidentally, Ted Happold was the first designer to introduce ETFE as a cladding material and it was used to skin the Mannheim Multihalle gridshell that he designed with Frei Otto (while Ted Happold was still working with Arup) and completed in 1975. Given Buro Happold's long and intimate history with the material, the ARTIC team was able to draw on three generations of knowledge of manufacturing, construction and performance.

Rationalizing the Facade Systems

In addition to the ETFE roof, the other major facade systems at work in ARTIC include two parabolic glass walls at the front and back of the building as well as metal panel walls that enclose the sides of the structure. Each of these systems went through rigorous rationalization, optioneering (evaluating multiple design options), and constructability assessments. Computation experts at Buro Happold created customized software and also used CATIA, Grasshopper, Excel, Robot and other tools to assess aesthetics and performance of the systems. Because of the fast project schedule, the team at Buro Happold was given six weeks to optimize the facade systems and provide a model in Revit, which was required by the client and enabled a 3d model of the project to be shared amongst the various architecture and engineering offices.

Not every shape can be easily built using simply fabricated or connected components, let alone perform as intended. Panelization of doubly curved shapes like the design for ARTIC can present a particular challenge. Ian Keough, senior technical designer, wrote software that helped the team generate the initial geometry. Through scripting and evaluation of the systems, the Buro Happold team reduced the depth of the structure by about a foot (30 centimeters) from the original scheme. Kurt Komraus of Buro Happold essentially became part of HOK's design team and worked almost every day in their office, which at the time was across the street. Komraus, an Associate, worked to define the prime geometry utilizing CATIA and custom scripts to create a constructible system. The "Geo Grid," as it became called by the team and contractors, was modeled in 3d and exported into a 35-page spreadsheet that defined each of the roof's x-y-z coordinates for the bid package. Buro Happold maintained several models in various software, each providing a different strategic purpose in design development. The prime geometry was articulated in CATIA and the Revit model was created to interface with HOK's interior model.

The rationalization process for the structure and facade was both intricate and multifaceted. Buro Happold used Thornton Tomasetti's structural geometry communicated through node identifications, which is industry standard. The Buro Happold team incorporated the primary geometry from TT into every analytical model that was created. Sanjeev Tankha, Associate Principal at Buro Happold describes the process,

> There is an inherent efficiency in analyzing the whole system and the interactions of the various components down to the details. Especially in this project where we had to drive the budget down and take as much fear out of the budget as we could, we had to analyze everything, which has an element of redundancy. Systems are a lot more efficient if you analyze them holistically.[15]

Given that each facade node needed to be normal to the surface, which was a form defined by HOK, each component of the structural anchorage, steel plates, and ETFE support channels were defined and modeled in order to evaluate the design. There were 3,000 stools that supported the channel extrusions that anchor the ETFE and each of these required a placement in space deciphered through a detailed CATIA model (Figure 16.8a–b). Komraus scripted the design of the componentry to adjust to the different angles and heights of plates needed to support the diamond-shaped cushions. Every time an adjustment was made to the form or materiality, the scripts were modified to generate new placements. This process was facilitated through parametric software and expert skill sets, but can take months when modeling in traditional CAD programs.

In the design of a complex facade, seemingly small details like the design of interstitial structures that connect panels to the load-carrying structure are critical to the success of the design. A number of factors played into the decision-making for the ETFE facade system (Figure 16.9a–b). Firstly, with constructability and aesthetics in mind, Buro Happold oriented the stools normal to design surface to limit the stools to only one type to support the ETFE foils. Each stool is a developable plate, allowing for ease of fabrication through waterjet cutting. Also striving for elegance in the design, the team worked to reduce the size of the clamps, which have a significant impact on the visual perception of lightness and buoyancy. Wind loads were also a huge factor in developing the

Figure 16.8 ETFE Pillow System. The Anaheim Regional Transportation Intermodal Center (ARTIC), PB/HOK, Buro Happold, Anaheim, California, 2014. Credit: (a) Buro Happold (b) Sinéad Mac Namara.

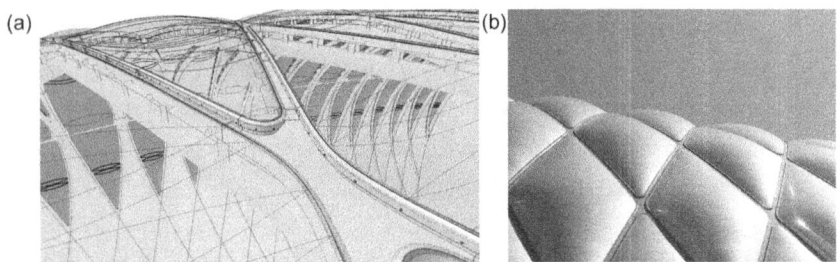

Figure 16.9 All of the ETFE framing components were modeled to analyze the system. The Anaheim Regional Transportation Intermodal Center (ARTIC), PB/HOK, Buro Happold, Anaheim, California, 2014. Credit: (a) Buro Happold and (b) Sinéad Mac Namara.

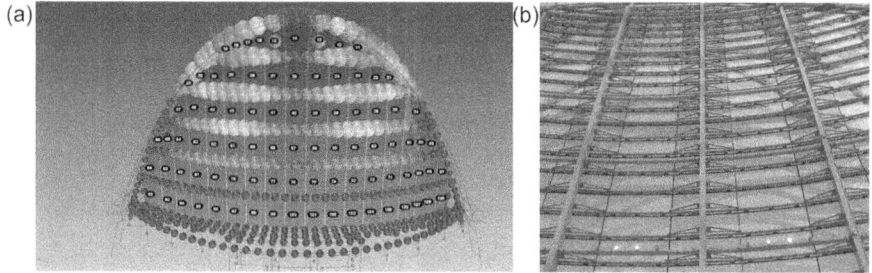

Figure 16.10 Grasshopper model to visualize the bubble deflection magnitudes. The Anaheim Regional Transportation Intermodal Center (ARTIC), PB/HOK, Buro Happold, Anaheim, California, 2014. Credit: (a) Buro Happold and (b) Sinéad Mac Namara.

detailing since the largest foil is an unprecedented 88-foot (27-meter) length. Stephen Lewis, Associate and Senior Engineer, developed a Grasshopper model to visualize the bubble deflection magnitudes and as a result, the team modified the detailing to include slip cables to restrain the cushions and reduce stress on the structural frame during high wind (Figure 16.10a–b). Lewis describes,

> In essence there are three key cushions over the surface of the structure and these cushions had to be form-found … We analyzed the cushions and looked at maximum stresses; if those were exceeded we modified the shape through another process of form-finding and added the slip cables.[16]

Each cushion is composed of three layers of foil that create an impressive insulating enclosure that can achieve a U value of 1.96 w/m^2°K (a thermal transmittance value comparable to that of triple glazed windows). The material filters infrared light and has an added frit pattern on the outer layer that reduces solar heat gain while allowing light penetration, further enhancing the sustainability measures that contributed to the LEED platinum goals.

The secondary structural system for the facade was also closely coordinated with TT's primary structural system. With wind and seismic loads, there can be instances of large deflection in the systems, which themselves needed to be flexible enough to move together. Lewis describes that design process saying that they "developed scripts in Grasshopper to process that data, describe it visually and used it to inform detailing to accommodate movement. We had 30 load cases from TT that we had to process."[17] That information was then integrated with the CATIA wire frame model, moved through Grasshopper and analyzed using Robot.

A holistic collaborative approach also guided the design of the faceted end walls, which required another customized structural system. The geometry, 120 feet (37 meters) tall at the highest point, was defined by HOK, and then

Buro Happold ran through multiple options to assess the aesthetic effects and costs of various systems. Komraus says,

> That was a big piece of geometric rationalization that directly affected the design. I sat with the designers and parametric models and said, well, if the glass panels are this size then it will interface with the diagrid this way ... You can see the geometry come together in a rational way, but there were so many decisions that had to be made with the architects and engineers concurrently.[18]

The team settled on a cable hung system to echo the roof design and reinforce the lightweight quality of the enclosure.

Tankha explains, "We conducted a series of studies within the price point for the wall system. Given the aesthetics that the architect wanted to achieve, we went through an 'optioneering' process (engineering options for the curtain wall system as opposed to value engineering which seeks primarily to reduce cost). We actually arrived at a system that was very close to the original aesthetic,"[19] and maintained the allowed budget for the system. When recounting the "optioneering" process the team went through, Tankha describes it as a collaborative process over nine months where the geometry was defined and the architects' aesthetic goals clarified. Contractors had to have a voice in the process to ensure the buildability and budget was also carefully considered. "We aren't working in isolation; we are working in tandem with the industry so all the feedback from them is looped back into the engineering. That's critical to working today. Working in a vacuum never helps."[20]

The side wall design also required a great deal of computation and rationalization. Komraus and the team worked to reduce the wall design in its original incarnation from more than 400 unique panel types to about 50. Given the curvature of the wall as a whole, there was an effort to eliminate customized forming of individual panels and so the geometry was defined as a series of planes formed by a translated polyline. The subdivisions, composed of 8–12 identical panels are planar parallelograms (Figure 16.11a–b). This process was hugely significant in reducing costs—the ETFE and structure were mostly fixed, however, the panels' portion of the budget was significantly reduced through the rationalization process. Tankha describes significant back and forth with suppliers and subcontractors during the design process. Once the geometry panelization was set, the team made very detailed designs of the various components. "Normally an engineer wouldn't go down to this level of detail in a model, but we wanted to make the system very clearly defined and transparent to get a realistic bid."[21]

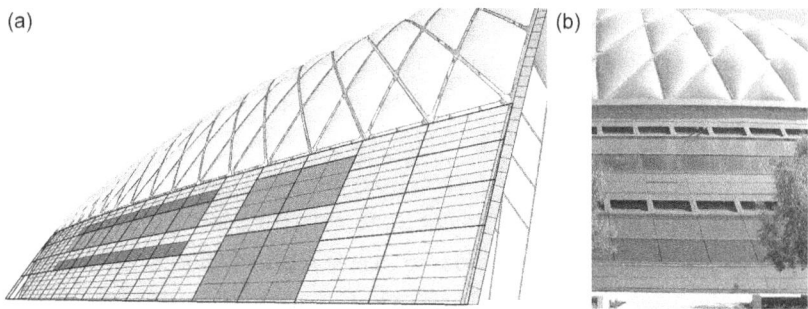

Figure 16.11 The team eliminated customized forming of individual panels for the side walls. The Anaheim Regional Transportation Intermodal Center (ARTIC), PB/HOK, Buro Happold, Anaheim, California, 2014. Credit: (a) Buro Happold and (b) Sinéad Mac Namara.

The systems were rationalized in CATIA with a series of customized scripts, analyzed in Robot and then imported into Revit for documentation for the enclosure drawing set, which was a collaboration with HOK on the detailing. All the dimensions were removed from the architectural drawings in order to make the geometry set the prime reference point for construction. Komraus wrote a visual key to enable the definition to be easily understood by the contractors, identifying thousands of points in space in both drawing and spreadsheet form. Although these drawings may have initially scared off some contractors from bidding on the project, the contractors embraced the team's method of relaying information, and Tankha reports that the Geo Grid "has been really successful with contractors. They are all on board."[22]

Bidding Process and Construction

With complex projects at the scale of ARTIC, risk plays a huge factor in the decision-making process. Through careful research, modeling and testing, the design team produced a bid set (the drawings that are issued to the contractors to estimate the final construction costs) on time and on budget. Otto explains that ultimately,

> If a design is not commercially intelligent then you have to ask yourself why … we took something incredibly complex and explained it and simplified it so that others could understand it so that various players could make a good bid and the client could get good value.[23]

Tankha agrees saying that "Technology is only here to make life easier, and if you keep it complicated, then it won't be buildable."[24]

Tanzmann describes that her firm had a contractual obligation to bring the project in on budget and had a cost estimating firm as part of the team and "spent serious time beating up on the design to figure out how to build this fabulous design on budget—not easy to do with a building as unique as this one."[25] She went on to explain, "[ARTIC's] got systems that are at the cutting edge and hard to estimate and the geometry is highly sophisticated ... part of my job is getting the design in control budget-wise."[26] The whole team was involved in getting the design to the point where interested contractors were confident they could build it and as such, the bids were on target. The city of Anaheim defines a "Successful Bidder" as the "lowest qualified, responsive and responsible bidder." Of the eight contractors that responded, six were within $1 million of each other on the estimated $125 million project. The low bid by Clark Construction Group LP of $126 million was selected (the budget increased by the time it was built, as is common, especially for large complex infrastructure projects).

In general, in the US and elsewhere, state-supported projects are publicly accountable and must adhere to strict rules that enable a competitive bidding process. BIM is now required as a deliverable for many state agency-sponsored contracts. In the case of ARTIC, the team was obligated to deliver a Revit model, although the bid set was still paper-based and included the drawing set as well as the 35-page spreadsheet defining the "Geo Grid" of x-y-z coordinates (Figure 16.12). Komraus describes that during the bid process, "the question would come up, 'Is this a tolerance?' It's not a tolerance, it's a definition. If you were looking at the computer, there'd be a lot more decimals on each number."[27] He is hopeful that more government-sponsored projects will be communicated through 3d information, rather than strictly 2d drawing sets. Given the

Figure 16.12 A portion of the Geo Grid. The Anaheim Regional Transportation Intermodal Center (ARTIC), PB/HOK, Buro Happold, Anaheim, California, 2014. Credit: Buro Happold.

complexity of projects like ARTIC, many contractors now use BIM models because it is the only way to understand the systems.

On September 18, 2012, just one month after the general contractor was selected, a ceremony was held to break ground, and the fast-track project was completed in 2014. The design team worked with fabricators to generate mock-ups for each of the facade types. The diagrid system was manufactured by Gartner in Chicago. Gartner's German plant had manufactured the facade for Coop Himmelb(l)au's BMW Welt and advised their Chicago colleagues about fabricating the roof facade system and refining detailing for ease of installation. One-to-one prototypes of the ETFE modules enabled the team to assess light qualities for both daylighting and an adhered RGB LED system that lines each cushion.

Tanzmann describes the hectic construction schedule: There was significant site work including grading, landscape, paving, roadwork, and new signalized intersections. Additionally, a railroad bridge had to be redesigned and replaced.[28] This particular site had suboptimal soil conditions due to existing backfill so the contractors carried out a process called deep dynamic compaction: a crane dropped a 30-ton weight from a height of 80 ft over and over again to compact the soil. Adam Sullivan, superintendent with general contractor Clark Construction Group described this process: "That's how we prepped the ground: We pounded it into submission."[29] After prepping the site, they poured the floating slab foundation. The advantage of the floating foundation is that you can have a rigid plane to support the structure but because it floats on the soil below it is less susceptible to cracking. The steel framing followed quickly and then the contractors placed the pressurized ETFE panels.[30]

There is no question that the nonstandard assemblies and the unusual doubly curved form of this project presented significant expensive challenges. However, the collaborative efforts of the team yielded improvements in cost-effectiveness and scheduling and there were a multitude of triumphs in the design process. The project achieved LEED platinum status, one of the first transit centers to do so.[31]

Tankha comments that "One of the successes of this project was HOK saying, let's collaborate and do this as a team as opposed to trying to drive the whole thing on their own."[32] Greg Otto agrees, saying,

> It's not an easy building. The world is now so complex—it's beyond an individual. The notion of the Beaux Arts architect with his cape and beret barking orders is an obsolete model. There are a lot of experts at the table and the challenge is how you get them to come together. Obviously, the digital prototype is probably the best because it's the way you get all that knowledge mashed up into something that

forces collaboration and coordination. But being able to communicate with other people is key ... In order to do this project right, you really had to have a view about what great design is, the total value for the project and how to achieve it. So it was the cross-disciplinary boundaries that mattered ... You have to be bigger than your own silo.[33]

Critics of the ARTIC project have questioned the suitability of the site for the intermodal transportation center, calling it disconnected from the city fabric and arguing that the existing transit network is not substantial enough to warrant the investment.[34] The high-speed rail line that ARTIC anticipates will not be completed until 2029. The absence of users led to an overall operating loss for the city of Anaheim in the first six months after opening.[35] *LA Times* architectural critic Christopher Hawthorne argues that it has a placeless style that does not have a regional character, but he allows that if transportation networks evolve as the California planners intend then critiques of the siting of the project will prove unfair.[36]

From the point of view of engineering and architecture collaboration, it is perhaps fair to critique the competition-winning form that necessitated so much rationalization to prove constructable. Although post-competition adjustments were made to the building height and other aspects, the rationalization process proved highly complex. By contrast, examples of doubly curved forms that can be resolved into straight and planar components relatively straightforwardly include ruled surfaces and hyperbolic paraboloids.[37] The formal and material ambitions of this project initially won out over pragmatic concerns, although the rationalization of the systems for cost and constructability proved to be interesting technical challenges. On balance, ARTIC might be argued to be an example where more rigorous interdisciplinary collaboration at the conceptual stage might have yielded a form that did not require such extensive rationalization.

Notes

1. LEED is an environmental ratings system officiated by the U.S. Green Building Council.
2. "Sustainability," HOK, accessed April 14, 2013, http://www.hok.com/about/sustainability/.
3. "Culture," HOK, accessed May 27, 2021, https://www.hok.com/people/culture/.
4. Peter Davey, *Engineering for a Finite Planet: Sustainable Solutions by Buro Happold* (Basel; Boston: Birkhäuser, 2009).
5. Greg Otto, Interview by the authors. In-person interview. Los Angeles, June 12, 2013.
6. Center for Demographic Research, "ORANGE COUNTY PROJECTIONS 2006: Population, Housing and Employment through 2035," Orange County Profiles, March 2007.
7. Arnold Lee, Interview by the authors. Phone interview. San Francisco, May 30, 2013.
8. Virginia Tanzmann, Interview by the authors. Phone interview. July 31, 2013.
9. Lee, Interview by the authors.
10. Lee.
11. Lee.
12. Otto, Interview by the authors.
13. Lee.

14 Lee.
15 Sanjeev Tankha, Interview by the authors. In-person interview. Los Angeles, June 12, 2013.
16 Stephen Lewis, Interview by the authors. In-person interview. Los Angeles, June 12, 2013.
17 Lewis, Interview by the authors.
18 Kurt Komraus, Interview by the authors. In-person interview. Los Angeles, June 12, 2013.
19 Tankha, Interview by the authors.
20 Tankha.
21 Tankha.
22 Tankha.
23 Otto.
24 Tankha.
25 Tanzmann, Interview by the authors.
26 Tanzmann.
27 Komraus, Interview by the authors.
28 Tanzmann.
29 Aileen Cho, "Plotting and Welding a Golden State Gateway | 2014-10-29 | ENR," October 29, 2014, https://www.enr.com/articles/5526-plotting-and-welding-a-golden-state-gateway.
30 Tanzmann.
31 "Anaheim Regional Transportation Intermodal Center (ARTIC)," HOK, accessed May 27, 2021, https://www.hok.com/projects/view/anaheim-regional-transportation-intermodal-center/.
32 Tankha.
33 Otto.
34 "Is High Traffic in the Future for Anaheim's ARTIC Station, Now 5 Years Old?," *Orange County Register* (blog), accessed January 20, 2020, https://www.ocregister.com/2020/01/20/is-high-traffic-in-the-future-for-anaheims-artic-station-now-5-years-old.
35 Art Marroquin, "Anaheim's ARTIC Sees $2 Million Deficit during First 6 Months," *TCA Regional News*, accessed April 18, 2015, http://www.proquest.com/docview/1674226695/abstract/7031FEDC97924F11PQ/1.
36 Christopher Hawthorne, "Review: ARTIC Bullet-Train Station a Curious, Conspicuous Bit of Symbolism," *Los Angeles Times*, accessed December 25, 2014, sec. Entertainment and Arts, https://www.latimes.com/entertainment/arts/la-et-cm-artic-train-station-review-20141225-column.html.
37 See for example the concrete shells of Mexican designer Feliz Candela that were constructed with straight timber boards for formwork.

CHAPTER 17

Groundwork to Support Collaborations

Owners, Project Goals, and Contracts

Drawing from the case studies and practitioners' working methods, it is clear that the structure of work and relationships sets the tone for the interdisciplinary collaborations that contribute to a project's success. Depending on the type of client and whether or not the proposed project derives from a competition or call for proposals, collaboration agreements may happen even before devising a contract. Laying the foundation for a solid and rewarding collaborative working relationship involves a number of key, interrelated factors: the support of owners, an early agreement about shared project goals, and the right contract.

Support of Owners

Owners play a vital role in setting the character, structure, and funding for an integrated, collaborative design and delivery process, often equating to increased project value, depending on the scale of the project at hand.[1] An owner's awareness of the costs and benefits of collaboration may depend on previous experience(s) working with architects, engineers, or contractors. As several case studies in this book demonstrate, such as the Gilder Center and the Kendeda Building, sophisticated owners may even evaluate the synergy among collaborators and their history of teamwork prior to offering a contract. By establishing integration as a baseline priority, owners create the foundation for an integrated team.

Owners may take on varying degrees of involvement in working periodically or alongside the project team to achieve project goals. Aside from rubber-stamping designs and making decisions, owners playing a more active role in team development may reap greater rewards. A study on the owner's role in successful delivery of green buildings argues that with motivation and commitment, owners can empower practitioners and encourage work performance through incentives, regular meetings, and rewarding innovative solutions.[2] In discussing the Frick Environmental Center, Larry Jones, Associate Director at Atelier Ten said the Living Building standards could not have been possible without the owner, who championed the project and "opened doors." He offers advice for talking with owners, "Ask questions, challenge when needed, but be open-minded to the answers you might receive. We love clients that ask the tough questions, because even better ideas can come out of those discussions."[3] By contrast, for those owners who may be hesitant to support early interdisciplinary work, it may be incumbent upon the architects to discuss the cost savings potential of early engineer or constructor involvement. See Chapter 3 for a discussion on the cost benefits of timely collaboration.

The role of owners will likely evolve, however, as future ownership scenarios may include new financing structures beyond the standard entities of owner, agency, or developer. As discussed in the Circularity chapter, designing out waste and planning for long-term use can involve borrowing materials or building components rather than purchasing them. Peter van Assche describes that a fully circular economy could change the finance structure for buildings, especially when considering the potential to lease materials, for example. With lowered starting costs, more diverse investors could enter into building "ownership," including architects and engineers.[4]

A Brief Note on "Clients"

Although owners create and finance projects, unless the project is a private home or office, the "clients" for a building extend far beyond the financiers to include a variety of community stakeholders impacted by the project. The "nonpaying" clients (i.e. community members) value the building outside its potential to generate economic gain. Programming, activities, pedestrian experience, aesthetics, and other factors contribute to community well-being. Therefore, integrating all "client" concerns enriches the design process, making it more inclusive, which is synonymous with collaboration.

Shared Project Goals

When owners, designers, and builders co-develop and agree upon the project ambitions at the start of a project, work can be more efficient and copacetic. Shared goals may involve conceptual, experiential, ecological, or community-oriented ambitions. When everyone is on the same page about what, ultimately, is most important, the shared values can guide design decisions at every scale and stage, alleviating disagreements and adversarial interactions. Likewise, revisiting the goals periodically can recenter the focus and drive of the work. In numerous discussions, including about the National Museum of African American History and Culture and the Billie Jean King Main Library, architects and engineers expressed that the team would often return to the shared goals as a way to guide decisions and reaffirm synergies. Simply put, commitment to project goals, especially sustainability or humanitarian goals, contributes to a project's success.[5]

Role of Contracts

Contracts define the roles and responsibilities of architects, engineers, contractors, and owners thereby guiding the relationships, and assigning roles and risk. The hierarchical organization for project delivery remained fairly stagnant throughout the 20th century: traditional contracts put the onus on architects to hire "consultants" to provide engineering drawings after which the project was bid by contractors. Recently, however, the industry developed

Figure 17.1 Guggenheim Museum in Bilbao, Spain, Gehry Partners, 1997. Credit: Clare Olsen.

alternatives to normative project delivery methods with the goals of improving design, communication, schedules, and costs through increased collaboration. In *The Demise and Rebirth of Professionalism*, Carl Saper points out that for Frank Gehry, the redesign of the firm's contract structures was more important than digital technologies for growth and success of the office (Figure 17.1).[6] Without a doubt, delivery methods significantly affect a project team's ability to deliver a building successfully, i.e. on time and on budget, while meeting the project goals.

Traditional Method of Project Delivery: Design-Bid-Build

The American Institute of Architects (AIA) developed its first contract in 1888, the precursor to the project delivery mode and contract type that has dominated the industry for over a hundred years, Design-Bid-Build. Using this conventional family of contract documents, the owner/client signs two contracts: one with the architects and after the design is completed, one with the contractors. It is possible for the architects and owner to develop the goals and schematic design for a project without asking for input from other experts. When consultants are hired (including civil and structural engineers, mechanical engineers, and landscape architects), the architects manage and orchestrate the design, development, and permitting processes. When the design is complete, owners often solicit multiple bids for construction from contractors. Generally speaking, the low bid is selected, especially in governmental projects where federal and state laws require selection of the "lowest qualified, responsive and responsible bidder." The architects often advocate for the owner and design during the building process, termed "construction administration."

As discussed in Chapter 3, however, depending on the circumstances of the project, consulting engineers and construction experts late in the design process can be costly, and quite possibly an adversarial process. Barbara Jackson, author of *Construction Management Jumpstart* and *Design-Build Essentials*, describes the problematic aspects of the traditional contract system, asserting,

> We're addicted to cheap in this country [U.S.] and design-bid-build, the low bid mentality, is the worst thing that ever happened to us as an industry … Our industry is so familiar with a reactive model of engaging with one another versus a proactive model--We're missing fundamental trust.

Jackson goes on to describe that the pervasive system of designing and delivering buildings "incentivizes distrust, incentivizes not communicating, and incentivizes keeping information close to the chest."[7] Many of the professionals interviewed for this text echoed that view and noted that concerns about being held responsible for delays or costs via the specific contract structure stymies collaboration and innovations that might ultimately yield lower costs or higher quality results.

More Collaborative Contract Types

For these reasons, in recent decades industry professionals have sought out new delivery methods and in response, the AIA, the main source for industry contracts, has developed numerous new contract types. The AIA Firm Survey Report 2020 indicates that in 2017, design-bid-build represented 59% of billings, remaining consistently more than half of the contracts in the US by billings, whereas the fastest growing contract type, construction manager as constructor, had increased rapidly in use from 11% of billings in 2017 to 19% of billings in 2019.[8] In the latter contract type, a single entity provides construction services and oversight. Generally, owners select the contract type, impacting the timing, selection and working relationships of project collaborators. The following contracts offer a range of those that lend well to early collaborative design processes.

Construction Manager

As mentioned, for these agreements, an owner contracts with a construction manager to provide preconstruction and/or construction services, depending on the construction manager contract type. Involving contractors in preconstruction, even predesign, enables early and continual discussions about constructability and cost concerns. Seeking input from contractors during preconstruction also reduces Requests for Information (RFIs), that have been pervasive in the industry since architects, engineers, and contractors have resided in separate silos. A Navigant Construction Forum analysis of over 1,300 construction projects worldwide found an average of nearly 800 RFIs per project and an average cost of a single RFI Review and Response of $1,080.[9] Reducing this costly process by integrating constructors into design and detailing discussions with architects and engineers contributes to more efficient construction with fewer cost-overruns. Other versions of this contract type include construction manager as constructor at-risk and/or with a guaranteed maximum price. These contracts tend to be used for institutional or public projects with sensitive budgets and schedules.[10]

Design-Build

Owners use design-build contracts to hire a single entity to provide both design and construction of the project while also assuming liability. Design-build modes of delivery offer the benefits of "cross-functional teams and integrated

Figure 17.2 The Billie Jean King Main Library under construction. The public–private partnership involved SOM and Clark Construction from the start of the project. Credit: © Skidmore, Owings & Merrill.

design of product and process,"[11] and as a result, they are an increasingly popular form of delivery. The Design-Build Institute of America works to advance the acceptance and use of the contract type in public projects, which often necessitate fast-track scheduling. A version of this contract, design-build-operate-maintain, a public–private partnership (P3), guided the working relationships for the Billie Jean King Main Library case study, demonstrating how partnerships between contractors and designers facilitate a smoother, more efficient and rewarding project design and delivery process (Figure 17.2).

Integrated Project Delivery

Generally speaking, integrated project delivery is a multiparty agreement where the contractor is brought on board from the start of the design process. Although IPD, by definition, involves an integrated team, the contract type is mostly used in the healthcare sector. The first "true" IPD project, the Fairfield Medical Office Building, began in 2005 and the AIA officially released an IPD contract as well as other associated documents (including a BIM agreement)[12] in 2008. Other legal strategies that guide integrated project delivery include liability waivers, shared risk/reward, financial incentives tied to goals, and fiscal transparency,[13] which IPD participants surveyed reported "had a positive effect on the teams' perception of trust and respect for project partners."[14] Integrated delivery provides the benefits of shared risks and rewards, easing the tension prevalent in traditional delivery modes that pit aesthetics or experience against costs.

Jackson acknowledges that new delivery modes require an entirely different way of working. "This is earth shaking for the design industry because nobody is accustomed to this, so psychologically, culturally, practically, educationally—it turns everything upside down."[15] Speaking from a construction management perspective, however, Jackson said that in her experience, early commitment from all concerned, especially the client, to the principles of integrated delivery is the key to success.

> The transition is very difficult: with the first roadblock everyone goes back to a silo mentality ... To me, the key to all this is leadership. The critical skills of that leader are facilitation, communication, the ability to dialogue, investigate and discover solutions together.[16]

Jackson's observations corroborates Kellogg School of Management collaboration researcher Leigh Thompson's, "[W]ith a few key insights and simple best practices, teams can dramatically improve their performance and generate a creative conspiracy."[17] Thompson describes those "best practices" to include establishing rules and a strong leader to guide discussions.[18] Incidentally, the AIA IPD case studies found benchmarks of IPD management strategies included *strong leadership* and *intensified planning/team building*.[19]

Lean Principles

The industry has adopted a number of delivery methods to use in conjunction with contracts as a way to address the problems of cost-overruns and waste. These include Lean Construction techniques introduced to the industry in the early 1990s based on lean manufacturing as demonstrated particularly in the automobile industry's successful reduction of costs, time, waste, and space; and Target Value Design (TVD), which "designates value, cost, schedule and constructability as basic components of the design criteria."[20] Lean Construction and TVD are often used in conjunction, where the value or project costs drive the design decisions from the very start of a project and value is assessed throughout each stage of project development. This way the project costs and differences in designers' versus contractors' cost estimations are aligned/realigned throughout the project (instead of being done after the bidding process as is the norm). Lean construction methods may also play an increasing role, as "lean and green" project delivery refers to eliminating waste (ranging from time to materials) to generate greater value both for the bottom line and sustainability goals.

"Full-Life Benefits" of Collaboration

Given the complexity and multiplicity of the practices of architecture, engineering, and construction, these contract types and their associated methods hold extraordinary potential and should not be undervalued, especially in their capacity to facilitate collaboration through more productive, less adversarial, more cost-effective ways of designing and delivering projects. Ultimately, AEC professionals recognize that although design-bid-build has served the building industry for 125 years, it is an antiquated paradigm and the industry has suffered as a result. Jackson summarizes her hope for the industry:

> I say it as gently as I can but I tell everyone on my project teams: this project is not about you. This project is about this community, this organization of folks and what they produce. This is what I call 'full life benefits'.[21]

She gives the example of hospital design to illustrate her point where the overarching goals are faster recovery and lower rates of infection for the patients. She places the onus on owners to invest in the concept of quality and longevity over immediate (apparent) cost savings.

> I think our industry is one of the noblest industries on the face of the planet. And look at what has been produced under design-bid-build and low bid mentality! Imagine what we could do if we started to consider that full life benefit instead of our own vested interest and identities. It's such a different outcome and everybody would walk away feeling they had a wonderful experience.[22]

Whether collaboration is contracted or not, laying the groundwork for open communication, empathy, and creating a shared vision for project goals contribute not only to a project's success but inevitably, each individual's work satisfaction and fulfillment. But given that contract structure can have such a significant impact on the nature of collaboration among engineers, architects, and especially contractors it is incumbent on the AEC professions to revise, refine, and interrogate the legal and financial frameworks we use to ensure that they align with larger, long-term goals for the greater good.

Notes

1. Lauri Koskela, Greg Howell, Glenn Ballard, and Iris Tommelein et al., "The Foundations of Lean Construction." In Rick Best and Gerard de Valence, eds. *Design and Construction: Building in Value*. 1st edition. Oxford; Boston: Butterworth-Heinemann, 2002..
2. Jingxiao Zhang et al., "A Successful Delivery Process of Green Buildings: The Project Owners' View, Motivation and Commitment," *Renewable Energy* 138 (August 1, 2019): 651–658, https://doi.org/10.1016/j.renene.2019.02.002.
3. Larry Jones, Interview with Atelier Ten, Larry Jones, Zoom, June 10, 2021.
4. Peter van Assche, Interview with bureau SLA, Peter van Assche, Zoom, May 4, 2021.
5. Zhang et al., "A Successful Delivery Process of Green Buildings."
6. Kiel Moe, "Automation Takes Command: The Nonstandard, Unautomatic History of Standardization and Automation in Architecture." In Robert Corser ed. *Fabricating Architecture Selected Readings in Digital Design and Manufacturing*. New York, NY: Princeton Architectural Press, 2010. 152–167. 164.

7   Barbara Jackson, Interview by the authors. Phone interview. Denver, August 21, 2013.
8   American Institute of Architects, "Firm Survey Report – The Business of Architecture 2020," 2020, https://www.aia.org/resources/6151-firm-survey-report.
9   Hughes Nigel, M. Wells, C. Nutter, and J. Zack, *Impact & Control of RFIs on Construction Projects*. Navig Constr ForumTM. 2013.
10 Caryn Brause, *The Designer's Field Guide to Collaboration*, 1 edition (New York: Routledge, 2017).
11 Koskela et al., "The Foundations of Lean Construction."
12 E202–2008, or Building Information Modeling (BIM) Protocol Exhibit, provides terms of use of a BIM model, see B. J. Novitski, "AIA to Release New IPD and Design-Build Documents." Architectural Record, accessed October 2, 2008, archrecord.construction.com/news/daily/archives/081002aia.asp.
13 AIA, AIA Minnesota, School of Architecture –University of Minnesota. "IPD Case Studies." www.aia.org/aiaucmp/groups/aia/documents/pdf/aiab093703.pdf.
14 AIA, "IPD Case Studies."
15 Jackson, Interview by the authors. Phone interview. Denver.
16 Jackson.
17 Leigh L. Thompson, *Creative Conspiracy: The New Rules of Breakthrough Collaboration* (Boston, MA: Harvard Business Review Press, 2013).
18 Thompson, *Creative Conspiracy*.
19 AIA.
20 AIA, 20.
21 Jackson.
22 Jackson.

CHAPTER **18**

Tools to Support Collaborations
Software

Similar to the typological and stylistic transformations that grew out of the Industrial Revolution, new technologies and materials are revolutionizing the architecture and engineering professions, creating new working methods and sensibilities. In the 1980s, graphic Finite Element Analysis software and Building Information Modeling emerged, followed in the 1990s by Computer Aided Manufacturing software that facilitated digital fabrication. Now, decades later, we can safely say that these technologies have had and will continue to have a profound effect on curricula, design, and construction methods as well as the forms and performance of the work produced. Technological developments in materials, construction techniques (including digital fabrication and offsite construction), and sustainable systems are just a few of the advancements that call for new approaches to design, analysis, and construction. Consequently, the work—and work life—of architects and engineers is becoming increasingly more complex.

Recognizing the complexity of contemporary design and practice, clear and consistent visual communication and project documentation are crucial to project development and realization. Greater coherence and integration can be achieved when communicating often and this certainly happens through numerous means: from verbal communication about the values and goals for a particular project to a highly intricate virtual construction model with coordinated building systems and details. Architects and engineers interviewed for this book agreed that fluid and continual visual communication is vital throughout the entire project from the initial stages, when designers use hand sketching and form-finding through analog and digital techniques, and ultimately, in coordinating the documentation for construction.

As software that facilitate representation, rationalization, analysis, design, prototyping, component fabrication, construction, and operations become ever more available, ever more widely used, and ever more cross-platform compatible, architects, engineers, and contractors increasingly use digital means for collaboration. These digital practices allow collaborators to literally "get on the same page" through cloud-based models or shared files, although the types of files exchanged or shared may change throughout the various stages of project delivery. Increasingly, as emerging software become more accessible and easier to use, digital tools have a significant role to play, potentially addressing a number of the challenges to architect–engineer–constructor partnerships, and making teamwork more efficient and integrated.

In basic terms, transformations in working methods result from expanding capabilities in computation ranging from BIM to digital twins[1] used in building operations. Ben van Berkel of architecture firm UNStudio, writing with the practice's Smart Parameter Platform, states,

> It is clear now that computation is ubiquitous, and form making and form controlling are no longer its most expedient uses. Whether it is through proprietary and customized software or a single piece of code, computation's primary potential lies in its flexibility to communicate design across multiple disciplines via associative data.[2]

Building upon this insight, this chapter discusses digital working methods that increase communication and integration of designs and ultimately aid in more thorough and efficient project design, construction, and operations processes.

Collaborative Workflows: Representation, Analysis, and Rationalization

Certainly, most engineering and architecture practices have long-shared use of hand drawing and 2D digital drawings using AutoCAD and similar programs. However, increasingly in early stages of collaborative design, practitioners cite the importance of 3D digital representation tools to their conversations and mutual development of design ideas.[3] Sharing files or transferring information across platforms facilitates common understanding while taking advantage of the fluidity of using 3d software such as Rhinoceros (Rhino) in form-finding. Architects and engineers alike are transforming their practices through ever-expanding digital workflows. George Keliris, structural engineer in Buro Happold's London office remarks that their tools and techniques have radically changed. Whereas visualization was usually left to the architectural designers, Buro Happold has integrated the tools into their working methods, helping to conceptualize complex, efficient structures in shorter lengths of time.[4] Similarly, the engineers at Thornton Tomasetti also use Rhino to integrate structural concepts with architectural intent at early stages.[5] Arup structural engineer Michelle Roelofs describes the technique of hand drawing over screen shots of a Rhino model and then slicing through the digital file to evaluate sections for structural potential and load flows.[6]

While engineers expand the use of digital tools for design and visualization, architects are embracing digital analysis software at earlier stages to develop and enhance the design of building performance. Patricia Culley, architect at Bohlin Cywinski Jackson describes that at various stages in project design, in-house specialists assess digital models and suggest energy reduction strategies.[7] An example of a multi-platform design and analysis process is demonstrated in the case study of the ARTIC project (see Chapter 16) where architects

Figure 18.1 Digital models for the Anaheim Regional Transportation Intermodal Center generated in various software including Catia and Grasshopper. Image courtesy of Buro Happold. Credit: Buro Happold.

and engineers rationalized the curvilinear form into constructible components, a challenge facilitated through the use of Grasshopper and CATIA (Figure 18.1).

Throughout the design process (from ideation to detailing), rationalization and analysis aid in making designs more safe, buildable, sustainable, and comfortable. Software performing these functions are available for multiple platform types including plug-ins that augment Rhino's capabilities to embedded functions within Building Information Modeling software such as Revit. For example, early in the design process, designers may use Ladybug, a Rhino Grasshopper plug-in that integrates weather data for analyzing form, whereas later, one might conduct energy analyses (Building Energy Modeling) using Revit with Insight or through another software such as DesignBuilder or Virtual Environment. Similarly, structural engineers may import Rhino geometry into finite element analysis (FEA) programs such as ANSYS and SAP2000 to analyze multiple performance criteria (stress, deflection, thermal performance, air flow) and find potential weaknesses or points of failure.

Digital applications facilitate more productive conversations between architects and engineers, in particular when they allow engineers to quickly communicate the technical implications of specific design decisions, and help refine their architectural collaborators' understanding of the engineering constraints and opportunities. Architects and engineers Besserud, Katz, and Beghini at SOM, a noted collaborative practice, use computational tools to facilitate collaboration, particularly in design processes that require architects and engineers to "jointly define performative goals and constraints;" for example, where complex shapes need to be geometrically defined and technical feasibility needs to be tested for multiple design approaches. They advocate for graphic visualization tools such as mapping flows or colored heat maps to easily and quickly communicate technical constraints such as stresses and magnitudes so that architects can easily understand the relationships between shape and structural capacity. "This ability to get a clear window into the structural performance of a given design scheme allows designers to speculate more intelligently and more immediately about possible modifications to improve the design."[8]

Of course, analysis software are crucial from material and energy efficiency standpoints. The benefits of digital analyses far outweigh the costs associated with poor or inefficient performance in the physical structure or in building operations over time. Creating robust digital models for design integration, analysis, and refinement requires investing in personnel time and software and hardware resources at the front end of projects, but this translates into invaluable cost savings when considering the benefits of construction efficiency and operational energy savings. For a discussion on investing in digital processes for environmental benefits, see Chapter 8 on net zero.

Expanding on Workflows Using Building Information Modeling (BIM)

A host of BIM software applications available to designers include Digital Project, Tekla, ArchiCAD, Bentley Architecture, and Revit. At a basic level, BIM software enable parametric modeling (modeling with embedded algorithms that create and maintain relationships between objects), thereby facilitating construction documentation and visualization. When these models are shared across multiple disciplines, design teams can more easily assess the impacts of integrating systems and monitor the consequent effects of changes to the design. Coordination is a matter of integrating systems and checking their compatibility. One of the major benefits of developing a shared information model is that one can see when systems are not working together, but there are also clash detection protocols that can be used to determine where conflicts occur.

For some practitioners, BIM is used from the start of a project, whereas others use Rhino[9] for design development and then export the model to BIM (using Conveyor or other means) once design ideas are more solidified, often after schematic design. But BIM offers many more uses and benefits beyond development of construction documentation including the ability to construct the building in digital space using time-based (4d) simulations (virtual construction) to determine project phasing and scheduling and to estimate costs (5d). Some municipalities also provide code assessments of the BIM model at multiple stages of the design. The program SMARTreviewAPR, for example, provides automated assessment of the information model for International Building Code (IBC) compliance. During and after construction, the building information model can be updated to include as-built conditions via drone to serve as a digital twin that building operations managers can use throughout the life of the project.[10]

As a result of the many advantages described, use of BIM software has grown markedly since they were introduced to the building industry in the 1990s. The AIA Firm Survey Report 2020 indicates that BIM adoption has grown steadily, and in 2019, was used by 100% of large firms, 88% of midsize firms and 37% of small firms.[11] In the UK, BIM is mandated for all projects in the public sector. Similarly, in the US, the General Services Administration (GSA) that oversees federal agencies and the US Army Corps of engineers both mandate the use of BIM in the design phase. The GSA also encourages its use for facility management, energy savings, more efficient building maintenance, renovation, and improved working environments.[12]

Value of BIM

These robust capabilities translate into numerous benefits for users and the built environment summarized succinctly by Adriana Sanchez et al. "Mature BIM is a socio-technical system that can be used to improve team communication throughout the project life cycle, produce better outcomes, reduce rework, lower risk, provide better predictability of outcomes and improve operation and maintenance of an asset."[13] Although using BIM in the design process can be costly for firms at the front end (associated with staff training, software acquisition, and time invested in detailed modeling), BIM can translate into significant cost savings during construction if project managers coordinate systems input from each discipline (clash detection) and use the software for scheduling and cost estimating. A McGraw-Hill survey of contractors in ten countries reported in *The Business Value of BIM in Major Global Markets* that the top five BIM benefits included reduced errors and omissions, collaboration with owners/design firms, enhanced organizational image, reduced rework, and reduced construction costs (Figure 18.2).[14]

Illustrating the benefits of a fully integrated model, the American Institute of Architects (AIA) carried out a study of Integrated Project Delivery (IPD), which often makes use of BIM. One of their case studies was the Cathedral Hill Hospital in San Francisco for which an integrated information model facilitated more efficient onsite work. There the team located all the studs in the

Figure 18.2 Screen view of the Navisworks model used by the SOM-Clark Construction team for the Billie Jean King Main Library in Long Beach, California. This view shows integration of structure, fire protection, plumbing, and ducts. Credit: © Skidmore, Owings & Merrill.

model so the handrail could be attached directly, and since a hospital has handrails along almost every foot of the corridors, the elimination of the continuous backing for the handrail saved $400,000 on total project costs.[15]

When designers integrate models and eliminate clashes of systems, BIM also offers an opportunity to reduce construction errors, rework (construction activities performed more than once), and construction waste. Research by the Navigant Construction Forum found,

> [a]verage rework on projects can cost between 7.25% and 10.89% of total construction cost (when both direct and indirect costs are included) and can cause an increase in the schedule (project delay) of approximately 9.8% of the planned project time.[16]

In other terms, a 2018 survey of 600 construction leaders in the US found that rework amounted to more than $31 billion that year.[17]

Interviewed in *Architecture*, Seattle architect Joe Pinzone extols the benefits of determining systems locations prior to construction, "One of the dirty little secrets of construction is how much re-work has to be done… Moving something three times is built into the cost of that sprinkler head."[18] Ultimately, a carefully managed BIM model translates into both cost savings as well as a reduction in onsite waste. On the other hand, if rework results from design omissions or lack of coordination among designers, these errors can also negatively impact the designers' bottom line. Conversely, a SmartMarket Brief on BIM Advancements reports that for half of respondents, successful use of BIM equated to a 5% reduction in construction costs and a 5% acceleration in project timelines.[19]

A further illustration of cost savings can be found in a project at the Stanford University Medical Center. Three Cath Labs of similar size and scope were designed and built. While the first lab was constructed based on 2D digital drawings, the second two labs were designed by Design Partnership LLP Architects and Planners who used BIM for some of the documentation process of the second and for the entire development and documentation of the third. In analyzing the differences and successes of the three projects, the owner–architect team discovered that the first cath lab, designed using traditional methods, had change orders[20] that totaled 12.4% of total costs, whereas the 100% BIM project had change orders below 0.1% of total construction costs! They also discovered that the BIM project saved 23% on total costs, had 44% fewer requests for information (RFIs) and was completed 35% faster.[21]

Testing BIM's jobsite capabilities, McKinsey & Company used a robust BIM process for the Venice Capability Center and integrated digital technologies within three key areas: *collaboration* (as information base for owners and contractors), *tracking, and forecasting* (using drones to document construction in relationship to the BIM model to determine errors and potential clashes), and worker safety and material workflows.[22] They note challenges to the process involve proper inputs into the BIM "control tower," personnel training and engagement with the tools, and management of the construction work schedule,[23] but an overall net gain in testing and integrating BIM in the construction process.

Yet, BIM's advantages extend far beyond cost and workflow efficiencies in design and construction: potential benefits accrue through the working life of a building if the model is used as a building management tool to facilitate maintenance, renovations and additions, and day-to-day management of building systems and operations. Investing in the accuracy of the model makes sense for long-term building maintenance goals[24] especially in large, institutional projects. Arnold Lee of HOK notes, "Almost all of our clients need a virtual database for record keeping and maintenance and so it's not uncommon to deliver a digital model at the end of a job."[25] Building operations and maintenance uses of BIM include locating building components, monitoring energy use, and space planning.[26]

Challenges to BIM Collaboration

Despite this growth in use and expansive capabilities, BIM is not without controversy. Early criticism was that it was a kit-of-"object" parts that proved very challenging to alter for customized, nonnormative design work. The software libraries of materials and components have inherent benefits and limitations—BIM programmers cannot possibly provide every system available in construction, leaving firms to develop their own element libraries. Furthermore, the databases can be challenging to manipulate when designing bespoke systems. The various BIM tools continue to evolve, however; not only are the interfaces becoming more user-friendly, but translation or interoperability between software platforms has also become easier.

Other barriers to BIM use include the challenges of transitioning personnel and workflows to use new working methods and managing the interoperability of different systems or integration of different models between architects, engineers, and constructors. For large projects, when different, complex parts are constructed by many people, a model manager inevitably invests significant time in coordination to fix inconsistencies and clashes and update ongoing changes. Describing this process for the Billie Jean King Main Library, SOM Senior Designer Roshanak Mostaghim explained that this was a challenging process, but well worth the investment because it led to significant efficiencies during construction.[27]

With the expectation of virtual construction, optimizing the accuracy of the BIM file proves a significant challenge. Stephen Kieran and James Timberlake advocate that an accurately constructed building "simulation" where dimensions can be derived from the 3d model will transform working methods, "rendering the once necessary dimensional drawings now obsolete."[28] In response to this idea, Dan Willis and Todd Woodward point out that if construction documents go by the wayside, "there will be unprecedented demands for accuracy of the architect's computer modeling, but there may also be the potential for increased control over the built work."[29] They go on to caution, however, that the

> virtual reality of the BIM is actually more precise than the material world ... We believe that the inevitable "errors" present in reality, including natural processes such as thermal expansion and weathering, make it impossible to achieve a *direct* correlation between digital data and a constructed building.[30]

Most projects are not entirely machine-fabricated—the finishes and materials are made by hand, like the paint on the drywall, and structural elements are still placed and connected by humans. This simultaneously provides opportunities for field adjustments when the real-world conditions do not match with the virtual construction, and represents an upper limit on the tolerance within which the final product can exactly match the model. For these reasons, constructors increasingly use drones on the construction site to document the built condition and discrepancies with the building information model, and update the digital model for future use in operation and maintenance.

Despite the challenges with BIM, the associated productivity gains mean that the tool is an integral part of the collaborative process for architects, engineers, and constructors. Software will continue to evolve to facilitate earlier and more integrated collaboration amongst all the AEC disciplines. Harif Kara, of AKT II warns, "[T]hese new media should also be approached cautiously since the ubiquity of digital media cannot replace human interaction that frames new questions and permits interdisciplinary creativity."[31] For a more in-depth discussion of the humanistic aspects of collaboration, please see Chapter 3.

Danelle Briscoe, author of *Beyond BIM: Architecture Information Modeling*,[32] recognizes that BIM provides fertile ground for design practices driven by the logics of materials and systems. Briscoe says,

> With conceptualization through BIM, the information becomes a recipe for exchange of aesthetics (among other things) ... The

open-source nature of information exchange means design of built space and form can be improving exponentially as a collective for a progressive process.[33]

As many case studies in this book demonstrate, BIM proves critical, not just for communication and coordination of designs, but also to achieve a more holistic understanding of the building and its future impacts on people and the planet.

Notes

1 For more information, see Dennis Shelden, "Cyber-Physical Systems and the Built Environment," *Technology|Architecture + Design* 2, no. 2 (July 3, 2018): 137–139, https://doi.org/10.1080/24751448.2018.1497358.
2 B. van Berkel, "Navigating the Computational Turn," *Architectural Design* 83 (2013): 82–87. 87.
3 For example, Hans Schober, Interview by the authors. Skype Interview. Stuttgart, June 19, 2013; George Keliris, Interview by the authors. Phone interview. London, England, June 21, 2013; Michelle Roelofs. Interview by the authors. Zoom Interview. New York City, March 4, 2021.
4 Keliris, Interview by the authors. Phone interview.
5 Bruce Gibbons, Interview by the authors. Phone interview. Los Angeles, July 8, 2013, and Roelofs, Interview by the authors.
6 Roelofs.
7 Patricia Culley, Interview with Bohlin Cywinski Jackson, Patricia Culley.
8 Keith Besserud, Neil Katz, and Alessandro Beghini, "Structural Emergence: Architectural and Structural Design Collaboration at SOM," *Architectural Design* 83 (2013): 48–55.
9 For more innovative and non-normative structures, many designers begin the design process in "looser" programs such as Rhino, Maya or even Sketchup and then import the geometry into a BIM model to serve as a basis for development of the details and constructability.
10 Kim Haugbolle and David Boyd, eds., *Clients and Users in Construction: Agency, Governance and Innovation* (Routledge, 2017), https://doi-org.ezproxy.lib.calpoly.edu/10.4324/9781315644783.
11 American Institute of Architects, "Firm Survey Report – The Business of Architecture 2020," 2020, https://www.aia.org/resources/6151-firm-survey-report.
12 GSA, "Facility Management," *General Services Administration*, accessed August 23, 2013, http://www.gsa.gov/portal/content/122555.
13 Adriana Sanchez et al., "BIM for Sustainable Whole-of-Life Transport Infrastructure Asset Management," 2014.
14 Chiến Phạm, "The Business Value of BIM for Construction in Major Global Markets: How Contractors around the World Are Driving Innovation with Building Information Modeling," https://www.academia.edu/27756523/The_Business_Value_of_BIM_for_Construction_in_Major_Global_Markets_How_Contractors_Around_the_World_Are_Driving_Innovation_With_Building_Information_Modeling.
15 AIA, AIA Minnesota, School of Architecture – University of Minnesota. "IPD Case Studies." www.aia.org/aiaucmp/groups/aia/documents/pdf/aiab093703.pdf, 21.
16 Jason M. Dougherty and James G. Zack, "The Impact of Rework on Construction & Some Practical Remedies," 2012, 21.
17 "New Research from PlanGrid and FMI Identifies Factors Costing the Construction Industry More Than $177 Billion Annually," accessed May 13, 2021, https://www.plangrid.com/press/fmi/.
18 Brian Libby, "Plugging In," *Architect the AIA Magazine* January (2013): 80–86.
19 BentleyTech Research Report 01. "BentleyTech Research Report 01 by Dodge Data & Analytics," accessed May 13, 2021, http://www.smartmarketbrief.com/.
20 *Change orders*, as they are called in the AECO industry, are changes to the scope of work agreement, discovered after the project has been bid and priced, translating to added total costs (beyond the expectations) for construction of the project. A 2006 AIA survey found that change orders averaged about 4% of total construction costs, although the survey found that in 23% of the jobs reported, change orders amounted to 5% or more of total construction costs. Change orders are caused by a range of circumstances: owners modify the scope of work after the bid, architects and engineers make mistakes on the original documents (RFI responses can result in change orders), and unpredictable circumstances arise. The cost of change orders depends on the scope and scale of the work, and regional costs of construction also play a large role. See Baker, Kermit, PhD, and Hon. AIA. "AIArchitect This Week | Economics: WORK-ON-THE-BOARDS SURVEY: Firms Enjoy a Late Summer Surge," http://info.aia.org/aiarchitect/thisweek06/0922/0922b_otb.cfm.
21 Eric Peabody, "Experimental BIM Use Comparison on Stanford Hospital Cath Labs," *Upload & Share PowerPoint Presentations and Documents*. http://www.slideshare.net/epeabody/shc-cath-7-9-10-comparison.
22 "Walking the Talk: Best Practices for Digital Construction | McKinsey," accessed May 14, 2021, https://www.mckinsey.com/business-functions/operations/our-insights/walking-the-talk-best-practices-for-digital-construction.
23 McKinsey & Company, *Digital Capability Center Venice Expansion Update – Capital Excellence Showcase*, 2021, https://www.youtube.com/watch?v=hlVpjYtOiMg.

24　Charles M. Eastman, *BIM Handbook: A Guide to Building Information Modeling for Owners, Managers, Designers, Engineers and Contractors.* 2nd edition (Hoboken, NJ: Wiley, 2011). 21.
25　Arnold Lee, Interview by the author. Phone interview. San Francisco, May 30, 2013.
26　A. H. Oti et al., "A Framework for the Utilization of BMS Data in BIM to Bridge Gaps between Building Design and Operation," *Automation in Construction* 72, no. 2 (2016): 195–210.
27　Roshanak Mostaghim, Interview with SOM, Zarmine Nigohos and Roshanak Mostaghim, Zoom, April 16, 2021.
28　Stephen Kieran and James Timberlake, *Refabricating Architecture* (New York: Mcgraw Hill, 2004): 61, quoted in Dan Willis and Todd Woodward, "Diminishing Difficulty: Mass Customization and the Digital Production of Architecture." In Robert Corser ed. *Fabricating Architecture Selected Readings in Digital Design and Manufacturing.* New York, NY: Princeton Architectural Press, 2010. 152–167. 183.
29　Willis and Woodward, "Diminishing Difficulty: Mass Customization and the Digital Production of Architecture."
30　Willis and Woodward, 184.
31　Hanif Kara, "On Design Engineering," *Architectural Design* 80 (2010): 46–51.
32　Danelle Briscoe, *Beyond BIM: Architecture Information Modeling* (New York: Routledge, 2015).
33　Danelle Briscoe, "Beauty + the BIM." ACSA 100th conference. Boston, 2012.

APPENDIX

Guidelines for Developing Interdisciplinary Courses[1]

The following guidelines are based on the Shells Structures course, co-taught by the authors at Syracuse University in two iterations. The faculty worked with Syracuse University education evaluators, Scott L. Shablak, Carolina B. Harris, who conducted focus groups and surveys and the beginning, middle, and end of the two courses.[2] The education evaluation reports have enabled us to develop the following guidelines for future engineering and architecture collaborative courses.

Logistics/Course Structure

1. *Interdisciplinary design can be taught at any point in the curriculum to either the same level of students or to a mix of levels.*

    In our experience where both classes were composed of engineers from the third year and architecture students from a wide range of years, we found no clear indicators that interdisciplinary design should be taught at a particular moment in the curriculum. Although intuitively it may seem that communication would improve amongst students who are at about the same level, at least in the Syracuse University context, the dominant personalities were not necessarily those in the higher age group.

2. *The course structure works well as a hybrid of the design studio, seminar, and technical lecture models, but because of time, should (ideally) run as a studio.*

    Lectures, lab instruction (on software or other technical topics), and group critiques enable general knowledge to be dispersed about vocabulary, history, precedents for the work, and technical skills. The group critiques are also an essential part of the design course so that students can understand the range of possibilities and learn from one another. At the same time, small group critiques, desk critiques and working sessions allow the instructors to give individual attention to groups and observe group dynamics more closely, which also facilitates intervention if there are communication issues in the group.

3. *Instructors from each of the disciplines should (ideally) be present in the classroom together as much as possible.*

   Given tight budgets, this may be difficult to achieve, however, key learning (on the part of the students and instructors) occurs when multiple perspectives are voiced in the classroom. In order to address communication dynamics amongst students, it is helpful to understand their perspective and the instructor's understanding can be gained, in large part, from observing and talking to the other instructor.

4. *Invite outside experts—equally—from both disciplines.*

   Emphasize that each discipline is complex and that feedback from colleagues is an essential part of the design and learning processes. We would usually invite outside critics to review the work (as presented by the students), but we found that some engineering colleagues were unaccustomed to the review process and did not always provide constructive feedback, especially regarding technical concerns. It may be helpful to invite colleagues who have some experience with design teaching or even interdisciplinary collaboration.

5. *Meet in a classroom that is not in the architecture school/department.*

   The Shells Structures courses met in the architecture school both years, and we now recognize (through the course evaluations) that the context alone provides comfort and sets a tone. Our goal was to emphasize creative thinking for the engineers, which naturally took them out of their mental comfort zone. Confidence-building and emotional comfort may result from teaching the engineers on their "home turf."

6. *A note to department heads: Flexibility and support are vital.*

   We were lucky enough to have the support of NSF and the two Deans, and this made logistical processes fast and relatively painless. Without administrative support, potential stumbling blocks may include obtaining permission to cross-list the course, determining the room, and deciding how to share equipment and material resources. Fingers crossed that your administration is as visionary as you are.

Content

7. *Choose a topic that is relatively new to the curriculum of both disciplines.*

   Shells Structures turned out to be a well-suited topic for the Syracuse University curricula because it was new for both the engineering and architecture students. Although it is important to recognize and harness varying types of expertise amongst the students, it is also helpful to achieve a level playing field—a sensibility that everyone is "in it together". When growth is happening in parallel amongst a diverse group of students, they tend to forge bonds and help one another through the process.

8. *In a 15-week semester, 3-credit course scenario, we recommend no more than three short assignments (without a high degree of resolution) and a final project of about six weeks, which is more resolved.*

In the case of the Shells collaboration, which emphasized open-ended problem solving and creativity, we introduced a series of short projects so that there would be multiple opportunities for collaborating with different partners. We attempted to isolate the key design elements for the group to tackle, acknowledging very clearly what was being left out to avoid misconceptions about the design process.[3] On the positive side, we observed that the short assignments were helpful in building confidence through multiple attempts. However, student surveys revealed that the students were frustrated by the lack of time to delve deeply into design (especially later in the semester when we had allotted four weeks for the final project).

Tips for Teaching

9. *Allow working sessions during class time in order to observe group dynamics and tactfully intervene when necessary.*

As faculty already know, the complex craft of teaching involves nuances that change from student to student. In our experience, teaching an interdisciplinary course requires even more close observation and attention to psychology than other non-collaborative courses. Observing group dynamics during working sessions is an important evaluative tool to assess communication and learning.

10. *Acknowledge and discuss disciplinary differences in vocabulary and training. Talk about ways to communicate so that students from each discipline feel they have valued expertise.*

Students develop disciplinary vocabularies early in their educational careers and may find communication about values and goals challenging. Addressing these gaps via faculty mentoring and by modeling communication behaviors helps students to address these challenges.

Notes

1. These guidelines were first featured in the following paper: C.J. Olsen and S.C. Mac Namara, *In Support of Pre-Professional Relations: Guidelines for Effective Educational Collaborations between Architecture and Engineering*, ACSA 100th conference, 2012.
2. For further discussion, see: S.C. Mac Namara, C.J. Olsen, Scott L. Shablak, Carolina B. Harris, *Merging Engineering and Architectural Pedagogy - A Trans-disciplinary Opportunity?*, 2010 ICEE Conference on Engineering Education, Silesian University of Technology, Gliwice, Poland, July 18–22, 2010.
3. For example, in the first assignment in Shell Structures, we asked for five connected shells with specific square footages, but the site and program (type of function or activity of the space) were abstract and materiality was ambiguous.

Index

Academy for Architectural Culture, Hamburg 245
Accademia di Architettura, Mendrisio 154
Accra, Ghana 38
accreditation 7, 9, 11, 13, 17
Accreditation Board for Engineering and Technology (ABET) 9, 11
acoustic engineering/design 62, 101, 109, 120, 145, 182
Activity Based Office (ABO) 196
Adams, Robin 148
Adjaye Associates 5, 37–61, 148
Adjaye, David 37–61
ADPi 227
AECOM Tishman 62, 70
African Diaspora 41–42, 51
aggregate 77, 239
Ahrens, Chandler 164, 166–169, 179
air conditioning/air handling 23, 91, 115, 121, 167, 208
Akron Art Museum 166
AKT II 31, 38, 145–163, 297
aluminum 46–47, 211–212
Alvar Aalto Medal 200
Amelar, Sarah 211
American Academy of Arts and Letters 39
American Institute of Architects (AIA) 20, 22, 27, 40, 125, 135, 200, 283–286, 293–294; CAE Award 135; Collaborative Achievement Award 40; COTE Award 135; Firm Survey Report 284, 293
American Institute of Architects Gold Medal (AIA) 200
American Memorial Library, Berlin 200–201
American Museum of Natural History 62–82
American Society of Heating, Refrigerating and Air-Conditioning Engineers (ASHRAE) 121, 134
Amerika Gedenkbibliothek 200–201
Amman, Jordan 231
Anaheim Regional Transportation Intermodal Center (ARTIC) 32, 260–279, 291

Anderson, Alissa 79, x
Anderson, Eric 266
Ann Arbor, MI 39
ANSYS 292
Anthony, Ron 101, 113
Antwerp, Belgium 182–198
Antwerp Port House 32–33, 182–198
Appelbaum, Ralph 53
Apple Park 228
Applied Acoustic Design (AAD) 145
Aqua Tower 63
arch 247, 255–257
ArchiCAD 293
Architect Magazine 40
Architectural Association 148
Architectural Design 171
architectural research 5, 28, 38, 63, 128, 147–148, 162, 165, 185, 200, 216, 222, 228, 245, 262
Architectural Review 63, 87, 211; Architect of the Year 63
Architecture 295
Architizer A+ Firm of the Year Award 63
Arcus Center for Social Justice Leadership 63
Arnsen, Eric 58
Arup 3, 10, 12, 24, 26, 28, 31, 39, 62–82, 83, 132, 166, 199, 208, 216–218, 220, 228, 262, 270, 291
Arup, Ove 12, 16, 24, 63–64
Atelier Ten 62, 130–132, 134, 281
Atlanta, GA 135–136, 138, 261
atrium 52, 65, 116, 171–172, 174–175, 177, 188, 194, 204–205
AutoCAD 290
automation: Robot 271, 273

Baghdad, Iraq 182
Balmond, Cecil 24–25
Baltimore, MD 42
B-architecten 183–184
Bard College 87
Beaux Arts 87, 277

INDEX

bedrock 54, 72–73
Beijing Airport 230
Bendheim 37
bending moment 52, 85, 95–96, 113, 177, 206, 255–257
bending moment diagram 256–257
Benedictine monastery 154
Benson Industries 116
Bentley Architecture 293
Bergdoll, Barry 154
Bergermann, Rudolph 242
Berlin Hauptbahnof 24, 242–259
Bevk-Perovic Arhiktekti 184
Biebauw, Gert ix, 192–194
Billettt, Neil 234
Billie Jean King Main Library 32, 101–124, 282, 285, 294, 296
Billings Design Associates 145
Billington, David x, 6, 14
Bjarke Ingels Group (BIG) 40, 148
blast protection 49
BMW Welt 277
Bocconi University 147, 153
Bohlin Cywinski Jackson 126, 130–134, 291
Bond, Max 42
Boston, MA 39
Brause, Caryn 3, 63
BREEAM 196, 198
bridge building 12, 14, 47, 92, 220, 250, 277
Briscoe, Danelle x, 297
British Museum Great Court 229
Broad Street Station, Philadelphia 267
bronze 45, 47
Bruder, Will 166
Brussels, Belgium 184
budget 9, 23, 49, 69–70, 73, 76, 78–80, 104, 108, 110, 121, 126, 134, 150, 167, 179, 192, 194, 263, 266, 269, 271, 274–276, 283–284, 302
building code 22, 86, 92, 113, 141, 169, 180, 218, 293
building information modelling (BIM) 15, 75, 109–110, 120, 128–129, 192–194, 196, 276–277, 285, 289–298; ArchiCAD 293; Bentley Architecture 293; Digital Project 293; general 15, 75, 109–110, 120, 128–129, 192–194, 196, 276–277, 285, 289–298; Revit 75, 128, 137, 194, 271, 275, 276, 292, 293; Tekla 293
Bullitt Center 135
Bunch III, Lonnie 41, 50, 55, 57, 59
Bureau Bouwtechniek 182–198
bureau SLA 217, 219
Buro Happold 18, 31, 62, 69, 227–241, 260–278, 291
Burwell Deakins 145

cables (structural) 48, 243–244, 250, 254–257, 273–274
cables (utility) 95, 221, 230
Calatrava, Santiago 264
California Department of Transportation (CalTrans) Headquarters 165
Cal Poly San Luis Obispo ix, x, 10
camber 95
canals 47, 87
cantilever 50–52, 156–157, 159–160, 165, 174, 176–179, 189, 203, 206, 236
capstone 11–12, 14–15
carbon 3, 101, 112, 114, 120–121, 125–129, 137–141, 162, 215–216, 223, 233; CarbonCure 139; carbon dioxide 125, 214; Carbon Leadership Forum 128; carbon neutral/neutrality 125, 139–140, 215, 220, 233; embodied carbon/energy 114, 126, 128–129, 138, 141; sequestration 112, 130, 138–139, 141
CarbonCure 139
carbon dioxide 125, 214
Carbon Leadership Forum 128
Carlise, Stephanie 126, 128
Carnegie Mellon University 16
catenary 268
Cathedral, Christ the Light 102, 113
Cathedral, Gothic 1, 2
Cathedral Hill Hospital, San Francisco 294
Cathedral, National (Ghana) 38, 148
Cathedral, Notre Dame de Paris 2
Cathedral, Reims 2
Cathedral, St. Patrick's 40
Cathedral, Wells 2
CATIA 271–272, 292
CCTV Headquarters 25, 64
Chapel of St. Ignatius, Seattle 200
Chapman BDSP 145
Charles David Keeling Apartments 166
Charles River 205
Charleston, SC 47
charrette 44, 69–70, 78, 136
Chek Lap Kok Airport, Hong Kong 230
Chhatrapati Shivaji International Airport Terminal 2 102
Chicago, IL 24–25, 63, 87, 102, 107, 277
Chicago Schoool of Architecture 24, 102
Chrysler Building 102
circularity 33, 214–223
Circular Strategy 215, 220
circulation 53, 64–65, 71, 152, 171, 188–189, 236, 268
City Hall, Montigny-Le-Tilleul 184
civic 32, 38, 41, 42, 64, 86, 101–104, 106, 112, 115, 121, 145, 147, 153–154, 162, 198, 214, 215, 228, 264
civil rights 41
Civil War 40, 59
cladding 128, 208, 219, 244, 270
Clandening, Kurt ix, 13, 167–170, 174, 176–179
Clark Construction Group 37, 101, 104, 107, 109, 111, 260, 276–277, 285, 294
clash detection 75, 96, 110, 293–296
Claus and Kaan Architecten 184
climate: building interior climate (design for) 91, 196; climate change (design for) 3, 112, 125, 141; greenhouse gases 125, 128–129; local climate (design for) 38, 136, 139

306

code compliance 22, 86, 92, 113, 141, 169, 180, 218, 293
Columbia University 200
column grid 92, 110–111, 113, 151, 156, 176
communication 11, 15–16, 24, 27–31, 69–70, 74, 107, 136, 170, 194, 196, 217, 283, 286–287, 289–290, 294, 298, 301–303
community: as collaborator/stakeholder 3, 30, 63, 70, 79, 106, 130, 131, 281; as program 59, 106, 115, 137, 147, 287
composite steel and concrete 52–53
computer aided design (CAD) 15, 272, 290; AutoCAD 290; CATIA 271–272, 292; general 15, 272, 290; Navisworks 109
Computer Numerically Controlled (CNC) machine 119, 239
concrete: carbon emissions 112–113, 139, 141, 216; curing of 55; glass fiber reinforced concrete (GFRC) 76; non structural 51, 76, 159; precast 149, 159, 205–211, 235, 237–239; shell structure 25, 84–85, 237–239, 265, 301–303; steel fiber-reinforced 239; as a structural material 24, 52–55, 73, 75–78, 85, 92, 103, 106, 110, 112–113, 120, 128, 139, 147, 149, 152, 156–157, 162, 167, 171, 174–179, 188–189, 194, 205, 207–212, 216, 218, 222, 233, 235–240, 250, 269; using low-iron portland cement 78
concrete shell structure 25, 84–85, 237–239, 265, 301–303
Congressman John Lewis 40
constructability, construction efficiency 17, 53, 64, 75–76, 147, 165, 182, 184, 192–196, 227, 235–236, 261, 268–273, 278, 284, 286, 293, 298
Construction Administration (CA) 86, 108, 240, 283
Construction Documentation/Drawings (CD/CDs) 108
Construction Industry Institute 119
Construction Manager (contract type) 284
contractors, constructors 49, 75–79, 107–109, 115–116, 118–122, 129, 136, 141, 176, 193–194, 207, 211, 216, 223, 235, 237–240, 271, 274–277, 280, 282–287, 290, 294, 296
contracts, contract structure 22, 23, 45, 70, 103–108, 119, 123, 184, 235, 265, 281, 282–286, 287; Construction Manager (contract type) 284; Design, Bid, Build (contract type) 22, 104, 283–284, 287; Design Build (contract type) 103, 108, 120–122, 184, 196, 284–285; Integrated Project Delivery (contract type) 285–286, 294; Public–Private Partnership (P3) (contract type) 103–104, 106–107, 114, 122, 285
Conwed 37
Cook, Mike 234
Cooper Hewitt 63, 200
Cooper Union 164, 166–181
Coop Himmelb(l)au 166, 277
Cornell University 165
Corning Museum of Glass 39
Corning, NY 39
corona 42–43, 45, 48–54, 57, 59
Cosentini Associates 83, 86–87, 90
COST of Wisconsin 75
Court, Brian x, 136, 139
Coussee & Goris Architecten 183–184
craft 38, 47, 77, 118, 139, 297
craftspeople 77, 79
Cramer, James 261
crane 56, 116, 194, 235, 239, 277
cross laminated timber 112–114
Cuff, Dana 17
Culley, Patricia x, 126, 131–132, 291
Cultural Centre De Grote 183
Cultural Centre De Waalse Krook 183
curriculum 7–18, 20, 290, 301–303
curtain wall cf facade 37, 115, 160, 274

Daidalos Peutz 182
Dallas, TX 86, 262
Daniel O'Connell's Sons 199, 207
Dar Al-Handasah 227
Davey, Peter 229
Davis Brody Bond 37–61, 62–82
Davis Langdon 227
daylight/daylighting 67, 71, 78, 103, 115, 138, 154, 171–172, 205, 209, 212, 237, 268
decarbonization 125, 130
deconstruction 114, 128, 218–220
Dee and Charles Wyly Theatre 86
deflection 52, 95, 116, 178, 255, 273, 292
De Kestelier, Xavier ix, 16, 28, 234, 235
demoliition 214
Denari, Neil ix, 13
Denver Union Station 102
Dermot Foley Landscape Architects 145
Design, Bid, Build (contract type) 22, 104, 283–284, 287
Design Build (contract type) 103, 108, 120–122, 184, 196, 284–285
Design Builder 128, 292
Design-Build Institute of America 285
design competition 42–43, 48, 51, 64, 69–72, 87, 103, 135–136, 146, 149, 152, 165, 183–185, 187, 189, 192, 196, 200–201, 246, 250, 265–268, 278, 280
Design Development (DD) 70–71, 86, 107, 109, 130, 266, 271, 283, 293
DesignIntelligence 261
Des Moines, IA 40
Deutsche Bahn AG 242
Digital Project 293
Disney Concert Hall 87, 166
diversity 22, 60, 147
Domus 212
doubly curved form 238, 271, 277
Dublin, Ireland 69, 147, 154
Dutch Design Week 217

earthquake loads 52, 98, 110
École Polytechnique Fédérale de Lausanne 84, 154
educational research 17

INDEX

Egyptian obelisks 45
Eindhoven, Netherlands 217, 219
electrical engineer/engineering 7, 22, 72, 95, 117, 120–121, 145
Ellen MacArthur Foundation 214–216
embodied carbon 128, 141
Embodied Carbon in Construction Calculator (EC3) 128
Emch + Berger 242
empathy 38, 130, 287
Empire State Building 102
energy: embodied energy 127, 129; energy efficiency or conservation 57, 121, 126–127, 130–131, 132, 134, 174, 180, 196, 231, 292, 296; geothermal 127; net positive 129, 132, 137; wind 127
energy modelling: Design Builder 128, 292; Honeybee 128; Insight 292; Integrated Environmental Solutions (IES) 128, 137; Ladybug 128; Virtual Environment 292
Engineering for a Finite Planet 229
engineering research 14, 22, 85, 96–97, 113, 184, 196, 219, 223, 229, 262, 275, 295
environmental engineer/engineering 22, 28, 127, 132, 228, 234
environmental impact 4, 106, 214, 216, 222, 262
Environmental Product Declarations (EPDs) 129
Erasmus School, Brussels 184
Erie Canal 87
ethylene tetrafluoroethylene (ETFE) 269–272, 274, 277
European Commission 215; Circular Economy Action Plan 215
European Green Deal 215
excavation 54, 90, 96, 194
exhibition (of design work) 39, 148, 184
exhibition design 43, 49, 56, 62–63, 65–67, 69–70, 72, 75–80, 170, 244–245
exoskeleton 212, 247, 250, 253

facade 32, 42–44, 46–52, 58, 62, 145, 159–162, 164, 166–167, 171, 192–194, 196, 203–207, 209, 211, 247, 250, 254, 267, 269–273, 277
Fairfield Medical Office Building 285
Fallingwater 40
Farnsworth, David x, 31
Farrell, Yvonne 147, 153–154
Federal Building San Francisco 165
filigree 45, 247, 255
finite element analysis (FEA) 289, 292; ANSYS 292; SAP 2000 292
fire: fire damage 130; fire engineering 145, 182; fire rating/protection 112–113, 156, 182, 294; fire sprinklers 117, 119
Fisher Marantz Stone 37
Fisher, Thomas 4
Fitwel 129
F.J. Sciame Construction Co., Inc. 164
floating slab/mat foundation 205, 277
Flor Ortiz, Ana x, 69, 71, 74, 79

Folan, John 16
Forest Stewardship Council (FSC) 138
form-finding 192, 229, 244, 273, 290
formwork 55, 75–76, 176, 210, 236; steel 238–239; timber 176, 210, 238
40th Precinct Station House 40
41 Cooper Square 32, 33, 164–181
Fort Worth, TX 39
Foster + Partners ix, 12, 16, 27–28, 64, 227–241, 264
foundation 53–55, 73, 79–80, 96, 106, 110, 112–113, 120–121, 130, 139, 155, 159, 189, 191, 194, 205–206, 239, 269, 277; pile 54, 159, 205, 218, 239; slab/mat 205, 277
FPC 182
Franchina, Joe x, 44, 49, 53
freehand drawing cf sketching 12, 14–16, 44, 70, 108, 218, 276, 290–291
Freelon Group 37–61
Freelon, Phillip 42, 58–59
Frick Environmental Center 125, 130–135, 140, 281
Front, Inc 83
Fuller, Buckminster 16, 39
funicular 85, 256

Garlock, Richard ix, 12, 15, 23
Gartner 277
Gaudi, Antoni 16, 85
Gautrey, John 166
Gehry, Frank 87, 166, 283
Gehry Partners 87, 166, 264, 282
Gensler 30
geometry 16, 71, 73–74, 85, 158–159, 176–177, 179, 229, 234, 236, 256, 265, 267–268, 270–276, 292
Georges Pompidou Center 24–25
Georgetown University 58
Georgia Tech 135
geotechnical engineer/engineering 54, 62
geothermal energy 127
Gerkan, Marg and Partners (gmp) 24, 242–259
Getov, Pavel 164
Ghana 37–38, 148
Ghent, Belgium 183–184
Gibbons, Bruce x, 24
Gifu Kitagata Apartment Building 84
Gilder Center 32, 62–82, 280
Giovannini, Joseph 196
Glasgow School of Art 200
glass 76, 83–100, 115, 174, 188–189, 192, 242–257, 268–270, 274; glass blowing studio/ hot shop 90, 96; glass fiber reinforced concrete (GFRC) 76; shell structure 244, 255
glass blowing studio 90
glass fiber reinforced concrete (GFRC) 76
Glass Pavilion at the Toledo Museum of Art 6, 32, 39, 83–100
glass shell structure 244, 255
glulam timber 112–114, 116
Goldberger, Paul 228

Goppion 37
Gordon H. Smith Group 164
Gothic 1, 2
Grace Farms 84
Grafton Architects x, 145–163
Graham, Bruce 24, 102
Grande Médaille d'Or 200
Grasshopper 128, 192–193, 271, 273, 292
gravity loads 54, 71, 110, 154, 155, 162, 256–257
gray water 58, 262
Green Building Initiative 262
greenhouse gases 125, 128–129
grid shell 244, 255, 265, 268, 269
Group Delta Consultants 260
Groven+ 182
Gruzen Samton, LLP 164
Guangzhou Opera House 183
Guerrero, Brian x, 30
Guggenheim Museum (Bilbao) 87, 282
Gustafson Guthrie Nichol 37
Guy Nordenson Associates (GNA) 13, 15, 25, 37–61, 83–100, 199–213

Hall Estate Winery 166
Hall of Mirrors, Versailles 88
Hamad International Airport Passenger Terminal Complex, Doha 261
Hamburg, Germany 245
handcraft, hand finished 38, 47, 77, 118, 139, 297
Happold, Edward (Ted) 228–229, 262, 270
Harlem Renaissance 41
Harris, Carolina B. 301
Hartsfield–Jackson Atlanta International Airport 261
Harvard Graduate School of Design (GSD) 165
Harvard University 28–29, 154, 165
Hasegawa, Takayuki 83
Hawthorne, Christopher 278
Heatherwick Studio 148
Heath, Piers 28
heating, venting and air conditioning (HVAC) 91, 121
Hebel, Dirk E. 220–221
Heintges 37, 45
Heisel, Felix x, 220–221
Helios House 262
Hellmuth, George 260
Hellstern, Chris x, 139
Herd, David 269
Herning Museum, Denmark 200
Herzog & De Meuron 64
Heydar Aliyev Center 148, 183
Hilmer, Jürgen ix, 242, 249, 255, 258
HOK 260–279
Holder, Darryn 234
Holl, Steven ix, 23, 25, 39, 40, 87, 199–213
Honeybee 128
Hongkong and Shanghai Bank (HSBC) Headquarters 228
Horton Lees Brogden Lighting Design, Inc. 164

Hughes, Thomas 11
Hunters Point Community Library 40
hydrostatic 54

Ian Simpson Architects 184
IBE Consulting Engineers 164
ice, ice loading 49
ice models 73
Idenburg, Florian 83
identity: architectural 102, 155; cultural 38, 287; professional 24
Illinois Institute of Technology 243
Imamura, Mizuki 83
Indianapolis International Airport 261
Indira Gandhi International Airport, New Delhi 261
Industrial Revolution 1, 8, 289
Ingenieurgesellschaft Höpfner 242
Ingenium Nv 182
Insight 292
Institute of Civil Engineers Special Award 229
insulation 90, 208, 220, 269; sound 2, 76, 90, 112, 208
Integrated Environmental Solutions (IES) 128, 137
Integrated Project Delivery (contract type) 285–286, 294
Interbuild 182
interdisciplinary education 12, 15–18, 301–303
interior design(ers) 107, 261
International Architecture Biennale of Venice 147
International Library Design Competition 200
ironwork 47
Ishigami, Junya 83
Isozakin, Arata 86
Istanbul 27
Ito, Toyo 25, 85–86, 92

Jackson, Barbara x, 283, 285–287
Jackson, Matt 69
Jefferson Memorial 47
Joannou & Paraskevaides (Overseas) Ltd 227
Johannesburg, South Africa 38
John A. Martin and Associates (JAMA) ix, 13, 164–181
John Hancock Center 25, 102
Johnson, Benton 113
Johnson Controls 104
Johnston Marklee 262
Jones, Alan 38
Jones, Larry x, 132, 281
Jordanian Royal Development Company 230
J&P-AVAX S.A. 227

Kahn, Louis 16, 24, 63, 201
Kakamigahara Crematorium 85
Kalamazoo College 63
Kamikatsu, Japan 215
Kara, Hanif x, 31, 38, 148–151, 155–156, 159, 162, 297

INDEX

Kassabum, George 260
Keliris, George 31, 38, 145–163, 234, 237, 291
Kellogg School of Management 286
Kendall Heaton Associates, Inc 83
Kendeda Building for Innovative Sustainable Design 125, 130, 135–140, 280
Kendeda Fund 135
Kentucky International Convention Center 261
Keough, Ian 272
Khan, Fazlur 24, 102
Kiasma Museum of Contemporary Art, Helsinki 200
Kieran, Stephen 297
Kieran Timberlake 126–128, 166, 297
Kilt Planning 83
Kimbell Art Museum 39, 202
Kimbell Museum 39, 202
King Abdullah University of Science and Technology (KAUST) 261
King's Office and Council of Ministers, Saudi Arabia 228
Kingston University 149
Kipnis, Jeffrey 165
Komendant, August 24
Komraus, Kurt ix, 267, 271–272, 274–276
Kondo, Tetsuo 83
Koolhaas, Rem 24–25
KPFF Consulting Engineers 101
Krause Gateway Center 40
Kubo, Michael 148
Kuhle, Silvia 164

Laberenne, Rebecca ix, 43–45, 48–49
labor 75, 128, 137, 194, 272, 275, 277, 293, 294
Ladybug 128, 292
Langan 62
lateral stability 2, 48–49, 52, 89, 93, 96–97, 110, 113, 189, 206, 238, 254, 257, 272–273
LA Times 278
lean principles: lean construction 286; lean manufacturing 286
Le Corbusier 201
Lee, Arnold ix, 265–268, 296
LEED 32, 57, 103, 106, 129, 135, 180, 228, 261, 265, 269, 273, 277
Leedham, Amy 141
Leslie E. Robertson and Associates (LERA) 12, 23
Lewis, John 40
Lewis, Stephen 267, 273
LG Science Park, Seoul 261
life cycle 126–129, 132, 150, 216, 220, 294; Life Cycle Assessment (LCA) 128–129, 132, 222; Whole Building Life Cycle Analysis (WBLCA) 129, 141
Life Cycle Assessment (LCA) 128–129, 132, 222
lighting/lighting design 37, 83, 108–109, 115, 132, 154, 164, 166, 196, 199, 227, 230, 233, 237, 242, 268; daylight/daylighting 67, 71, 78, 103, 115, 138, 154, 171–172, 205, 209, 212, 237, 268

Lima, Peru 147, 153
Lincoln Center for the Performing Arts 42
Lincoln Park 103, 115
Lincoln's Inn Chapel 152–153
Lincoln's Inn Field 145–146, 151, 159
Linda Demmers 101
Linked Hybrid 86
Living Building Challenge (LBC) 129, 131–132, 134–136, 139, 281
loading dock 56, 72
load path 70, 73–74
Locke, Alan 166
London Aquatics Center 183
London 2012 Olympic Stadium 229
London School of Economics and Political Science (LSE) 145–163
London, UK 28, 33, 37, 148, 149, 151, 166, 182, 183, 228–230, 234, 261, 291
Long Beach, CA 101–124
Long, Eric ix, 10, 14, 30, 107, 112, 113, 115, 118
Lord Aeck Sargent 135
Los Angeles, CA 24, 87, 107, 165–166, 260, 262
Louisiana State Penitentiary 56
Louis I. Kahn Memorial Award 63
Louvre 84
low-iron glass 87
low-iron portland cement 78

MacArthur Fellowship 63
Mackintosh School of Architecture 200
Madrid 27
Maillart, Robert 14, 243
maintenance 76, 103, 106, 130, 294, 296–297
Maisam—Dar Al-Omran JV 227
Majidi, Mouzhan 27
Mangelsdorf, Wolf 229
Mannheim Multihalle 270
Marcus Prize for Architecture 63
Marg, Volkwin 245
Marshall Building, LSE 145–163
Marshall, Paul 159
Martin Luther King, Jr. Center for Nonviolent Social Chang 42
Massachusetts Institute of Technology 9, 39, 199–213
mass timber 101–124, 130, 138; cross laminated timber 112–114; glulam timber 112–114, 116
Maxfield, Claire 141
MAXXI Museum 183
Mayne, Thom 164–166
McGowan, Rory ix, 3, 69, 71, 75–78, 80
McKinsey & Company 4, 295
McNamara, Shelley x, 147, 149–155, 158–160, 162
mechanical engineer/engineering 5, 7, 22, 32, 37, 108, 127, 135, 145, 164, 166, 167, 169, 179, 199, 208, 242, 266–267, 283
mechanical systems cf utilities 53, 67, 71–72, 79, 91–92, 94–96, 99, 106, 117, 132, 138, 162, 167, 179, 230, 267
Mendrisio, Switzerland 154

310

mentorship 4, 12, 30, 86, 303
Mercedes Benz Stadium, Atlanta 261
Merkel, Jayne 171, 204
Merrill, John 102
metalsmithing 46–47
Mettam. Kirk 40
Mickus, Ben ix, 30
microclimate 51
Milan, Italy 147, 153–154
Millennium Bridge 12
Miller Hull Partnership 135–140
minimalism 83, 258
MIRA 63
mockup cf protoype 76–77, 108–109, 194, 219, 240, 254, 277, 290
module/modularity 115–117, 158, 193–194, 207, 209, 219–221, 227, 230, 235–238, 277
Moens, Jan 184
morphology 71, 74, 204, 212
Morphosis 164–181, 262
Mostaghim, Roshanak ix, 108, 120–121, 296
Mouton, Guy ix, 183–185, 189
Moynihan Train Hall 102
Mumbai, India 102
Munich Olympic Arena 243
Museum aan de Stroom (MAS) 184
Museum of Modern Art (MOMA) 39
Museum of the African Diaspora 42
mycelium 220

NACO 227
National Aquatics Center (Beijing) 64
National Architectural Accrediting Board (NAAB) 9, 13
National Design Award 63, 200
National Museum of African American History and Culture (NMAAHC) 5, 32, 37–61, 86, 282
National Museum of American History 41
National Science Foundation (NSF) vii, ix, 302
National Stadium (Beijing) 64
natural light 67, 71, 78, 103, 115, 138, 154, 171–172, 205, 209, 212, 237, 268
Nature Reserve Het Zwin 184
Navigant Construction Forum 284, 295
Nervi, Pier Luigi 152, 243
net positive energy 129, 132, 137
net positive waste 129
net positive water 129, 135, 137
net zero 33, 125–142, 165, 293
Net Zero Carbon Buildings Commitment 129
Neutelings Riedijk 184
Nevada Museum of Art 166
New Museum of Contemporary Art 39, 84
New Orleans, LA 47
Newson Brown Acoustics 101, 120
New York City, NY 27, 38–40, 63–65, 68–69, 72, 80, 83–84, 86–87, 102, 140, 148, 165, 166–168, 199–200, 267
New York City Public Design Commission 39
The New York Public Library (53rd St) 86

New York Times 88
Nigeria 45
Nigohos, Zarmine ix, 107, 109, 120–122
Nishizawa, Ryue 83–84, 87, 90
Noguchi, Isamu 39
Nordenson, Guy ix, 13, 15, 25, 39, 42, 48, 83, 86, 91, 92, 96, 98, 200, 201–202, 205, 207–208, 211–212
Novitski, B. J. 27

Oakland, CA 102, 113
Obama, Barack 42
Obata, Gyo 260
Ochsendorf, John 9
Oei, Jean 164
Office dA 262
Office for Metropolitan Architecture (OMA) 26, 63–64, 69, 86
Oki, Toshihiro x, 16, 83, 91, 96–97
Olowe of Ise 45
Oppenheimer, Nat 40, 42, 53
optimization 85, 139, 167, 196, 235, 267, 271, 297
Origin 182
orthotropic plate 92
Otto, Frei 228, 243, 270
Otto, Greg ix, 18, 262, 267, 277–278
Ouroussoff, Nicolai 88–89
outrigger truss 51–52
Overtreders W 217, 219
Owings, Nathaniel 102

PAE 135–140
Palacios, Jose 106–107, 109, 115, 118
Parr, Jonathan ix, 234–237, 240
Parsons Brinckerhoff 260–279
Passive House 129
passive systems 23, 57, 58, 106, 130, 132, 165, 208, 233, 262
Pauwels, Joris x, 185, 188, 194, 196
Pearson, Clifford 89
pedagogy 7, 9, 11, 13, 18, 29, 303
Pelli Clarke Pelli 262, 264
Pennsylvania Station, New York 267–268
Pentagram 164
People's Pavillion 214, 217–220
perfcon 205, 209
Perkins + Will 37–61
Perot Museum of Nature and Science, Dallas 262
Perry Dean Rogers and Partners 199
Peter Andres + Conceptlicht GmbH 242
Peter B. Lewis Library 87
PHA Consult 28
Phaeno Science Center 183, 188
phenomenology 200
photovoltaic panels 58, 121, 127–128, 132, 137
physical model(s) 28, 70, 75, 85, 193, 202
Piano, Renzo 24–25, 39, 40, 202
piles/pile foundations 54, 159, 205, 218, 239
Pinzone, Joe 295

INDEX

Pittsburgh, PA 130–131, 133–134
PJ Dick 130
Platt, Christopher 200
Plenary-Edgemoor Civic Partners 103–104
pollution 214–215
porch 43, 46, 50–51, 115, 137
porosity 153–154, 158, 203–204, 212
Port Authority, Antwerp 182, 184, 188
portland cement 78
post-occupancy: assessment 129–130, 132, 135, 222; maintenance 76, 103, 106, 130, 294, 296–297
Prada Store (Arezzo Italy) 84
Pratt Institute 200
precast concrete 149, 159, 205–211, 235, 237–239
prefabrication 103, 110, 114, 117–118, 121, 176, 192, 194, 196, 205, 220, 237–238, 262
President Barack Obama 42
Princeton University x, 12, 15, 38, 39, 87
Princeton University Art Museum 38
Pritzker Prize 24, 84, 147, 165, 183
progressive collapse 50
prototype cf mockup 76–77, 108–109, 194, 219, 240, 254, 277, 290
Proving Ground 75
PTW Architects 64
Public–Private Partnership (P3) 103–104, 106–107, 114, 122, 285
Pullman Train 56–57
Pure + FreeForm 37

Queen Alia International Airport 32, 227–241
Queen Elisabeth Hall, Antwerp 184

radiant ceiling 179–180
radiant floor 132
Rahe Kraft 227
Ralph Appelbaum Associates 62, 69
rationalization 148, 159, 182, 192–193, 235, 260, 267, 270–271, 274–275, 278, 290, 292
RCR Aranda Pigem Vilalta 184
rebar (steel reinforcing bars) 24, 52–53, 75–78, 206–207, 211, 239
recylcing 47, 130, 141, 214–216, 220–221, 269
Reed Hilderbrand 69–70
Reginald F. Lewis Museum of African American History and Culture 42
Reichstag, Berlin 228
Renzo Piano Building Workshop 39
Requests for Information (RFI) 284, 295
research: architectural research 5, 28, 38, 63, 128, 147–148, 162, 165, 185, 200, 216, 222, 228, 245, 262; educational research 17; engineering research 14, 22, 85, 96–97, 113, 184, 196, 219, 223, 229, 262, 275, 295; research as an architectural program 64–67, 137, 146, 150, 154, 219, 220; scientific research 4, 65–67, 137, 141
research as an architectural program 64–67, 137, 146, 150, 154, 219, 220

RESET Air 129
resuse 110, 135, 216, 220, 222, 238, 262
Revelle College 166
Revit 75, 128, 137, 194, 271, 275, 276, 292, 293
REX 86
Rhinoceros (Rhino): general 15, 73–75, 128, 193–194, 291–293, 298; Grasshopper 128, 192–193, 271, 273, 292
Rice, Peter 24–25
Richard B. Fisher Center for the Performing Arts 87
Ridsdill Smith, Roger 28
river 72, 205, 246; Charles River 205; riverbed 73; River Spree 246
Riverside Studios 28
River Spree 246
Robinson, Julian 146
Robot 271, 273
Rocky Mountain Institute 37
Roelofs, Michelle ix, 69, 71–72, 74, 77–78, 291
Rolex Learning Center 84
Rome, Italy 183
Ron Anthony 101, 113
Rosenberg, Ben x, 41, 44–46, 51, 53–56, 58
Rotterdam, The Netherlands 63, 69
Royal Courts 145, 152
Royal Institute of British Architects (RIBA) 38, 147, 150, 200
Royal Institute of British Architects Gold Medal 38, 147, 198
Royal Institute of British Architects International Award 200
Royal Museum for Fine Arts, Antwerp 184
Ruby City 38
Russell 37

Safran, Yehuda 212
Salesforce Transit Center 262
SANAA 6, 32, 39, 83–100
San Antonio, TX 38
Sanchez, Andriana 294
Sanchez, Brenda 58
Sanders, Ken 30
San Francisco, CA 42, 63, 107, 165, 294
SAP 2000 292
Saper, Carl 283
Sarkisian, Mark ix, 102, 107, 113–114
Sasaki and Partners (SAP) 6, 32, 39, 83–100
Sasaki, Mutsuro ix, 39, 84–86, 91–92, 98
Schlaich, Bergerman und Partner (SBP) 12, 24, 242–260
Schlaich, Jörg 242–244
Schober, Hans ix, 12, 15, 24, 243–244, 248–250, 253–257
School of Art and Art History at the University of Iowa 200, 202
Schreiber, Amy 208, 211
Schumacher, Patrick 185
scientific research 4, 65–67, 137, 141
sculptural 38, 147
Sears Tower 102

312

Seattle Public Library 64
security 43, 153, 230
Sejima, Kazuyo 83–84, 87
Sempergreen Series Seating 37
sensitivity analysis 85
Serpentine Pavilion 148
Shablak, Scott L. 301
shading (solar shading) 43, 137, 196
shell structure 25, 268–269, 301–303; concrete 25, 84–85, 237–239, 265; glass 244, 255; grid shell 244, 255, 265, 268, 269
ship-building 92, 238–239
shotcrete 76–78
Silman 37–61
Silman, Robert 39–40
silos (of expertise) 2–4, 7–19, 18, 118, 217, 278, 284, 286
Simmonds, Peter ix, 167, 169, 179–180
Simmons Hall 39, 199–213
Simpson Gumpertz & Heger (SGH) 199, 211
Skanska 136, 139
sketching *cf freehand drawing* 12, 14–16, 44, 70, 108, 218, 276, 290–291
Skidmore, Louis 102
Skidmore Owings and Merrill (SOM) 10, 14, 24, 27, 30, 101–124, 168, 285, 292, 294, 296
skylight 78, 117, 230
slab/mat foundation 205, 277
slave trade/ slavery 41, 46–47, 55, 58
Smith Group 37–61
Smithsonian Institution 37–61, 63, 200
Smoot 37
Sobek, Werner 220–221
social (aspects of design) 13, 16, 22, 33, 38, 42, 104, 131, 171, 204, 212
social condensation 176, 277
social justice/change/advocacy 22, 42, 63, 214
software 30, 73, 75, 128, 130, 137, 218, 268, 272–272, 290–299; *see also* automation; building information modelling (BIM); computer aided design (CAD); energy modelling; finite element analysis (FEA); Rhinoceros (Rhino)
soil, soil conditions 53, 57, 73, 79, 110, 205, 218, 269, 277
solar gain 57, 172, 192
solar panels 58, 121, 127–128, 132, 137
sound insulation 2, 76, 90, 112, 208
Spaceport America 230
Sport Center of Boerekreek 183
Stanford University Medical Center 295
Stansted Airport, London 230, 235
Staples Center 166
steel: carbon emissions 112–113, 141; non structural 167, 171–172, 174–175, 177, 179–180, 255; reinforcing for concrete structure 24, 52–53, 76, 78, 206–207, 211, 239; as a structural material 46, 51–55, 75–76, 87–88, 92–93, 95, 97, 109, 112–114, 128, 141, 156, 167, 179, 189, 194, 207, 222, 247, 250, 253, 268–271, 277

steel fiber-reinforced concrete 239
steel formwork 238–239
Steer Davies Gleave 145
stereotypes 22, 31, 170
Steven Holl Architects 87, 199–213
St. Louis, MO 260
30 St. Mary's Axe 64
Sto 37
Structural Engineers Association 102
Studieburo Mouton Bvba 182–198
Studio Gang 62–82
Stuttgart, Germany 242–243
Stuttgart University 242–243
STV 260
substructure 53–54
Sullivan, Adam 277
superstructure 42, 44, 49, 51–54, 78
sustainable, sustainability 17, 23, 27, 32, 37, 47, 57, 62, 79, 86, 103, 104, 106, 107, 113, 121, 125–142, 146, 162, 165, 166, 196, 214–223, 237, 255, 261, 262, 264, 267, 273, 282, 286, 289, 292
Swiss Federal Laboratories for Material Science and Technology 220
Sydney Opera House 25–26
Syracuse University vii, ix, x, 301–302
Syska Hennessy Group 101, 164

Taniguchi, Yoshio 39
Tankha, Sanjeev ix, 267, 271, 274–275, 277
Tanzania 37
Tanzmann, Virginia ix, 266, 275, 277
Target Value Design (TVD) 286
Taylor, Albert 148
Technical University of Berlin 242
Tekla 293
TEN Arquitectos 86
Thabo Mbeki Presidential Library 38
Theodore Roosevelt Park 70
thermal expansion 250, 297
thermal mass 208, 233
thermal performance 51, 112, 117, 137, 208, 222, 233, 262, 273, 292
Thie, Edwin ix, 10, 216, 218, 220
Thomas Phifer and Partners 39
Thompson, Leigh 286
Thornton Tomasetti (TT) 24, 30, 128, 260–279, 291
threat assessment 49
3d printing 16, 28, 70, 106, 202, 265
Thuwal, Saudi Arabia 261
tidal estuary 205
timber 101–124, 130, 138, 218, 220; formwork 176, 210, 238
Timberlake, James 297
TIME 63
Tocumen International Airport, Panama 230
Tokyo, Japan 84, 215
Toledo Museum of Art 32, 39, 83
Toledo, OH 83, 87
tolerance 239, 276, 297

INDEX

Tom Bradley Terminal, LAX 166
Tortorella, Joe 40
Tottenham Hotspur Football Club Stadium 229
Town House 149
transfer girder 155, 162, 177–178
truss 48–49, 51–52, 77, 155, 189, 206, 253–258
tunnel 77
21st Century Museum of Contemporary Art (Kanazawa, Japan) 84

UC Berkeley 39
Uchiyama, Keiko 83
UC San Diego 166
UNESCO 40
United States Army Corps of Engineers 293
United States Bureau of Labor and Statistics 21
United States General Services Administration (GSA) 293
United States Green Building Council 57, 106
University College Dublin 154
University of Amsterdam 219
University of California Los Angeles (UCLA) x
University of Southern California 164
UNStudio 290
Urban Mining and Recycling (UMAR) 220–221
USG Ceilings 37
UTEC 147
utilities cf mechanical systems 53, 67, 71–72, 79, 91–92, 94–96, 99, 106, 117, 132, 138, 162, 167, 179, 230, 267

V+ 184
value engineering 48–49, 108, 274
van Assche, Peter x, 216, 218–220, 222–223, 281
van Berkel, Ben 290
van der Rohe, Mies 201, 243
Venice Capability Center 295
vernacular 51, 137
Versailles, Hall of Mirrors 88
The Vessel 148
Victor Buyck Steel Construction 182
Vierendeel truss 206

Viollet-le-Duc, Eugène Emmanuel 1
Virtual Environment 292
vocabulary 24, 29–30, 301, 303
von Gerkan, Meinhard 242, 245–246

Walker, Weston x, 67, 69–71, 73–74, 76, 79–80
Walt Disney Concert Hall 166
Washington, DC 39, 43, 49, 58
Washington Mall 41, 50, 52
Washington Monument 41, 45, 47
wastewater 135
watercolor 201–202, 204
water proofing 54–55, 103, 128
water table 53, 159
weather 51, 115, 194, 196, 220, 292
weather proofing 54
Weidlinger Associates 39
WELL Building 129
Whole Building Life Cycle Analysis (WBCLA) 129, 141
Willis, Dan 297
Willis Tower 102
wind energy 127
wind loads 2, 48–49, 52, 96–97, 110, 189, 206, 254, 257, 272–273
wind tunnel 49
wind turbines 127
Woodward, Todd 297
workflow 73–75, 108, 290–291, 293, 296
World Bank 231
World Green Building Council 125, 129
World of Lights 227
World Trade Center 39
Wright, Frank Llyod 40
WSP Flack + Kurtz 37–61

Yale University 154

Zaha Hadid 148, 182–198
Zaha Hadid Architects 182–198
Zero Emission Tokyo Strategy 215
Zubatkin Owner Representation, LLC 62
Zuhair Fayez Partnership 227

For Product Safety Concerns and Information please contact our EU representative GPSR@taylorandfrancis.com
Taylor & Francis Verlag GmbH, Kaufingerstraße 24, 80331 München, Germany